threads.
Sewing Guide

threads. Sewing Guide

A COMPLETE REFERENCE FROM AMERICA'S BEST-LOVED SEWING MAGAZINE

edited by Carol Fresia

The Taunton Press

The Taunton Press
Inspiration for hands-on living®

The Taunton Press, Inc., 63 South Main Street,
PO Box 5506, Newtown, CT 06470-5506
e-mail: tp@taunton.com

Editors: Erica Sanders-Foege, Judith Neukam, Carol Fresia, Beth Baumgartel
Copy editor: Betty Christiansen
Indexer: Lynda Stannard
Jacket/Cover design: Teresa Fernandes
Interior design: Teresa Fernandes
Layout: Cathy Cassidy

Threads® is a trademark of The Taunton Press, Inc., registered in the U.S. Patent and
Trademark Office.

The following names/manufacturers appearing in *Threads Sewing Guide* are trademarks:
Bemberg™, Calgon®, Carbona®, Fray Check™, Hump Jumper®, Jean-a-ma-jig™,
Lycra®, Nymo®, Orvus® Paste, Post-it® Note, Res-Q Tape™, Rigilene®, Synthrapol®,
Teflon®, Tencel®, Thread Heaven®, Tiger Tape™, Tyvek®, Ultrasuede®, Velcro®,
Woolly Nylon™

Library of Congress Cataloging-in-Publication Data
Threads sewing guide : a complete reference from America's best-loved sewing magazine /
edited by Carol Fresia.
    p. cm.
  Includes index.
  ISBN 978-1-60085-144-5
  1. Sewing--Handbooks, manuals, etc. I. Fresia, Carol Jean. II. Threads magazine.
  TT705.T494 2011
  646.2--dc22
                            2010048738

Printed in the United States of America
10 9 8 7 6 5 4 3 2 1

Preface

At *Threads* magazine, we have more than just a passion for what we do. We live and breathe all things sewing. More than anything, we love to make new sewing discoveries, to hotly debate their implications, and to brainstorm the clearest way to convey them to our readers. We understand that garment sewing is a constantly evolving craft.

For the past 25 years, we at *Threads* have been engaging our readers in the debate. It's our readers, after all, who push us to be our best, to test and test and test again the steps for projects, tips, and techniques. To make sure that we provide the latest market knowledge about the equipment, tools, and notions involved in sewing. And to help our readers be the best home sewers that they can be.

The result is the beautiful book you now hold in your hands. *Threads Sewing Guide* represents 25 years of the very best articles and columns written by the most experienced and knowledgeable sewing professionals, industry leaders, teachers, *Threads* staffers, and the readers themselves—each indispensable contributors. Two contributors in particular warrant special mention: Carol Fresia, who took on the monumental task of compiling the book from so much material, and her editor, Judith Neukam, *Threads* technical editor, who ensured that it all made good sense.

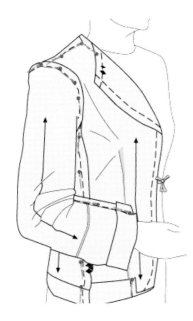

For all skill levels, this garment-sewing encyclopedia answers questions about everything from maintaining a sewing machine to installing an invisible zipper to repairing vintage fabric. A timeless collection of invaluable reference material, *Threads Sewing Guide* is a must-have for any home sewer's library, and one that will sit on your shelf forever. May you enjoy each and every page!

—Deana Tierney May, Editor, *Threads*

Contents

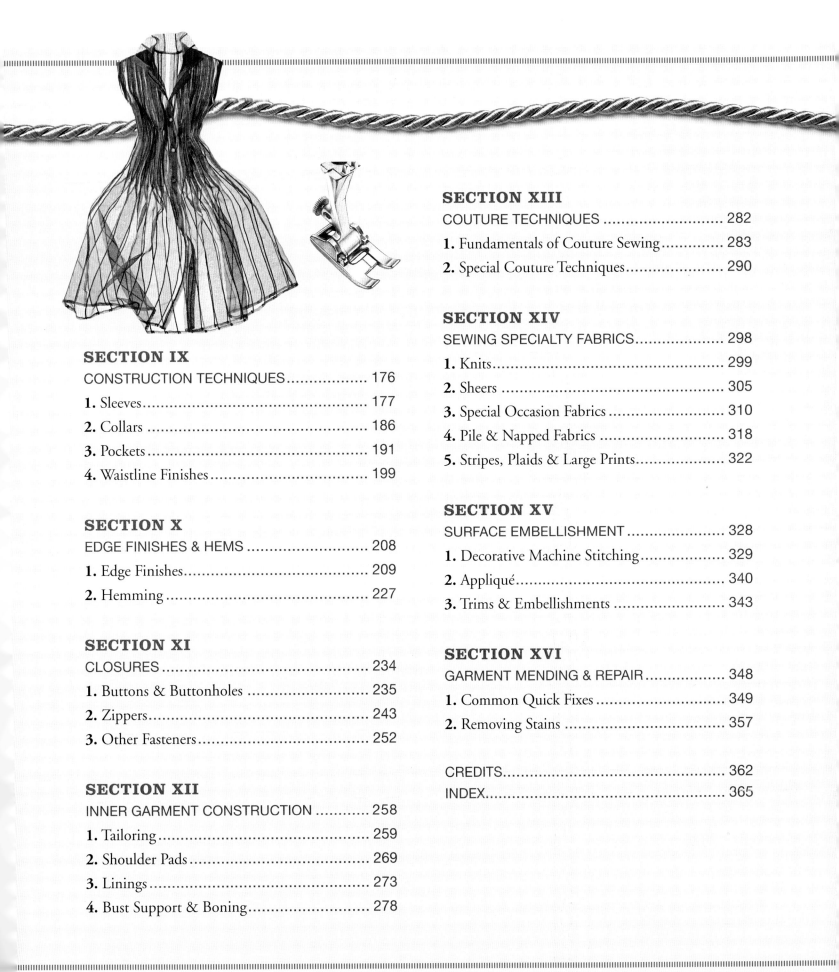

I
SEWING EQUIPMENT

1
Sewing Machines & Sergers

good sewing machine is the key piece of equipment you need to pursue sewing as a hobby or career. As a new or returning sewer looking to tap into your creativity, you're likely to have lots of questions about machines. Today's sewing machines offer much more than a few basic stitches. From entry-level mechanical models to top-of-the-line computerized embroidery machines, there are plenty of options. Whatever your needs and budget, you can find a machine to suit.

MACHINE TYPES

Before buying a sewing machine, it's important to assess your sewing needs. For garment construction and repair, crafts, quilting, and most home décor sewing, a relatively simple sewing machine with a straight stitch, a zigzag stitch, and a buttonhole function is sufficient. These machines are available at the lower end of the price range. If you're interested in creating elaborate embroidery, prepare to spend considerably more on a computerized machine. A serger, or overlock machine, adds speed and efficiency to your sewing, but it doesn't take the place of a basic machine. Your options for sewing machines include the following:

- **MECHANICAL MACHINES** are driven by a single motor and use cams, gears, and/or levers to move the needle shaft and feed dogs. Most mechanical machines include 10 to 20 stitches and a multistep buttonhole feature. Though very basic, mechanical machines can handle nearly every sewing project you undertake. These are the most affordable choices.

- **ELECTRONIC MACHINES** work like mechanical models, but incorporate electronic parts for labor-saving features, such as a speed adjustment switch, a needle position option, and a low-bobbin warning. They're available in the low to middle price range.

- **COMPUTERIZED MACHINES** use an entirely different drive system. Rather than one large motor, they contain a series of tiny motors controlled by a single microprocessor, which creates a smooth-running machine with dozens of decorative stitches. From automatic thread cutters, to alphabets for monogramming, to color touch-screen controls, computerized machines offer convenience and creativity. Some computerized machines contain programmable memory, enabling you to create and store your own stitch combinations. These machines include mid- to high-priced models.

- **COMBINATION SEWING/EMBROIDERY MACHINES** both sew, with many decorative stitch options, and stitch digitized embroidery motifs onto hooped fabric, using a special embroidery attachment. When a digitized embroidery design is loaded into the machine (via

a special memory card, a flash drive, or direct connection with a computer), the unit moves its attached embroidery hoop under the needle to stitch out complex motifs. These top-of-the-line machines are typically the most expensive.

- **EMBROIDERY-ONLY MACHINES** perform only digitized embroidery on hooped fabric driven by the embroidery unit. They aren't designed to sew seams or straight lines of stitching, so an embroidery-only machine is best used as a complement to a regular sewing machine. Embroidery-only machines are available at medium to high prices for home models. Semi-professional models, with multiple needles and threads for fast, production-style embroidery, are more expensive.

- **SERGERS** are a boon in the sewing room, but aren't a replacement for a regular sewing machine. A serger can't sew a single line of straight stitching, make buttonholes, or stitch anywhere but along the edge of the fabric, so for many garment-construction tasks, the serger won't do. On the other hand, the serger sews, trims, and overcasts seams quickly and in a single pass; creates seams that stretch; and makes fast work of finishing raw edges. It's ideal for sewing knits and can speed up some home décor projects. Sergers are priced similarly to computerized sewing machines.

SELECTING A SEWING MACHINE

All sewing machines, no matter the type, create a stitch by interlocking a top thread, threaded through the needle, with a lower thread, wound around a bobbin. The fabric is held beneath the needle by a presser foot and moved along by the feed dogs, a set of little teeth that protrude from the throat plate.

A straight stitch is the fundamental utility stitch offered in every machine, and you can sew nearly any project with it. Most machine models offer a variety of sewing features and a greater assortment of decorative and utility stitches, allowing for seemingly unlimited creativity.

When you start shopping for a new sewing machine, spend some time getting to know the main parts and features. Research various models and brands in your price range, using the websites of the machine manufacturers. When you find a few machines that meet your criteria, take the time to test-drive them. The first step is to lift the levers, turn the wheels, and listen to the machine purr. Also be sure that its speed works for you. Next, sew a variety of fabric swatches, from denim to silk. Look for smooth, regular stitches, even tension, and feed dogs that feed the fabric evenly.

Become familiar with the physical features shown in the photographs on pages 6–7 and the operational features listed in the chart on pages 8–9, and decide which are important to you. Two considerations worth investigating are the machine's ability to easily make consistent buttonholes and its variety of built-in stitches.

Stitch Variety

Utility stitches, including the standard straight stitch and zigzag stitch, are used for hemming, finishing seams, sewing elastic and trims, and sewing novelty fabrics to prevent raveling, stretching, or "popping" seams. Utility stitches make sewing easier, faster, and more professional looking. And often they're only visible on the inside of a project.

Decorative stitches, which are sometimes intricate, can be very appealing. Most sewing machines offer some decorative stitch patterns, which stitch out in a line on unhooped fabric. Depending on the type of sewing you plan to do, you may not need or want many of these fancy stitches.

Buttonholes

Today, most machines feature an automatic buttonhole setting. Although this function is useful, the truth is that any machine that zigzags can produce a buttonhole. All it takes is two parallel rows of satin stitches and a bar tack at each end. Nonetheless, for convenience, most sewers consider an automatic buttonhole function a must-have feature.

Some machines offer a four-step automatic buttonhole, for which each of the four sides is sewn individually and in succession; you must manually switch the control to move through the steps. A one-step buttonhole is stitched on all four sides with just one command. Some machines feature a special foot that automatically sizes the buttonhole to fit your button.

Anatomy of a Sewing Machine

Most sewing machines contain these basic features or their equivalent. To identify the features of your machine, consult your sewing machine manual.

NEEDLE BAR
Holds the needle and moves it up and down and side to side to sew a stitch. A screw releases and tightens the needle. Sometimes referred to as the needle shaft or clamp.

PRESSER FOOT
Keeps the fabric flat against the feed dogs, allowing it to be fed underneath the needle. There are various types of feet for different techniques and stitches.

FEED DOGS
"Teeth" located beneath the presser foot, which pull the fabric under the needle. They can be lowered so the fabric can be moved freely in any direction.

THROAT PLATE
Metal plate in the sewing surface below the presser foot. It contains openings for the feed dogs and needle, and seam guide markings.

BOBBIN, DROP-IN OR VERTICAL
Thread-wound spindle positioned inside the machine. It is inserted either into the sewing surface or into a removable metal case, which is then inserted vertically into the front or side of the machine.

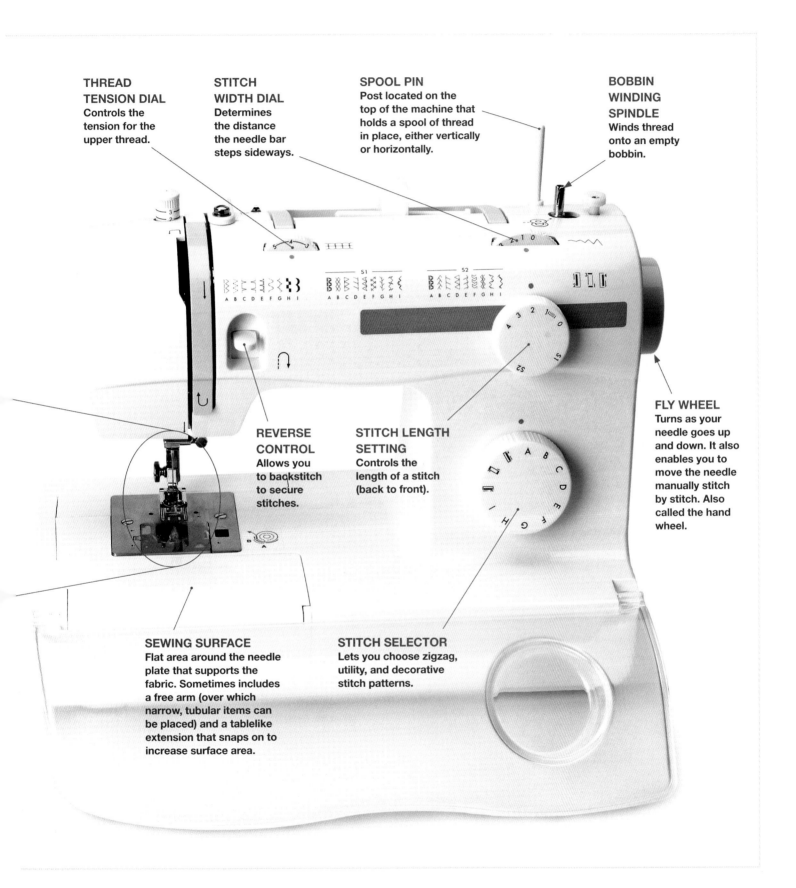

THREAD TENSION DIAL
Controls the tension for the upper thread.

STITCH WIDTH DIAL
Determines the distance the needle bar steps sideways.

SPOOL PIN
Post located on the top of the machine that holds a spool of thread in place, either vertically or horizontally.

BOBBIN WINDING SPINDLE
Winds thread onto an empty bobbin.

REVERSE CONTROL
Allows you to backstitch to secure stitches.

STITCH LENGTH SETTING
Controls the length of a stitch (back to front).

FLY WHEEL
Turns as your needle goes up and down. It also enables you to move the needle manually stitch by stitch. Also called the hand wheel.

SEWING SURFACE
Flat area around the needle plate that supports the fabric. Sometimes includes a free arm (over which narrow, tubular items can be placed) and a tablelike extension that snaps on to increase surface area.

STITCH SELECTOR
Lets you choose zigzag, utility, and decorative stitch patterns.

Specialty Machines

As mentioned on page 5, embroidery machines and sergers can enhance your sewing efficiency and creativity. The neatly overlocked seams and edges a serger creates add a professional touch to garments, improve the longevity of your projects, and make fast work of long seams on large home décor projects. The more you work with a serger, the more uses you will discover. Many sewers consider a serger an indispensable addition to their sewing room.

See "Serger Sewing" page 164.

An embroidery or a combination sewing/embroidery machine introduces nearly unlimited creative options in sewing. If you like embroidered embellishment on garments or soft furnishings, an embroidery machine is worth considering.

There's a steeper learning curve with these machines: In addition to learning how to prepare and hoop fabric, install the embroidery unit, and get the stitching started, you need enough technological savvy to manage the digitized design files that tell the machine what to stitch. Once you become more comfortable with the machine, you can purchase separate software that enables you to design and digitize your own embroidery motifs for custom embellishment.

Sewing Machine Features

	WHAT IT IS	
MACHINE PARTS	BOBBIN, DROP-IN OR VERTICAL	
	ADJUSTABLE FEED DOGS (FABRIC TEETH)	
	FOOT CONTROL (FOOT PEDAL)	
	LCD PANEL	
	SEWING SURFACE, EXTENSION, AND FREE ARM	
	THROAT PLATE (NEEDLE PLATE)	
FEATURES FOR CONVENIENCE AND SEWING ACCURACY	VARIABLE NEEDLE POSITION	
	NEEDLE UP/DOWN FUNCTION (NEEDLE STOP FUNCTION)	
	NEEDLE THREADER	
	ADJUSTABLE PRESSER FOOT PRESSURE	
	THREAD CUTTER, MANUAL OR AUTOMATIC	
SEWING FUNCTIONS AND SETTINGS	BUTTONHOLE FUNCTION, 4-STEP AND 1-STEP	
	DECORATIVE STITCHES	
	AUTOMATIC FIX STITCH (TIE-OFF)	
	STITCH LENGTH SETTING	
	STITCH WIDTH SETTING	
	UTILITY STITCHES	
	COMPUTER MEMORY	

WHAT IT DOES

Carries lower thread, drops horizontally into machine from an opening near the needle (amount of thread in bobbin is easily visible), or is loaded into a removable metal bobbin case that is inserted vertically into machine. Some machines feature a low bobbin warning.

Feed dogs in raised position move fabric under presser foot. Dropped feed dogs give the sewer total control over the movement of the fabric under the needle; useful for darning and free-motion embroidery. Some machines without adjustable feed dogs provide a cover to block the teeth from moving the fabric.

Supplies power to the machine like a gas pedal does to a car: starts, stops, and sets speed. Some foot controls have other features like half stitch, full stitch, and needle lift, which are activated by tapping the control.

If present, displays stitch selections, settings, and other information applicable to the machine.

The flat area around the needle plate, which supports the fabric. It consists of a free arm (a projecting arm over which narrow, tubular items can be pulled for easier sewing) and one or more tablelike extensions that slide around the free arm to increase surface area. Some machines do not include extensions; others are flat bed only.

Metal plate in sewing surface, below the presser foot. Contains openings for the feed dogs and needle to move above and below the throat plate. Some machines provide a straight stitch plate (and a zigzag plate that can be changed). The straight stitch plate has a smaller needle hole and produces a more attractive straight stitch. The throat plate often has seam guide markings to the right and/or left of the foot.

Realigns needle to left or right of its typical position, centered within the presser foot. Provides greater control for sewing in tight situations, such as near edges.

Changes needle stop position from up to down or vice versa, with the push of a button or a tap on the foot pedal. Saves you from making manual adjustments with the hand wheel. A related feature allows you to set the machine to stop automatically with the needle in an up or down position.

Built-in mechanism pulls thread through the eye of the needle.

Increases or decreases the pressure of the foot on the fabric. Influences the ease and balance with which fabric passes between the feed dogs and the presser foot. Though not used often, this adjustment can be helpful, especially with very lightweight or heavyweight fabrics.

Manual thread cutters may be mounted on the left side of the machine. Pull thread over the cutter (a small blade) to separate your work from the machine without the need for scissors. Automatic cutters clip threads close to fabric at the touch of a button, before you remove the fabric from beneath the presser foot; these produce less thread waste and nearly eliminate thread clippings on the floor.

Stitches a buttonhole. A four-step buttonhole requires the sewer to execute each part (two bar tacks, two sides) individually. A one-step buttonhole creates the entire buttonhole in a single operation. Use an auto-size foot if provided. Look for a machine that allows you to adjust stitch width and length to fine-tune the results.

Either a row of straight stitches shaped into a design/pattern or satin stitches configured into linked shapes such as scallops or diamonds. Used for special finishes, borders, and embellishment.

Push-button control that secures stitches at the beginning and/or end of seam. May also cut thread.

Controls the length of the straight stitch, from very short (for fine, sturdy stitching) to very long (for machine basting). Varies the length of zigzag, utility, and decorative stitch patterns as well.

Controls the side-to-side dimension of zigzag, utility, and decorative stitch patterns. On some machines, the width setting also controls needle position when straight stitching.

Preprogrammed stitch combinations designed to serve a specific purpose, such as overcasting raw edges, sewing elastics, making invisible hems, darning, and sewing stretch knits.

Enables sewer to store stitch combinations for future use.

MACHINE ACCESSORIES

Presser feet, bobbins, and sewing machine needles are essential equipment. New machines usually contain a few of each in the package, but as you sew, you'll need to replace or supplement your supplies. Purchasing the right items makes your sewing easier and neater, and protects your machine from potential damage.

Presser Feet

Almost every sewing machine comes with a zigzag (also called a general-purpose) presser foot, a zipper foot, and a buttonhole foot. These are the most-often-used presser feet in general sewing. Many machines include a few additional presser feet designed to make specific sewing tasks easier. You're likely to find feet for blind hemming, roll hemming, overcasting, and darning. Consult your machine's manual to identify the feet you have and their intended purpose.

Although all presser feet contain the same basic parts (see "A Guide to Commonly Used Presser Feet" at right), foot design can differ from brand to brand, so feet aren't always interchangeable between machines. The most obvious difference is in the manner of installation. Some feet contain an integral shank, which snaps directly to the machine. Others must be attached to the machine with a screw; finally, some simply snap onto the machine. Review your machine's operating manual for more details about the feet that come with the machine. You can purchase specialty feet from your machine dealer; in some cases, you can use generic feet, as long as they are designed to fit the shank setup of your machine.

A Guide to Commonly Used Presser Feet

The appearance of specialty feet, even those with the same function, varies with machine brand, and may not match the feet pictured here.

GENERAL-PURPOSE FOOT
Wide stitch hole is good for most straight and zigzag stitching.

STRAIGHT-STITCH FOOT
Small stitch hole accommodates straight stitch only; good for sewing lightweight and sheer fabrics.

ZIPPER FOOT
Narrow foot allows stitching close to the zipper coil or teeth. Accommodates stitching on either side of the foot. Also good for attaching piping and cording.

AUTOMATIC SIZING BUTTONHOLE FOOT
Use with automatic buttonhole function to stitch buttonholes the correct size for the button.

NARROW HEM FOOT
Rolls the edge of lightweight fabric to form a narrow hem.

BLIND HEM FOOT
Guides the fabric for blind stitching, so stitches are barely visible on the right side of the fabric.

WALKING OR EVEN FEED FOOT
Feeds the top layer of fabric at the same rate as the bottom layer to keep layers and patterns perfectly aligned during stitching.

OVEREDGE FOOT
Used with an overcasting stitch, helps wrap the stitches over the fabric's raw edge.

SATIN STITCH FOOT
Also referred to as an embroidery foot. Has a channel on the sole, so it glides over raised stitching or narrow folds of fabric; often has an open front for greater visibility.

PIN-TUCK FOOT
With between three and nine grooves on the bottom, this foot enables you to create multiple equidistant, parallel rows of raised pin tucks when used with a twin needle.

Bobbins and Bobbin Cases

Not all bobbins, which hold the lower thread, work the same way. Some drop directly into an opening near the machine's throat plate, and others are inserted into a removable bobbin case, which is then placed vertically into the front or side of the sewing machine. Use only bobbins that are recommended for your machine, and make sure they don't have any dents or rough spots that could snag the thread and thus distort your stitch. Refer to your sewing machine owner's manual for bobbin-winding and installation instructions.

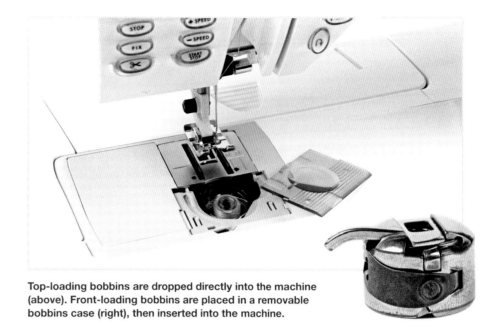

Top-loading bobbins are dropped directly into the machine (above). Front-loading bobbins are placed in a removable bobbins case (right), then inserted into the machine.

Sewing Machine Needles

The correct machine needle is the key to making well-formed stitches, so choose the right one to cleanly pierce the fabric. The two factors to consider when selecting a needle are the fabric and the thread. Choose a needle type based on the fabric ("universal" is designed for most wovens, but special styles may be needed for other fabrics, like knits), then a needle size based on thread type and fabric weight. This ensures that the thread lies in the needle's front groove without wiggling and fits through the eye with little friction. If the needle is too large for the thread, the stitch may be uneven. If the thread is too large for the eye of the needle, it can shred or break. But when the combination is just right, the stitches form beautifully.

Change the needle often. A dull or damaged needle can snag the fabric, affect stitch tension, break threads, and cause irregular or skipped stitches. It can also nick or damage the machine's throat plate or bobbin. The average needle is good for a maximum of eight hours of sewing on average fabric. Some fabrics, including synthetics, dull needles faster. To keep sewing smoothly, change the needle after completing every other project, and dispose of used needles safely.

ANATOMY OF A NEEDLE
If you think all sewing machine needles look the same, try peering at a few of them through a magnifying glass. You'll be surprised at the different shapes and sizes of their main components.

- **POINT** The tip that pierces the fabric; point style is the main difference among needle types.
- **EYE** The hole that the thread passes through.
- **SHANK** The top part that's inserted into the sewing machine; most needle shanks are flat on one side, so they can only be inserted into the machine facing the right way.
- **SHAFT** The diameter of this center part determines the size of the hole created in the fabric.

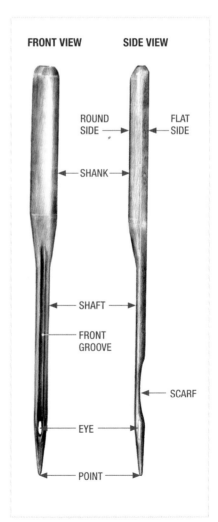

FRONT VIEW   SIDE VIEW

ROUND SIDE →   ← FLAT SIDE

← SHANK

SHAFT →

FRONT GROOVE

← SCARF

EYE →

POINT →

Standard Machine Needles

NEEDLE TYPE		FABRIC
	UNIVERSAL General-purpose needle with a slightly rounded point	Most wovens (and with some brands, knits), synthetic leather, and synthetic suede
	BALLPOINT The rounded tip slips between fabric yarns rather than piercing them—necessary for the loop configuration of knits.	Knits such as interlock, rib knits, fleece, double knits, and jersey
	STRETCH A rounded tip and small hump between the eye and scarf causes the thread to make a large loop, which helps prevent skipped stitches on very stretchy knits.	Slinky knits and knits containing spandex
	JEANS/DENIM A stiff shaft, sharp point, and slender eye	Denim, canvas, and other thick, tightly woven fabrics
	LEATHER The slightly twisted cutting edge at the point penetrates hides.	Natural leather or suede; *not* for synthetic leather or suede
	QUILTING A thin, sharp, long point and tapered shaft for sewing multiple layers	Cotton quilt fabrics and batting
	MICROTEX/SHARP A supersharp point pierces the finest yarns and produces quality topstitching.	Fine, delicate, and tightly woven fabrics

- **SCARF** The back indentation where the stitch is formed; when the bobbin shuttle swings into this indentation, it catches the looped thread to make a stitch.
- **FRONT GROOVE** This front indentation protects the thread from the friction of the needle piercing the fabric.

TYPES OF NEEDLES

Choosing the right needle type depends on the fabric you are using. The standard needles in the chart above can handle most sewing needs and fabrics. For decorative stitching, specialty needles are helpful. Refer to the chart on the facing page for suggestions.

NEEDLE SIZE

The thickness of the thread you are sewing with determines which size needle you use. Needle size is listed as two numbers. The first is the European system, the second the American system (for example, 60/8). The European sizing convention refers to the diameter of the needle shaft as represented by the percent of 1 mm that the shaft measures. The American number also relates to diameter, but is a gauge system, not an actual measurement. In both systems, the smaller the number, the finer the needle. As a general rule, use the smallest needle you can to accommodate the thickness of your thread.

Specialty Needles

These needles are configured to handle special threads, fabrics, or sewing tasks.

NEEDLE TYPE	USES	CONFIGURATION	TROUBLESHOOTING
TOPSTITCHING	Topstitching	Has extra-acute point, extra-large eye, and large groove for heavy thread	Use smallest size needle that accommodates your thread to avoid punching large holes in fabric.
EMBROIDERY	Machine embroidering or embellishing with decorative thread	Has light point (neither sharp nor ballpoint) and enlarged eye to keep decorative threads from shredding or breaking and to prevent skipped stitches	If thread still shreds on dense or heavily stitched design, use larger size needle or metallic needle.
METALLIC	Sewing with decorative metallic threads	Has universal or standard point; large, elongated eye; and large groove to allow fragile metallic and synthetic filament threads to flow smoothly	Metallic threads are very sensitive to problems in machine; the tiniest burr on thread path or needle can cause problems.
QUILTING (STIPPLING)	Piecing, quilting, and stippling	Has special tapered shaft to prevent damaging fabrics when stitching multiple layers	Move fabric smoothly without pulling on needle when free-motion stitching to prevent breaking needle.
HEMSTITCH (WING)	Hemstitching or heirloom embroidery on linen and batiste	Has fins on sides of shank to expand holes as you sew	Stitch is more effective when needle returns to same needle hole more than once. If needle pushes fabric into machine, put stabilizer under fabric.
TWIN (DOUBLE)	Topstitching, pin tucking, and decorative stitching	Two needles on single shaft produce two parallel rows of stitches. Measurement between needles ranges from 1.6 mm to 6 mm, and needles come with universal, stretch, embroidery, denim, and metallic points	Be sure throat plate allows for distance between needles. Check the machine manual to determine what stitches can be used with this needle.
TRIPLE	Same uses as for double needle	Cross bar on single shaft connects three needles to sew three parallel stitching rows. Comes with universal point in 2.5-mm and 3-mm widths	Same as for double needle
SPRING	Free-motion stitching with dropped feed dogs	Has wire spring above point to prevent fabrics from riding up onto needle, eliminating need for presser foot and protecting fingers	Before using, practice free-motion stitching with heavy regular needle, paper, and dropped feed dogs. Don't pull paper/fabric; instead gently guide it through stitching. Wear safety glasses for free-motion work, since needles often break.

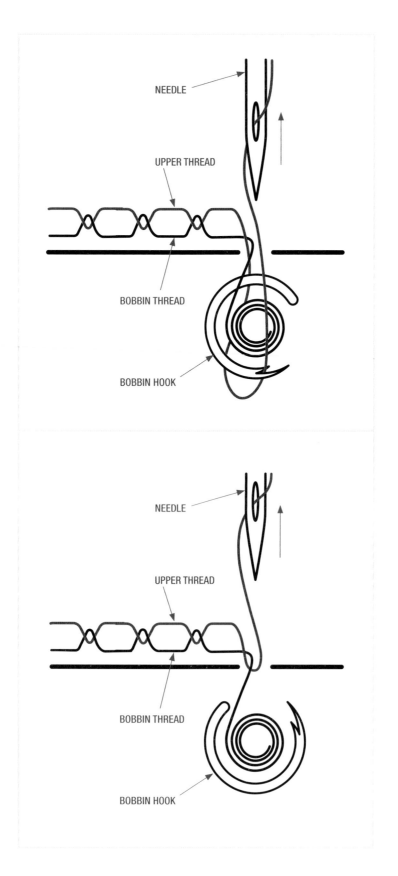

NEEDLE

UPPER THREAD

BOBBIN THREAD

BOBBIN HOOK

NEEDLE

UPPER THREAD

BOBBIN THREAD

BOBBIN HOOK

PREPARING TO SEW

When you know how to operate your sewing machine properly, you'll learn more than simply how to sew straight seams. Before long, you'll handle turns, corners, and bumps easily, for fabulous results. Part of your success depends on how you use your hands to control the fabric as you sew. Naturally, you need to develop a feel for your sewing equipment. When you've sewn on a machine for a time, you acquire an intimacy with the way it accelerates and how it sounds. You become familiar with its vibration, pings, and knocks, and you can hear the difference when it's not running smoothly.

Smooth sewing depends on starting with a machine outfitted with the correct needle and thread for the fabric you're using.

See "Sewing Machine Needles," page 11.

Make sure the machine is threaded properly. Refer to your owner's manual and sew a practice swatch to make sure the thread tensions are correctly set.

If there is any problem with the quality of the seam, the first step in troubleshooting is to rethread the machine to be sure you didn't miss a thread guide or tension disk. Take care that the thread hasn't caught on the spool.

Stitch Formation

The formation of a stitch begins when the needle penetrates the fabric and descends to its lowest point, carrying the upper thread with it. The bobbin hook then slides by the needle's scarf, catching the upper thread, then carrying it around the bobbin and bobbin thread. The thread is then pulled up into the fabric, completing the stitch. In order to form a row of stitches that looks the same on both sides of the fabric, the same amount of thread needs to flow from the spool and the bobbin simultaneously. This is accomplished by running the upper thread through various thread guides, tension disks, and tension regulators, and the lower thread through the bobbin tension spring.

RECOGNIZING BALANCED TENSIONS

When the tensions are balanced, the stitched line looks regular and even on both sides of the fabric, and when they are unbalanced, there are visible knots or loops at the end of each stitch on one side or the other. A perfect stitch pulls both the spool and bobbin thread to the center of the fabric layers.

If the bobbin thread shows on the fabric right side, the needle tension is too tight or the bobbin tension too loose. If the needle thread shows on the wrong side, the needle tension is too loose or the bobbin tension too tight. Of course, if you're sewing on very thin or lightweight fabrics, both threads may show on both sides when the tension is balanced, simply because the fabric is so thin.

It's possible that the tensions still need adjustment even if they're balanced. For example, if both tensions are too tight, the seam may pucker or break easily when stretched. If both are too loose, the seam will gap when pressed open, exposing the threads between the sections.

UPPER-THREAD TENSION ADJUSTMENTS

The tension disks and tension regulator together are called the tension assembly. The tension disks, which resemble small cymbals, squeeze the thread as it passes between them, while the tension regulator controls the amount of pressure on the disks. On older machines, there are only two tension disks, which are controlled by a screw or knob. On newer models, there are three disks controlled by a dial or keypad on the front of the machine, which can regulate two threads at once. Thread guides also direct the thread along its path, each one exerting a small amount of resistance on the thread, adding to the tension from the disks to achieve an overall balanced tension.

The tension regulator for the *needle thread* is elementary: When adjusted to a higher number (turned clockwise), the disks move closer together, increasing the amount of pressure. Turned to a lower number (counterclockwise), the disks move apart, decreasing the pressure. A change in thread thickness usually calls for a tension adjustment. Some newer machines adjust upper tension automatically to accommodate varying thread weights.

BOBBIN-THREAD TENSION ADJUSTMENTS

The bobbin tension is not self-regulating, but you almost never have to adjust the bobbin-thread tension unless you are working with decorative and heavy threads. With a removable bobbin case, bobbin-thread tension adjustments are relatively easy: Turn the small screw on the case a quarter turn (clockwise to increase the tension, counterclockwise to decrease it, as for heavy threads) and

test the tension by sewing on a fabric swatch. To easily return the tension to its original setting, mark the screw position before turning it. Alternatively, keep one bobbin case set for normal sewing and never change its tension. Purchase a second case for use with specialty threads in the bobbin.

A drop-in bobbin may occasionally require tension adjustment, in particular if you're using especially heavy thread. Some machines come with instructions for adjusting bobbin-thread tension. If yours doesn't, you may be able to bypass the tension springs and let the thread flow directly through the hole in the throat plate.

TESTING THE THREAD TENSION

Make a test seam to determine whether the thread tension needs to be adjusted. Thread the machine, and set the stitch length for 2 mm (12 stitches/in.) or for the length you expect to use most frequently. Set the upper-tension regulator at the middle of its range (on most machines, this is 4 or 5). Sew a test seam on the project fabric, and examine the stitches. If an adjustment is necessary, first change the upper-thread tension. If that doesn't work, get out your second bobbin case and start moving the screw in quarter turns to loosen or tighten it, as your sample dictates.

Typically, when you use a lighter-than-normal thread for both needle and bobbin, the tension stays balanced. This is often just what you need to avoid puckering lightweight fabrics, so no adjustment may be necessary. A heavier thread in top and bottom usually calls for a decrease in both upper- and bobbin-thread tension.

So many things can affect the tension that it's worthwhile to run through the following checklist in the order given before you reach for the tension regulator:

- Check for incorrect threading, which is responsible for more "tension" problems than any other factor.

- Remove any thread on the bobbin before you wind on new thread. Wind at a consistent slow or medium speed, especially with polyester and nylon threads.

- Clean your machine regularly.

See "Regular Cleaning," page 17.

- If you are using different thread sizes and types on top and in the bobbin, double-check that these are not throwing off your tension settings.

Using Convenience Features

Mid- to-high-priced machines typically offer features to help you maneuver corners, curves, and tight spots without ever taking your hands off your fabric to hand-crank a stitch or needle position. Once you learn to rely on these features, you'll never want to give them up.

- A HALF-STITCH FUNCTION A foot control that takes a half stitch when you heel-tap the control, enabling you to either raise or lower the needle. Alternatively, some machines offer a needle up/down button that performs the same function, which requires a free finger to operate.

- A PRESSER-FOOT LIFTER On some machines, the presser foot lifts automatically when you stop sewing—just enough to pivot the

fabric, but not so much that you lose control of it. Other machines offer a knee-operated presser foot lifter, which enables you to lift and lower the foot without using your hands. Still others have a button to partially raise the presser foot, allowing you to adjust the fabric or pivot a corner.

- AN AUTOMATIC THREAD CUTTER These cutters clip the upper and bobbin threads close to the fabric surface, eliminating thread ends. The cutter is controlled either by pressure on the foot pedal, or as a preset function on the machine.

CARE AND MAINTENANCE

Regular maintenance is essential for sewing machines, keeping them running smoothly and safely for years. Some maintenance can be done at home with household tools. It's a good idea to have your machine serviced every year or two (depending on how much you use it) by a sewing machine repair professional.

Routine Care

The following guidelines should keep your machine in great working order.

- Keep your machine covered when not in use to avoid a buildup of dust, lint, grit, and animal hair.

- Change the needle often to prevent damage to the machine.

- Match the needle size to the thread weight.

- Use a bobbin designed specifically for your machine to avoid poor stitching as well as permanent damage to the machine.

- Keep the bobbin case clean. Every time you use your machine, take

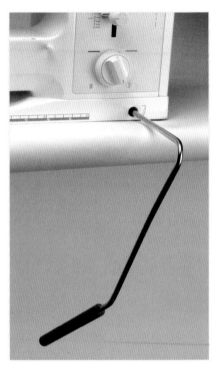

This knee-operated presser-foot lifter leaves your hands free to control the fabric.

out the bobbin case and brush it clean with a clean makeup brush, a paintbrush, a cotton swab dipped in alcohol, or the small brush that comes with the machine's accessories.

- Remove the throat plate and brush away any lint accumulated around the feed-dog mechanism. Clean the spool holders so they are free of dust, lint, and stray threads.

- Wind the bobbins correctly (refer to the owner's manual). Be sure there are no thread tails hanging from the bobbin, as they can hinder the bobbin rotating smoothly and affect stitch quality.

- Use good-quality thread. The short, brittle fibers of old or inexpensive thread create lint. Buildup of lint can shorten your machine's life.

Regular Cleaning

Regular cleaning is essential, so get in the habit of cleaning your machine after each project. Follow the instructions in your manual, or ask your machine mechanic to show you how. You'll need a small brush for removing lint, a piece of clean muslin, and sewing-machine oil. Also helpful is a hand vacuum or a mini vacuum-attachment kit.

Some fabrics leave dye behind, so wipe down the entire machine using a paper towel lightly sprayed with glass cleaner. Never spray the machine directly to avoid getting moisture in the working parts.

Start at the top and clean the tension disks with a folded piece of fine muslin. Be sure the presser foot is up, so the tension disks are loose and the muslin can move easily between the disks, dislodging any lint or fuzz. Use a vacuum to remove loose particles from around the tension disks and to clean other areas inside the machine. Don't blow into the machine yourself, because your breath's water vapor can eventually cause corrosion.

Remove and discard the needle. Then consult the machine manual for

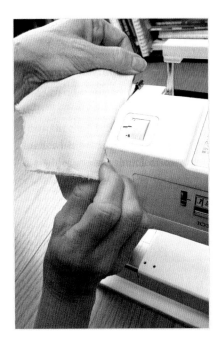 

instructions on removing the throat plate and all applicable parts of the bobbin assembly. Clean under the feed dogs and around the bobbin area with a small brush and/or vacuum cleaner.

Wipe the removable parts of the bobbin assembly with a clean piece of muslin (if instructed to do so in the machine manual, moisten the muslin with a drop of sewing machine oil).

Read your machine manual before

oiling any parts, as some new machines are entirely self-lubricating, and additional oil may cause damage. If your instruction manual recommends oiling other machine parts, remember it is always better to oil too little more often than too much at one time, and avoid oiling any plastic parts. Wipe off any excess oil with a scrap of muslin, then sew on another scrap until there is no residue on your thread.

- Don't sew over pins. If you hit a pin, the needle may strike the throat plate or other parts under the plate. This creates burrs, which catch the thread and cause it to break or fray. It may also affect the timing and alignment of the needle and bobbin case.

- Sew slowly through heavy layers, and set the machine for a longer-than-usual stitch length. This

prevents jamming or skewing of the needle.

- Use a presser foot designed for your machine.

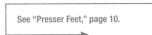
See "Presser Feet," page 10.

- Watch for buildup on the needle when using fusible interfacings, stabilizers, or spray adhesives, as

glue may collect on the needle and thread. Clean with an alcohol wipe.

- Plug the machine into a surge protector to protect against surges and dips in electricity.

2
Essential Tools & Supplies

aving the right tools and knowing how to use them is essential to the mastery of sewing. For ease and accuracy, you need tools for measuring, marking, cutting, securing materials, pressing, and more.

You can start with the bare bones—straight pins and a pincushion, a seam ripper, shears and scissors, hand and machine needles, a ruler or seam gauge and a tape measure, chalk or a fabric-marking pen, and a steam iron. As you continue to sew, you'll discover all sorts of gadgets that enhance your sewing skills.

PINS

A single type of pin can't successfully tackle all fabrics and sewing tasks. Simply stated, different jobs require different pins. Start with a basic, all-purpose pin, then add specialty pins as needed. Discard bent or damaged pins to avoid marring your fabric.

Pin Characteristics

There are five pin characteristics that distinguish pins and that suit pins to different tasks: length, diameter, point shape, head style, and metal content.

LENGTH

Some sewing projects require long pins; other ventures may do better with short, stubby pins. Most pin manufacturers list the actual pin length on the packaging.

- Appliqué/sequin pins are the shortest, ½ in. to ¾ in. long, and are the best choice for applying appliqués, trim, or sequins, as you can position many pins close together.
- Dressmaker/all-purpose pins (also called silk pins) are medium length, 1¹⁄₁₆ in. to 1½ in. long, and are

appropriate for all sorts of garment-sewing tasks.

- Quilting pins are 1½ in. to 2 in. long and are made especially for pinning through many layers of fabric and batting. Their long length and ball-shaped or flower-shaped heads make them easy to grasp, and their length helps them stay in position in heavier fabrics and quilts.

DIAMETER

To avoid marring fabric with pin holes, choose the thinnest pin to accomplish the task at hand. Pin shafts range from exceptionally thin at 0.4 mm for sheer fabrics to quite thick at 0.7 mm to 0.8 mm for use with very thick fabrics. For most sewing projects, choose 0.5-mm or 0.6-mm diameter pins.

POINT SHAPE

The points of pins should slide cleanly into fabric without causing snags or unsightly holes. Different fabrics require different types of points.

- Sharps are all-purpose points, and a fine choice for loosely woven, medium-weight, and heavyweight fabrics.

- Extra-sharps are more defined and tapered, so the point passes cleanly through delicate fabrics.

- Ballpoints are created especially—and only—for knits. This point is rounded so it slips between the loops of the fabric and doesn't pierce or pull the yarns.

HEAD STYLE

The head is the most recognizable part of a straight pin. What it is made of dictates whether it can withstand the heat of an iron, and the shape determines where you should use it in the construction process.

- Flat-head pins can usually be pressed with a hot iron. They're good for handwork, as thread doesn't get caught around the head, but they can be difficult to see on busy or textured fabrics.

- Plastic ball-shaped heads come in different sizes and colors and may be pearlized. They are easiest to see and are a good choice for lace, eyelet, and loose weaves, as the large heads won't slip through the holes in the fabric. These melt when touched with an iron.

Sharp

Extra-sharp

Ballpoint

- Glass ball-shaped heads are fairly easy to see and won't melt when touched with an iron.

- Metal ball-shaped heads aren't common, but they can be pressed with an iron without fear of melting.

METAL CONTENT

A pin's metal content is important, especially if you are allergic to certain metals. There are five types: stainless steel, nickel-plated steel, nickel-plated brass, brass, and chrome-plated steel, which is the strongest option. If you aren't sure of the metal, test it with a magnet; stainless steel and brass pins won't cling. Knowing the metal content is also important if you live in a humid climate, as some pins may rust, causing damage to the fabric if they have been left in for a long period of time.

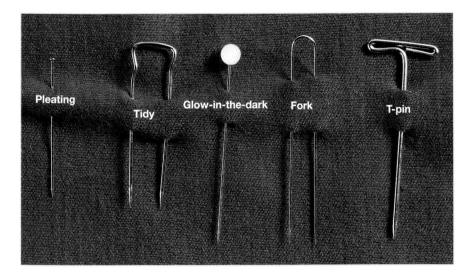

Needle threaders

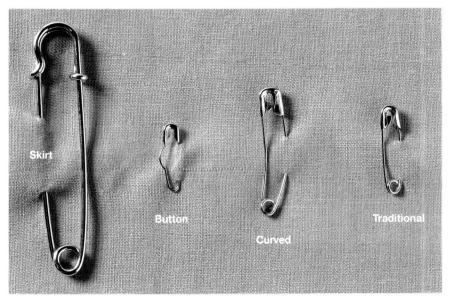

- Safety pins won't wriggle free or stab you as you sew. They are available in a range of metals and colors, as well as sizes: size 00 (¾ in. long), size 0 (⅞ in. long), size 1 (1¹⁄₁₆ in. long), size 2 (1½ in. long), and size 3 (2 in. long). Some types include skirt, button, curved, and traditional.

HAND-SEWING NEEDLES

Having the right needle for the job makes hand sewing that much easier. Needle size refers to the needle's diameter: The larger the number, the finer the needle (just the opposite of machine needles).

All the needles shown in the chart on the facing page have sharp points, and most are available in both multisize and single-size packages. Since needle quality has a major effect on its performance, it's worth the small extra cost for good-quality needles. Choose a needle that feels most comfortable in your hand and is the smallest or finest needle possible for your thread and fabric.

Specialty Pins

For certain projects, you need special pins. Check your local fabric store for availability, or search for an online source.

- Pleating pins are fine, strong, and 1 in. long, which allows you to perfectly pin out pleats.

- Tidy pins are similar to fork pins, but flat and square. They are used to secure doilies, arm covers, and slipcovers to furniture.

- Glow-in-the-dark pins are handy if you drop one; simply turn off the light and look for its glowing head.

- Fork pins are fine and 1⅝ in. long. They have two prongs and curve up at the end. This allows you to align stripes and plaids and pin hard-to-handle fabrics, like lining, without lifting.

- T-pins are thick and 1¾ in. long, and they can pierce and hold hefty upholstery and outdoor fabrics.

Hand-Sewing Needles

NEEDLE TYPE	USES	SIZES	MOST COMMON SIZE FOR HAND SEWING	NEEDLE LENGTH	SIZE OF EYE
BEADING	Beadwork; too thin for most hand sewing. Largest size (10) works well for sheers and delicate fabrics.	10 to 13	10	Extremely long	Extremely small
MILLINERS (STRAW NEEDLES)	Basting, gathering, pleating, delicate embroidery, craft/doll work, with all threads and fabrics.	1 to 10	8 to 9 for basic hand sewing; 10 to 12 for fine or sheer fabrics. A 12 also works well for some beadwork.	Long	Small
BASTING (LONG DARNERS)	Quilt basting, general basting, decorative stitching, appliqué, and craft/doll work, with all threads and fabrics. The combination of the needle's large size and large eye makes it easy to hold and thread.	1 to 9	7	Extremely long	Large, elongated
EMBROIDERY (CREWEL)	Craft, needlework, and general hand sewing due to large eye and small needle sizes.	1 to 10	8 to 10	Medium	Large, elongated
SELF-THREADING	Slotted eye makes threading a snap (although the thread may pop out of the eye during use). Multipurpose needle for visually impaired, for all threads and fabrics. Otherwise, not fine enough for most handwork, but will do in a pinch. Helpful for burying thread tails and knotting short tails.	4 to 8	4 to 8	Short	Small, slotted
SHARPS	All-purpose needle for all types of hand sewing with all threads and fabrics.	1 to 10	7 to 9	Medium	Small
BETWEENS (QUILTING NEEDLES)	Hand quilting and applying delicate trims and sequins; short length difficult for everyday hand sewing.	1 to 12	7 to 9	Very short	Extremely small

Hand-Sewing Aids

These tools make working with pins and needles easier.

- **NEEDLE GRABBER** Make a needle grabber by cutting a small circle of textured rubber to help you grip the needle as you pull it through stiff or thick fabrics or bulky seams.
- **NEEDLE THREADERS** The tried-and-true needle threader, available from notions counters, works for most needles. Look for sturdy threaders with embedded wire loops to avoid breakage.
- **THIMBLES** Thimbles come in a wide range of sizes and materials, including metal, plastic, and leather. Open-tip, ring-style, and disk-shaped finger protectors provide coverage for any task.
- **THREAD WAX OR CONDITIONER** This helps keep thread from tangling and knotting as you sew. After waxing your thread, iron it to melt the wax into the thread. Thread conditioner, like Thread Heaven®, is a synthetic alternative that doesn't require melting and protects thread against moisture and light.

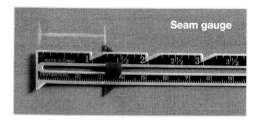

Seam gauge

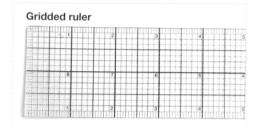

Gridded ruler

French curve

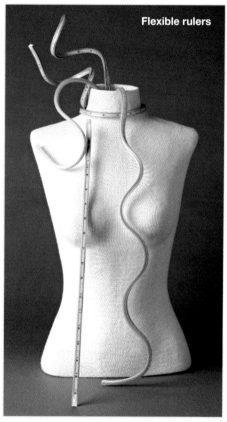

Flexible rulers

Tape measure

MEASURING AND MARKING TOOLS

Accurate measuring and marking tools are essential for sewing garments—or soft furnishings—that fit and drape properly. You'll use them for measuring the body, doing pattern work, and throughout construction. Here's an overview of tools that ensure accuracy for sewers of every skill level.

Measuring Implements

Use these tools for measuring the body and adjusting or drafting patterns.

- **TAPE MEASURE** Most tape measures are 60 in. long. An extra-long (120-in.) flexible tape measure is helpful for measuring and fitting a body, a dress form, or large home décor projects. You'll also find yourself using it throughout the construction process.

- **SEAM GAUGE** This small, adjustable guide is helpful in determining and marking the width of a seam allowance, depth of a hem, or length of a buttonhole.

- **18-IN. GRIDDED RULER** This 18-in. by 2-in. acrylic ruler is marked with a ⅛-in. grid. Because it is transparent, it's a great guide for marking topstitching lines and adjusting or drafting patterns. A thicker, rigid transparent ruler can be used as a guide when using a rotary cutter.

- **FRENCH CURVE** Use this as a guide for drawing new curved lines or to reconnect and smooth altered, shaped pattern lines. Slide and pivot the edge of the French curve until it matches the existing curve or smoothly bridges the gap between two nonconnecting curves.

- **TAILOR'S SQUARE** This L-shaped ruler has fractional divisions printed along one or both edges, and the right angle allows you to establish perfect lengthwise and crosswise grainlines and make accurate square corners.

- **HIP CURVE** Shaped in a long gentle curve, this measuring and drafting tool enables you to draw perfect hiplines, hems, flared shapes, and lapels.

- **FLEXIBLE RULERS** A flexible ruler's inner lead core allows it to contour to and hold almost any shape. Use it to duplicate the shape of any curve, and to transfer a curve from the body to the pattern.

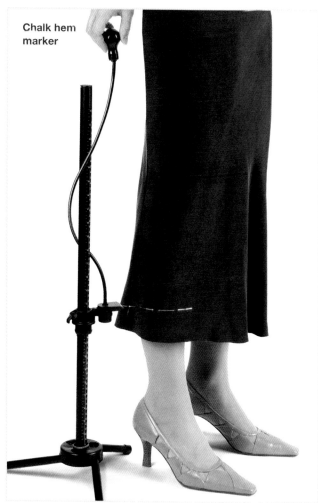

Chalk hem marker

Marking Tools

To transfer measurements, shapes, or markings from muslin to a pattern or from a pattern to fabric, or to note adjustments during a muslin fitting, use a tool designed for the task at hand. Test any marking method on fabric scraps to ensure that the marks are removable.

- **MARKING WHEELS AND DRESSMAKER'S TRACING PAPER** Use a notched or smooth tracing wheel with dressmaker's tracing paper to transfer marks from patterns to fabric prior to sewing. Some tracing papers wash or brush away easily, while others dissipate with air. A pinpoint tracing wheel is used without tracing paper. It leaves a punctured trail beneath any line it passes through, making this wheel ideal for transferring a pattern onto paper. This wheel can mar a tabletop, so work on cardboard or foam-core board.

- **CHALKS** Tailor's chalk is used to mark clothes for alteration or to record seamlines and match points on muslins that have been pin-fit. It is inexpensive, is long-lasting, and won't evaporate or dissolve in water. Wax chalk leaves marks that disappear when touched with a hot iron; use it on thick fabrics that readily absorb the mark as it melts. Use clay chalk on thinner or delicate fabrics because you can brush it away. Chalk markers dispense a thin line of powdered clay chalk via a tiny, serrated wheel, which is set into a handle that doubles as the chalk container. They come in a variety of handle shapes and colors, can be refilled, and never require sharpening. A chalk hem marker offers a way to mark hems on yourself or on others.

- **FABRIC MARKING PENS** Water-soluble and air-erasable pens produce fine lines for accuracy. Test for removal on your fabric before using, as some inks may stain some fabrics and spread on others, leaving unclear marks. Rubbing with a damp cloth or laundering removes water-soluble ink. Air-erasable ink disappears automatically from the fabric in four or five days, depending on humidity; avoid pressing over the marks, as this can set the ink. They are best used to mark dots and other matchpoints.

SHEARS

SCISSORS

Embroidery scissors

General-purpose scissors

Trimmers

CUTTING TOOLS

A wide variety of cutting tools is available for the many tasks associated with sewing, from scissors of many sizes and shapes to rotary cutters. You don't need all of them, but it's helpful to have a couple of choices at hand, then add to your collection as needed. Three basic types can handle most sewing tasks: dressmaker shears for cutting out patterns and heavier-weight fabrics, sewing scissors or trimmers for clipping and trimming, and small embroidery scissors or thread snips for snipping threads and fine detail work. And always test scissors before you buy to determine if they'll do the job and feel comfortable in your hand.

To keep scissors sharp and in tip-top condition, wipe the blades after each use with a clean, soft, dry cloth. Even the slightest lint buildup can affect the smooth cutting action. Store scissors in a protective sheath to avoid damage, and keep all cutting tools in a dry location to prevent them from rusting. Every few months, place a drop of sewing machine oil on the pivot screw, open and close the blades a few times, and wipe off the excess.

Shears

Shears are usually longer than 6 in., and they're designed for heavy-duty rather than detailed cutting. Shears are easily identified by their finger openings: The top is a round ring (for the thumb), and the lower opening (called the bow) is an elongated oval that can accommodate two or more fingers. Some have a bent handle to make it easier to cut fabric on a flat surface without lifting the fabric. Pinking shears have jagged-edge blades, which make a decorative zigzag cut and prevent the cut fabric from raveling.

Scissors

The term *scissors* usually refers to double-blade cutting tools with the following characteristics: They're 6 in. to 6½ in. long or less, and they sport two round finger openings (called rings).

They're designed for detailed cutting, such as clipping seams and cutting intricate shapes.

- **SEWING/GENERAL-PURPOSE** Sewing scissors feature one pointed tip and one slightly rounded tip for clipping seams and light/medium trimming.

- **EMBROIDERY** The fine, narrow-pointed blades of these smaller scissors (less than 6 in. long) make easy work of close detail cutting on fine, lightweight fabrics.

- **TRIMMERS** These scissors are similar in size and shape to sewing/general-purpose scissors, but are created especially for trimming. Both blades are pointed so you can clip right up into a corner.

Snips

Also called "clips" or "nippers," these scissors fit into the palm of the hand. There are a variety of styles—some have a ring for the middle or ring finger,

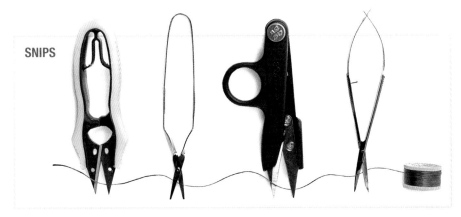

SNIPS

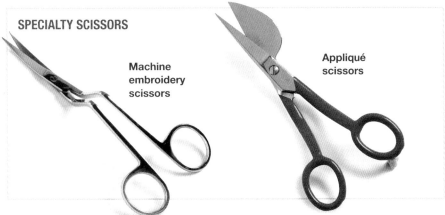

SPECIALTY SCISSORS

Machine embroidery scissors

Appliqué scissors

TIP

Truly "left-handed" scissors are made completely in reverse of right-handed scissors, which eliminates all hand position and visibility problems for left-handed sewers. "Ambidextrous" scissors have handles that are usable either right- or left-handed, but the blades are arranged for righties only; the blades may block the view of a left-handed cutter.

Seam ripper

Rotary cutter

and some are spring-action for lefties or righties—but their sole purpose is to clip threads.

Specialty Scissors

Specialty scissors have blades shaped to make specific tasks easier and neater.

- **SERRATED-EDGE** Fine serrations on one blade edge keep slippery fabrics or threads from slipping while being cut. These work well on lightweight, silky fabrics.

- **MACHINE EMBROIDERY** These scissors have fine blades, often curved, and the shank is offset to aid in clipping threads in embroidery hoops.

- **APPLIQUÉ** These scissors are designed to trim excess fabric from appliqué stitching. The narrow/wide blade combination of the duck- or pelican-bill appliqué

scissors assists in close trimming, enabling you to trim away an upper fabric layer without cutting the lower.

Seam Ripper

A seam ripper, with its small curved blade, is designed especially to cut through stitches, without cutting the surrounding fabric. Use these for removing any unwanted stitches. You can also cut open buttonholes with a seam ripper. (See also page 240.)

Rotary Cutters and Mats

A rotary cutter has a circular blade that cuts as it rolls. Unlike scissors, this tool cuts through multiple layers of fabric and a pattern without having to lift the stack off the table. Rotary cutters come

in a variety of sizes and shapes, and most cutters work for either the right or left hand.

Blade diameters correspond to the handle size and range from 18 mm to 65 mm (approximately ¾ in. to 2½ in.). Smaller cutters navigate tight curves such as armholes and necklines. Larger ones cut through heavier fabrics, loftier thicknesses, and more layers, and they move effortlessly along a straight or moderately curved seam.

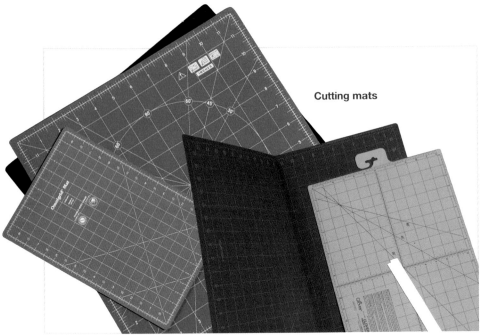

Cutting mats

When working with a rotary cutter, protect the table and cutting blade with a cutting mat. Cutting mats, typically made of plastic, are usually printed with a right-angle grid and show a 45-degree diagonal line for bias cutting. They come in an unlimited range of sizes, shapes, and custom cuts. Unless the mat was designed to fold or roll, store it flat or hang it on a wall in an environment where it's protected from extreme temperatures and buckling. To prolong the life of your mat, never iron on it.

Rotary cutters are extremely sharp. Be vigilant about where you position your free hand, always use a sharp blade (dull ones require more force to use), keep the blade retracted and locked in position when not in use, and store the cutter out of the reach of children.

PRESSING TOOLS

There are many specialized tools for pressing. For garment sewing, a good steam iron, pressing ham, sleeve board, and clapper are the most helpful. A needle board is useful if you plan to work with napped fabric. Analyze your pressing needs and, starting with an iron, consider the tools you need to get the job done right.

Irons and Ironing Boards

A steam iron is essential in the home sewing room. A domestic model, designed more for ironing than for garment construction, contains an internal water tank, and when set to steam, water is released from the tank, hits the hot soleplate, and converts to steam. This activity all happens inside the iron. The soleplate temperature must be at least 300°F for steam to form. (If the iron is set to steam but the temperature is less than 300°F, water may dribble or spit from the soleplate and spot your fabric.) Along with a good iron, you need a good ironing board that offers enough space for effective pressing, as well as a pad that moves moisture away from the fabric you're pressing.

IRONS AND IRONING SYSTEMS

Professional irons have heavy soleplates, narrow shapes, superior temperature dials and thermostats, and greatly enhanced steam capacity—all necessary elements for great results in garment sewing. Domestic versions of gravity feed and boiler system (or steam generator) irons and vacuum boards—all similar to those used in the garment industry—have been introduced to the home sewing market.

The advantages of a gravity feed iron, in which the water tank is suspended above the iron itself, are a nearly constant supply of pressurized steam on demand; a larger water tank capacity, which will produce steam for as many as six hours; and a heavier iron head. A gravity feed iron can be switched back and forth between dry and steam heat instantly. It produces steam when held upright as well as in the conventional horizontal position, but steam is produced only when the soleplate is heated to at least 300°F. In a boiler system, the water is held in a separate tank, where it is heated and converted to steam. The steam is delivered by high pressure through a hose to the iron, so continuous steam is available at any soleplate temperature.

WHAT TO LOOK FOR IN AN IRON

- Heavy weight, about 3 pounds
- Wide temperature range
- Water reservoir to produce steam
- Adequate number of holes on the soleplate to deliver even steam. (Some are confined to the tip area, offering superior control; others are spread across the entire soleplate, offering wider steam distribution.)
- Pointed tip or nose to press and open even hard-to-reach seams effectively
- Automatic shutoff, which some sewers love and others don't

IRONING BOARDS

A sturdy ironing board covered with a pad and topped with a cover is essential. The pad should do more than simply cushion the surface; it should help move moisture away from the fabric being pressed. An effective combination is an uncoated cotton cover over a dense, needle-punched nylon pad. Together, these wick moisture away from the project, speeding a smooth, even press.

Specialty Pressing Tools

To create attractive, smooth lines on a garment, use these pressing tools to mold and shape the fabric. A press cloth, positioned between the iron and the fabric, is critical because it protects the fabric while also allowing use of the highest temperature the fabric can withstand.

- **SLEEVE BOARD** This looks like two miniature ironing boards joined together. It's great for pressing open seam allowances in sleeves or other tubular garment sections.
- **CLAPPER** This block of wood, often attached to a point presser, is used to form flat seams and crisp creases. Press the project with steam, remove the iron, and apply firm pressure with the clapper on the hot area until it cools. Traditionally used on woolens, a clapper is also useful for pressing synthetic fabrics that can't withstand high heat.
- **TAILOR BOARD** This wooden tool contains multiple shaped pressing surfaces, including large and small curves, as well as points for pressing inside corners in collars and miters. Removable, padded covers are available.
- **TAILOR'S HAM** The rounded surfaces of a ham mimic various body parts, including the neck, shoulder, and hip. Press darts, sleeve caps, necklines, and other curved areas over a ham to retain shaping.
- **SLEEVE ROLL** This is like a tailor's ham, but cylindrical in shape. Use it to press seams in sleeves and pant legs and for shaping smaller curves. Alternatively, use a wooden dowel, uncovered or wrapped in a towel, for pressing seams on long, tubular garment pieces.
- **VELVABOARD** This is a fabric mat with deep, flexible pile on one surface to cushion the nap on fabrics such as velvet and corduroy. A needle board, covered with fine vertical metal pins, does the same thing. Lay velvet fabrics facedown on the board's surface to press, using minimal pressure from the iron.

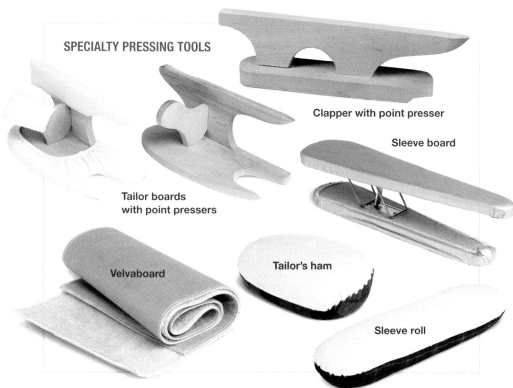

SPECIALTY PRESSING TOOLS

Clapper with point presser

Sleeve board

Tailor boards with point pressers

Velvaboard

Tailor's ham

Sleeve roll

CONSTRUCTION AIDS

Specialized sewing tools can improve your sewing results while making specific tasks easier. Consider adding these to your collection as your interest and skills grow.

- **Awl** A supersharp awl is indispensable for punching holes in heavy fabrics, for pattern drafting, for steering little bits of fabric under the presser foot, and for positioning beads or sequins.

- **Bodkins** Bodkins come in all sorts of shapes and sizes, and are used for threading cords, ribbons, and drawstrings through stitched channels and casings.

- **Clamp and bird set** Also called "the third hand," this nifty device attaches to your sewing table, preferably right next to your sewing machine. When the clamp is holding the fabric taut, you can use both hands for other tasks. This tool is great for trimming seams and hems, especially on fine, slippery fabrics, and also holds seams taut for ripping.

- **Dress form** A dress form is a body double that lets you adjust a garment's fit, drape, and design directly on it.

- **Gauges** Use a hem gauge to turn up and mark an even hem allowance. The gauge is marked for straight hems from ¼ in. to 4 in. deep and for curved hems from ¼ in. to 2½ in. deep. Use a buttonhole gauge to mark evenly spaced button and buttonhole placements within a given span. It also simplifies positioning and measuring pleats, tucks, or anything else that calls for regular spacing.

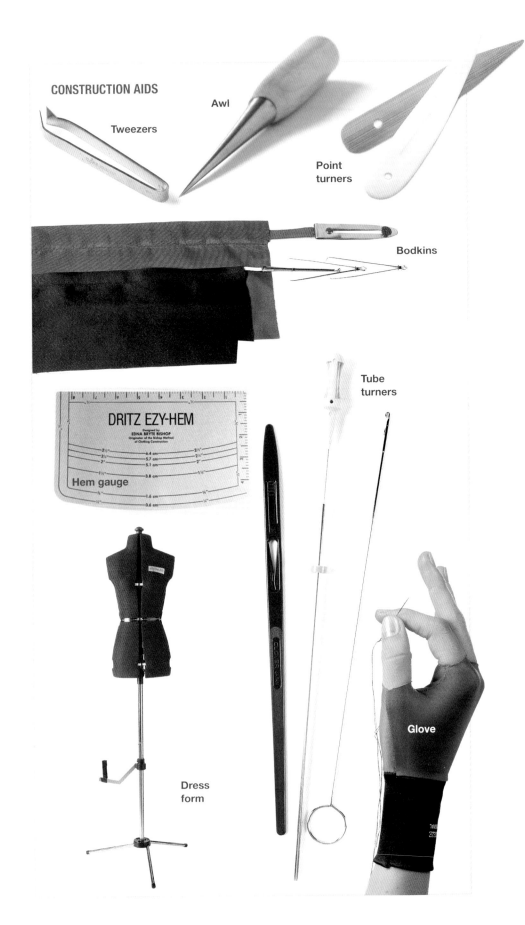

CONSTRUCTION AIDS

Tweezers

Awl

Point turners

Bodkins

Tube turners

DRITZ EZY-HEM
Designed by
EDNA BRYTE BISHOP
Originator of the Bishop Method
of Clothing Construction

Hem gauge

Dress form

Glove

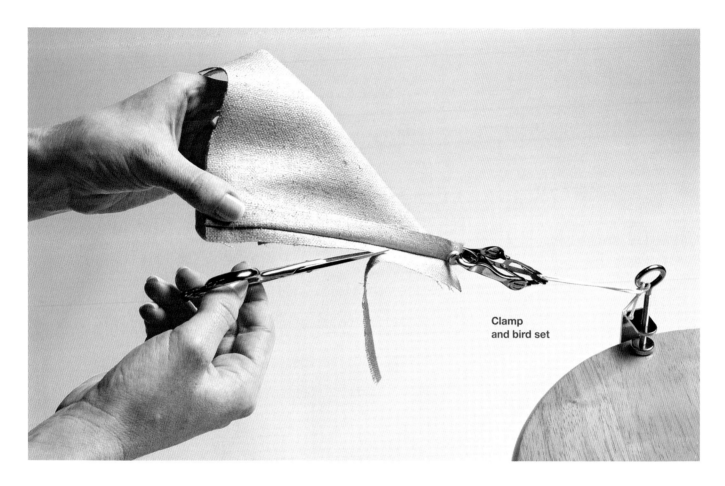

Clamp
and bird set

- **Gloves** Spandex-reinforced gloves are like support hose for your hands. These fingerless gloves cling gently to your hands to alleviate stiff muscles and provide relief from the pain of repetitive-stress injuries.

- **Tube turner** A tube turner is basically a long wire with a tiny latch hook at the end used for turning spaghetti straps, button loops, and fabric tubes for things like frogs and knot buttons. The tool is also perfect for retrieving elastic or cording that has gotten lost while being fed through a casing.

- **Point turner** A wooden or plastic point turner helps turn out sharp corners on pockets and collars without poking through the fabric.

Also use the flat side to push out a straight edge before pressing.

- **Tweezers** Tweezers make pulling out stitches even easier. The tweezers shown here are not the ordinary drugstore variety. Imported from Japan, they have a flat front edge and an ultrasharp point for easier use. And, if you are having a problem seeing those tiny threads, look for magnifying tweezers for all your close work.

TIP

Chopsticks and bamboo skewers make great substitutes for point turners. The long, skinny shapes get into places a regular point turner can't.

II

NOTIONS

Thread

Y
ou can't stitch a seam without thread. But all threads aren't the same, and it's important to choose the right thread for your project. As you browse the thread section in a fabric store, you'll discover many varieties of thread, each intended for a specific purpose.

Selecting the right thread is more than a matter of picking the best color. For some projects, any of several thread choices may be suitable. For others, the finished results are affected for better or worse by the type of thread used. In all cases, the thread must perform well on your machine, work with your fabric and needle, and yield the look and wear you want.

SELECTING THREAD

Whatever thread you choose, always check its quality. Inferior thread can leave a residue in your machine or clog it with lint. For general machine sewing, look for a smooth, nub-free strand that doesn't twist easily (and is as free as possible of fuzz) by unwinding a strand and holding it toward a light. Test any thread you are considering on your project's fabric. Experiment with stitches, trying various stitch and tension settings.

For general construction, thread the machine with the same thread on the top and in the bobbin; it's practical and simplifies balancing the tension. Choose a thread by the attributes of your particular project, such as fabric type and care requirements. For example, if your fabric requires high

heat for pressing, choose a thread fiber that withstands high temperatures as well. If you're constructing a heavy cotton denim bag, choose a polyester thread for its strength and durability rather than a weaker cotton thread.

Similarly, most children's clothing requires durable polyester thread to withstand rough wearing and heavy-duty washing and drying. For swimwear, choose a strong thread with stretch, plus ultraviolet (UV) and chemical resistance—you don't want to risk fading your decorative stitching or rotting your seams in chlorinated water. And remember, one project might use several thread types.

See "Fiber Chart," on page 32.

For seaming, match the color of thread to the fabric. The traditional rule for selecting thread color when an exact match to your fabric isn't available is to choose thread that's a shade darker than the fabric. On the other hand, you can choose a lighter color thread (often white or ivory) when stitching on pale-colored, fine, lightweight fabrics. Lighter thread colors blend better on

Fiber Chart

FIBER	DESCRIPTION	USES
COTTON	Little stretch, low sheen, matte appearance	Heirloom sewing, decorative stitching, embroidery, sewing lightweight natural fibers, patchwork, and quilting
COTTON-WRAPPED POLYESTER	Strong, with low sheen	All-purpose sewing
NYLON	Strong, clear, and limited colors	Invisible sewing and blind hems
POLYESTER	Strong, colorfast, some stretch, heat and mildew resistant, tremendous color variety	Spun polyester for all-purpose sewing Trilobal polyester for machine embroidery Textured polyester for serging
RAYON	Lustrous shine, minimal stretch or strength, heat resistant, takes dyes beautifully, sometimes fades with repeated washings	Decorative stitching, not strong enough for garment construction
SILK	Strong, smooth, and lustrous	Fine and sheer fabrics, suitable for fabrics that stretch

pastel fabric colors than darker shades do. Unroll a few inches of any threads you are considering, lay them over your fabric in natural light, and then decide which color blends best.

When stocking your sewing room, purchase spools of black, white, off-white, mid-range gray, khaki, navy, and red thread. In a pinch, one of these colors can blend with nearly any color of fabric. And for decorative stitching, anything goes. Choose by color, texture, or weight.

Thread Sizing

There isn't a universal sizing convention for thread, so there's no way to compare size among all types. However, you can learn how the basic sizing systems work so you can distinguish thinner from thicker threads in all varieties.

- **WEIGHT/PLY** Expressed as a slashed number (e.g., 50/3 or 60/2), this sizing convention indicates the number of kilometers of thread per kilogram of weight, as well as the number of plies in the thread. The higher the weight number, the thinner the thread.

- **DENIER** Used for synthetic threads like polyester, rayon, and nylon, the size number indicates the weight in grams of 9,000 m of thread. A higher number means a thicker thread.

- **TEX** The weight in grams of 1,000 m of thread. Higher numbers indicate thicker threads.

SPOOL PIN DIRECTION

If you have a choice of spool pin direction on your machine, use a vertical spool pin for spools with thread wound parallel to the spool ends. This is especially important with sensitive threads (like metallic thread) or spools with a notch for securing the thread tails. If your machine has only horizontal spool pins, put the spool on the machine with the notch to the right, toward the fly wheel, to prevent the thread from catching in it. Some thread is cross-wound, i.e., wrapped to form V-shapes on the spool or cone. Spools wrapped this way may be used successfully either horizontally or vertically. But thread that is cross-wound on cones or large, heavy spools should come off over the top of the spool, so use a separate stand to keep the thread feeding in the right direction.

NOVELTY THREADS

Part of the fun of sewing is using novelty threads. They can be as much a part of the design of the garment as the fabric and silhouette.

- **BASTING THREAD** Fine, soft, and weak, making it easy to remove.

- **BOBBIN THREAD** Fine and lightweight, and used for machine embroidery where the wrong side won't show. It comes in limited colors and is sometimes available on prewound bobbins.

- **BUTTONHOLE TWIST (TOPSTITCHING THREAD OR CORDONNET)** These heavy threads are available in silk, polyester, cotton-covered polyester, and cotton. Use for heavy-duty utility sewing, open decorative machine stitching, bold topstitching, hand-stitched buttonholes on heavy fabrics, and corded machine buttonholes.

- **ELASTIC THREAD** Has a continuous elastic core wrapped with thread. Hand-wind it onto the bobbin for decorative machine stitching for smocking and shirring.

- **FUSIBLE THREAD** Melts when ironed, forming a bond with fabric. Use it in the bobbin or lower looper on a serger to outline applied details so they can be temporarily fused in place instead of basted.

- **LIGHT-SENSITIVE THREAD** Either changes color in sunlight or glows in the dark. Use it for topstitching and machine embroidery.

- **LINGERIE THREAD** Soft and fine, and available in polyester or nylon fibers. It comes primarily in pastel colors and is for lightweight, delicate fabrics.

- **MACHINE-EMBROIDERY THREAD** Designed to fill in designs smoothly and evenly. This fine thread comes in cotton, rayon, long-staple polyester, or with a wrapped polyester core, and is available in hundreds of colors. Use for decorative stitching and embroidery where strength is not a concern.

- **METALLIC THREAD** May be wrapped in metal or have a foil-like appearance and is used for decorative stitching and embroidery. It is known to be temperamental on some machines, so stitch slowly, loosen the tension,

use a specialty needle, and pair with all-purpose thread in the bobbin. Some newer wrapped-core versions have a veneer-type finish that helps prevent separation.

- **MONOFILAMENT THREAD** A single strand of nylon or polyester filament. Polyester withstands higher heat than nylon. Almost invisible, it comes in clear or neutral gray, and can be shiny or matte. Thicker thread sizes may feel abrasive next to the skin.

- **QUILTING THREAD** Intended for actually quilting, not piecing or patchwork. Some may indicate whether they are for hand quilting only (due to the finish), for machine quilting, or for both.

- **SERGER THREAD** Finer than all-purpose thread, it has a special finish for high-speed sewing and comes on cones or tubes.

- **TEXTURIZED THREAD** Fills in stitches on rolled hems and overlock stitches, and makes soft, stretchy seams for swimwear or children's clothes. Available in nylon or polyester. Used almost exclusively in serger loopers.

- **UPHOLSTERY THREAD** Always a synthetic fiber, usually nylon but can be polyester, and extra strong—too strong for clothing. It has built-in UV protection, making it ideal for outdoor furnishings.

- **WATER-SOLUBLE THREAD** Use to temporarily baste hems and position pockets and pleats.

SEWING WITH SILK THREAD

The old school of thought was that silk thread was too strong for garment construction. If you use the right thread for your fabric, however, you can add years to the life of the finished product, which is worth the extra expense (good silk thread costs more than $5 a spool). Silk thread produces strong, flexible, and nearly invisible seams, edge finishes, and hems, particularly when you are working with lightweight and sheer fabrics.

Silk thread appears to sink into and become part of the garment fabric. Seams and finished edges are nearly invisible. When silk stitches are removed, they leave imperceptible holes in the fabric—that's why silk thread has traditionally been recommended for marking and basting.

The 50-weight workhorse is the most useful thread, suitable for use with most fabrics. The thicker, loftier, 30-weight thread works well for decorative stitching, while the heavy 8-weight thread is the choice for hand-sewn buttonholes, but it also lends itself well to decorative machine stitching and handwork. On the other end of the spectrum, the 100-weight, two-ply filament silk is perfect for fine, sheer, and delicate fabrics like chiffon.

2 Interfacing

Used to reinforce, stiffen, support, or add body to your fabric, interfacing contributes to the appearance and longevity of a garment. Nearly every garment needs interfacing of some kind. Using the right interfacing, in the right place, in the right way helps your garments look professionally finished, even though the interfacing itself remains entirely invisible from the outside of the garment.

PURPOSE AND FUNCTION

Your choice of interfacing ultimately depends on its intended purpose. In fact, several types of interfacing may be needed in one garment to fulfill the following functions.

1. Reinforce edges such as hems and front openings.

2. Provide added body to parts of a garment, such as jacket fronts.

3. Create stability in buttonholes, seams, and armholes.

4. Prevent stretch in areas like the waistband or upper back.

5. Build shape in lapels and collars.

6. Provide a crisp finish to details such as pockets.

TYPES OF INTERFACING

Home sewers have many different types of interfacings to choose from, but selecting among them needn't be confusing. To select an interfacing that's appropriate for your garment design and fabric, determine the most appropriate structure type and then look for compatibility of weight, hand, application, color, and fiber content.

Structure Type

Choose a type of interfacing: woven, knit, or nonwoven. As you may expect, woven interfacing behaves like woven fabrics.

See "Fabric Structure," on page 56.

It doesn't stretch in the lengthwise grain, has minimal cross-grain stretch, and has the most stretch on the bias. Use woven interfacing with woven fabrics.

Knit interfacing behaves like knit fabric. It freely stretches in at least one direction and therefore allows the fashion fabric to stretch slightly. Use a knit interfacing with knit or woven fabrics.

Nonwoven interfacing is created by melding fibers together with heat and steam. It doesn't have grain or much stretch, but it works well for handbags, totes, and other accessories, like belts.

Weight and Color

Ranging from featherweight to heavyweight, interfacing should usually be the same weight as or a lighter weight than the fabric. Test it by slipping a piece under your fabric and draping it over your hand. An interfacing that's too heavy for the fabric distorts the garment design and silhouette. One that's too light doesn't hold the shape or maintain stability in the garment. Interfacing should complement the hand of your fabric and at the same time provide support, to give the garment longevity.

A loosely woven fabric may require a more stable or firm interfacing than a dense or tightly woven fabric.

Most interfacing products are available in a limited choice of colors: white, off-white or beige, black, and gray. As a general rule, use white or beige interfacing for light-colored fabric, and gray or black interfacing for dark-colored fabric.

Fiber Content

Interfacing fiber content (natural, synthetic, or a blend) is important in terms of comfort and care requirements. The interfacing's fiber content must match your fabric's care requirements. Shrinkage or distortion may occur when a dry-clean-only interfacing is paired with a fabric that will be laundered. When used in large areas, like a jacket front, a natural fiber interfacing is more comfortable in warm weather.

Fusible or Sew-in

Each of the three types of interfacing—woven, nonwoven, and knit—is available in sew-in and fusible forms. Sew-in interfacing must be anchored to the garment with stitches, either by incorporating it into a seam or by sewing it to a layer of fabric before the garment is constructed. Fusible interfacing is attached to the fashion fabric with a glue that's activated by heat from the iron. Choose between sew-in and fusible interfacing based on the project fabric, the garment's requirements, and your preference. Some sewers find sew-in interfacings more reliable; others like the convenience of fusibles.

Sew-ins provide the widest range of minimal, ultralight support options. Some of the best sew-ins aren't in the interfacing section of your fabric store, but are ordinary fabrics like cotton batiste and high-quality cotton organdy or silk organza. Remember, too, that the garment fabric itself can serve as an interfacing in some instances. Because a sew-in interfacing isn't glued to the fashion fabric, it doesn't substantially change the fabric's hand, and it can be more supple and flexible as it allows the layers to shift separately. A sew-in interfacing is the only choice if the fashion fabric can't withstand the heat or pressure of fusing (as with pile or napped fabrics, or synthetics with a low melting temperature), when the fusing agent shows through (as with sheer fabrics), or when the fabric just won't stick to the fusing agent.

Fusible interfacings are easy to use. Once fused, the fabric and interfacing become a single layer, which is easier to handle than two layers of basted-together fabric. Fusibles also do a great job of stabilizing loosely woven fabrics and of strengthening lightweight fabrics when used in a project that calls for heavier material. The fusing agent or glue yields a slightly firmer finish than a similar-weight sew-in provides, so it's important to test-fuse interfacing candidates to a scrap of fashion fabric and see how the hand is changed.

The size of the adhesive dots on fusible interfacing determines how deeply the adhesive seeps into the fabric, which affects the quality of the bond and the final hand of the fabric. Small dots work well on lightweight fabrics, and larger dots on heavyweight, loosely woven, and coarse fabrics.

A finished garment with fused interfacing has fewer separate layers inside it, and is therefore often easier to press. Fusibles are especially useful in tailoring and have replaced more traditional tailoring processes for almost everyone, from manufacturers to home sewers.

See "Sewing and Fusing Interfacing," on page 113.

3

Elastic

lastics are a blend of stretch fibers like rubber or spandex and natural or man-made nonstretch fibers such as cotton or polyester. There is a type of elastic for virtually every stretch project you can envision. From waistbands to decorative shirring, elastic makes clothes easy to sew, straightforward to care for, and comfortable to wear.

TYPES OF ELASTIC

There are three basic types of elastic: waistband, specialty, and lingerie. They are sold either packaged in precut lengths or by the yard. There are common widths for each type (indicated in inches or millimeters), but they differ slightly by manufacturer, as do colors. White is the most common elastic color, with black and beige following. Decorative varieties for lingerie are available in a rainbow of hues.

The main difference between the types of elastic is that some can be sewn through and some cannot. Some should only be threaded through a casing, as stitching through them breaks the inner bands of rubber, stretching the elastic out of shape and destroying its recovery (ability to spring back to its original, unstretched length). Sew-through elastics can be sewn or serged directly to your fabric without damaging their stretch recovery.

Elastics may be constructed by knitting, weaving, braiding, or extruding. The construction technique causes various elastic types to behave differently. The fiber content dictates how elastic should be laundered, so study the label and follow the cleaning recommendations.

Λ Guide to Elastics

No-roll

Cut-through

Sport

Drawcord

Buttonhole

Action

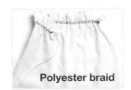
Polyester braid

Gripper/cycling

Elastic thread

Clear

Swimwear

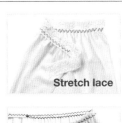
Stretch lace

Picot edge

Plush

WAISTBAND ELASTICS are specially designed for use in stretch waistbands.

SPECIALTY ELASTICS have unique characteristics, distinctive purposes, or out-of-the-ordinary applications that set them apart.

LINGERIE ELASTICS are designed specifically for undergarments and sleepwear. They are soft, pretty, and comfortable.

NO-ROLL
This stiff, fairly thick elastic is available in a variety of widths. Evenly spaced ridges prevent it from rolling or bending in a waist, cuff, or ankle casing.

SPORT
This soft, flexible elastic is a good waistband choice for boxer shorts, pajamas, and athletic pants, and it comes in 1¼-in. and 1½-in. widths. Rubber is removed from four visible rows, and stitching in these rows allows you to secure the elastic directly to the fabric without damaging its inherent stretch recovery.

BUTTONHOLE
This unique, adjust-to-fit, ¾-in.-wide polyester elastic has buttonholes spaced 1 in. apart along the center. It's an ideal choice for maternity and children's clothing, and for anyone with a changing waistline.

CUT-THROUGH
Used by many garment manufacturers, this high-quality, sturdy elastic is available in 1-in., 1¼-in., and 1½-in. widths. It can be cut lengthwise (for custom widths as small as ¼ in.) without raveling.

DRAWCORD
A seemingly magical elastic: 1¼ in. wide, with an encased cord that, when pulled out, expands to twice the elastic length. This comfortable, adjustable elastic is popular in sportswear and athletic garments.

ACTION
Available in 1¼-in. and 2-in. widths, this rugged elastic behaves and looks best with multiple rows of topstitching.

POLYESTER BRAID
Lightweight, narrow (⅛-in. and ¼-in. widths), and very stretchy, polyester braid makes easy work of gathered sleeves and cuffs. Note that braided elastics get narrower as they're stretched, and they are not as resilient as woven elastics.

GRIPPER/CYCLING
One side of this 1-in.-wide elastic features three rows of exposed rubber compound that gently grips skin. This ability to hold garments in place makes gripper elastic a popular choice for activewear, especially in hems of bike shorts, in wrists and ankles of ski wear, and across the top of strapless tops and dresses.

ELASTIC THREAD
Although this threadlike nylon elastic (available on a spool) is too thick to pass through your sewing machine needle, it can be used in the bobbin to produce shirred effects on lightweight fabrics.

CLEAR
Transparent as well as thin, lightweight, strong, and very stretchy, clear elastic resists oil and chlorine, withstands dry cleaning, and is available in many widths (¼-in. and ⅜-in. widths are most common). In addition to its use in swimwear, it's also great for gathering fabric and as a stay-tape for knit seams.

SWIMWEAR
Although this sturdy cotton-based elastic (available in ¼-in., ⅜-in., ¾-in., and 1-in. widths) is specially treated to withstand chlorine, it can also be used in many other garments.

STRETCH LACE
Available in a variety of widths (from ¼ in. to 3 in.) and patterns, this fine, soft, elastic produces a pretty edge on panties, slips, camisoles, and knit tops. It can also be used as straps.

PICOT EDGE
One edge of this elastic, available in ¼-in. or ½-in. widths, has decorative loops that are meant to just peek over the top of the fabric in panties, slips, camisoles, and knit tops.

PLUSH
One side of this sturdy, ¼-in.- to 1-in.-wide product (also called felt-back elastic) is soft and fuzzy, making it the ultimate in terms of comfort. It's a great choice for sport and bandeau shelf bras, as well as waistbands. One edge may feature decorative loops, similar to picot-edge elastic.

Closures

Closures—zippers, buttons, hooks and eyes, and more—perform an important role in garment construction. They enable you to get into and out of your garment easily and comfortably, keep openings from gaping, and offer the opportunity to make garments convertible (e.g., zip-off jacket hoods or pant legs). Whatever their function, closures should look right. They can be an eye-catching design feature or can do their job invisibly. Selecting closures can be a lot of fun, and you may find yourself just as inspired by the perfect button as by the right fabric and pattern.

ZIPPERS

Zippers are the most versatile of closures. From invisible types that are perfect for special occasion gowns to the heavy-duty metal-toothed variety found in jeans, there's a zipper for every application. A garment pattern lists the size and type of zipper required, but you can substitute a different style if desired. Once you start looking, you'll discover a host of choices regarding types of teeth, sizes and weights, slider variations, and zipping access options.

Types of Zippers

The vast range of zipper types, sizes, and colors can be sorted into one of three teeth styles.

METAL TEETH

Used most often on jeans, heavy leather jackets, and men's trousers, metal zipper teeth are made from brass, nickel, or aluminum. These are workhorse zippers. The teeth are first stamped out of the metal, then crimped around the tape edge and engaged by a metal slider. (Losing a tooth usually means you'll need to replace the whole zipper.) Once used in all women's clothing, metal dress zippers are now delegated to uses where extra strength is needed.

MOLDED PLASTIC TEETH

Unlike most metal teeth, plastic teeth don't corrode or have sharp edges. Zippers with molded plastic teeth are used in jackets, sports gear, tents, and sleeping bags. From rhinestones embedded into molded teeth to the wide color range available, plastic zippers are splashy, fun, and a good choice for novel, decorative applications. They are stronger and more abrasion-resistant than coil zippers, but they're not as flexible.

COIL TEETH

Coil zippers are the first choice for most garments and are becoming popular for slipcovers and luggage. A nylon coil is either sewn to or woven into the tape edge, and each loop on the coil serves as a tooth. Most coil zippers are self-fixing: Simply zipping the slider over a problem area reengages the chain. They take a curve better than molded plastic or metal zippers, and they won't jam. Of all three types, they're the most flexible and the smoothest for the majority of garments.

Anatomy of a Zipper

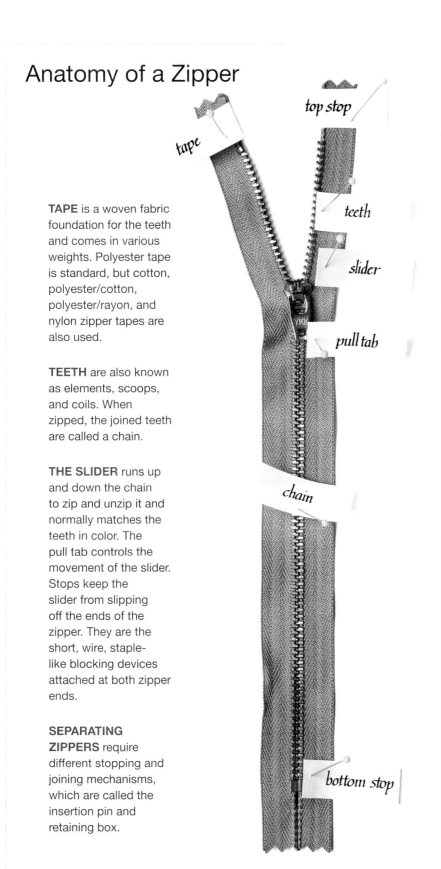

TAPE is a woven fabric foundation for the teeth and comes in various weights. Polyester tape is standard, but cotton, polyester/cotton, polyester/rayon, and nylon zipper tapes are also used.

TEETH are also known as elements, scoops, and coils. When zipped, the joined teeth are called a chain.

THE SLIDER runs up and down the chain to zip and unzip it and normally matches the teeth in color. The pull tab controls the movement of the slider. Stops keep the slider from slipping off the ends of the zipper. They are the short, wire, staple-like blocking devices attached at both zipper ends.

SEPARATING ZIPPERS require different stopping and joining mechanisms, which are called the insertion pin and retaining box.

tape

top stop

teeth

slider

pull tab

chain

bottom stop

Invisible zippers (a type of coil) are so called because from the right side, when sewn in, they can't be distinguished from the seam. They have fine teeth and are perfect for silk, polyester, or rayon fabrics.

Zipper Size

Zippers are measured by width and length. The width of the chain (the closed teeth or coil) determines the size of a zipper, from size 1 for doll clothes to size 10 for luggage, totes, and sleeping bags. Dress zippers range from size 3 to 4.5. Zippers for jeans and denim clothing start at size 4.5. For jackets, use size 5 to 10, depending on the weight of the fabric.

The precut, standard-length zippers normally available for garments and home sewing are intended for pants plackets, skirt plackets, and longer dress plackets and do not include any reference to teeth size. Teeth size designations come into play when you are purchasing zipper by the yard or are having custom zippers made. All three teeth types come in standard lengths and in separating versions.

See "Preparing the Zipper and the Garment," on page 243.

Continuous zippers are rolled onto reels, like ribbon, and are sold by the yard or roll, with sliders either included or purchased separately. You can cut continuous zippers to any size and configure them with sliders any way you want. They're available in all three teeth types and from size 4 to 10. These zippers aren't commonly used for garments, but they can be useful for home décor projects like slipcovers or accessories like large bags.

BUTTONS

If you collect buttons, you know that they come in many shapes, sizes, and materials. But for all their variety, there are basically two types of buttons: buttons with holes and buttons with shanks. Sew-through buttons have two, three, or four (or more) holes and are usually more casual and less expensive than shank buttons. Shank buttons

Anatomy of a Zipper

Zippers open in different ways. They can be purchased or assembled with a variety of zipping configurations. They can separate at one or both ends with either single or multiple sliders, and they can open from one or the other end or in the middle, or they can be used in reversible garments and open from both sides.

Closed-end for pants and skirts

Closed-end, two sliders for coveralls and jumpsuits

Separating or open-end for jackets

Two-way separator for outerwear

Head to head, two sliders, tape closed at both ends for sports bags and luggage

End to end, two sliders, tape closed at both ends for luggage

**NEW LIFE
FOR OLD BUTTONS**
Update your old buttons
or hide discoloration with
nail polish; it can create
some very interesting results.
Air-dry your garments sewn
with this type of button
because the heat from the
dryer might cause the button
to stick to the fabric.

COVERED BUTTONS

For a closure that matches fashion
fabric perfectly, or that provides unique
contrast, make a covered button. The
basic components of a covered button
are fabric, a form to support the fabric,
and a back that finishes the button and
provides a shank to attach the button to
the garment. Use coordinating fabrics,
or feature a motif woven or printed in
the fabric by intentionally positioning
the motif on your button form. If the
fabric is sheer or lightweight, consider
strengthening it with a layer of fusible
interfacing on the wrong side.

have a loop on the back that lifts them
from the fabric surface.

Sew-through buttons are best suited
for light- to medium-weight blouses,
shirts, dresses, pants, and skirts. Shank
buttons are generally used on jackets,
coats, and sweaters, where fabric bulk at
the buttonhole must be accommodated.
Button size indicates its diameter,
which can range from ¼ in. to 2 in. or
even larger for novelty effects.

Select buttons whose care
requirements match those of the
garment. If you want to use delicate
buttons on a wash-and-wear garment,
attach them with curved safety pins
or plan to remove the buttons before
washing.

See "Pins," on page 18.

Button forms and kits are readily available at fabric stores. Wrap a fabric circle snugly over a commercial button form (such as the ones shown at the bottom of page 41), tuck the fabric edges into the form, which often has little metal teeth, and attach the snap-on back to anchor the fabric and supply the shank. Refer to the package for specific instructions.

HOOKS AND EYES AND SNAPS

These little bits of metal or plastic, used to hold finished edges together, can fasten anything from the most delicate heirloom garment to bulky fur coats. You can hide hooks and eyes and snaps inside garments or feature them front and center for an updated style statement.

Hooks and Eyes

The sizing convention for hooks and eyes is entirely logical: The lower the number, the smaller the fastener. A 00 hook and eye is about ¼ in. long when fastened; a size 3 is just over ½ in. Sizes 0 through 3 work for most garments, aside from very delicate pieces or bulky outerwear. With standard dress hooks and eyes, from sizes 0 to 3, you have a choice of two eye styles. The round style is often simply called an eye. The straight or bar style is sometimes called a straight eye or bar. Choose a round eye to close abutting edges, and a bar style for overlapping edges.

Other specialty types of hooks and eyes are available for specific uses, like metal trouser hook sets for waistband closures, large covered hooks to secure fur garments, adjustable hooks and eyes for waistband size options, and swimwear hooks. A whole range of hooks and eyes has been developed for

stage costumes. Hooks and eyes are often preferred to zippers in couture garments. Hooks and eyes are also available preattached to twill tape for cases when you want to use several in a row, as in bridal wear.

See "Sewing Hooks and Eyes," on page 252.

Snaps and Snap Tape

Snap closures, which are used to hold overlapping edges together, are a good alternative to buttons or zippers, especially in garments that need to be put on and taken off easily, like clothing for children or adults with arthritic hands. The most common snap closures are sew-on snaps, snap tape, and gripper snaps, which all feature interlocking parts called a ball and socket. The type

of snap closure you choose depends on the look you want and the garment's function.

- **SEW-ON SNAPS** These most common snaps come in a variety of sizes, from size 4/0 for fine fabrics to size 10 for heavier, jacket-weight fabrics. Some larger sizes are available for fashion applications designed to be seen on the outside of a garment. They come in brass, nickel, and clear finishes and have "guide holes" in the center of the stud (ball) and socket for perfect alignment. Some clear snaps are heat resistant, so you don't have to worry about melting if you press over them. Check the package for details.

- **SNAP TAPE** This closure features the ball and socket portions of gripper snaps mounted onto separate pieces of twill tape. It is most often found applied to the crotch and leg areas of infant and toddler clothing and pillow and duvet closings. It's readily available in white and black, but the white tape can be dyed to match your fabric.

- **GRIPPER SNAPS** No-sew snaps are strong, sturdy, and often decorative. These four-part snaps are hammered or set into the fabric with a tool. There are two different types of gripper snaps: post style or prong style. The prong style has teeth that penetrate through the fabric and is most suited to loosely woven or knit fabrics, and on cardigans, shirts, vests, and

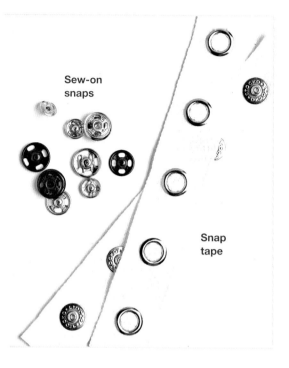

Sew-on snaps

Snap tape

BUCKLE OPTIONS

Bar prong

Bar/slide

Clasp

Quick release

lightweight jackets. The post style has a shaft that penetrates the fabric and is best used on densely woven or natural/synthetic fabrics, and on leather and outerwear jackets, denim jackets, jeans, and bags.

BUCKLES

Buckles are used for more than belts. You'll find them on the back of vests, the straps of overalls, totes and other bags, pillows, luggage, and sporting equipment. They're available in many sizes, shapes, colors, and materials, including cover-your-own options. Choose the size according to the width of the strap to which it will be attached, and keep the weight compatible with the weight of the project fabric. These are some of the most common buckles and their uses.

- **BAR PRONG** Prong buckles sport a single or double prong, depending on the buckle size, and require eyelets for adjustable positioning.

Use with webbing or covered belts and on straps and ties.

- **BAR/SLIDE** These buckles don't hold as securely as other styles because one belt end is simply woven through the bars. On some, the center bar is stationary; on others, it slides under tension from the tightened belt. To minimize slippage, the belt width should be slightly larger than the center bar length. Use with ribbon or trench-style belts.

- **CLASP** The click-and-lock mechanism of these buckles is similar to those on jewelry, so they are often decorative and used on all belt types and some bags.

- **OVERALL** Used with a button, this type of buckle is used to connect a strap to a garment or bag.

- **QUICK RELEASE** These heavy plastic stationary buckles allow for single-handed release and are used mostly in sporting gear. Use with webbing

or trench-style belts, on luggage, on sporting equipment, and on tote bags.

- **RING PAIR** D-shaped, O-shaped, square, or oblong rings are fastened on one end of a belt, tie, strap, or purse. Weave the other strap end through the rings to secure.

GROMMETS, EYELETS, AND LACING

Although traditionally used to reinforce functional openings in fabric, leather, or paper, eyelets and grommets are showing up as decoration on everything from scarves to boots. The terms *eyelets* and *grommets* are used nearly interchangeably, with size usually being the differentiating factor: Smaller sizes are referred to as eyelets, and finishings with larger holes are referred to as grommets.

These one- or two-piece metal or plastic reinforcements are used to cover the raw edges of precut holes in fabric. Use the smaller versions for belts, drawstrings, laced closures, bags, and decorative accents. Use the larger versions for window treatments, shower curtains, sport and duffel bags, and tarps. Once the eyelets or grommets are inserted, you can thread them with cording, rattail, ribbon, or any type of lacing that will hold the opening closed.

Anatomy of a Traditional Grommet/Eyelet

1. **BARREL** The barrel passes through the right side of the material and is joined to the washer on the wrong side. The barrel's dimensions (length, outside diameter, and inside diameter) are sized for material thickness, the size of the cut hole, and the intended lacing.

2. **FLANGE** The flange frames the hole's raw edge on the fabric's right side. Its width adds support to the hole.

3. **WASHER** The washer reinforces the fabric behind the flange. The barrel is crimped into the washer.

HOOK-AND-LOOP TAPE

This two-layer fastener is best known by the trade name Velcro®. It's an ideal closure for clothing worn by children or adults with limited hand mobility, and it is best suited for loose-fitting casual clothes. One layer has soft loops and the other has tiny hooks, so the two layers catch when they are pressed together. Variations include sew-on, fusible, and adhesive-backed. Hook-and-loop tape is available in white and black, a variety of tape widths, individual squares or dots, and different weights. For garments, look for the softest, lightest tape that can hold the garment closed.

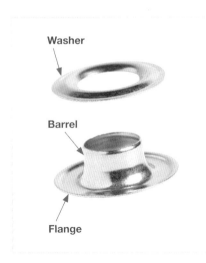

Washer

Barrel

Flange

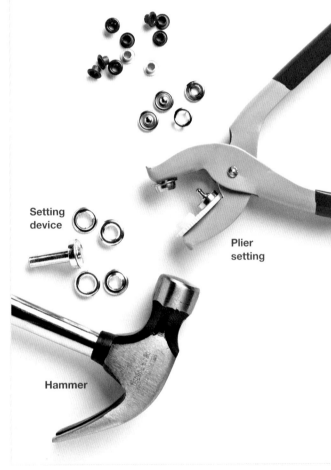

Setting device

Plier setting

Hammer

Trims & Embellishments

5

Decorative trims and embellishments are meant to be seen. Use them to enhance the design of your garment or accessory. Functional trims are used inside garments to add stability, strength, and a finished appearance. Peruse the notions department of your fabric store, and you're sure to be inspired. Be sure that the care requirements of any trims you use match those of the project.

FUNCTIONAL TRIMS

These trims perform specific construction jobs in a garment, either finishing raw edges or supporting and stabilizing key areas.

- **BIAS TAPE** Whether single- or double-folded, these bias-cut fabric strips have prefolded edges that meet in the middle (or slightly off center) to bind raw fabric edges. It is prepackaged in several widths and comes in a large variety of colors, but it's easy to make your own.

See "Bias Strips," on page 158.

- **FOLDOVER BRAID** Prefolded and slightly off center, with a knitted or braided band, foldover braid is used as a binding. Like bias tape, the wider section goes on the fabric underside.

- **HEM FACING TAPE** A wide strip of bias fabric with both long edges folded to the wrong side, this trim is used to finish/face hem edges. It can also be used to bind a raw edge.

- **SEAM BINDING** This woven tape is used to finish hem edges, reinforce

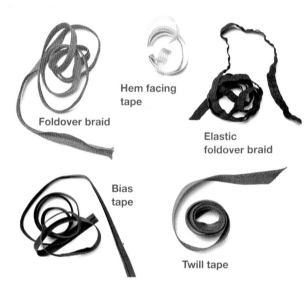

Foldover braid

Hem facing tape

Elastic foldover braid

Bias tape

Twill tape

seams, and extend seam allowances. It is often used in place of twill tape and tailor's tape.

- **TAILOR'S TAPE** This woven cotton or linen tape is traditionally used in tailoring to stay shoulder seams, roll lines, patch pockets, and more. It is also called stay tape and is commonly confused with twill tape, which is also used in tailoring, but is heavier, with a herringbone weave. There are several types of stay tape, including clear elastic and fusible.

- **Twill tape** A diagonally woven band perfect for reinforcing seams, drawstrings, or decorative applications.

DECORATIVE TRIMS

Decorative trims, whether subtle or over-the-top, are an ideal way to make a garment or accessory truly unique. Look for trims in the fashion fabric section of the store, and also in the decorator fabric area.

- **Appliqué** Fabric or embroidery motifs that are applied to a fabric background by sewing or fusing with an adhesive backing.

- **Band trims** Any number of trims with two finished edges that are either fused or topstitched in place. Variations include braid, gimp, ribbon, rickrack, soutache (narrow braid with a center indentation for stitching), and flat lace.

- **Chain** Metallic link chains are available for belts or accent trim in all sizes, colorations, and link shapes.

- **Continuous sequins, pearls, rhinestones** These single-stranded trims are glued or stitched to garments or craft projects. A special presser foot with a channel on the bottom allows you to machine-stitch some of them in place.

- **Cord** Available in twisted, knit, or braided form, cord can be used as a drawstring, sewn on top of fabric in a passementerie style, or used as an edging. It can be found in numerous colors and diameters. Combine or twist cords for belts and purse straps.

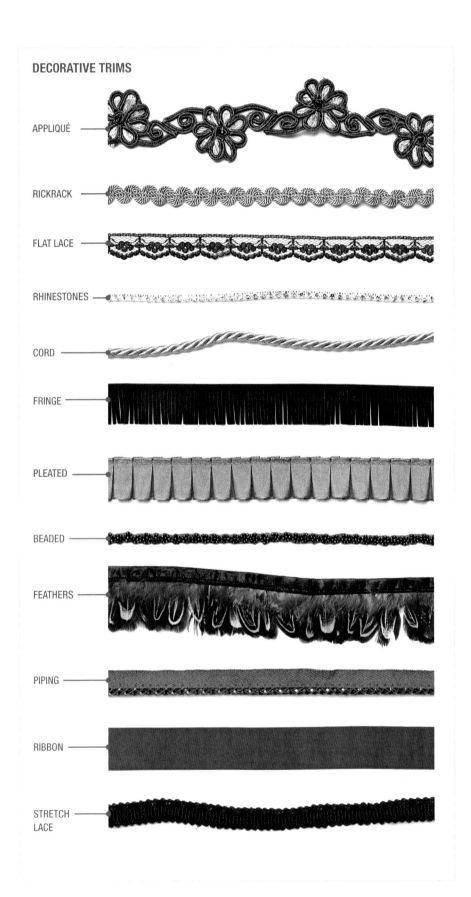

DECORATIVE TRIMS

APPLIQUÉ

RICKRACK

FLAT LACE

RHINESTONES

CORD

FRINGE

PLEATED

BEADED

FEATHERS

PIPING

RIBBON

STRETCH LACE

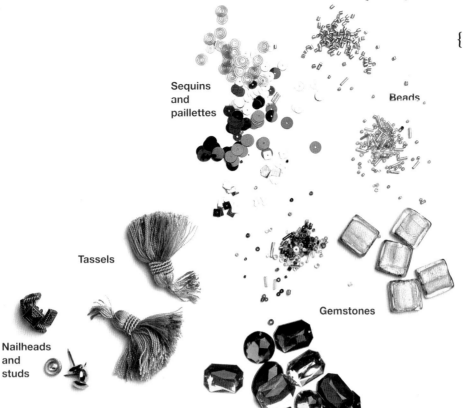

Sequins and paillettes

Beads

Tassels

Gemstones

Nailheads and studs

- **EDGINGS** Trim with one finished edge, which can be caught in a seam or topstitched in place. The opposite edge is decorative, as in fringe, pleated trim, beaded trim, ruffling, and piping. Lace and eyelet trims are often edgings.

- **FEATHERS** String individual feathers together to make continuous trim, buy them prespaced on a ribbon or fabric band, or buy them in the form of a boa. A feather boa has a corded center with feathers attached; it can be glued or hand-stitched in place.

- **PIPING** Piping has a twisted cord or fabric-covered cord, plus a lip of fabric or braid for attaching the corded edge to fabric, usually within a seam or along a hem edge.

- **RIBBON** Ribbon is a type of banded or edged trim. Enjoy the textures, colors, and patterns of so many wonderful choices. A popular variation has a picot edge of small thread loops.

- **STRETCH TRIMS** With elastic incorporated into the design, stretch trims offer flexibility and are suitable for sewing on stretch-knit garments. Stretch lace, sequins, and even rickrack are good examples.

EMBELLISHMENTS

Beads, sequins, feathers, and all manner of surface ornaments make your projects original. They take some time to apply, but the results are worth the effort. Match the weight of any embellishments to the fabric, and add interfacing or stabilizer to support the elements, if necessary.

See "Stabilizers," on page 336.

- **BEADS** Bugle and seed beads are the beads most often used on garments, but other bead types may also be used as long as the weight of the beads isn't too heavy for the fabric.

- **FEATHERS** Before applying individual feathers, cut away the calamus (hollow shaft) and the downy feathers near the base, then hand-stitch them. Apply them from the bottom of a garment up, overlapping rows like roofing shingles.

- **GEMSTONES** In all shapes, sizes, and colors, gems can be glued, heat-set, or applied with a prong backing and setting tool.

- **NAILHEADS AND STUDS** These embellishments usually have pronged backs so you can push the prongs through the right side of the fabric and fold the prongs down to secure them in place. Alternatively, you can use a setting tool to attach them. Heat-set versions are also available.

- **SEQUINS AND PAILLETTES** Like beads, individual sequins can be sewn directly on most fabrics, or they can be applied as prestrung strands. Paillettes are extra-large sequins and, like sequins, come in lots of colors, sheens, shapes, and sizes.

- **TASSELS** Perfect hanging from home decorating items and specialty clothing or accessories, tassels are easy to make or can be purchased ready-made.

Adhesives

Adhesives have been used for decades to bond fabric to itself or other surfaces in nongarment and garment sewing applications. The most common types of adhesive products are sprays, tapes, glues, and fusibles. Assess the requirements of your project to select a suitable adhesive.

SPRAY ADHESIVES

Contemporary spray adhesives fall into three basic categories: permanent, temporary, and repositionable. All sprays have toxic qualities, so refer to the package directions, and use them with care.

- **PERMANENT SPRAYS** As their name suggests, these adhesives create a lasting bond between two surfaces. Spray-on fusible web enables you to make any fabric fusible by simply spraying its underside and allowing it to dry. You can then cut the fabric into any shape or size you want, place it sprayed-side down in the desired position, and iron with medium heat to permanently adhere it.

- **TEMPORARY SPRAYS** Over time, these sprays lose their effectiveness. They will hold for hours or days and then release their hold. These sprays are often used to hold quilt layers together during quilting, to secure a stabilizer to an embroidery project, to adhere layers of fabric when making faux chenille, to position appliqués or lace on a garment while you try it on, to spray two masked-off seam allowances of velvet together

for shift-free sewing, and even to hold buttons securely for machine stitching.

- **REPOSITIONABLE SPRAYS** With these sprays, the sprayed surface can be positioned, removed, and repositioned without losing its stickiness or leaving behind a residue, somewhat like the ubiquitous Post-it® Note. Use a repositionable spray to hold stencils, which once used can then be picked up and positioned for reuse, or to preview appliqué placement choices before sewing them in place.

The safest practice is to use glues and adhesive sprays outdoors. The next safest plan is to create cross ventilation, for example, with a fan placed on the far side of the sprayed object, blowing toward an open window and away from the sprayer. Keep sprays away from your kitchen and all food or drinks. Never spray when children or pets are nearby. Be sure to read the product directions before use.

ADHESIVE TAPES

The range of sewing tasks that tapes can assist with is astounding. These non-toxic alternatives to sprays can be used to mark, measure, baste, and bond.

- **TIGER TAPE™** This pressure-sensitive, reusable tape is printed with stripes at various intervals and comes in ⅛-in. and ¼-in. widths. Position the tape next to the stitching line, and use the stripes as guides for hand-sewing precise, even stitches. You can also use it to position buttonholes, beads, or other repeating embellishments.

- **IRONABLE TAPE** Sold in ½-in. and 1-in. widths, this cellophane-like tape doesn't shrivel and distort when ironed. It also can be lifted and repositioned easily, making it especially useful for adjusting or repairing tissue patterns.

- **WATER-SOLUBLE BASTING TAPE** This tape is temporary, double-sided, and transparent, and it holds fabrics together for sewing. It won't gum up the needle (a common problem when sewing through tape), and it disappears after washing. Common uses include applying zippers, attaching trims before sewing, and holding slippery fabrics together within the seamline until they can be seamed.

GLUES

Like spray adhesives, the vast selection of glues is divided into temporary and permanent bonding categories.

- **PERMANENT GLUES** Bond fabric, lace, leather, trims, and embellishments instead of sewing them. You'll find multipurpose glues that work on many fabrics, as well as fabric-specific types.

- **BASTING GLUES** These removable adhesives provide a water-soluble, temporary bond that washes away the first time a garment or quilt is laundered. These are created specifically for sewing use. Conventional glue-stick products can be used as basting adhesive, but test that it washes out before applying to your project.

FUSIBLES

Fusible products that bond fabric to fabric, trim to fabric, and even fabric to hard surfaces make some sewing tasks much faster and easier to accomplish. Most of them require heat, pressure, and moisture to apply, so they can be used only in a project that can be ironed.

- **FUSIBLE WEB** A man-made adhesive fiber, which melts when heated by an iron. Placed between two layers of fabric, or between trim and fabric, and heated, fusible web bonds the layers permanently. Some web has a paper backing, allowing the web to be fused to one layer of fabric, after which the paper can be removed to expose the other web surface for fusing. This product is sold in prepackaged sheets or by the yard and is useful for applying appliqués and patches.

- **FUSIBLE TAPE** Fusible web sold in ¼-in. and ½-in. widths. Some fusible tapes provide a temporary bond before ironing. This product is available in different weights; choose a weight that corresponds to the weight of the fabric you're working with. Fusible tape is used for hemming, applying ribbons and trims, and making no-sew straps and belts.

- **FUSIBLE THREAD** Creates a temporary bond, and it shouldn't be used alone to make permanent seams. Thread the fusible thread through the machine needle or in the bobbin, and stitch so that it lies on the surface to be fused. Use fusible thread to baste seams, zippers, or appliqués before permanently sewing them in place.

TIP

Res-Q Tape™ is a clear, double-sided tape that can hold fabric to skin and fabric to fabric. It can also bond paper and leather and leaves no residue. This tape offers a quick fix for plunging necklines as well as for the gaps that form between blouse buttons and for hems that have come unsewn. Use Res-Q Tape instead of pins to keep lapels flat and scarves tucked or looped.

III
FABRIC

Fiber Selection

Selecting fabric is one of the most inspiring aspects of sewing, but with so many fabrics to choose from in every fiber, color, design, and texture you can imagine, you need some basic knowledge to ensure that you're picking the right fabric for your project. Fiber content establishes many of the characteristics of a particular fabric, so it's important to know what a textile is made of. From natural fibers—both plant- and animal-derived—to today's nearly miraculous synthetics, you're sure to find a fabric that suits your needs.

FIBER TYPES

Fibers fall into three basic categories: plant-based, animal-derived, and man-made. Many sewers are unwaveringly loyal to natural-fiber fabrics—and with good reason. Natural fibers are comfortable, are easy to sew, and produce attractive, easy-care garments. Although these fabrics have been around for millennia, they always look current and fresh. But 21st-century man-made materials have remarkable properties, too, and sometimes are exactly what you need for a particular garment.

- Plant-based fibers such as cotton, linen, hemp, and ramie are strong whether wet or dry, take dye well, are easy to launder, and press nicely. However, they also soil and wrinkle easily. Insects won't gnaw at them, but they are susceptible to mildew. They're rather dense, heavy fibers, and while they're absorbent, they don't wick moisture or dry quickly.
- Animal-based fibers include silk, wool, and hair fibers such as angora, mohair, camel's hair, cashmere, and alpaca. Fabrics made of these fibers tend to be light in weight relative to their bulk, insulating, and able to absorb moisture without feeling soggy. They are naturally elastic, resist wrinkling, and take dye well. However, you must protect them from damage by moths and carpet beetles. Chlorine bleach, strong detergents, hot water, and agitation damage distort, or even dissolve, these fibers. Dry cleaning is often recommended, but in many cases hand washing is gentler and safer.
- Man-made fibers are quite varied in their derivation and characteristics. Rayon, Tencel®, acetate, and triacetate are made from plant cellulose formed into threads. Petroleum-based synthetic fabrics, such as acrylic, nylon, polyester, and spandex, mimic—and sometimes improve upon—properties of natural fibers. Qualities of today's synthetics include elasticity, soil and water resistance, moisture wicking, durability, colorfastness, and excellent insulating properties. Thanks to new technologies, man-made textiles are easy to care for and comfortable to wear.

Sheer

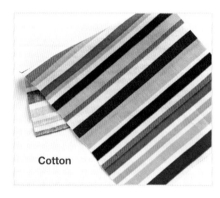

Cotton

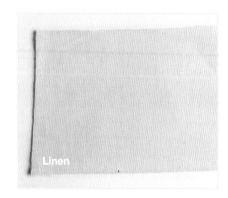

Linen

FIBER AND FABRIC EXAMPLES

Fibers can be woven or knitted into a wide variety of fabric types.

See "Fabric Structure," on page 56.

Below are descriptions of fabrics you'll encounter both in ready-to-wear garments and in fabric stores. Familiarize yourself with these as a starting point to understanding how to evaluate textiles for sewing projects.

Plant-Based Fibers

BATISTE AND VOILE

Sheer and semi-sheer cotton fabrics, such as batiste and voile, are fine, soft, and lightweight. Use them for lingerie, eveningwear, summer clothing, and heirloom sewing, as well as for comfortable, absorbent linings and underlinings. These fabrics are machine washable and can go in the dryer, but require ironing if you want a smooth, wrinkle-free look.

COTTON

Cotton (and cotton/polyester blend) plain-weave fabrics are commonly used for children's clothing, quilts, handcrafts, and home décor. They are easy to sew and easy to launder. Polyester content of up to 40 percent helps prevent

Silk dupioni

wrinkling without substantially altering the absorbency of cotton fibers.

LINEN

Linen fibers, from the flax plant, are the toughest of the vegetable fibers and are used to make fabric that is refined, strong, and comfortable. Linen is an airy but crisp and cool fabric that is also durable, quick drying, lint free, and easy to dye. It has a tendency to wrinkle, a characteristic some admire in a finished garment. Linen is available in many weights, appropriate for everything from fine lingerie to tailored suits. You can launder simple garments; dry cleaning is recommended to maintain any complex construction layers.

Animal-Based Fibers

SILK DUPIONI

Silk dupioni is a natural-filament fiber made of two strands of silk, the result

Silk noil

of two silkworm cocoons spun together. Dupioni has an irregular, slubbed surface texture with a reflective sheen. It's soft, with a crisp drape and little stretch. It also comes in a wide range of colors from jewel tones to pastels, is relatively inexpensive for silk, and doesn't wrinkle much. To maintain the fabric's sheen, you must dry-clean dupioni. Laundering it is an option, but this dulls the surface, producing a subtler, less formal finish.

SILK NOIL

Silk noil is made from the short waste fibers of silk, called *noils*. (Noil is sometimes incorrectly called "raw silk.") It is more casual than other silks with its matte, almost cottonlike surface. A coarse fabric that is also lightweight, silk noil takes dyes beautifully and comes in terrific colors. This durable fabric also has a gentle drape, travels well, and resists wrinkles. It doesn't

Wool bouclé

Wool jersey

Fleece

Microfiber

Rayon

show pin holes and is reasonably priced. Hand washing, rather than dry cleaning, is recommended.

WOOL BOUCLÉ

Wool bouclé is made of textured wool yarns, giving it a nubby effect. The yarns often include a three-ply strand, in which one ply is looser than the others and forms small, closed loops. Crimped, chenille-textured, or tufted yarns occur on novelty bouclé fabrics. Wool bouclé is easy to shape with heat and moisture, and the soft loops trap air, creating warmth. Its loft and surface texture make this a forgiving fabric to sew and a comfortable one to wear.

WOOL JERSEY

Wool jersey, a single knit characterized by lengthwise ribs on the right side and horizontal rows of purl stitches on the reverse, is a favorite for comfort, wrinkle resistance, and flattering drape

on the body. It skims the figure but isn't clingy, and it has a good amount of stretch. Jersey shrinks dramatically when laundered, producing a dense, felted fabric—sometimes a desirable effect. To prevent felting and shrinkage, dry-clean jersey garments, or hand-wash them very gently, with minimal agitation, and lay flat to dry.

Man-Made Fibers

FLEECE

Fleece fabrics are usually made of polyester or acrylic fibers. They are soft, lofty, warm, and water resistant, and they come in a variety of weights, colors, and patterns. Fleece is easy to sew and launder; it doesn't shrink and the colors don't bleed. Use lightweight fleece for jackets, scarves, and children's clothing, and heavier weights for outerwear jackets and blankets.

MICROFIBERS

Microfibers are made of ultrafine strands of synthetic fibers, usually polyester, nylon, acetate, or rayon. You'll find woven and knit varieties; woven versions are dense and often difficult to press crisply. They're strong, durable, and repel moisture. These nicely draping fabrics can be machine washed and dried.

RAYON

Rayon, sometimes called viscose, is a man-made fiber created from natural cellulose (wood pulp). Rayon comes in both woven and knit versions and is very versatile—it can mimic silk's drape and the feel of wool, cotton, or linen. It takes dye well and is soft, smooth, comfortable, and highly absorbent. Depending on the finish and weave, rayon fabric can shrink noticeably, so dry cleaning may be recommended.

Fiber Characteristics

FIBER	CHARACTERISTICS
COTTON	Absorbent, comfortable, durable, wrinkles, shrinks, easy to launder
LINEN	Absorbent, natural luster, quick drying, wrinkles, frays, little stretch
SILK	Absorbent, natural luster, insulating, strong, resilient, dyes well
WOOL	Absorbent, strong, elastic, shrinks when laundered improperly, wrinkle resistant
RAYON	Soft and comfortable, drapes beautifully, blends well with other fibers, shrinks, poor shape retention, wrinkles, dyes well
ACETATE	High luster, drapes well, loses shape, wrinkles
TRIACETATE	Drapes well, poor durability and elasticity, wrinkle resistant
ACRYLIC	Resembles wool, soft, warm, nonabsorbent, pills, heat sensitive, can shrink or stretch
NYLON	Strong, elastic, water repellent, colorfast, frays easily
POLYESTER	Good shape retention, easy to launder, wrinkle resistant, colorfast, blends well with other fibers
SPANDEX	Very elastic, adds stretch when blended with other fibers, requires stretch-stitching techniques, shrinks

Determining Fiber Content

The label on the fabric bolt should identify its contents, but if there is no label available, the burn test is a simple way to make an informed guess as to any fabric's general fiber content.

You'll need a small candle—short, wide, votive candles are perfect. Place the candle on an aluminum pie tin, which provides a stable, fireproof base and a safe place to drop the sample after burning. Use a pair of tweezers to grasp the fabric swatch.

Unravel several yarns from both the lengthwise and the crosswise directions of the fabric (if they appear different, test each separately), or cut a small sliver from a seam or hem if you're testing a garment. Burning too large a swatch can be hazardous.

Pass the yarns horizontally across the flame, watching the fiber both as it approaches the heat and as it ignites. Then remove it from the flame before it's entirely consumed, and note how it reacts. Put your nose to work, too: The odor of a burning fiber can be an excellent clue to its content. Feel the cooled ash with your fingers or with the tweezers to test the texture of the residue. Compare your results to the chart on the facing page to identify the fiber content of your fabric.

Fiber Characteristics

FIBER	APPROACHING FLAME	IN FLAME	REMOVED FROM FLAME	ODOR	ASH
COTTON	Scorches; ignites quickly	Burns quickly; yellow flame	Continues to burn rapidly; has afterglow	Burning paper	Light and feathery gray ash; ash is black if mercerized
LINEN	Scorches; ignites quickly	Burns less quickly than cotton; yellow flame	Continues to burn	Burning paper	Light and feathery gray ash
RAYON, TENCEL	Scorches; ignites quickly	Burns more quickly than cotton; bright yellow flame	Continues to burn rapidly; has no afterglow	Burning paper	Light and feathery gray ash
SILK	Smolders and curls away from flame	Burns slowly; sputters	Burns with difficulty; ceases to flame	Burning hair	Round, shiny black bead; easy to crush
WOOL	Smolders and curls away from flame; ignites slowly	Burns slowly with small flickering flame; sizzles and curls	Ceases to flame	Burning hair; stronger odor than silk	Crisp, dark ash; round, irregular bead; easy to crush
NYLON	Fuses (melts without burning) and shrinks away from flame	Melts, then burns slowly	Flame ceases and dies out	Celery	Round, hard grayish bead; won't crush
POLYESTER, POLYFLEECE	Fuses and shrinks away from flame	Melts, then burns slowly	Burns with difficulty	Chemical	Round, hard black bead; won't crush
ACETATE	Fuses away from flame; turns black	Blazes and burns quickly; sputters, melts, and drips like burning tar	Continues to melt and burn	Vinegar	Hard black ash; irregular bead; difficult to crush
ACRYLIC	Fuses and shrinks away from flame	Flames rapidly; sputters and melts	Continues to melt and burn	Chemical	Irregular, hard black bead; won't crush
SPANDEX	Fuses and shrinks away from flame	Melts and burns	Continues to melt and burn	Sharp, bitter	Soft, sticky, gummy

Fabric Structure

2

Fabric is made of fibers and yarns. Most conventional garment fabrics are either knit or woven from yarns. Some fabrics are made of fibers bonded together by heat, mechanical, or chemical treatment. Understanding how these fabric types are formed and being able to recognize their distinct yarn and fiber configurations helps you correctly match fabric to garment design, minimizes sewing and fitting frustrations, and improves the overall look, comfort, and fit of your final creations.

KNIT, WOVEN, OR NONWOVEN FABRIC

While the fiber content of a fabric determines its overall feel, its construction method contributes to its hand, drape, and stretch. The major difference between the two types of fabric is the way the yarns are configured. Note that differences in fiber type and manufacturing processes can alter the basic characteristics of any fabric type, resulting, for example, in a stretchy woven or a stiff and stable knit.

In woven fabrics, separate yarns cross each other at right angles. Each yarn is stretched as it is woven, producing a relatively stable fabric that doesn't give either along or across the grain.

See "Understanding Grain," on page 103.

In general, wovens retain their shape reliably. They're good for structured and tailored jackets, dresses, pants, and skirts.

In a knit, the yarns interlock in many small loops. These loops provide built-in give in a knit fabric (called mechanical stretch), making knits comfortable and easy to wear, but not particularly stable. Because many knit fabrics bag or stretch out of shape during wear, they're often reserved for casual clothing.

Nonwoven fabrics include a wide variety of materials, from wool felt to faux suede to PVC (vinyl). Leather and skins may be included in this category, too. Some of these fabrics stretch, others are quite rigid; some are breathable, others are entirely water- and vapor-proof. The one common property of these fabrics is that they don't have a defined grain.

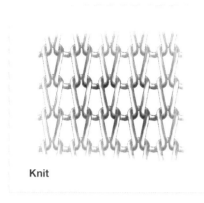

Knit

Woven

Knit

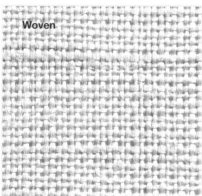

Woven

WOVEN FABRICS

In woven fabric, yarns cross each other at right angles. A loom arranges one set of yarns lengthwise (called the warp), then crosswise yarns (called the weft) are interlaced, or woven in, at right angles. Woven fabrics are either yarn dyed or printed and are stable with some inherent give on the bias.

Because they don't offer much mechanical ease (stretch that's built into the weave itself), woven garments offer support and, when properly fitted, conceal bulges. Most woven fabrics don't stretch along the lengthwise grain (the length of the fabric), and there is minimal give along the crosswise grain (the width of the fabric). When fabrics are woven from a yarn that's blended with spandex, they gain some built-in stretch. If you treat a woven garment well, you can count on it to hold its shape over time and many wearings.

Types of Weaves

Different weaves behave differently. Plain weaves in which the lengthwise and crosswise yarns are joined in a simple over-one-under-one pattern, like muslin, are smooth and often finely textured, but they tear easily along the grain and are prone to wrinkling.

Twill weaves, such as denim, gabardine, and some tweeds, have a diagonal rib on the surface. They're quite strong, but they fray badly and can be bulky due to the yarn density.

Satin weaves (these can be made of fibers other than silk, including cotton, wool, and synthetics) look glossy and smooth on the surface, but the long float threads on the surface are susceptible to snags.

Muslin

Denim

Satin

Types of Patterns

Woven fabrics can be given surface patterns by several dyeing and printing methods. Piece dyeing is the most common and economical dyeing method. These fabrics are fully immersed in a dye bath after they're woven, resulting in a solid color.

Yarn-dyed fabric is made with yarns that have been dyed before the cloth is woven. Yarn dyeing can create

Tartan plaid

Ikat

Chintz

ginghams, stripes, checks, and tartans or plaids, depending on the weave pattern.

Ikat is a unique fabric in which the warp and/or weft threads are resist-dyed before weaving. These patterned yarns are woven, creating an intricate, reversible pattern.

Printed fabric features designs applied to one side of a (usually solid-color) fabric. The wrong side of printed fabric remains solid, or shows a partial, faded version of the print, depending on the dye penetration. There are several ways to create the design on the cloth surface. Transfer, roller printing, and screen printing are common.

KNIT FABRICS

Knit fabric, as mentioned above, is created by the interlocking of yarns. A knitting machine forms a row of loops, then another row of loops is drawn through that row, again and again in a process similar to hand knitting. Because they're made of interlocking loops of yarn, knits stretch and mold close to the body, thus they're forgiving of a less-than-perfect fit.

Where woven fabrics have a straight and cross-grain, knits are properly described as having courses (horizontal rows, traveling from selvage to selvage) and wales (parallel to the selvages). However, in general parlance, courses are considered the cross-grain, and wales the straight grain. When laying out patterns on knits, align the grain-line along a wale.

See "Layout and Cutting," on page 301.

Knits are created in a number of ways, with each method producing a fabric with distinct properties. No matter how they're made, all knits have some degree of mechanical stretch. Even fabrics made in the same way may vary in stretch, however, so it's important to assess the properties of a fabric and compare them to the requirements of your project.

The fiber content of a knit deter-mines, to a large degree, its degree of stretch and recovery. While most knits stretch somewhat across the grain, and a little along the grain, those made with fibers containing a percentage (2 to 10 percent) of spandex have greatly enhanced recovery. They'll spring back to their original size after stretching, and sag much less than non-spandex-blend knits.

The stretch factor in a knit is often described in terms of a percentage: how far a knit can stretch beyond its unstretched width. To test the amount of stretch in a knit fabric, fold a sizable swatch (larger than 8 in. square) on the cross-grain, and mark a 4-in. interval on the fold. Grasp the fabric along the fold, beyond the ends of the marked area, and pull firmly. Measure the width of the marked area. If it measures 5 in., it has a stretch factor of 25 percent (fine for T-shirts and fleece jackets). If it measures 6 in. to 7 in., its stretch factor is 50 to 75 percent (good for leotards and swimsuits). If it measures 8 in., its stretch factor is 100 percent (ideal for high-performance activewear).

TIP

Many fabrics undergo some type of finishing process after knitting or weaving that changes their texture or performance. Fabric finishes can be as common as napping to create a soft, raised surface or as useful as a wrinkle- or crease-resistant or even a water-repellent finish. Be sure to check the label on the fabric bolt so you know exactly what you are buying.

Weft knit

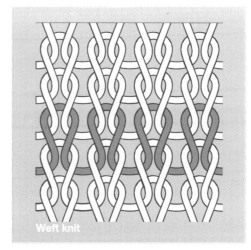

Weft knit

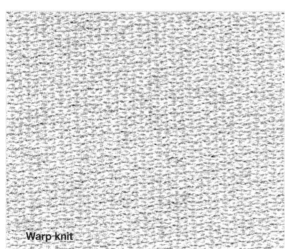

Warp knit

Warp knit

NONWOVEN FABRICS

Although weaving and knitting are the most common fabric production methods, fabrics can also be made by bonding, molding, and felting. Real and faux leather and suede belong in this group, as do nonwoven interfacings and paperlike "fabrics" such as Tyvek®. Each has its own characteristics and sewing requirements.

Felt vs. Fulled Fabrics

Felt is probably the most widely recognized of all nonwoven materials. It's made by the application of heat, moisture, friction, and pressure to wool and/or synthetic fibers, causing them to shrink and lock together to form a matted fabric. Fine-quality, all-wool felt is warm, dense, and drapable, and is suitable for coats and jackets. Unspun wool fibers, called roving, can be felted to other textiles, such as silk gauze or chiffon, to produce a hybrid fabric that has the qualities of pure-wool felt, with the added structure provided by the woven foundation. Synthetic felt, readily available in craft and fabric stores, won't wear well in a garment application, although it's fine for use in crafts and costumes that won't receive much wear.

Fulled fabrics are often incorrectly called "felt" or "felted." They're made by wetting, heating, and agitating woolen fabrics, which respond by shrinking considerably, becoming more dense, and developing a soft, fuzzy surface. Boiled wool, loden, and melton are made from fabrics that have been shrunk and felted. Wool knits are particularly well suited to fulling, yielding lofty fabric that tends to drape and conform to the body better than actual felt.

3

Choosing & Purchasing Fabric

Every sewer has his or her own approach to fabric shopping. Some have a particular garment style, or even a specific pattern in mind when they enter the fabric store, and they focus on selecting the perfect fabric to make that garment. Others shop speculatively, allowing the bolts of fabric to inspire them to creativity. Even if you're buying on impulse, it's important to determine whether the fabric you've fallen in love with is actually suitable for a garment you'd like to sew and wear. For a successful pairing of fabric to design, consider characteristics such as stability or stretch, weight and density, absorbency, opacity, drape, hand, surface texture, and color, pattern, or print.

HINTS FOR CHOOSING FABRIC

Fabric is fabric, but it's often categorized in stores by its intended purpose. Thus, you'll find stores or departments within stores specializing in fashion fabric, quilting fabric, and decorator fabric, and further subdivisions within those classifications. Even if you intend to sew garments, it's still worth visiting other shops. Quilting cottons are often just right for colorful blouses, children's clothes, and casual wear. Among decorator fabrics, you can find hefty, textured weaves that are perfect for unique jackets, or brilliant silks for special-occasion sewing.

A resourceful sewer realizes that the inherent properties of some fabrics can be altered. Interfacing, lining and underlining, quilting, pleating, and even more complex manipulations can totally transform a fabric.

See "Lining & Interior Fabrics," on page 66.

It's possible to add body, weight, and stability to flimsy yardage, and a run through the washing machine and dryer can soften stiff material. If you're determined and creative, you can persuade fabrics to work in unexpected and wonderful ways.

When shopping, though, bear in mind a few fabric-selection essentials.

- Patterns with the indication "for knits only" or "for knits with two-way stretch only" should only be used with knit or stretch woven fabrics whose stretch matches the gauge printed on the pattern envelope. The pattern's fit depends upon the fabric's inherent stretch.

- Drape describes how a fabric hangs. The silhouette of the garment determines whether the fabric needs to drape softly or stand away from the body. Unroll a length of fabric from the bolt and hang it over your arm to assess its drape.

- Dense fabrics are suitable for cold-weather garments. Sheer fabrics are suited for warm-weather and special-occasion garments.

- Plaids, stripes, and some other patterns require matching at seamlines, so garments with fewer seams make sewing with these fabrics easier.

- Heavyweight and bulky fabrics are best suited to garments without a lot of complicated design details. Conversely, garments with many design details are better showcased in solid or small-print fabrics.

- Fold and crush the fabric to see if it holds a crease or springs back. Fabric that holds a crease is a good choice for pleated designs.

- Certain fabrics stretch, slip, or cling and require extra skill and care for the best results.

- Fabrics with nap (see page 318) require special layouts to maintain consistent shading in the garment.

- Natural fabrics like cotton, silk, and linen are comfortable for clothing worn in hot, humid weather because they absorb moisture. Use them in loose fitting clothing for the coolest effects.

BUYING COORDI-NATING FABRICS

Although it's fine to buy a fabric just because you love it, you'll get the most use from your fabrics and resulting wardrobe—with fewer gorgeous pieces languishing in the back of the closet—if you purchase with a plan in mind. Shop for fabrics in groups to create garments that you can mix and match perfectly. Try to buy fabrics that work in an outfit grouping of at least three fabrics, as either a bottom (skirt or pants), a jacket, or a top. Not all outfits must have three pieces, or need three different fabrics, but it's a useful place to start.

In a group of three fabrics, the "speaking fabric" draws your attention (in the groups shown below, the center swatch is the speaking fabric). It's the strongest visually, the one you see first. The others, the "listening fabrics," are chosen to bring out, or in some cases to subdue, selected aspects of the speaking fabric. Speaking fabrics can include heavy tweeds, stripes, multicolor jacquards, and embroidered fabrics. Soft, muted fabrics are the easiest to combine with a variety of fabrics and work well as listening fabrics.

For the most versatile wardrobe, buy fabrics in groups of three. Include one strong, "speaking" fabric, and two "listening" fabrics that coordinate with it.

TIP

RECORDING BOLT-END INFORMATION

Keep your digital camera handy and take a photo of the information on the label on the end of the fabric bolt. Include a bit of the fabric in the photograph. Print the photo for a great fabric collection reference file.

be quite flexible, whereas a lightweight one that's tightly woven may be stiff.

Check out the drapery section for eyelets, batiste, lawn, lightweight cottons in pierced and embroidered versions, stripes, and madras plaids perfect for blouses and sundresses. You'll likely buy silk dupioni at a garment fabric store, but you'll find that home décor dupioni is usually heavier and often wider, and consequently a bit more expensive.

TIP

TIPS FOR SEWING WITH HOME DÉCOR FABRICS

- Prewash cotton fabrics. Plan for shrinkage, especially in the length.
- Sew or serge seams with all-purpose polyester thread.
- Use a universal or sharp needle in a size suitable for your fabric—as fine as 70/8 for sheer fabrics or as heavy as 100/16 for denim and canvas.
- Most of these fabrics will ravel, so bind or serge raw edges.
- Most of these fabrics are at least 54 in. wide and may be up to 110 in. or 118 in. wide. Extra-wide fabrics are meant to be "railroaded," or run sideways with the selvage at the top and bottom so curtains and other home décor projects can be made without seams. The pattern is oriented so that it's upright when the selvages are at the top and bottom. This technique may or may not work when using it for a garment, depending on the pattern and fabric design.

USING HOME DECORATING FABRICS FOR GARMENTS

When shopping for garment fabrics, don't hesitate to visit a home décor fabric store or department. The advantages of decorator fabrics are many: They're usually stronger, heavier, and, in some cases, wider than similar garment fabrics. They are often in a comparable price range as their garment-weight counterpart, and they have other advantages, too. They're usually treated with finishes for stain protection. Patterns are sold in several colorways and in coordinating groups, making wardrobe building convenient. Turnover in home décor fabrics is much longer than in fashion fabrics, so a year from now you can still buy the same fabric or a coordinating piece from the same collection. This enables you to continue to add to your wardrobe for several seasons.

For top-notch garment-sewing results, look among the tapestries, brocades, and damasks for a fabric that has body without being stiff. Because weight and stiffness work independently of one another in upholstery weaves, a heavy fabric can

ONLINE AND MAIL-ORDER FABRIC SHOPPING

Purchasing fashion yardage on the Internet and through the mail is easy, is safe, and multiplies your sewing options exponentially. If your local stores don't have what you need, you can send for it.

Whatever you're in the market for, from basic garment material to specialty decorator fabrics, quilt cottons, bridal silks, bargain yardage, high-end designer cuts, waterproof outdoor fabrics, or the finest heirloom batiste, you'll find it on the web. If you're hesitant to make a purchase online, your best bet is to start with a company that offers service either by e-mail or telephone.

Matching Fabric

Matching colors can be tricky, because each computer monitor displays images differently. If you're looking for something specific, the best solution is to work with a swatching service, which is like having a mini fabric store sent to your home at regular intervals for an annual fee. Some swatching services sell or give swatches of fabrics shown on their websites. Other sites provide a custom swatching service: You e-mail or phone the store with your color and fabric preferences, and they mail you swatches that fit those criteria.

Online descriptions vary from detailed information, including weight in ounces, to a quick notation of fiber content and fabric width. Look for phrases like "appropriate for tailored jackets," "lots of drape," or "great for full skirts," to help you determine if a fabric suits your needs. Search for clues in the photos, as well. Click to enlarge pictures, and note rulers, gauges, or other objects in the photo to assess the fabric's scale.

Some sites display fabrics in coordinated groups, or offer a "fabric coordination" feature, which allows you to cluster photo swatches as if physically grouping bolts in the store. Finally, for a safe transaction, look for the designation "https" before the site name to indicate a secure shopping site.

MAKE A STASH REFERENCE FILE

When you buy fabric, immediately cut a 2-in. square swatch and fuse or glue it onto an index card. Record the fiber information, width, yardage, and care instructions on the card. Punch a hole in one corner and keep all your file cards together on a split ring. This is a portable file when you're shopping or just a handy reference when your fabric stash is stored out of sight.

raw silk basketweave 88" wide

YARDAGE CONVERSION

Fabrics come in several standard widths: 110 in. (home décor fabric), 60 in., 54 in., 45 in., and 35 in. Most pattern envelopes call for fabric in 45-in. or 60-in. widths. If your fabric is wider or narrower, you need to calculate how much yardage to buy. Refer to the chart below to convert from one width to another.

Yardage Conversion Chart

The chart shows yardages for fabrics 110, 60, 54, 45, and 35 in. wide. If, for example, your pattern calls for 1 yd. of 60-in.-wide fabric, but you find a gorgeous 35-in.-wide fabric you'd like to use, simply read across the row to the 35-in. column on this chart, and you'll discover you need 1¾ yd. of fabric.

(36 IN. = 1 YD.)

110 IN.	60 IN.	54 IN.	45 IN.	35 IN.
⅝	1	1⅛	1⅜	1¾
¾	1⅜	1½	1¾	2¼
1	1¾	1⅞	2¼	2⅞
1⅛	2	2¼	2¾	3⅜
½	2⅜	2⅝	3⅛	4¼
1⅝	2¾	2⅞	3⅝	4¾
1⅞	3	3¼	4	5¼

Estimating Yardage without a Pattern

If you don't have a pattern for a favorite fabric, you can still find a way to sew with it. Determining the yardage for a particular project is straightforward. Start by measuring key body lengths, as shown below.

See "Body and Pattern Measurements," page 92.

Then follow the directions on the facing page for the garment you plan to sew. If you're buying a patterned fabric, you'll need a bit more to match the design lines at the seams and to make sure the print is pleasingly arranged in the garment. Depending on the print's repeat, you may need ¼ yard to 1 yard more fabric.

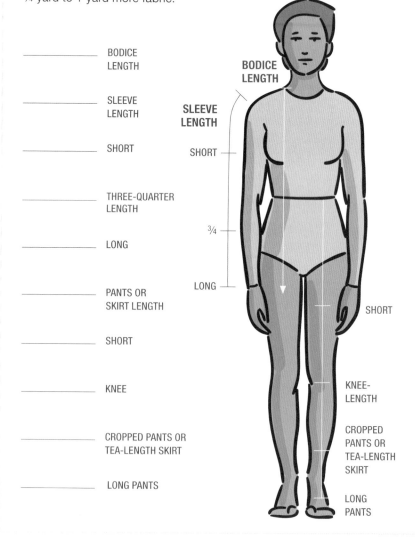

BODICE LENGTH

SLEEVE LENGTH

SHORT

THREE-QUARTER LENGTH

LONG

PANTS OR SKIRT LENGTH

SHORT

KNEE

CROPPED PANTS OR TEA-LENGTH SKIRT

LONG PANTS

BODICE LENGTH

SLEEVE LENGTH

SHORT

¾

LONG

SHORT

KNEE-LENGTH

CROPPED PANTS OR TEA-LENGTH SKIRT

LONG PANTS

USE KEY LENGTHS TO ESTIMATE YARDAGE

Take a guess at the lengthwise dimension of a pattern piece, basing the guess on a corresponding body measurement. Use this number to make the calculations explained here, then divide the totals by 36 to obtain the yardage requirements for most basic garments.

ESTIMATING YARDAGE

To figure out how much fabric you will need for a particular garment, all you need are a few body measurements and simple calculations.

Conveniently, estimating yardage this way automatically accommodates details such as pockets, collars, and waistbands, since these smaller pieces fit nicely between the key pattern pieces.

TOPS

- For 45-in. and 54-in. fabric, add one sleeve length and two bodice lengths. If your largest body circumference is greater than 40 in., add three bodice lengths.

- For 60-in. fabric, add one sleeve length and one bodice length.

SKIRTS

- For a straight skirt, if the difference between your hip circumference and the fabric width is 7 in. or more, you need one skirt length (that is, the skirt length you desire plus hem allowance). If the difference is less than 7 in., you need two lengths.

- For a flared skirt, divide the hem circumference by the fabric width. Round the resulting number up and buy that many lengths of any width fabric.

DRESSES

For any fabric width, simply calculate the lengths needed for a top and skirt, then add them together.

PANTS

The distance from crotch point to side seam at the crotch level is key to estimating yardage for pants. It determines how you will arrange the pattern pieces on the fabric.

- For 45-in. fabric, buy two lengths (plus hem allowance), unless your hip circumference is less than 30 in., in which case you need only one length.

- For 54-in. and 60-in. fabric, you may or may not be able to fit the four pieces across the fabric width. Do a test layout to determine whether the front and back patterns can fit side by side. If so, purchase one length; if not, purchase one-and-a-half lengths. The width of your measurement at the crotch level determines how much yardage you need to buy to allow for the proper length.

Lining & Interior Fabrics

Several fabrics are used inside garments to add support to the fashion fabric or to conceal inner construction, so that the garment wears better, holds its shape, and is more comfortable. These fabrics include interfacing (see pages 34–35), lining, underlining (sometimes referred to as interlining), and batting. Many different types of fabric can be used to perform these functions, so don't hesitate to think creatively when selecting inner fabrics.

Interfacing is used in most garments and is often considered, and listed on the back of the pattern envelope, as a necessary notion. Underlining and lining are used most often in tailored garments, and batting is used to add insulation to jackets and outerwear.

LININGS

A lining hides the interior construction of a garment. It reduces the transparency of the fashion fabric, increases the life of your garment, and makes it more comfortable and easier to wear.

Choose a lining fabric based on compatibility with your fashion fabric in weight and care requirements. A lining fabric should be slippery, flexible, colorfast, durable, wrinkle resistant, and comfortable to wear.

Types of Lining

Most traditional lining fabrics are lightweight and silky or slippery, but you can use other types of fabrics depending on the requirements of your garment. Natural fibers and man-made fibers with a natural base, like rayon, absorb moisture more readily than synthetic types, meaning they wrinkle more but are often more comfortable to wear.

• **ACETATE** linings are common in ready-to-wear and are available to the home sewer. They press very flat and are inexpensive, but they

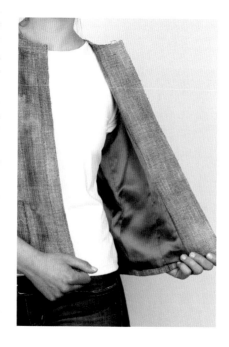

must be dry-cleaned. Acetate has a tendency to water-spot and discolor from perspiration, and an acetate lining may shred in areas that receive continuous abrasion. Use acetate linings in garments that will have limited wear, such as the skirt of a wedding dress. Acetate fabrics can also crock, or transfer dye when rubbed, so avoid pairing dark colors with light-colored fashion fabric.

- **Cotton batiste or lawn** can be used for lining some garments. These lightweight cottons are cool, absorbent, and soft, but they're not slippery, so they're most suitable for lining fitted bodices and other areas of a garment that don't need to slide on. When using cotton, always remember to preshrink the fabric.

- **Cotton flannel** makes a warm lining in a roomy garment like a barn jacket. It's soft, adds body, and always needs preshrinking.

- **Flannel-backed satin** linings offer added insulation. They're heavier but have good drape and are suitable for all types of outerwear.

- **Knit** lining fabrics are important when you're lining a garment made of a stretch woven. Stretchy tricot, used mainly for lingerie, is a good choice for sweater knits and closely fitted garments in stretchy woven fabric. For lining lightweight knits, there's stretch illusion, which is very transparent and soft, and can be cut clean without finishing the raw edges.

- **Polyester** linings are washable and available in various weights and weaves, and are usually quite affordable. Unlike acetates, they take stress very well. Polyester traps moisture near the skin, however, so

Lining Fiber Guide

FIBER	PROS	CONS	BEST FOR	CARE
SILK	Luxurious, antistatic, breathes	Expensive, breaks down over time	Eveningwear	Hand wash, high-quality dry-clean items
ACETATE	Inexpensive, breathes moderately	Frays and rips, least durable, perspiration	Coats	Dry-clean only, dry-clean-only garments
COTTON	Comfortable, soft/breathes	Dries slowly, wrinkles, doesn't slide over	Casual items	Machine-wash
RAYON	Durable, antistatic, comfortable	Shrinks, expensive	All fabrics	Machine-wash or dry-clean, all garments
POLYESTER	Widely available, inexpensive, easy care	Hot/sticky, pills/puckers	Man-made fabrics	Machine-wash

it can feel hot and sticky or clammy in some situations.

- **Rayon** is a great fiber for linings because it's breathable and wears very well. It is usually lightweight, soft as silk, firmly woven, strong, washable, easy to press, and cool to wear. It's a little more costly than acetate and polyester linings, but it pairs beautifully with most fabrics and is suitable for a wide range of garments.

- **Sheer** linings are needed for sheer or lacy fabrics. Chiffon, organza, or stretch illusion are suitable if you want to maintain the sheer quality of the fabric. For a completely transparent, "nude" look under sheers, match the lining color to the skin tone.

- **Silk** lining is a hidden luxury. The most common silk lining is China silk, which is very lightweight, has a slightly crisp hand yet drapes well, and is cool to wear. It's a little fragile, so it's not recommended for garments that receive a lot of

TIP

If you can't find a stretch lining to match a stretch-woven garment, try using a rayon, silk, or polyester lining that's cut on the bias for stretch.

wear. For longer wear and a richer hand, consider silk charmeuse, jacquard, dress-weight crepe de Chine, washed silk twill, or silk broadcloth.

Lining Weights

To determine the best lining weight for your garment, first consider how much structure and warmth you want. Then layer the lining and fashion fabric, and drape them over your hand to test compatibility.

- **LIGHTWEIGHT** China silk is the lightest of the lightweight linings and is perfect for delicate blouses, jackets, dresses, and soft skirts and pants. Silk charmeuse is another lightweight choice that provides a little more structure.

- **MEDIUM WEIGHT** Midweight linings are the most versatile for jackets, skirts, and pants. They include most polyester linings as well as silk taffeta, jacquard, and broadcloth. Bemberg™ rayons are available in many weights but commonly fall under this category.

- **COAT WEIGHT** Silk satin, polyester satin, acetate twills, and acetate satins have a dense weave, which makes them heavy, durable, and warm—perfect choices for outerwear. There is also a water-repellent acetate overcoat lining for trenches and rainwear.

- **HEAVYWEIGHT** Quilted lining is durable but bulky. It is the warmest offering for coats because it traps air in the batting. Most are acetate or polyester and require dry cleaning. Flannel-backed lining (also called fleece-backed lining) is the stiffest option but has a silky side to slip over clothes. It provides about the same warmth as a quilted lining but without bulk. It's also acetate and requires dry cleaning.

UNDERLINING

The job of underlining is to add support and durability to fashion fabric, helping it keep its shape and resist wrinkling. Underlining hides between the garment's outer fabric and lining. It's cut from the same major pattern pieces as the garment and is hand-basted to the wrong side of the fashion fabric. From then on, throughout the gar-

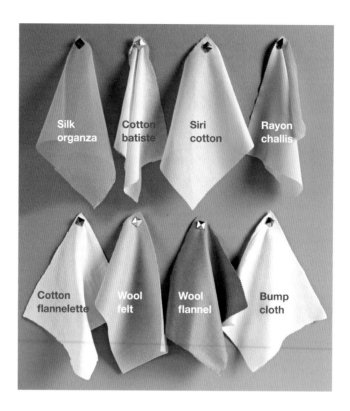

ment's construction, the fashion fabric and underlining are sewn as one, with the underlining supporting the garment from the inside out. An added benefit is that seam and hem allowances can be stitched to the underlining, anchoring them invisibly for a smooth appearance on the outside of the garment.

Types of Underlining

Underlining can perform several functions, depending on the garment. It can add featherweight support or warmth, structure, and subtle padding to conceal foundation elements such as boning. The samples shown above are some of the most commonly used underlining fabrics.

SILK ORGANZA

Silk organza makes an exceptional underlining fabric because it's very lightweight, strong, and flexible. Because of these traits, it's naturally able

to mold to a fashion fabric and invisibly strengthen and support it without bulk. It reinforces loosely woven fabrics, gives life to limp fabrics, supports a garment's shape, reduces wrinkles, and keeps a garment from becoming disfigured with wear and cleaning. Use it in garments that range from tweed suits to charmeuse dresses to summer-weight garments.

COTTON BATISTE

In cotton garments, substitute cotton batiste for silk organza.

SIRI COTTON

This white, plain-weave cotton broadcloth is a little thicker than organza. It's similar to a shirt-weight cotton, which would be a good substitute. It is suitable for tailoring, when making a summer-weight jacket out of silk dupioni or moiré.

RAYON CHALLIS

This limp, lightweight twill weave, which is usually made into women's dresses, is a bit hard to find in solid colors (it's usually printed). Yet it's the best underlining for wool crepe. It keeps the fluidity of the wool crepe, but the twill weave inhibits bagging at elbows and seats of skirts.

COTTON FLANNELETTE

Use cotton flannelette for underlining tailored moiré, faille, and bengaline clothes. It also makes silk dupioni jackets warmer. It provides weight and warmth, and when sewn with a slight zigzag stitch (0.5 mm wide, 3.5 mm long), it makes a seam without any puckers.

WOOL FELT

Wool felt is used in limited amounts. Collars and cuffs, especially when made from velvet or satin, benefit from having wool felt underlining.

WOOL FLANNEL

When you want warmth and substance for an otherwise thin fabric, using wool flannel gives you the best of both worlds.

BUMP CLOTH

Bump cloth is used to underline the most expensive draperies, hence you'll find it in the decorator fabric department. This is the top end of the thickness scale; it looks like a thin cotton flannel blanket.

BATTING

Quilted garments are warm, comfortable, and stylish. But all the qualities depend on the type of batting you choose and how it pairs with the fashion fabric of your garment. Consider loft, fiber content, and flexibility when selecting filling for quilted clothes, as well as care requirements (which should be labeled on the packaging). Batting is sold either by the yard or in prepackaged pieces intended for quilts. The price varies, usually depending on the fiber content.

Loft is the thickness of the batting. For garments, especially fashion pieces that aren't intended as outerwear, opt for a very thin batting. Some battings can be separated into two layers for even thinner quilted results. Polyester batting tends to maintain its loft longer than cotton or silk, but it can make a garment look stiff.

Like fabric, batting comes in a variety of fibers, including polyester, cotton, and wool, as well as luxury blends with cashmere, alpaca, or silk. Natural-fiber batting is more comfortable to wear than polyester, providing insulation and breathability. Silk batting, though very lightweight and luxurious, sometimes sheds fibers through the fashion fabric.

There are two types of batting: bonded and needlepunched. In bonded batting, the fibers are held together with a resin. In needlepunched batting, the fibers are interlaced by being punctured repeatedly by many needles. Bonded batting is lighter and loftier, while needlepunched batting is denser.

Batting can soften and grow thinner with use. To test how a particular batting will change with time and wear, knead a sample of it in your hands for several minutes and observe whether it loses body, wads up, or holds its

shape. It's important to select a batting that will react the way you want your garment to react, either softening gently over time or maintaining its original form and structure. After feeling the hand of the batting on its own, you should layer a sample between a piece of your fabric and lining. Again, work them in your hands to test the layers for flexibility, loft, and weight.

TIP

You can quilt garments using fabric as "batting." Cotton flannel or flannelette makes lovely batting for drapey garments, and so does muslin or gauze. These yield a very thin, pliable quilted fabric but with less texture and loft than batting provides.

5

Fabric Care & Storage

Fabrics often change, sometimes drastically, when laundered. To avoid unwanted shrinkage, color bleeding, puckered seams, and other similar problems, it's best to pretreat fabric before you cut and sew it. If you decide ahead of time how you want to care for the finished garment, you'll know, too, how to pretreat the fabric. Machine washing and drying, hand washing and air drying, and dry cleaning are the most common methods of pretreating and cleaning fabrics and garments.

PRETREATING FABRIC

Pretreating fabric serves two main functions: It prepares fabric for sewing by removing excess dyes as well as any finishes or sizing, and it takes care of shrinkage ahead of time, so that the finished garment reliably maintains its size and shape. Additionally, you can use pretreating methods to make deliberate changes to the fabric's characteristics.

See "Creative Laundering," on page 72.

Pretreating methods depend on the type of fabric you're using (both fiber and structure), the kind of garment you plan to make (structured or unstructured), and the cleaning method you'd like to use for that garment.

As a general rule, treat fabrics more harshly during the pretreating phase than you would handle the finished project. You want any changes to the fabric's texture or size to occur before you cut and sew. If you know the fabric's fiber content, you can make informed decisions about how to pretreat. If you don't, cut swatches and test-treat them to see which method provides the most satisfactory results.

Bear in mind that nearly any cleaning method changes fabric in some way. It's up to you to decide how much and what kind of change you're willing to accept.

Cotton and Linen

Most cotton and cotton-blend fabrics can be machine-washed and -dried, but they are prone to shrinkage, including, in some cases, progressive shrinkage over several washings. Pretreat cottons by washing them in hot water and tumble drying them in a hot dryer. If you're concerned about progressive shrinking, repeat this process two or three times. Then, launder the finished garment in cold water and machine-dry at a warm temperature.

Many linen fabrics have been treated with finishing processes that soften the fibers and at the same time reduce or eliminate shrinkage. Still, you should wash and dry yardage before sewing— even if you're making a structured garment that you plan to dry-clean.

Wool and Animal Fibers

Wool and animal fibers such as camel hair, angora, and alpaca, as well as many wool blends, should not be laundered unless you're deliberately trying to shrink or felt them. Pretreat them by steaming or using the "London shrink" method described below.

For the most consistent results with steaming, take the yardage to a dry-cleaner for a professional steaming, asking that the fabric be shrunk, if possible. Alternatively, you can steam the fabric yourself using a steam iron. Lay the fabric on a large surface or over an ironing board, supporting the overhanging sections on a chair or table to avoid stretching. Press the yardage with steam, allowing each steamed area to dry thoroughly before shifting the fabric.

A simple, iron-free method for shrinking wool is called the "London shrink." First, dampen a bedsheet (put it through your washing machine's rinse and spin cycles without detergent). Lay the sheet flat and spread the wool fabric on top of it, keeping the grain straight. Fold the sheet ends in to completely cover the fabric, then roll it into a loose tube. Slip the tube into a garbage bag, squeeze out any air, knot the bag closed, and leave it for 12 to 24 hours. Open the bag, and unroll the damp sheet and now-damp wool. Lay a dry sheet on a table and spread the wool on it, again making sure the selvages are straight. Leave the fabric to dry, then press it. Garments made from wool treated this way should be dry-cleaned.

If you want to felt, full, or shrink wool fabric, machine-wash it with a nondetergent soap or shampoo in hot water with a cold-water rinse, and tumble-dry it. Maximum felting effects may require more than one wash/dry cycle. Garments made from fabric treated in this way must be dry-cleaned or, in some cases, very gently hand-washed.

Silk and Rayon

Ready-to-wear silk and rayon garments are almost invariably labeled "dry-clean only," but silk fabric, and garments made from it, can be laundered. To maintain the shiny surface and/or crisp hand of some silks, such as dupioni or brocade, don't prewash the fabric. Use it as is, and dry-clean the garment. Note that dyed silk and rayon fabrics can bleed, so prewashing is recommended if you're using multiple colors in a single garment.

To create softer textures for silk fabrics, however, prewash the fabric with shampoo or a special product such as Synthrapol®, which removes dirt, oil, and silkworm gum, as well as excess dye. Machine- or hand-wash, depending on how you plan to clean the finished garment, then lay flat or tumble-dry (you can machine-dry on warm until the fabric is slightly damp, then air-dry). Machine washing and drying silk charmeuse can result in a sueded surface, and laundering dupioni dulls the sheen and softens the hand noticeably. If you prewash silk fabric, you can wash the finished garment the same way, unless it's tailored or otherwise structured (as in special-occasion wear).

Synthetics

Most man-made fabrics are completely machine-washable, and many can be machine-dried. They don't tend to shrink, but some melt or degrade when subjected to hot temperatures in the

Test swatches of your fabric to determine the best pretreating (washing, drying, and pressing) method.

Creative Laundering

While prewashing is always recommended if you want to sew a machine-washable garment, there are other reasons to launder fabric. The idea behind creative laundering is not to make perpetually washable fabrics, as is the case with typical prewashing, but instead to improve the surface and hand of a fabric for more elegant sewing. There's always a small risk involved in machine washing fabric that's not specifically labeled with those instructions, but it's worth experimenting if you'd like to alter the fabric's characteristics.

The most marked changes occur in silk, wool, rayon, and blends of these fibers. Cotton and linen, known for withstanding regular laundering, don't change much.

If you're not sure you want to change the fabric dramatically, start by washing a small swatch. Use hot water, strong agitation, and hot machine drying. Recommended soaps include shampoo, grease-cutting liquid dishwashing soap, and Synthrapol. Note that some fabrics change progressively after several launderings.

Rayon

Silk brocade

Tropical wool

dryer. Unless the fabric is treated with a finish that inhibits sewing, you may not need to prewash a synthetic at all. If you do wash the fabric and garment, note that nylon and spandex, in particular, can be damaged by drying with heat; hang or lay these items flat to dry.

Polyester fabrics, like lining and fleece, are best left unwashed before sewing. They're often treated to resist static electricity, and they're easier to handle during construction if you don't remove that finish.

Notions

Pretreat any notions to be used in a project, such as zippers, lace, elastic, and trims, using the same laundering method as the fabric. Toss them into a mesh bag, then wash and dry with the fabric. Also pretreat sew-in interfacing in the same manner as your fabric. Pre-shrink fusible interfacing by folding it into a manageable size and submerging it in warm water for 5 to 10 minutes. Remove it from the water, carefully unfold it, and place it on an absorbent towel or a drying rack to dry, smoothing out any wrinkles.

CARING FOR AND STORING GARMENTS

Cleaning and storing garments properly ensures that pieces you've created last and look good for many seasons, or even years. The purpose of cleaning is to restore a garment to a condition as close to "new" as possible without damaging it. Check the fabric content of clothes you wear often. On ready-to-wear clothing, use the manufacturer-recommended cleaning method. For custom-made clothing, use the cleaning method indicated on the fabric bolt.

Consider fiber content and finishes such as dyes, trims, linings, embellishments, or buttons before you proceed. The fashion fabric may be washable, but the trim or lining may not be. If the garment is soiled, consider the types of stains that must be removed.

Dry Cleaning

Most dry-cleaners use the liquid solvent perchloroethylene (or "perc") in their cleaning processes. Unlike water, it does not penetrate fibers, so the process protects the fabric from the swelling and shrinking associated with water saturation. After garments are immersed in cleaning liquid, the fluid is drained, and the clothes are machine-spun to extract remaining solvent. They are then tumble-dried with hot air and removed for ironing.

Dry cleaning usually maintains dye colors, but the heat used can melt pearls, buttons, and other embellishments. It is the best choice for removing oily stains and for materials that shrink, such as wool. Look for a Certified Professional Dry Cleaner (CPD) and one that is a member of the Drycleaning & Laundry Institute (DLI).

Washing in Water

Water washing with detergent or soap can remove grease, oil, dirt, mud, and body fluids. Most detergents have whiteners, but whiteners can fade dark colors; check product labels. Sugar- and salt-based stains such as food and beverages are best treated by washing, but if the item must be dry-cleaned, ask for a treatment specific for sugar-based stains. Stains can set if allowed to stay in the fabric for too long, and not all stains can be removed.

Storing Garments

Protect your clothing from dirt, moisture, heat, light, and insects. Store clothing in a dry, climate-controlled area such as a closet or under a bed (avoid attics and basements). Store it away from light and heat sources as well as areas where pets sleep to avoid flea infestation. Cover clothes that are seldom worn with a garment bag made of clean muslin or an old sheet that has been laundered without fabric softener.

Garments should never be stored on metal hangers. Prolonged hanging on a narrow edge can result in weakening fibers and stretching. Instead, use padded, scent-free hangers with broad surfaces.

If the garment is too heavy to be supported on a hanger, an archival box is the best choice for long-term storage.

These boxes shield your heirlooms from ultraviolet rays, fluorescent lighting, dust, and dirt. Use unbuffered or acid-free (pH neutral) tissue to wrap and stuff garments. Pad the bust and arms to give them natural form and support. Do not seal the box.

After two to three months, check to see if yellow sugar spots have formed. Reclean the garment at the dry-cleaners for sugar spots. Some stains may remain, and they will be permanent. Once a year, remove the garment from the box, air it for one to two days, and return it to the box with fresh acid-free tissue paper, folding it in a slightly different way to avoid permanent creases.

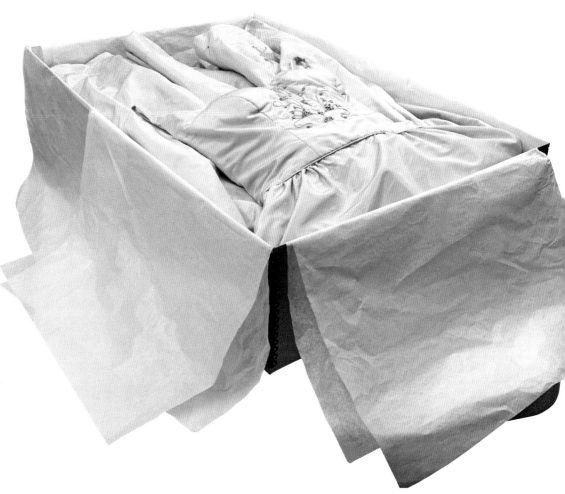

IV
WORKING WITH PATTERNS

Shopping for Patterns

Shopping for patterns is nearly as much fun as shopping for clothes—only you know that if you sew your own garments, you can have exactly the fit, style, and color you want, no compromises. You may have explored the pattern department of your local fabric store, and that's a great place to start. But there's a world of patterns beyond the fabric store, where you can find unique styles and fit. And remember, patterns aren't law. Once you know how to use them, you can change them any way you like. If you're an aspiring designer (even if just for yourself), you're sure to find the wealth of patterns available today a wonderful source of information and inspiration.

TYPES OF PATTERNS

Whatever the level of your sewing skills, your interest in designing original garments, and your personal style, there are patterns to suit. Prices range from very low (for paper patterns at in-store sales) to substantial (for full-featured pattern-drafting software), so consider what your needs are before purchasing.

Standard "Commercial" Patterns

The most familiar type of pattern is the printed tissue pattern, sold in envelopes at fabric stores (some smaller brands print their patterns on heavier paper stock for durability). Most patterns contain one garment with style variations, or several garments intended to coordinate in a wardrobe. You'll find everything from the most basic garments to the latest trends. You cut the tissue templates and follow the sewing instructions included on the pattern guide sheet. When on sale, tissue patterns are very inexpensive; full-price designer patterns cost more, but still represent a good value compared to purchasing a designer garment.

Pattern Magazines

International pattern publishers often sell fashion magazines with patterns included for sewing the fashions pictured. The styles offered tend to be fashion-forward. Each issue usually contains 20 to 40 separate, multisized designs, which are printed on removable pattern sheets. The patterns are often printed in "road-map" style, with each garment's pieces outlined in a different color, and all the pieces overlapped and nested. To use them, you need to trace the appropriate pattern pieces.

See "Duplicating Patterns," on page 77.

Typically, the patterns don't include seam or hem allowances. You must add them during tracing.

Independent Patterns

Independent or boutique patterns are designed and published by individuals, and usually come in much smaller lines. The lines strongly represent the designer's aesthetic, and if you find a designer you like, you may be able to work exclusively with his or her patterns. Most independent

75

patterns are printed on tissue, like standard commercial patterns, but the instructions sheets are not standardized. Some provide minutely detailed directions, others a simple step-by-step guide, assuming a fair amount of sewing knowledge from the user.

Vintage Patterns

Older patterns are available either through Internet retailers or at local outlets such as thrift or antique stores. They offer unique styles, often with interesting details that don't appear on contemporary designs. These patterns are usually made of tissue paper; some are printed, like modern patterns, but others are outlined with perforated lines. Working with a vintage pattern, therefore, requires some sewing experience. Most vintage patterns are single-size designs, with sizing that doesn't correspond to modern patterns or ready-to-wear. It's recommended that you make a muslin to adjust the fit. Some pattern companies have reissued vintage patterns, with modern sizing and updated instructions.

Computer-Drafted Patterns

For those who are comfortable working with computers, pattern-drafting software can be a useful tool. With full-featured programs, you can input your measurements, select a style from a collection of options (in some cases you can modify the style), and print out a pattern to fit. More complex programs enable you to design your own garments from scratch. Additionally, there are companies who sell patterns via the Internet: You select the size, download the pattern, and print it at home.

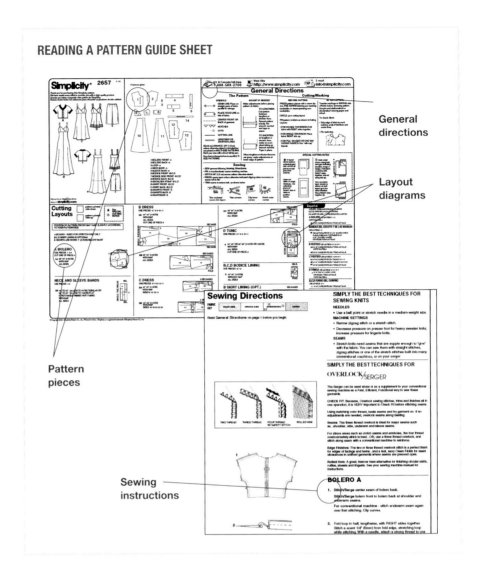

READING A PATTERN GUIDE SHEET

General directions

Layout diagrams

Pattern pieces

Sewing instructions

WHAT TO EXPECT IN A PATTERN

In a standard commercial pattern, you'll receive tissue paper sheets printed with the pattern pieces for each garment included in the packet. Along with the pattern tissue, you'll find a set of guide sheets, usually printed on newsprint. These are the instructions for making the garments. Somewhere on the guide sheet, usually on the first page, are diagrams and lists indicating which pattern pieces are required for the individual garments included in the pattern envelope. Highlight the pieces you need.

Note that on the pattern tissues, the pieces are laid out for maximum efficiency in printing, so all the pieces for a single garment aren't necessarily on the same sheet. Be prepared to unfold all the sheets to locate the pieces you need. Start by roughly cutting out the appropriate pieces you marked on the guide sheet.

See "Navigating the Pattern Tissue," on page 84.

Read the guide sheet through before cutting and sewing. In addition to the pattern piece drawings and list, note the following:

- **LAYOUT DIAGRAMS** Follow these diagrams to cut the garment from the amount of fabric listed on the envelope. If you have less fabric than recommended, a creative layout could accommodate the pieces.

- **SEWING INSTRUCTIONS** These provide the step-by-step sequence for constructing the garment. Read through the directions fully before starting, and note where steps are shared between several garment views. Highlight any potentially confusing steps.

- **GENERAL DIRECTIONS** These directions help you interpret the symbols and terms found on the guide sheet and pattern tissue.

TIP

SINGLE OR MULTISIZE?

In most cases, pattern companies print multiple sizes together on the pattern tissue. Although the pattern appears more complicated with all those lines, it is advantageous to have multiple size offerings in one envelope. Not all designs can be grouped into multisize offerings. Those with closer fit or many design details remain as single-size patterns.

Duplicating Patterns

If you want to reuse a pattern multiple times, make adjustments while retaining the original pattern, use more than one size from a multisize pattern, or use a pattern from a pattern magazine, you need to make a duplicate pattern. Tracing is the easiest way to copy a pattern.

The tools you need are a long ruler, preferably transparent; a curved ruler; a short ruler; pencils, pens, or markers; and pattern paper. You can use any paper that's transparent enough to see through: pattern paper marked with dots at 1-in. intervals; lightweight, nonwoven interfacing with or without a printed grid; medical exam-room paper; or tissue paper work well.

Tape the pattern piece to the table so it won't shift. Lay a sheet of tracing paper over it, and anchor it with tape or weights. Start by tracing the grainline. Then trace all straight lines, using the long ruler as a guide. To trace curves, either work with a curved ruler or use a short ruler to make dashed lines that you can connect freehand.

Transfer all markings from the pattern, including darts, fold lines, and notches. Write the pattern company name, pattern number, pattern piece identification number, seam and hem allowance widths, and size on the duplicate piece, and add a date if desired.

If you want to make a whole pattern piece from the half piece that's intended to be cut on the fabric fold, trace the pattern piece onto a folded piece of pattern paper, cut, and open it.

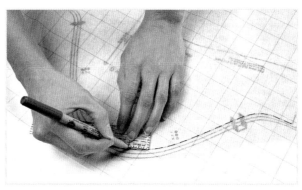

Use a ruler as a guide for tracing pattern cutting lines.

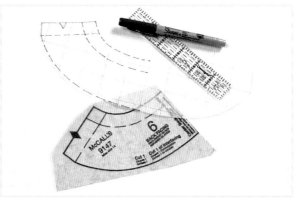

If desired, make a full pattern piece by tracing a half piece onto folded pattern paper.

Determining Your Pattern Size

The first step to making a well-fitting garment is to choose the pattern size closest to your body measurements. Taking accurate body measurements is imperative, so you can compare them to the pattern measurement chart and make any alterations needed before cutting. You must also take into account any ease—added room beyond the body measurements—included in a garment's design. If you start with the right pattern size, you'll have fewer alterations to make and will end up with a garment that fits better than most ready-to-wear.

PATTERN SIZING

Your correct pattern size is almost never the same as your ready-to-wear size. Pattern manufacturers haven't changed their sizing standards in decades, while clothing manufacturers have steadily applied the same size numbers to increasingly larger-proportioned clothing. Therefore, most women need a larger pattern size than they wear in purchased clothing. Check the body measurement chart on the pattern envelope or in the pattern catalog, and refer to written descriptions (loose-fitting, and so on) to select a size.

See "Body and Pattern Measurements," on page 92.

Sizing and fit standards vary from pattern company to pattern company, especially among independent manufacturers. However, key sizing terms give you a place to start. The major pattern companies produce patterns in the following categories.

Juniors

Size range for youthful figures: slim hips, smaller busts, less waist definition.

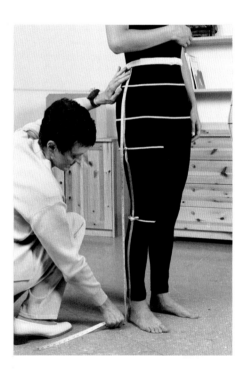

These dimensions reflect the sizing convention in junior ready-to-wear.

Misses

Size range for well-proportioned, developed figures with more pronounced curves through bust, waist, and hip. The measurements use the same sizing numbers as in misses' ready-to-wear, but the actual measurements are smaller than in purchased clothing.

Petites

Sizing for women under 5 ft. 4 in., or those with short limbs and torsos. Most juniors, misses, and women's size patterns can be made "petite-able," that is, applicable pattern pieces have lines indicating where to shorten the bodices, skirts, sleeves, and/or pant legs.

Women's/Plus

Size range for the larger, fully developed, mature body. Plus sizes refer to women with bust measurements 40 in. or more.

Men's

Men's patterns are designed for an average build and a height of 5 ft. 10 in. The key consideration in choosing a pattern size for a jacket or shirt is the chest measurement, neck circumference, and sleeve length, and for pants, the waist measurement. Men's pattern sizes are closer to their ready-to-wear equivalents than women's are. Nonetheless, you may need to make just as many adjustments to a men's pattern.

Children's

Pattern sizing for children falls into five categories, based on age and body maturation. "Infants" is generally used for newborns to crawling babies, and "Toddlers" for children who are learning to walk; the patterns in both of these categories include enough ease for bulky diapers. The "Children's" category is for the walking child who no longer wears diapers, and "Boys" and "Girls" are for preteens about 4 ft. to 5 ft. tall. There's also "Girls Plus" for girls who are 4 ft. to 5 ft. tall and weigh more than average. Once preteens begin maturing into young adult figures

(adolescence), they graduate to "Juniors" (for girls) and "Teen Boys."

UNDERSTANDING EASE

Ease refers to additional space within a garment, beyond the actual body dimensions. There are two types of ease that are built into every fashion pattern: wearing ease and design ease. They work together to produce a well-fitting garment.

Minimal design ease

Generous design ease

Wearing Ease

Wearing ease enables you to breathe and move in your clothes, and sit comfortably in pants or a skirt. This basic amount of ease, typically 2 in. added to the bust, waist, hip, and other key points, is built into any commercial pattern by the companies. Wearing ease is critical. Too little causes unflattering wrinkles and limits movement. The strain of a too-tight garment also lessens its durability. Recommended amounts of wearing ease are listed below.

An exception to the rule of wearing ease occurs in the case of patterns designed especially for use with stretch knits. In activewear, swimwear, and some lingerie, patterns are drafted with "negative ease," that is, the pattern is smaller than the body measurements, and the fabric's stretch ensures the proper fit. Cutting the pattern too large can result in a baggy garment. In these cases, it's essential to assess the fabric's stretch and recovery. If the fabric isn't stretchy enough, the garment will be too small.

WEARING EASE RECOMMENDATIONS

- Bust: 2 to 4 in.; 3 to 5 in. for coats and jackets
- Chest width: ½ to ¾ in.
- Back width: ¾ to 1 in.; 1 to 2 in. for jackets and coats
- Biceps: 1½ to 2½ in.; 3 to 4½ in. for jackets; 4 to 6 in. for coats
- Waist: 1 in.
- Hips: 2 to 4 in.
- Crotch length: 1 to 2 in.
- Crotch depth: ½ to 1 in.

Design Ease

Design ease is the amount of ease added to the basic pattern, in addition to wearing ease, to create a desired style or silhouette. The amount of design ease varies with current trends, as well as with the fit or activity the garment is intended for. Design ease also takes intended wearing situations into consideration. A winter coat meant to be worn over heavy sweaters generally has more ease than a spring trench coat. Similarly, a sleeveless top has less ease than a vest that is to be layered over shirts and turtlenecks.

When determining how much design ease to include in a pattern, designers take into consideration the type of fabric recommended for the style. The same jacket sewn in lightweight silk has a very different fit than when made of thick cotton or wool. If you're using a fabric that's significantly different in weight or thickness from what's recommended on the pattern envelope, consider sewing a different size to preserve both wearing and design ease.

On most patterns, the garment description on the envelope indicates the amount of design ease with the terms *close-fitted, fitted, semi-fitted, loose-fitting,* or *very loose-fitting.* The ease built into a garment can range from 0 in. (or less) for a close-fitting garment up to 12 in. (or more) for a very loose-fitting garment (see ease allowances chart on the facing page, which is the standard for the four major pattern companies: Vogue, Butterick, McCall's, and Simplicity). The chart below gives an approximate measurement to help determine the amount of design ease to expect in patterns.

You're free to adjust that amount as you desire, either by adjusting the pattern or by simply sewing a larger or smaller size than indicated by your measurements. Note that most garments fit somewhat closely at the neck and shoulders or waist, with the greatest amount of design ease elsewhere. If you change sizes, double-check that any close-fitting areas are still ample enough for comfort.

Determining Ease in a Pattern

You can figure out how much total ease (wearing plus design ease) is included in a pattern by comparing the body measurements given on the pattern company's size chart to the finished garment measurement chart (if present). For example, if the pattern company's size 12 has a bust measurement of 34 in., and the finished garment measurement is 40 in., there's 6 in. of ease in the pattern. If the finished garment

Design Ease

CLOSE-FITTED   FITTED   SEMI-FITTED   LOOSE-FITTING   VERY LOOSE-FITTING

Besides the wearing ease, patterns include design ease to create the silhouette. Design ease, sometimes called fashion ease, is the extra inches added after the wearing ease. Designers create or subtract fullness by adjusting design ease. You can tell how much design ease is added to a commercial pattern by the way it is described on the envelope. The chart below gives an approximate measurement to help determine the amount of design ease to use in your own patterns:

FIT	DRESSES AND TOPS	JACKETS	COATS	SKIRTS, PANTS, AND SHORTS
CLOSE-FITTED	Up to 3 in.	Up to 3¾ in.	Up to 5¼ in.	Up to 2 in.
FITTED	3 to 4 in.	3¾ to 4¼ in.	5¼ to 6⅞ in.	2 to 3 in.
SEMI-FITTED	4 to 5 in.	4¼ to 5¾ in.	6⅞ to 8 in.	3 to 4 in.
LOOSE-FITTING	5 to 8 in.	5¾ to 10 in.	8 to 12 in.	4 to 6 in.
VERY LOOSE-FITTING	More than 8 in.	More than 10 in.	More than 12 in.	More than 6 in.

measurements aren't printed on the envelope, look at the pattern tissue. Often, a finished bust, waist, and hip measurement is printed on the pattern pieces themselves.

Sometimes, especially if you're between sizes or are a larger size in one area than another, you need to determine exactly how much ease is built into a pattern at a specific point (such as the hip of a pair of pants). To do so, measure the pattern tissue paper. You must measure the width of all pieces that are involved—usually a front and back on a basic pair of pants. Don't include the seam allowances, and fold darts, pleats, or tucks. Add these measurements and, if each pattern piece is for only half the body (as is generally the case in pants, but may not be so with tops or skirts), double that result. Subtract your own body measurement at that point to find out how much ease you'll have. You may be able to make do with less design ease than was intended for the pattern, but don't skimp on wearing ease.

USING BODY MEASUREMENTS TO SELECT A PATTERN SIZE

The most important information for choosing a pattern size is the body's measurements, both length and circumference. Most figures don't conform exactly to the dimensions given on a company's size chart, but it's still possible to select a pattern that's a close starting point. The major pattern companies base their sizing on a standard set of body measurements, noted on each pattern envelope and in the back of the pattern catalogs. You can determine your pattern size by comparing your measurements with those standards.

Finding the Ease

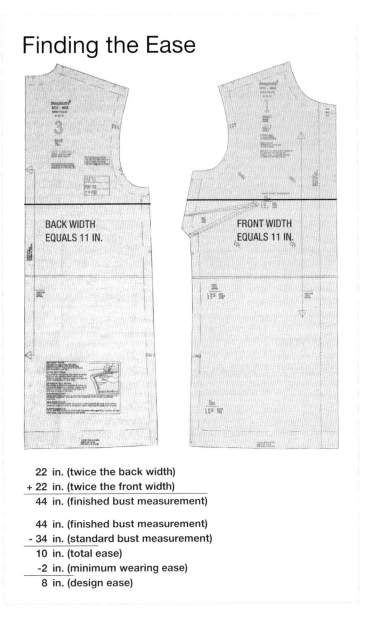

BACK WIDTH EQUALS 11 IN.

FRONT WIDTH EQUALS 11 IN.

	22 in. (twice the back width)
+	22 in. (twice the front width)
	44 in. (finished bust measurement)

	44 in. (finished bust measurement)
-	34 in. (standard bust measurement)
	10 in. (total ease)
	-2 in. (minimum wearing ease)
	8 in. (design ease)

Measuring for Proper Fit

Taking accurate measurements is easy, and it's important for working toward a good fit. For the most basic measurements, you need a measuring tape, a short chain necklace, and a length of string, ribbon, or narrow elastic. For more detailed measurements, you may also use pins, washable markers, narrow adhesive tape, and flexible rulers.

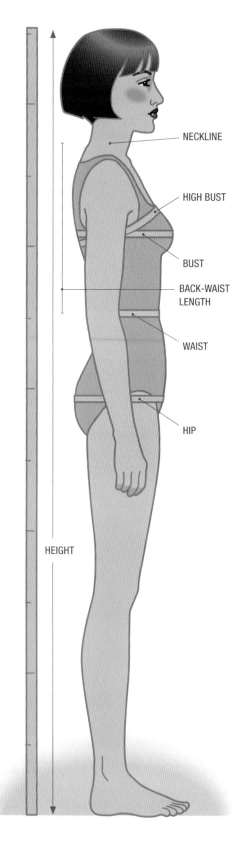

NECKLINE

HIGH BUST

BUST

BACK-WAIST
LENGTH

WAIST

HIP

HEIGHT

Enlist the help of a friend, if you can. It's difficult to get accurate body dimensions if you have to twist, raise your arms, or otherwise distort your body while measuring.

Wear your best-fitting undergarments or any special foundation garments you plan to wear with the garment you're making (for example, a strapless bra or body shaper). You may wear a leotard or swimsuit over your undergarments, but nothing that adds bulk or girth. Stand up straight, with natural posture. Tie a ribbon or narrow elastic around your natural waist (the narrowest part of your torso; this may be higher than where you like to wear pants) to mark it. Keep the tape measure smooth and parallel to the floor when measuring around the body, and don't measure loosely or with a finger under the tape to build in ease.

Take and record the measurements shown in the drawing at left.

- **HEIGHT** Stand up straight against a wall, without shoes. Mark the wall at the top of your head and measure the wall from the floor to the marking.

- **BACK-WAIST LENGTH** Measure from the prominent bone at the base of the back of your neck to the ribbon at your waist.

- **NECKLINE** Put on the short chain necklace so that it hangs at the level of a jewel or crew neckline. Measure around the base of the neckline as defined by the chain.

- **HIGH BUST** Measure high up under your arms, above the bust. Use this with the full bust measurement to determine bust cup size.

- **FULL BUST** Measure straight across your back and around the fullest part of your bust.

- **WAIST** The ribbon marks your natural waist. Measure directly over it.

- **HIPS** Measure around your body at the fullest part of your hips, upper thighs, or seat, usually between 7 in. and 9 in. below your waist.

Body Measurements vs. Pattern

Referring to the height and back-waist-length measurements you took, determine which size category (misses, women's, petites) your body type fits into. Then compare your bust, waist, and hip measurements to the standard measurements within the category you've selected. It's unlikely that your measurements match those used by the pattern exactly, so you must choose one or two key measurements to work from, and make adjustments elsewhere.

When you choose a blouse, dress, or jacket pattern, look at the bust circumference measurement. Note that most patterns are drafted to fit a B-cup bust. If your bust cup size is B or smaller, use the full bust measurement.

If your bust cup size is larger than B, compare your high-bust measurement to the standard bust measurement on the chart to get the best fit in the shoulder area. This keeps the pattern in better proportion to the body's frame through the shoulder area; you can more easily increase the bust size.

When choosing pants and skirt patterns, compare the waist and hip measurements. Select a pattern to fit your hips and plan to adjust the waist to fit. If you're making a very full skirt, select a pattern to fit your waist and let the extra ease in the skirt design accommodate the larger hip measurement.

Determining Bust Cup Size

Most pattern companies design bodice patterns to fit a B cup, but if that's not your size, you'll likely need to choose a different pattern size or make adjustments to the pattern. To find your correct bust cup size (and bra size), use three measurements.

MEASURE FIRST

Put on your best-fitting bra to measure the circumference under your bust (1). Keep the tape measure snug. To this measurement, add either 4 in. or 5 in. (to get an even number). This total is your bra band size.

Next, measure the high-bust circumference above your bust and high under your arms (2). This is the measurement of your chest, excluding your bust.

Then, measure around your full bust (3).

**CALCULATE
THE BUST CUP SIZE**

Subtract the high-bust measurement from the full-bust measurement. The difference determines your cup size.

DIFFERENCE	BRA CUP SIZE
LESS THAN 1 IN.	AA
1 IN.	A
2 IN.	B
3 IN.	C
4 IN.	D
5 IN.	DD or E
6 IN.	DDD, EE, or F

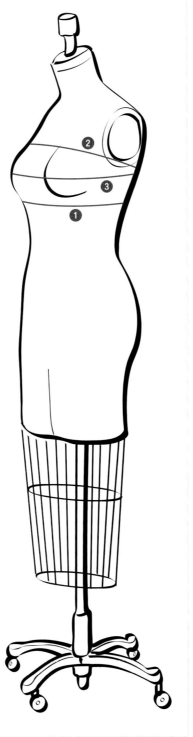

A pattern size usually lists just one measurement, but is intended to be used for figures that fall in the range between that dimension and the next size up. However, if your measurements fall between two sizes, consider your bone structure. Small-boned people may get a better fit with the smaller size, and large-boned people with the larger size. Often, there's a substantial difference—one full size or more—between the upper and lower body. If this is the case, and you're making a dress, take advantage of the multisize cutting lines on the pattern to cut different sizes, adjusting at the waist to fit.

TIP

STYLING TIPS

- Ease is dependent on body type. For a comfortable, flattering fit, a fuller figure usually needs more ease than a thinner body.
- Garment ease should be proportional to height. A taller figure can support more ease; a petite frame can be overwhelmed by a loose-fitting, flowing garment.
- Revisit your preferences often, as the amount of ease you find comfortable can change with size, age, and lifestyle. Fashion and pattern silhouettes (and ease) also change from season to season.
- Be sure to account for interfacing, lining, and other interior supports that may infringe on a garment's ease.

Navigating the Pattern Tissue

A sewing pattern is more than just a template to trace and cut. It's a detailed map of how a garment is constructed, piece by piece. The markings on the pattern tissue help you adjust for fit, lay the pattern pieces out properly on the fabric, and assemble the pieces in the proper position and sequence. Learn to read the markings on the pattern, and with some experience, you may not even need the pattern instructions.

MULTISIZE CUTTING LINES

Most commercial patterns today are sold in multisize packages. Each pattern piece is printed in several sizes (from three to more than a dozen). Typically, the sizes are printed in a nested format, with increasingly larger sizes overlapping smaller sizes. (Note that in European patterns, the lines you see on the pattern are not cutting, but rather are seam lines.) One advantage of using a multisize pattern is that you can combine two or more sizes into a single pattern piece. For example, you can use a size 12 hip with a size 10 length. This makes easy work of basic fitting adjustments.

When you unfold the pattern tissue and determine which pieces you need for your project, outline or highlight the cutting line for the size you want to sew. Some companies use different line weights, styles, or colors to distinguish among sizes, making it easier to find the one you want. If you plan to merge two sizes, for example, a size 10 waist with a size 12 bust, draw a smooth transition line from one cutting line to the other.

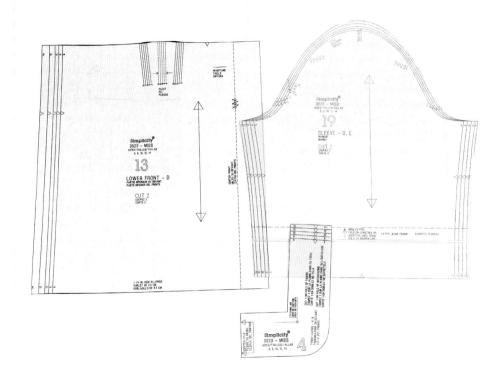

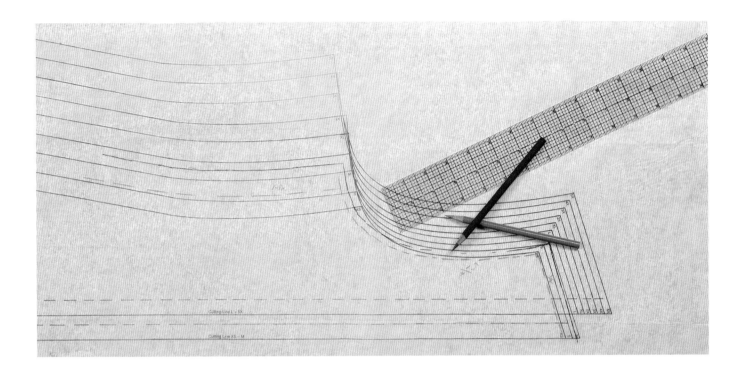

SEAM ALLOWANCES

Seam allowance is the distance between the cut edge of the fabric and the stitching line. Patterns published for distribution in the United States typically include the seam allowance. That is, each pattern piece is drafted with an extra margin around the edges for sewing. A conventional seam allowance width is ⅝ in., but it can vary from ¼ in. to 1 in.

On multisize patterns, the seam allowance is not marked, although the width is usually noted on the instruction sheet and on the pattern pieces. If you're making fitting adjustments, you may want to draw the seamline on the pattern tissue after you've selected your size. Vintage patterns and some specialty patterns that are printed in one size only include both cutting lines (usually solid) and seamlines (dashed lines).

European patterns, especially those published in magazines, usually omit the seam allowance. The printed pattern lines are seamlines, and you must add a seam allowance either when you trace the pattern or when you cut the fabric.

See "Duplicating Patterns," on page 77.

GRAINLINE AND FOLD MARKINGS

One of the most important symbols is the grainline arrow, which is found on all pattern pieces. (Pattern pieces cut on a fold generally don't have a marked grainline because the fold is on the grainline.) This arrow should always be aligned along the lengthwise straight grain of the fabric (parallel to the selvage) to ensure a correct fit and drape, unless otherwise indicated. For ease of layout, extend the grainline along the entire length of the pattern piece.

Foldlines, such as where a self-facing is to be folded to the inside of the garment, or where the hem allowance is to be folded up, are usually marked with a dashed line.

See "Placing Patterns on Grain," on page 106.

CONSTRUCTION NOTES

Notes printed on the pattern tissue are brief but essential. To identify the pattern, you'll find the pattern company name and the design's style number, its identification number and name (keyed to the pattern piece diagrams on the guide sheet), and a label telling you which garment view the piece belongs to, along with the size of the piece. Other instructions printed on the pattern indicate how many of the piece to cut from which fabric (fashion fabric, lining, underlining, interfacing, etc.), and how wide a seam or hem allowance is included.

Fit/Alteration Symbols

SYMBOLS	DESCRIPTION	PURPOSE	WHERE LOCATED	TIP
BUST AND HIP INDICATORS ⊕	Circle with enclosed cross; usually includes a list of garment measurements nearby.	This pattern mark gives the finished circumference measurement of the garment at the level of the symbol.	The bust symbol is generally located at the fullest point of the bust. The hip symbol is located at the hipline (about 7 in. below the marked waistline).	Refer to the bust and hip indicators to quickly determine the difference between the garment and body measurements.
LENGTHEN/ SHORTEN GUIDE lengthen or shorten here	A double solid line running across pattern piece, a single dashed line, or a single line with a dotted rectangle above it and mini-rulers at either end, depending on the pattern brand.	Recommended area in which to lengthen or shorten the pattern piece.	Below the knee on pants, below the elbow on sleeves, between the bust and waist on tops, below the hip on skirts. These may change depending on figure variations.	Use "petite-able" lines (spaced ½ in. apart on some patterns) to alter patterns for a petite figure.

Layout Symbols

SYMBOLS	DESCRIPTION	PURPOSE	WHERE LOCATED	TIP
CUTTING LINE	The outermost line on the pattern, often accompanied by a scissor icon. A solid line on single-size patterns. The line style is different for each size included in multisize patterns.	Indicates where you cut both the pattern tissue and the garment fabric.	On all pattern pieces.	Cut exactly on or slightly outside line to ensure that you maintain the correct size and shape of the pattern piece.
SEAMLINE	Dashed or broken line inside the solid cutting line. On single-size patterns, often accompanied by a presser-foot icon.	Indicates where you sew garment pieces together. Corresponding seamlines (sleeve, armscye) always have the same width seam allowance.	Rarely noted on multisize patterns.	Pencil in seamlines if they aren't marked. This enables you to accurately measure and alter the pattern, as well as match plaid and directional prints.
GRAINLINE	Solid line with an arrow point at one or both ends.	Use the arrow to orient the pattern on the fabric for cutting. The arrow usually indicates the lengthwise grainline (parallel to selvage). "Foldline" replaces the arrow and should be placed on a fold along the lengthwise grain, unless otherwise indicated (see below).	On all pattern pieces.	Extend the grainline to the pattern edge to help match stripes and plaids exactly. The crosswise grain is rarely used but may be used with four-way stretch fabric, in home decorating, and in quilting.
ON THE FOLD foldline	Rectangular bracket with arrow tips pointing toward folded edge.	For cutting efficiency, pattern pieces are often produced as "half" pieces, and laid out on doubled fabric. The on-the-fold edge is never cut. The pattern piece must be placed along a folded edge of fabric to create a full piece.	At center front and/or center back.	To ensure straight cutting of stripes or plaids, double the pattern at the on-the-fold edge, and cut fabric in one layer.

FITTING, LAYOUT, AND ASSEMBLY SYMBOLS

The symbols you encounter on the pattern tissue can be grouped into three categories based on their purpose: fit/alteration, layout, and assembly. Fit/alteration and layout symbols are important in the preparation stage of any sewing project. Assembly symbols tell you how to align, fold, shape, and join pieces together.

Assembly Symbols

SYMBOLS	DESCRIPTION	PURPOSE	WHERE LOCATED	TIP
NOTCHES	One diamond, a pair of diamonds, or a triple set of diamonds, usually half inside/half outside the cutting line. Some patterns use a half-diamond (triangle pointed into seam allowance). Tick lines or hatch marks, used in European patterns, are small solid lines.	Used for matching seamlines during construction. One diamond usually indicates the garment front. A pair of diamonds usually denotes the garment back. A triple set of diamonds indicates a seam reference other than the front or back.	On most pattern pieces, in a variety of spots, including center-back, sleeves, armscye, side, waist, and shoulder seams.	Instead of trying to cut out the diamond tip, cut straight along the cutting line, and clip ¼ in. into the center of the diamond on a ⅝-in.-wide seam allowance.
DOTS, SQUARES, TRIANGLES	Solid circles, squares, or triangles of varying sizes; they sometimes appear as unfilled shapes with different outline styles.	Use them to match patterns at seamlines and for details within the garment.	They appear most often on collar, neck, and shoulder points.	Use a paper punch or awl to cut out the marks on tissue only, then mark the fabric through the hole. Or you can apply small adhesive dots to the cut fabric piece.
DART SYMBOLS	Darts are either open or closed. The sides can be straight or slightly curved. Little dots in various increments aid in matching dart seamlines.	Marks the dart points and legs at the seamline and in the leg middle. Used to align the dart legs for stitching.	Bust, waist, hip, and occasionally at the shoulder, armscye, or elbow.	To quickly and easily match open dart ends, make a small scissor clip at the seam edge.
BUTTONHOLES AND BUTTONS	Buttonholes are marked as horizontal or vertical I-bars. Buttons are noted with an X.	Placement and spacing of buttons and buttonholes.	Either illustrated on the pattern piece or provided as a separate overlay pattern piece.	Use the button placement only as a guide, and adjust to the size and shape of the buttons you choose.
PLEATS, TUCKS, AND GATHERS	For pleats and tucks: Spacing is denoted by a series of straight lines extending from the cutting line. The line length reflects how deep detail is. Small dots, generally at the interior end of line, note end of detail or end of stitching line. Sometimes, an arrow or pair of arrows indicates which way to fold the fabric for pleating. For gathering: A dotted or wavy line in the area to be gathered, or dots marking the ends of the gathering area.	Symbols indicating pleats and tucks are very similar. They show the width and depth of the folded detail. The only difference is that pleats are folded in place, and tucks are sewn in place. Gathering symbols show how much of the seamline is to be gathered, and indicate where those points match the adjacent pattern piece.	Bodice, skirts, and pants, common at the waist and shoulder.	The cutting line may be distorted (offset) before pleat or tuck is formed. Once tucks or pleats are folded into place, cut edges align.

Evaluating the Pattern Draft

Patterns are professionally drafted, but sometimes grading (drafting larger or smaller sizes from one standard size) or fitting alterations you make yourself result in pattern pieces that are the wrong shape or size. Seamlines on adjacent pieces may not be the same length, edges may be distorted and hang incorrectly, or grainlines may have gone awry. For the best sewing results, check the pattern before cutting the fabric. If you plan to make fitting adjustments, do that first, then follow the guidelines in this section.

GENERAL PATTERN PRINCIPLES

No matter the type of garment, there are universal principles governing its pattern. These principles describe how certain flat-pattern shapes turn into three-dimensional garments, how adjacent pieces join correctly, how edges must be shaped to create hemlines that hang straight, and how garments must be drafted to fit the human body's general contours. Patterns vary by style, of course, and also by fit (especially if you alter them for your personal size and shape), but with very few exceptions, they all follow the principles outlined in this checklist.

- The upper shoulder point—where a jewel neckline crosses the shoulder seam—is the key pattern reference point on a garment. The garment hangs from this point, and it marks where you should begin most length and depth measurements.

- Lengthwise grainlines usually run parallel with the center front and center back lines, and perpendicular to the hipline and biceps line.

- At the point where two pattern piece corners join front to back—for example, at a pants waist side seam, the underarm side seam, or each end of a shoulder seam—the combined corner angles equal 180 degrees, usually from the right angles at each corner. This prevents seams from having undesirable bumps at the edge.

- On contoured body styles when the side seam angles in or out, or when the garment is A-line or flared, use a curved hem. This is true for bodices, coats, skirts, and any garment that flares or angles.

- A standard jewel neckline width is approximately a third of the total shoulder width. The front neckline depth is approximately half of the neck width. The back neckline is generally ¾ in. deep on most sizes.

- Darts must always point toward the apex on the body, i.e., the bust point, but they don't reach it. Keep the dart point ½ in. to 1¼ in. from the apex so it ends gracefully and doesn't accentuate the bust point.

- The shoulder slope is essentially a dart, hidden in the seam, allowing the garment to hang on the straight of grain. The slope on your pattern must match your own shoulder slope for a bodice to fit properly.

- When adding more than 1½ in. of flare to a pattern piece (to each garment quadrant), make the addition internally, not on the side seam. The allowable amount of flare you can successfully add at the side seam increases as the pattern piece becomes longer. Adding excessive flare at the side seams can leave you with a garment that looks like it has fins.

- Use seam allowances on large darts and fold and sew smaller darts as a wedge, without cutting up the middle of the dart. Removing the extra fabric in wide darts provides a smoother fit.

- The front waistline is generally longer than the back by approximately an inch. Conversely, the back hipline is longer on the back by the same amount.

- The upper chest width is generally narrower than its corresponding shoulder point. On a size 10, the armhole curves in approximately ¼ to ⅜ in. on each side.

- The front armhole angles toward the center front from the shoulder point down about two-thirds of the armhole depth before starting its curve around to the side seam.

- The back armhole curves toward the side seam halfway down the armhole depth. You need the greater scoop in the front to accommodate forward arm movement.

- The lower armhole flattens for approximately a quarter of the armhole inset. As garments become less fitted, the lower armhole points drop and widen.

- The side seam curve on pants and skirts should curve to the depth of the fullest part of the hip, and then

fall straight. The fullest part on some people may be the abdomen or thighs.

- Commercial pants and skirts generally have, on each side, one dart in the front and two darts in the back. The front hip curve is a sharper curve than the back, and is essentially a hidden dart. Front darts generally drop 3½ in. and back darts drop 5 in.

- To allow for longer crotch lengths that accommodate a full abdomen or buttocks, raise the center front or back seam above the normal waistline.

- The sleeve cap height on a fitted garment measures approximately two-thirds to three-fourths of the length of the armhole depth, which is measured vertically from the shoulder point to the underarm.

- When you deepen an armhole, you need to increase the biceps circumference and shorten the cap, creating a looser-fitting sleeve.

- When you increase the width of a garment at the side seam (resulting in a greater armhole inset on the pattern), the cap height of the sleeve needs to increase.

PROOFING THE PATTERN

To ensure that a pattern will go together properly, proof it by following the process shown here. This is an especially important and worthwhile step when you've made substantive fitting alterations to the original pattern, or when working with a pattern generated by drafting software. Even commercial patterns may have drafting errors that can affect how the garment fits and drapes, and even whether the pieces can be joined smoothly.

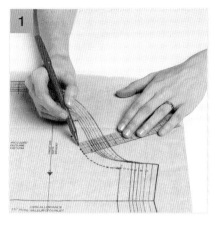

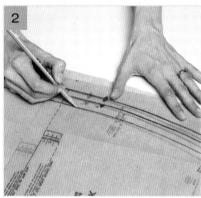

1. Prepare the pattern. Press the pattern pieces and extend the grainlines along the length of each pattern piece. Draw seamlines on each piece. Make your normal fit adjustments.

See "Flat Pattern Adjustments," on page 91.

2. "Walk" the adjoining seamlines to check that they are the same length and can be stitched together without easing or gathering. Work on a sheet of foam-core board, using pushpins and a pencil. Layer two pieces that will be sewn together, as if to stitch the seam. If one piece attaches to two joined sections, pin those sections together first and treat them as one unit. For vertical seams, match the bottom ends of the seamlines perfectly, and anchor them temporarily with the pencil point. Shift the uppermost

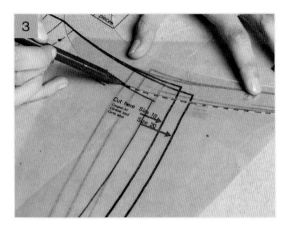

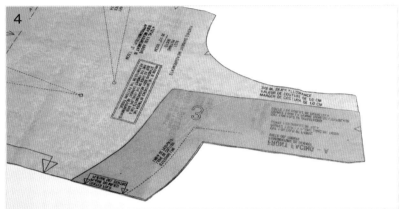

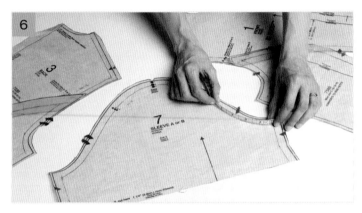

pattern piece so that the first few inches of its seamline are aligned directly on top of the corresponding seamline. Holding the pattern pieces in place, move the pencil point to the top of this segment and anchor the pieces again. Repeat until you reach the top of the seam, walking shorter segments for more sharply curved seamlines. If existing notches don't meet when you're walking the seams, correct them.

At the top of the seam, pin the pieces in place, with the last seam segment properly aligned. If the upper ends of the seamlines don't meet, redraw them as shown in step 3.

3. If, after walking a seamline, you discover that one seamline is longer than the other (and this isn't due to intentional ease built into one of the seamlines), correct the difference. To do so, lay both pattern pieces right sides up, abutting the vertical seamlines at the

upper, mismatched end. The seam corners will form a "step" from one pattern piece to the other. Using a curved ruler as a guide, blend the horizontal, intersecting seamlines, as though drawing a curved ramp over the step (the dotted purple line in the top left photo). You might have to shorten one seam, lengthen the other, or split the difference. Transfer the new seamline or edge to the underlapped pattern piece.

4. Make sure a facing matches its corresponding garment section. Lay the facing pattern on top of the garment pattern to check whether they are identical along the seam of attachment. Redraw the facing if necessary. (Some facings, such as lapels, are drafted slightly large to account for rolling or turn-of-cloth. This is intentional, so don't remove this allowance.)

5. Locate match points for collars. Beginning at center back, walk the collar seamline toward the shoulder seam, and mark a notch on the collar at that point. Walk the collar on the bodice front pattern, starting with the collar notch at the shoulder seam, and proceed toward center front. Mark the collar termination point with a notch on the bodice neckline.

6. Evaluate ease. When you're walking seamlines, mismatched seam ends may indicate built-in ease, which should be left as is. This occurs in waistlines, sleeve caps, two-piece sleeves, princess lines, the back shoulder, and the inseam of pants. In most places, small amounts of ease (¼ in. to 1 in.) are standard. On sleeve caps, the sleeve cap seam should be no more than 1½ in. longer than the corresponding armscye seamline.

Making Basic Fitting Adjustments

5

As you likely discovered when using your personal measurements to select a pattern size, most figures don't exactly match the standard dimensions for which commercial patterns are drafted. Simple fitting adjustments to the pattern remedy this, enabling you to create garments with a custom fit that outshines most ready-to-wear. With some basic pattern work, you can alter the pattern to accommodate differences in height and length, circumference, bust size and position, and seat fullness. Tissue fitting and working with muslin test garments are two other useful methods for perfecting fit.

FLAT PATTERN ADJUSTMENTS

Many potential fit problems can be solved before you even cut the fabric. By comparing your measurements to the dimensions of the pattern itself, you'll discover where you need to add or remove fabric for a good fit.

Measuring the Pattern

To determine how a pattern will fit your figure, measure it in the areas that correspond to key body measurements. Start by drawing in the seamlines, if they're not marked on the pattern. Work with a transparent ruler marked with a ⅛-in. grid to establish a seamline that's ⅝ in. inside the cutting line (unless another seam allowance width is indicated on the pattern). Omit seam and hem allowances from your measurements. Fold out fullness that's controlled by darts, tucks, or pleats so you don't include it in your measurement.

For most garments, circumferential measurements of the body at the bust, waist, and hip, as well as limb length measurements, are all you need to make basic alterations. The closer the desired fit of the garment, the more measurements you may need

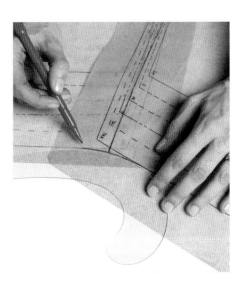

to compare. Following the guidelines on pages 92–93, measure the pattern and compare its dimensions with your body's. Be sure to take into account recommended wearing ease and as much design ease as you like.

See "Understanding Ease," on page 79.

For example, if your bust measures 34 in., and the pattern is 36 in. at the bustline, the garment will be quite close-fitting, so consider adding at least an inch of width around the bodice.

Note how much width or length you want to add or subtract at each part of the pattern, and proceed with the alterations described below. Remember that the pattern represents only half of the body's front or back, so double half-pattern dimensions to compare to the body measurement.

Pattern Alteration Basics

Flat pattern alterations aren't difficult. Keep in mind the following guidelines as you proceed.

- Many patterns have a length adjustment line, which indicates the right place to make an adjustment.

- You must make the same length adjustment to adjacent pattern pieces (such as front and back).

- If you are adding length or width to the pattern, cut along the length adjustment line, spread the pattern open, and place tissue paper or pattern paper under the pattern. Tape the pattern to the paper to fill in the gap caused by the addition.

- Remember that each front or back pattern piece actually represents a quarter of your body.

- After you make an alteration, "true" the cutting line (redraw the line to smooth any uneven jogs created by your alteration). Use a ruler or curve to guide the new line.

- If you are making multiple alterations, adjust the length first.

Length Adjustments

The beauty of making your own clothes is that you can add or subtract length exactly where you need it. Use the printed length adjustment line(s) on the pattern to lengthen or shorten.

Body and Pattern Measurements

Understand which areas on the pattern correspond to which body parts so you can accurately adjust the pattern to fit. You won't need all of these measurements for every pattern. Take the measurements that are most crucial for a good fit in the garment you're planning.

BODICE MEASUREMENTS
Compare both vertical and circumferential measurements. Add at least ¼ in. to length measurements (for minimal ease), and whatever wearing and design ease is desired in the girth.

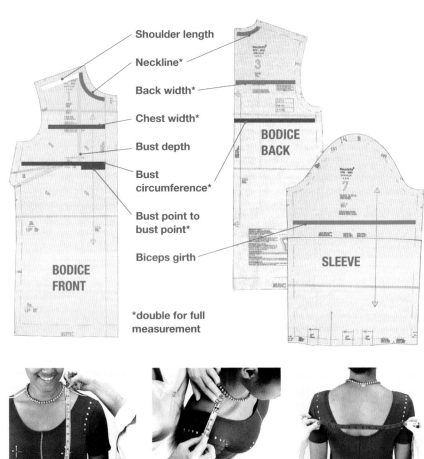

Shoulder length
Neckline*
Back width*
Chest width*
Bust depth
Bust circumference*
Bust point to bust point*
Biceps girth

BODICE BACK
BODICE FRONT
SLEEVE

*double for full measurement

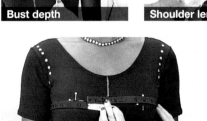

Bust depth
Shoulder length
Back width
Bust circumference

Chest width

LIMB LENGTH MEASUREMENTS

Arm and leg lengths are easy to determine, and just as simple to fit on pant and sleeve patterns. Assume at least ¼ in. of ease for these length measurements. Fuller styles, cuffs, flaring or tapering, and heel height may change how much ease is desirable.

PANTS CIRCUMFERENCE MEASUREMENTS

For pants (and skirts), waist and hip circumference measurements must be compared. Crotch length and depth measurements can be helpful in determining if a pant pattern will fit properly. Add recommended ease plus any desired design ease.

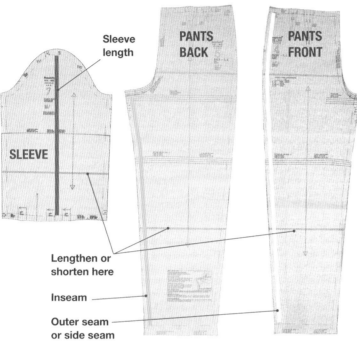

Sleeve length

SLEEVE

PANTS BACK

PANTS FRONT

Lengthen or shorten here

Inseam

Outer seam or side seam

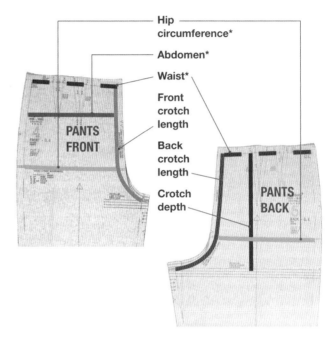

Hip circumference*

Abdomen*

Waist*

Front crotch length

Back crotch length

Crotch depth

PANTS FRONT

PANTS BACK

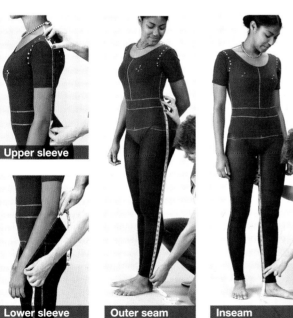

Upper sleeve

Lower sleeve

Outer seam

Inseam

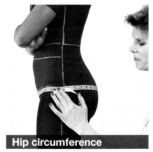

Hip circumference

Abdomen

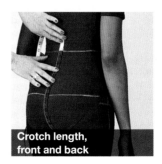

Crotch length, front and back

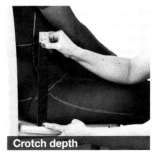

Crotch depth

LENGTH ADJUSTMENTS

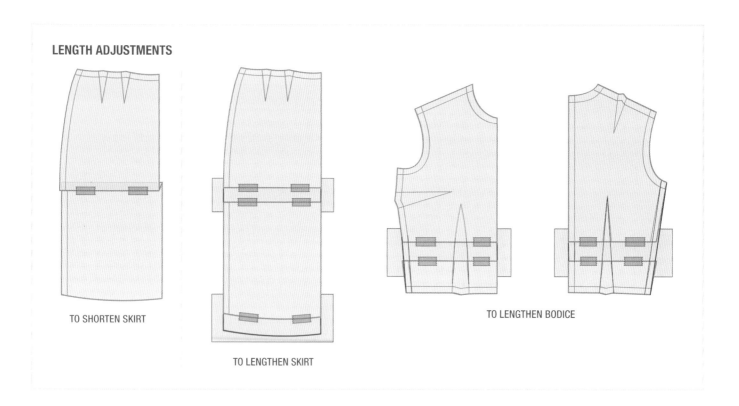

TO SHORTEN SKIRT

TO LENGTHEN SKIRT

TO LENGTHEN BODICE

If there are two adjustment lines within the body area, divide the total adjustment between the two lines. If you are adjusting a dress, determine if you need to make your adjustment in the back-waist length or the waist-to-hem length and use the appropriate adjustment line. If the pattern doesn't have a length adjustment line, draw a line perpendicular to the grainline from side seam to side seam. On styles that don't taper or flare, you can alter the length at the hemline. The illustrations show a skirt and bodice, but altering the length of pant legs and sleeves is done the same way.

To shorten, make a pleat in the pattern tissue at the adjustment line, half the desired amount. True the cutting lines and the dart markings (if applicable). For straight styles, you can cut away excess pattern tissue at the hem, following the shape of the pattern; however, be sure to leave enough for a hem or a last-minute length change.

Keep in mind that when you shorten from the lower edge, you reduce the circumference of the hem edge—small amounts aren't noticeable, but if you need to alter the length significantly, use the adjustment lines to maintain proportions.

To lengthen, cut along the adjustment line and spread the pattern tissue the desired amount. Be sure to spread evenly and tape a piece of tissue or craft paper in the opening. True the cutting lines. For straight styles, you can add length at the hem by taping tissue paper to the lower edge and drawing a new cutting line. Keep the original hem shape, and extend the cutting lines on the sides to the new bottom edge.

Width Adjustments

Simple adjustments of girth, at the waist, at the hip, or around the torso, can be made at the side seams or in the middle of a pattern piece. If the adjustment is large (2 or more in.), or involves a prominent bust or derriere, you may need to make a more involved alteration. For tops with sleeves, adjustments at the side seams require that the sleeves be altered, too.

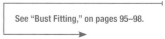

See "Bust Fitting," on pages 95–98.

PANTS

To adjust pants at the hip, simply add or subtract near the side seam, as shown. Use a curved ruler as a guide when you redraw the cutting line. Adjustments at the waistline are made similarly, with the side seam gradually straightening as it nears the waist.

BODICES

Blouses, tops, and jackets can be made wider or narrower by tucking or adding vertically from the shoulder seamline to the hem. This alteration can accommo-

WIDTH ADJUSTMENTS

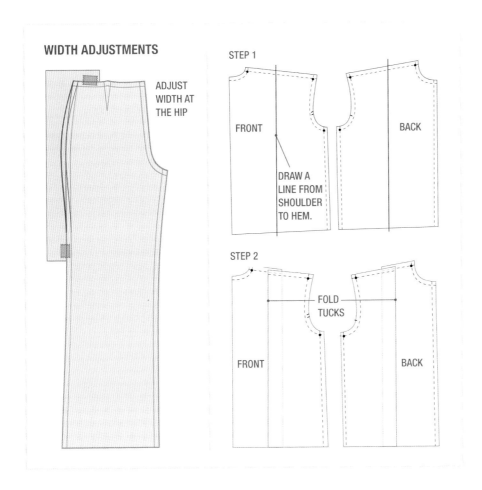

ADJUST WIDTH AT THE HIP

STEP 1

FRONT

BACK

DRAW A LINE FROM SHOULDER TO HEM.

STEP 2

FOLD TUCKS

FRONT

BACK

TIP

Measure patterns that you already love and know fit well, and then look for a pattern with similar measurements (at bust, waist, hip, and shoulder width, as well as garment length and hem width).

date an increase or decrease of up to 2 in. total, without substantially changing the fit at the shoulder seam. On the pattern front and back, draw a line parallel to the grainline from the mid-point of the shoulder seam to the hem. If there are bust or vertical darts, shift the line to avoid them as much as possible.

To make the bodice narrower, fold a pleat along the line, on both the front and back, with a depth equal to one eighth of the total desired reduction in size (this removes one quarter of the total from each quarter of the bodice). To increase the bodice width, cut the pattern along the line in front and back, and spread the pattern apart, filling the opening you create with tissue or pattern paper. You can spread the pattern evenly from top to bottom,

one quarter of the total desired increase, as shown.

SLEEVES

Too-tight sleeves are a common fitting issue. If the width of a sleeve is too small to accommodate your biceps measurement with at least a couple of inches of ease, you can gain ease by working with the multisize pattern lines. Typically, you'll need to increase the sleeve from the elbow to the sleeve cap by one size.

Trace the sleeve pattern, using one size larger for the upper half of the sleeve, and tapering smoothly to the original size you chose at the elbow. You must also use a larger size for the armscye so this new, larger sleeve cap can be smoothly attached to the bodice.

Trace the bodice front and back, but use the armscye from the size that corresponds to the sleeve cap; align it in the same position as the smaller armscye so that the shoulder seam isn't altered.

Bust Fitting

Fitting the bust is often more than a matter of simply increasing or decreasing the total bodice circumference. Sometimes, the bodice fits well everywhere but over the bosom, or the fullness of the bodice is not properly placed to accommodate the bust. Moving or adding darts, strategically enlarging the bodice front, and reshaping princess seams can improve the fit for both full or slight busts. The less ease built into the garment, the more crucial bust-fitting adjustments are. Very loose-fitting tops and jackets may fit fine, even over a full bust.

Shoulder Slope

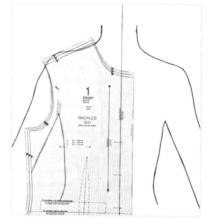

The shoulder seam is typically no longer than 5 in., but it plays a critical part in fitting the bodice. If the slope of that seam—the angle at which it slants from the neck to the top of the arm—doesn't match the body's shoulder slope, you may see excess fabric at the upper back, or diagonal wrinkles from the neck to the underarm. Altering the shoulder slope is an easy process, and is based on the actual silhouette of the body rather than body measurements.

TRACE THE SHOULDERS
Draw a line down the center of a large sheet of paper. Hang the paper on the wall, so the upper edge is just above your head, and the line is perpendicular to the floor. Dressed in a close-fitting top, stand with your back against the paper and the line centered at the top of your head. Let your arms hang naturally. Have a friend trace your torso with pencil, from the neck to the waist, including the upper arms. Keep the pencil

perpendicular to the wall. Step away from the paper and refine the pencil line by drawing over it with a marker, smoothing out irregularities in the line.

ASSESS THE PATTERN
Lay the tracing flat on a table, and use it as a template. Lay the garment pattern (front or back) over the tracing, aligning center-front/back lines with the center line, and matching the neckline end of the shoulder seamline to the drawing. Compare the slope of the pattern with the shoulder line on the tracing to determine if you need to raise or lower the outer end of the shoulder seam. Overlay the pattern on the tracing to make the correct adjustments.

CHANGE THE ANGLE OF THE SHOULDER SEAM
For square shoulders, the end of the shoulder seam needs to be moved up. For sloping shoulders, the end of the shoulder seam must move down. Cut around the armscye in an L-shape, and slide the armscye section up or down until the outer

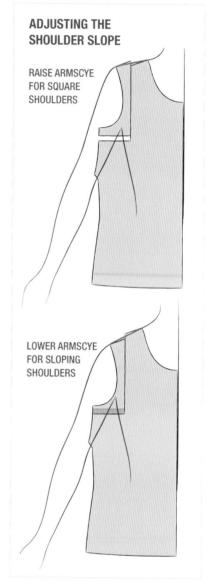

ADJUSTING THE SHOULDER SLOPE

RAISE ARMSCYE FOR SQUARE SHOULDERS

LOWER ARMSCYE FOR SLOPING SHOULDERS

end of the shoulder seam meets the shoulder on the body tracing. Tape the pieces together, then true the shoulder seamline by connecting the ends with a straight line. (Add tissue under the pattern if necessary to redraw the shoulder seam.) Adapt both the front and back patterns.

WIDTH ADJUSTMENT

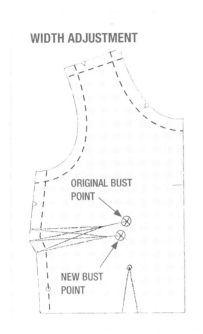

ORIGINAL BUST POINT

NEW BUST POINT

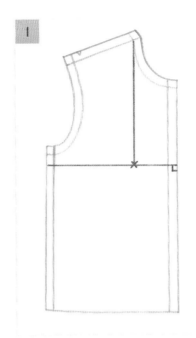

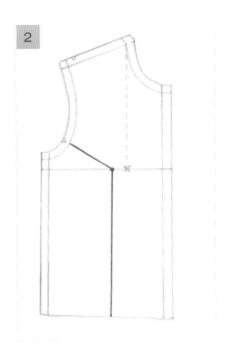

MOVE THE DART

Frequently, a top, blouse, or jacket includes sufficient ease for the bust, but it still isn't flattering. This may be because the side dart isn't correctly positioned to deliver fullness where it's most needed. The tip of the dart should point directly at the fullest part of the bust. If the point is too high—as is often the case with a mature or full-busted figure—the fabric bulges slightly above the bosom and strains across it. The dart tip may be too low on a youthful figure, causing the opposite effect.

To find out how much to raise or lower the dart, find the difference between the bust depth measurement on the body and on the pattern. Mark a new bust point that distance below or above the one printed on the pattern. Draw a line along the middle of the existing dart, pointing toward the new bust point. Measure the length of the original dart and mark that on the line you drew. Using the original dart-leg starting points, draw in the new dart, finishing at the new bust point.

When you reposition a dart, especially a wide or long one, the dart seamlines may end up quite uneven in length, resulting in a jog along the garment side seam. Correct this by adding a band of tissue along the side seam. After redrawing the dart, fold the dart, starting at the point and working toward the side seam. Fold the dart down and pin it in place, then redraw the side seam smoothly from above to below the dart. Cut the tissue along this line, and unfold it. This new side seam shape enables you to sew the adjusted dart correctly.

ADD A DART

Patterns designed without bust darts may yield an unflattering silhouette, particularly on full-busted figures. The extra fabric that's needed to fit the full bust isn't controlled elsewhere, causing loose fabric folds to develop around the armscye, or below the bust. You can add a bust dart as follows. Note that even small-busted people can benefit from this adjustment. To add a correctly

positioned dart, you need to know your bust depth measurement and the distance, on the body, from center front to one bust point.

1. Transfer your measurements. From the intersection of the neckline and shoulder seam down the front of the pattern (parallel to the grainline), measure the bust-depth distance you measured on your body, and make a dot. Draw a line perpendicular to the grainline from the center-front line through the dot to the side seam.

2. Starting at the center-front line, measure the distance along the horizontal line, the distance to your bust point, and draw a large dot. This dot is the correct bust point. Draw a second line from the bust point to the notch in the armscye. Draw a third line parallel to the grainline from the bust point to the bottom of the garment.

3. Cut the pattern along the horizontal line from the side seam to—but not through—the bust point. Slide a piece

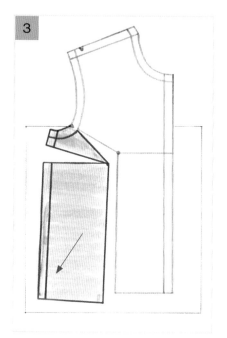

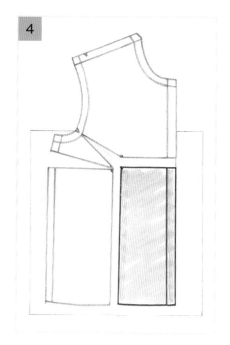

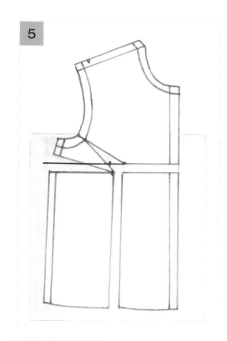

of tissue under the pattern. Cut from the bottom of the garment front to the bust-point dot. Continue to cut to the armscye seamline, and leave a hinge. Cut the tissue at this same point from the edge of the armhole to the seamline; keep the hinge. Carefully spread the vertical line by sliding the pattern tissue in the direction of the arrow, keeping the vertical slash lines parallel. Spread the pattern as follows: C cup, ½ in.; D cup, ¾ in.; DD/E cup, 1¼ in.; DDD/EE cup, 1½ in.

4. Cut from the bust point to the center-front line. Slide the pattern section down until the two pattern hemlines align. Tape the vertical cut edges to the tissue underneath. Draw a center-front line to connect the upper and lower portion of the pattern.

5. The wedge shape that has formed is not the true dart. To find the true dart, draw a line from the bust point to the side seam in the center of the wedge opening. This is the center foldline of the dart. Mark according to size. If you are making a

size smaller than 16, mark a dot on the foldline 1 in. away from your original bust-point dot. If you are using a size 16 or larger, place the dot 2 to 2½ in. away from the bust-point dot. The dart point should never end exactly at the bust point.

6. Mark a line from the top and bottom edges of the wedge shape to the new dart-point dot. Fold the dart center line, and bring the two legs together. Then fold the dart up, as if pressing it into position. Cut off the excess paper along the side seam. When the paper dart is released, a small divot of paper will form along the side seam. This will be needed when sewing your garment.

TISSUE-FIT THE PATTERN

Tissue fitting is a practical, time-saving, and creative process that helps you sort out fitting and design issues before you ever pick up the scissors. Tissue fitting involves pinning or taping the pressed pattern pieces together, trying on the paper half-garment, noting areas that

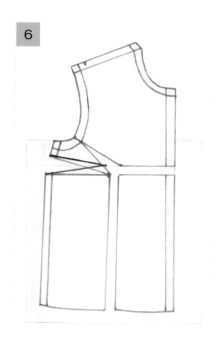

need correcting, making fitting adjustments to the pattern, and then repeating the process until you're happy with the fit. Because you're working with a pattern, you'll have only a half-garment to use for visualizing.

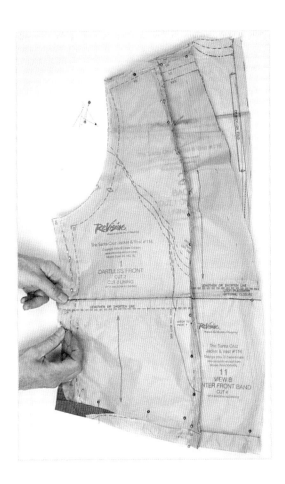

Prepare the Pattern

Tape the seamlines of individual pattern pieces to prevent tearing while fitting. This is especially important at armhole and neckline edges, or at other areas of stress. Clip curves through the tape.

Make flat-pattern alterations, such as length, width, or bust adjustments, that you typically make. If the waistline is relevant to the design, draw it in with marker by connecting the waist markings at center front, center back, and side seams.

Assemble the Tissue "Garment"

Pin the pattern together with seams and darts facing out. Pin the darts first, positioning the pins along the stitching lines. Then pin together the front and back main pieces at shoulders and side seams, all princess seams, and panels. Don't include the facings, collars, or other small pieces. Pin up the hems. For patterns with seam allowances, it's easiest to fold back one seam allowance (clipping the edge, if needed) and lap it over the second one, matching the seamlines.

Pin the sleeve together and attach the cuff, if any. If you plan to use a shoulder pad, pin it in place now. If the pattern has a skirt, attach it to the bodice, matching seamlines. Pin up the hem, then pin a length of seam tape or ribbon around the waistline of the pattern, even if there isn't a waistline seam. On a close-fitting garment, put the ribbon on the outside; on a loose-fitting garment, pin the ribbon loosely to the inside to hold it at the waistline.

Evaluate the Fit

Now, evaluate your pattern in front of a full-length mirror, using a hand mirror to see the back. Since a pattern hangs from the shoulders, begin at the top and check the following points.

- The shoulder seam should lie on the top of the shoulder and end at the shoulder joint.
- Bust darts should point to the bust and end about 1 in. before the fullest point.
- Check to make sure the pattern tissue reaches the center front and center back. If it is too narrow, let out the side seams.
- Vertical seams should hang perpendicular to the floor. If they don't, adjust them at the shoulders or waist.
- The sleeve should fit comfortably around the arm; check to be sure that any elbow shaping actually occurs at the elbow. Bend your arm to check the length.
- Make sure the marked waistline is at your natural waist.

Take the paper pattern off and make any necessary adjustments to it, then try the tissue on again and check the fit. When you're finally happy with the pattern, you're ready to cut the fabric, but be sure to leave generous seam allowances in the fitting seams (shoulder, side, waistline, and sleeve) for any additional adjustments you make as you sew.

WORKING WITH A MUSLIN TEST GARMENT

Trying out the pattern in inexpensive unbleached cotton, or muslin, allows you to fine-tune the fit and garment-making process. In fact, a test garment is often referred to as a muslin. Even if you adjust the flat pattern ahead of time, certain fitting issues are better resolved in the three-dimensional form of a muslin. If you have doubts about how a garment will fit or whether you can

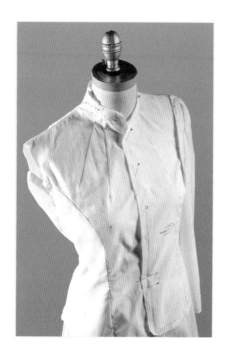

confidently sew it, make a muslin. Muslin fabric comes in various weights and blends, so choose one similar to your garment fabric, or use other inexpensive fabric for a test run.

How to Make a Muslin

Press all the pattern pieces with a warm, dry iron. Make any of your usual flat-pattern alterations. From muslin, cut out the main garment pieces. Omit cuffs, facings, pockets, and other details. Mark the darts, grainlines, waist, and bust points with permanent marker as shown in the top right photo. Mark the center-front line, zipper, or buttonhole placement, and the seam-lines, too, so that if you make any fit or style changes, you'll know exactly where your starting points are.

Machine-sew a line of stitches at the neck seamline and hem foldline, and then baste the garment pieces together, back-tacking only at stress points. Attach one sleeve to start. Only if things look too tight or too loose across the shoulders will you need to sew on

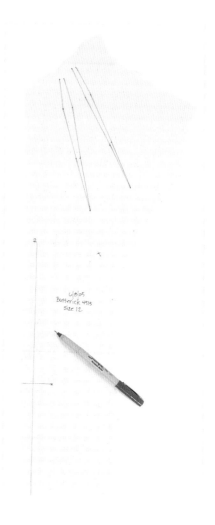

the other sleeve. Don't sew closures like zippers or buttonholes; you'll simply pin those areas in place. Also, just press up and loosely pin the hems. Don't add any waist finish for pants or skirts.

Press the seams as usual, because the garment must be smooth for a proper evaluation of fit. Whenever possible, don't trim or clip seam allowances in the muslin, as you might need to let out seams in the fitting process.

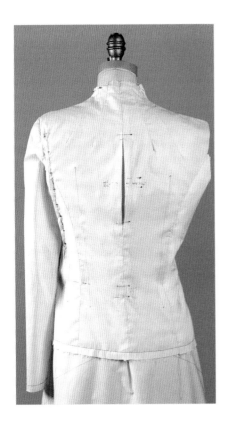

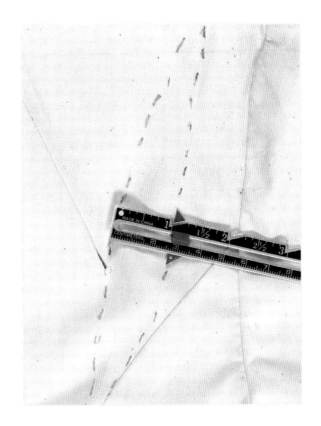

Evaluate the Fit

Try the garment on, or use a dress form to evaluate fit and style. Pin out any changes or release basting stitches to enlarge. You can pin or release anywhere on the garment, but it's easiest to start by making adjustments at shaping seams and darts. For pants and skirts, pin a band of stable interfacing or ribbon around your waist where you want the garment to fit, and slide the garment up or down until it fits comfortably and hangs evenly. Pin the garment to the band.

Remove the muslin and lay it flat on a hard surface. Using a dotted line, trace along both sides of any pinned sections with a permanent marker. You can write your adjustment notes directly on the muslin. Release the pins and press the muslin flat. Transfer your changes to your pattern. If the adjustments aren't at a seamline or dart, mea-

sure the width of the change, and add or subtract it at a nearby seamline. If you make major adjustments, consider making another test garment to double-check the fit.

WHY MAKE A MUSLIN?

* **You can practice construction techniques needed for the garment.**
* **You'll get refined fit and style since you can tweak the fit in areas impossible to adjust in fashion fabric.**
* **Fashion fabric is spared wear and tear from repeated fittings and corrections.**

V
LAYOUT, CUTTING
& PREP WORK

Pattern Layout & Cutting

①

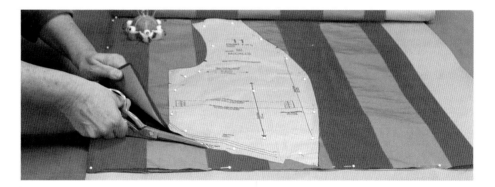

A well-sewn garment begins at the cutting table. Laying out your pattern on the fabric for cutting is an important step that must be done accurately for great-looking results. If you don't observe the grain of the fabric, the finished garment won't hang correctly, no matter how carefully you sew it. Whether you use scissors or a rotary cutter, take the time you need to follow the pattern contours precisely, so the pieces fit together properly and the garment fits as it should.

ORGANIZE YOUR MATERIALS

First, consult the pattern instruction sheet to make sure you have the right pattern pieces for the garment you're making. Make any necessary changes or fitting alterations to the pattern.

See "Making Basic Fitting Adjustments," on page 91.

Press the pattern pieces with a low-temperature, dry iron to remove folds and wrinkles. When cutting out the pattern, you have two choices. You can trim the tissue pattern on the cutting line before pinning it to the fabric, or you can cut away the excess tissue paper as you cut the fabric. If you decide to precut each tissue pattern to the correct size, cut down the center of the correct printed cutting line with scissors or a rotary cutter. If you decide to cut the paper layer along with the fabric layers, working with sharp cutting tools is imperative.

Set up a cutting surface that's large enough to accommodate the fabric folded lengthwise. If the surface isn't long enough, support any fabric that extends over the ends on a chair or ironing board, so it doesn't stretch or become distorted. When using a rotary cutter, be sure to cover the cutting surface with a cutting mat.

UNDERSTANDING GRAIN

Grain is the direction of a fabric's yarns in a woven fabric, lengthwise and crosswise. The selvage is the tightly woven edge formed by the crosswise yarns—it

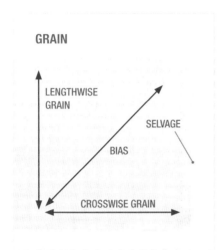

GRAIN

LENGTHWISE
GRAIN

SELVAGE

BIAS

CROSSWISE GRAIN

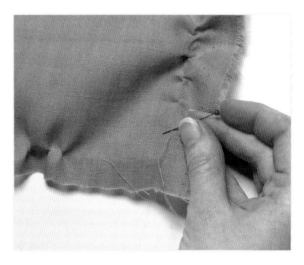

A foolproof way to find the grain is to mark one yarn, or a dominant line in the pattern or weave, along the fabric edge with chalk or an air-erasable marker. You can also pick out a yarn with a pin along the cut edge; the space it leaves behind is your straight-grain guide. Fold the fabric lengthwise, matching selvages, to see whether the ends match.

runs parallel to the lengthwise grain. The grain behaves differently in each direction, so you should always identify, then carefully align your pattern pieces with, the straight (or lengthwise) grain. In knit fabrics, the yarns loop together, so follow a "rib" in the fabric as a grainline.

Lengthwise Grain

Lengthwise fabric threads, also called warp, are commonly referred to as "grain" or "straight grain" on commercial patterns. It's marked by an arrow on the pattern piece indicating the direction in which the pattern should be placed on the fabric. Lengthwise grain lies parallel to the selvages and has little or no stretch. Therefore, in most garments, lengthwise grain runs vertically on the body.

Crosswise Grain

Crosswise fabric threads, also called weft or filling, are made from the yarns woven over and under the lengthwise yarns at a 90-degree angle. Crosswise grain has more stretch than lengthwise grain, thanks to the over/under weaving, which naturally provides less ten-

sion. In most garments, crosswise grain runs horizontally around the body.

Bias Grain

Bias—not technically a grain—refers to any diagonal direction in relation to the lengthwise and crosswise grains. "True bias" is a 45-degree angle from the selvage. Fabric hanging at this angle has a flowing drape and plenty of give. This inherent stretch means you need to take special care in cutting and sewing to use the stretch without distorting the fabric.

Finding the Straight Grain

When a woven fabric's filling yarns interlace the warp exactly at right angles, the fabric is said to be on grain, or grain perfect, as opposed to off grain, when the warp and weft yarns aren't perfectly perpendicular. A garment doesn't hang properly if the fabric is off grain, so avoid purchasing fabric that's badly distorted. The simplest way to check for straight grain in the fabric store is by looking at the cut or torn crossgrain end. If the fabric has been torn, fold the fabric to align the

selvages, and the torn edges should line up perfectly. If the bolted fabric has a cut edge, try to unravel a single thread across the very end of the fabric. If the fabric ends don't help, gently pull one crossgrain thread. Fold the fabric, matching the selvages, and check that the pulled thread is perfectly aligned.

Straightening the Grain

Most fabrics are on grain, but stretching or rolling on a bolt may temporarily distort the threads. You may be able to straighten the grain of a length of fabric by holding it at its opposite corners and stretching it away from the center. Preshrink the fabric first, then try

STRAIGHTENING THE GRAIN

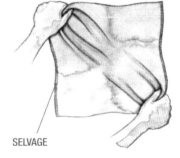

SELVAGE

straightening the grain, and finally press the fabric.

If a fabric has been permanently heat-set in an off-grain position in its finishing process, however, no amount of pulling and tugging will straighten the grain. Even if you can straighten the fabric temporarily, once it's laundered, it will revert to its original position. Avoid using off-grain fabrics for garments. They may be suitable for patchwork or smaller projects.

PATTERN LAYOUT

Once you have established straight grain, the fabric is usually folded lengthwise for cutting. The pattern instructions provide suggested layouts for different fabric width and are intended to make the most economical use of the fabric. If your fabric is a different width, or you don't have as much yardage as the pattern asks for, you can try to invent a new layout. Just be sure to maintain the grainlines as indicated on the pattern.

Many fabrics are cut with a double-layer layout, in which the fabric is folded in half, usually lengthwise along its grain, for cutting two layers of fabric from one pattern piece. Fabrics with asymmetrical prints or weaves need to be cut out in a single layer. To use a single-layer layout, make a full pattern for pieces originally intended for cutting on the fold. When cutting singly, flip over some pattern pieces for their second cutting to create both a left and right half.

A crosswise layout is often needed for wide pieces, and sometimes a layout shows a double fold, in which both selvages are brought to the center. In all cases, fold the fabric with the right sides out to view the designs that must be centered or matched and when cutting pile fabrics like velvet or corduroy.

LAYOUT ALTERNATIVES

Different folding methods accommodate hard-to-fit pattern pieces, or make more efficient use of yardage.

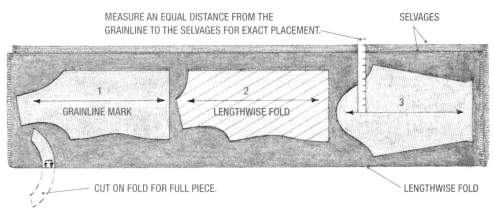

MEASURE AN EQUAL DISTANCE FROM THE GRAINLINE TO THE SELVAGES FOR EXACT PLACEMENT.

SELVAGES

GRAINLINE MARK
LENGTHWISE FOLD

CUT ON FOLD FOR FULL PIECE.

LENGTHWISE FOLD

WITH-NAP LAYOUT ON A LENGTHWISE FOLD
A with-nap layout has all pattern pieces placed in the same direction, so any patterning or nap on the fabric is consistently positioned on the garment.

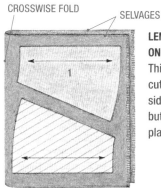

CROSSWISE FOLD
SELVAGES

LENGTHWISE LAYOUT ON A DOUBLE FOLD
This layout is used when cutting two pieces that fit side by side on the fabric, but both need to be placed on the fold.

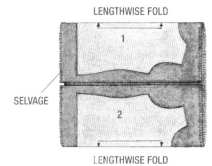

LENGTHWISE FOLD

SELVAGE

LENGTHWISE FOLD

WITHOUT-NAP LAYOUT ON A CROSSWISE FOLD
In a without-nap layout, the pattern pieces can be placed in opposing directions without variations in appearance.

Placing Patterns on Grain

The grainline on each pattern piece should be aligned with the lengthwise grain of the fabric, unless otherwise indicated. Lay out the pattern by positioning it on the fabric, as shown on the pattern guide sheet, and use a ruler to be sure each end of the grainline is the same distance from the selvage. Pin one of the arrows in place, and measure from it to the fabric's selvage. Then measure and adjust the other arrow so that it's the same distance from the selvage.

MEASURE FROM THE SELVAGE

Selvage

Fold

Grainline

Lengthwise grain

2

McCALL'S 3677

1

FRONT A B C D (TOP)

McCALL'S 3677

Avoid placing pattern pieces on a slight angle off grain, even if this enables you to fit the pieces more efficiently. Exceptions to this rule occur when you're working with some laces and real or synthetic leathers and suedes, as long as designs or nap don't indicate otherwise.

Layout Considerations for Special Fabrics

Any fabric with a nap (a surface texture that looks different when the fabric is turned crosswise or upside down) or pile, and any asymmetrical print, needs a one-way layout. That is, all the pattern pieces must be placed with their upper edges in the same direction. If your pattern recommends avoiding napped fabric, do just that. When planning for a with-nap layout, you may need to purchase extra yardage. Plaids, stripes, and large prints also often require additional fabric for matching designs.

See "Pile & Napped Fabrics," on page 318, and "Stripes, Plaids & Large Prints," on page 322.

Pinning the Pattern

Once the fabric is smooth, the grainlines are straight, and the pattern pieces are accurately laid out, pin them in place without lifting or shifting the fabric. Place the pins parallel to the seamlines within the seam allowance. Parallel pinning doesn't disturb the fabric and ensures that the pins never wander out past the cutting line. You can damage your scissors if you accidentally snip a pin that's placed perpendicular to the seamline.

Place the palm of your free hand on the fabric to keep it flat on the table, and use your index finger to guide the pins up through the fabric.

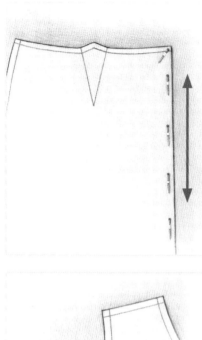

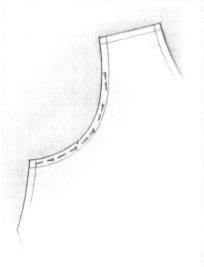

Weights are a fast, easy way to anchor a pattern. You can use weights specifically designed for this purpose, or raid your cupboard for soup cans, silverware, or something smooth and heavy enough to hold your pattern in place.

Start by diagonally pinning any pattern edge marked with two connected arrows (the universal foldline marking) exactly on the fabric fold, which, if you've matched the fabric's selvages accurately, will correspond to the fabric's grain. Then, to ensure that the fabric doesn't shift, place pins every 3 in. along the fold.

Pin nonfold pieces through all layers around each pattern piece's edges, spacing pins every few inches and at each corner, making sure to keep the pins well inside the cutting lines. Space the pins closer around necklines, armscyes, curved hems, and crotch curves to secure the fabric. To pin corners, place the head of a pin at the corner, and face the point in toward the garment. Make sure the pin does not cross the cutting line.

CUTTING

The more precise your cutting, the better your finished garment will look and fit. Whether you cut out pattern pieces with a rotary cutter or shears, cut with the bulk of the pattern to the left of the scissors or rotary blade (reverse if you're left-handed).

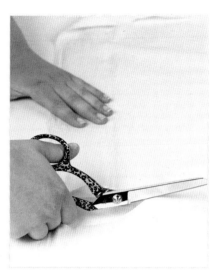

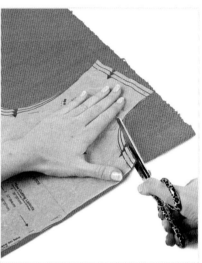

Using Scissors

Cut corners, thick fabrics, and big pattern pieces with scissors. Right-handed sewers should hold down the pattern with their left hands, and left-handed sewers, the opposite. Scissors snip into inside corners beautifully and handle thick fabrics with ease.

Hold scissor handles perpendicular to the table. If you tilt them even slightly, you can inadvertently add or shave off fabric along the edges of the pattern piece. Keep the bottom scissor blade in contact with the table and slide it along the table as you cut. To prevent

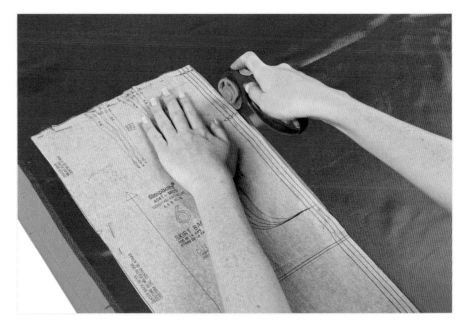

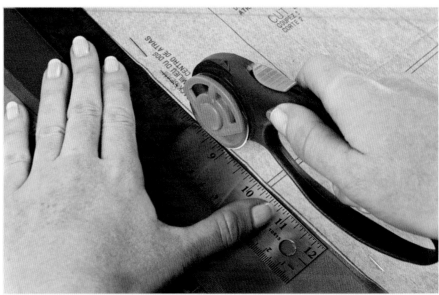

jagged edges, employ the full cutting motion of the scissors (just shy of the tip). Open and close the blades fully with each cut. Move the noncutting hand along with the shears as they cut in order to keep the fabric as close as possible to the table.

Whenever possible, move yourself around the layout to cut from all directions. Moving the pinned fabric can disrupt your careful layout.

As you cut, you can reposition a section as needed to accurately cut an area that would otherwise be awkward to reach. When you approach an outside corner, clip past it. This gives you room to turn the scissors without distorting the fabric.

Using a Rotary Cutter

Use a rotary cutter to cut delicate or slippery fabrics, curves, and long, straight edges, keeping the blade perpendicular to the table. Hold the pattern as you would for scissors; however, for safety's sake, keep some distance between your hand and the edge of the

pattern in case the blade slips. Roll the cutter in a continuous motion with even, firm pressure.

To cut a long, straight line, position a metal or plastic straightedge on the cutting line. Place the rotary cutter at one end, and roll, running the rotary blade along the straightedge.

TIP

TAG THE RIGHT SIDE

Before you unpin the pattern tissue, put a safety pin on the right side of each fabric piece if the fabric looks the same on both sides so you don't get confused when you start to sew.

Marking the Fabric

U se a marking tool suitable for your project's fabric to transfer the fitting symbols and other important construction information from the pattern tissue to the fabric after you have cut the pieces, but before you remove them from the cutting surface. These marks are meant to be temporary, and they help you assemble the pieces correctly.

As a general rule, mark the pattern details on the wrong side of the fabric, except for surface details, such as pocket placement. Remember to test any marking tool on a fabric scrap or within the seam allowance to make sure it will come off later and doesn't harm the fabric.

WHAT AND HOW TO MARK

Transfer fit-related and construction markings, as well as an indication of the center front and center back, even if they're not indicated on the pattern. For any pieces cut on the fold, use the fold to find the center. Mark darts, gathers, pleats, zipper placement, foldlines, plackets, and notches. You don't need to mark elements like hems, and buttonholes, since you may want to reposition them as the garment starts to come together. You can pull out the pattern tissue and use it as a guide when you need it, adjusting hem depth and placement to suit your size and shape. There are many methods and tools for transferring pattern symbols onto

fabric. Use a method that lasts through handling and construction, but is removable. Scissor snips, chalk or pen markers, pins, or thread marks are some of the options.

Scissor Snips

Mark notches, dots, center back, and center front with snips, about ¼ in. long, into the seam allowance at the marking position. Use only the tips of the scissors to prevent cutting beyond the stitching line. Make a single snip for a single notch, two snips for a double notch, and three snips for a triple notch. This method works best on garments with ⅝-in. seam allowances and fabric that doesn't ravel excessively.

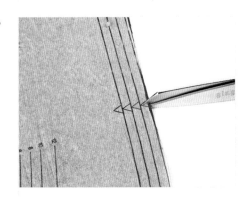

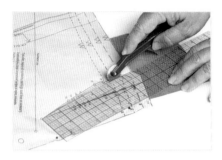

Dressmaker's Tracing Paper and Tracing Wheel

The colored surface of dressmaker's tracing paper is either air soluble or water soluble (marks come off with a damp cloth) or waxed (these marks can be more difficult to remove). Choose the lightest color paper that is visible on the fabric and mark on the wrong side of the fabric (you can use white paper on white fabric). Work on a protected surface or self-healing cutting mat. For most fabrics, use a serrated tracing wheel, which leaves a dotted line. A smooth wheel is a better choice for delicate or textured fabrics.

Position the colored side of the tracing paper on the wrong side of the fabric or between two fabric layers (fold the paper so a colored side touches both layers), with the pattern on top. Unpin a section of the pattern tissue if necessary to position the paper, but keep as much of it pinned in place as possible. Roll the tracing wheel over the marking. Use a ruler as a guide when you are marking long, straight lines. Remove the pattern tissue and the tracing paper when finished.

Chalk and Fabric-Marking Implements

Chalk is the best tool for marking fabric, because it makes a clear, fine line that's easily removable. Pens and markers are either air soluble or water soluble. Use a marking pen or chalk that contrasts with your fabric, and mark on the wrong side of the fabric whenever possible. If you must make marks on the right side of the fabric (to indicate pocket placement, for example), opt for using pins or thread marks. To see where to mark, insert straight pins vertically through the pattern tissue and fabric at the markings and mark the fabric wrong side at the pin location.

When selecting a marking option, bear these points in mind:

- Air-soluble pen markings disappear with exposure to air within a few days. Therefore, use these marking pens only on items that will be constructed promptly.

- Water-soluble pen markings disappear by applying a damp cloth to the fabric.

- Chalk comes off easily with your fingers or a brush, so it's not an appropriate marking tool for fabric that will be handled a lot, or for a project that might sit for a long time.

Tailor's Tacks and Thread Tracing

Thread marks are useful when you need to see the mark on both the right and wrong sides of the fabric. They're fully removable with no risk of ink or chalk residue. Tailor's tacks are used for marking discrete points, and thread tracing is suitable for transferring linear marks.

To make a tailor's tack, slit the pattern mark with the needle point. Then, with a double strand of thread, take crossed stitches through all layers, leaving long tails and a loop. Remove the pattern tissue, separate the fabric layers, and clip the threads.

Thread tracings are long, straight basting stitches used to mark straight lines, such as grainlines, with a single length of unknotted thread. To make them, fold the pattern back at the line, and make a row of large running stitches close to the fold, through a single layer of fabric.

Applying Interfacing

Selecting, preparing, and applying interfacing can make the difference in whether your garment looks, feels, and hangs well. Interfacing supports the fashion fabric, adding body, retaining shape, strengthening at points of stress, and sometimes increasing opacity. Whether you choose a sew-in or fusible type, it's important to pretreat and apply it properly, so that it does its job effectively through the life of the garment.

PRESHRINKING INTERFACING

Shrinkage after construction of either the fashion fabric or the interfacing—or both—is the most likely culprit when interfacings, especially fusibles, cause trouble. Common problems include puckering, bubbling, or delaminating (in the case of fusible). Be sure to preshrink both the interfacing and the fashion fabric (pages 70–72), and reassess the pairing of fabric and interfacing after both have been pretreated. Make sure you know the care requirements of the interfacing, either from reading the label or by asking when you purchase it.

Preshrinking Sew-Ins

If possible, preshrink sew-in interfacings in the same way as you'll care for the finished garment. Steam-shrink nonwoven or dry-clean-only sew-ins by holding a steaming iron 2 in. above the interfacing, letting the steam flow over it for several seconds until the entire surface has been treated. A washable sew-in such as silk organza (which shrinks only minimally in any case) can also be steam-treated if you want to preserve its unwashed crispness and the fashion fabric will only be dry-cleaned.

Preshrinking Fusibles

Hang the interfacing on a coat hanger, and steam it thoroughly with a commercial or travel steamer. Alternatively, fill a bowl with hot water and submerge the interfacing, leaving it until the water is cool. Shake it out onto a towel and roll it up to absorb the moisture. Stable interfacings can be hung over a rod to dry, but dry knits flat to avoid stretching.

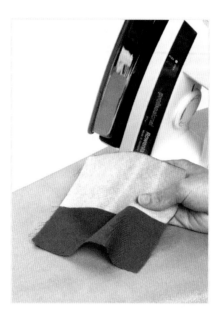

Not enough interfacing to cut all the pieces? With lightweight interfacing, you can simply overlap two pieces about ⅛ in. to ¼ in. Cut with pinking shears to avoid a ridge. With heavier interfacing, cut the pieces so the edges abut.

TESTING INTERFACING

Preshrunk interfacing should always be tested before it's applied to fabric. Here are a few suggestions.

Testing Sew-Ins

Drape the fashion fabric over the interfacing. Move the fabric/interfacing around to test movement, weight, and hand. A good interfacing lends the support you need, yet should be virtually undetectable when sewn properly. Also check for any undesirable change in color or texture.

Testing Fusibles

Draping won't tell you much with fusibles because the interfacing always feels crisper when fused to fabric. Fuse swatches of the fusible you'd like to use to the fabric to see how they look and feel together. Keep a selection of fusibles at home to pick from, and don't hesitate to use several different interfacings in a single garment to achieve just

the results you're looking for. Fusibles can also be layered if desired.

CUTTING INTERFACING

The pattern instructions indicate which pieces should be interfaced, and they usually include a layout diagram for those pattern pieces on the narrower width of the interfacing. Smooth out the interfacing on a flat surface. Follow the diagram, and pin your pattern pieces on it just as you did on your fashion fabric. With nonwoven interfacing, which has no true grain to follow, you may be able to adjust the layout to use less interfacing. If you are cutting a single layer of fusible interfacing, cut with the fusible side up. Use scissors or a rotary cutter.

With most interfacing, trim the seam allowance on interfacing pieces to ⅛ in. to reduce bulk. It's possible to leave lightweight interfacing on the entire seam allowance. If you're using a sew-in interfacing, trim the seam allowances after the seam has sewn. For fusibles, trim before fusing.

SEWING AND FUSING INTERFACING

Interfacing shouldn't show at all from the right side of the fabric.

Applying Sew-Ins

To apply sew-in interfacing invisibly, pin the interfacing to the wrong side of the fabric. Machine- or hand-baste within the seam allowance, then treat the interfaced fabric as a single unit for the rest of construction. The interfacing in the seam allowance facilitates sewing and stabilizes the seam. If the interfacing extends to a free edge, as in a neck or armhole facing, choose a stitched (rather than pinked) seam finish, and catch the interfacing in the stitching to secure it.

See "Seam Finishes & Specialty Seams," on page 156.

Applying Fusibles

Fusing instructions vary widely from product to product, even those made by the same manufacturer. Most require high heat, even moisture, and a press cloth. Placing a purchased, transparent press cloth between your interfacing and iron protects your fabric and your iron, but you can still see through it. Follow the manufacturer's instructions or, if you've lost them, use the method described below.

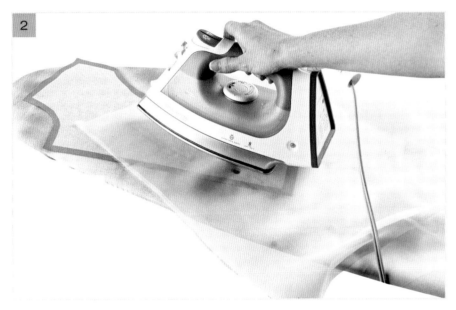

1. Identify the adhesive side of your interfacing. Follow the manufacturer's instructions for fusing temperature. On delicate fabrics, the press cloth will protect the fabric. Let the iron heat up for at least 15 minutes.

2. Press the fabric wrong side up to eliminate wrinkles and to warm it in preparation for fusing. Center the interfacing over the matching fabric piece, adhesive side down. If the instructions call for a damp press cloth, spritz the press cloth with water until it's evenly damp, then lay it down over the interfacing.

3. Starting in the center, place the iron on the press cloth, lean in firmly, and hold for 20 seconds. Lift the iron straight up, place it straight down on the next unfused section, and repeat until all areas are fused. Overlap areas as needed to fuse the entire piece.

4. Let the fabric cool completely, then lift the press cloth and flip the fabric over. Lay the press cloth back in place, and press from the fabric's right side to anchor the bond.

Block Fusing

When you have numerous small pattern pieces to fuse, you can save cutting and fusing time by interfacing a length of uncut fabric large enough to accommodate all the pieces. Fuse as described above, then lay out and cut the pieces. If the interfacing is heavy and you don't want to include it in the seam allowances, cut and fuse the pieces separately.

Basic Order of Construction

Most patterns come with detailed, step-by-step instructions for sewing the garment. When you're learning to sew, it's useful to read and follow these carefully. However, you may encounter situations where you have no instructions. They may be missing, or you may have made significant changes to the pattern and can no longer follow the original how-to steps. Sewing without instructions isn't difficult, and a set of general guidelines applies to almost any garment, whether it's simple or complicated.

BUILD SECTION BY SECTION

Sewing a garment section by section is logical. It ensures minimal handling of the fabric, increases sewing accuracy (because most of the detail work is completed on flat fabric pieces), and provides an efficient way of managing the separate processes that are involved in creating a finished garment.

Before you begin sewing, make a plan using the guidelines outlined here and on the pages that follow. Write down or sketch the sequence you've decided to follow. If you're unsure of the best way to proceed at certain stages of construction, consider making a partial or full muslin test garment to practice. The three general steps to constructing a garment are these:

1. *Get the small pieces ready: Prepare or construct small garment pieces or details (pockets, waistbands, facing sections, collars, and cuffs), then set them aside.*

2. *Complete each section in its entirety: Choose a section, such as a pant front. Start on the inside, move out to the edges, then layer small pieces or details on top. For example, sew interior darts, staystitch, then attach a patch pocket.*

3. *Join all the sections together: When all sections are completed, simply sew them together.*

   For basic skirts, pants, and blouses, see the sequences on pages 115–117.

Basic Order of Construction

Most basic garments follow the sequences pictured here, plus or minus individual details.
Revise the order of construction as needed to suit your project.

SKIRTS

1. GET THE SMALL PIECES READY

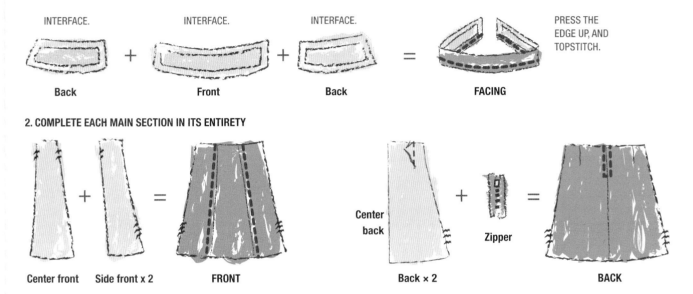

INTERFACE.

INTERFACE.

INTERFACE.

PRESS THE EDGE UP, AND TOPSTITCH.

Back

Front

Back

FACING

2. COMPLETE EACH MAIN SECTION IN ITS ENTIRETY

Center front

Side front x 2

FRONT

Center back

Zipper

Back x 2

BACK

3. JOIN ALL THE SECTIONS TOGETHER

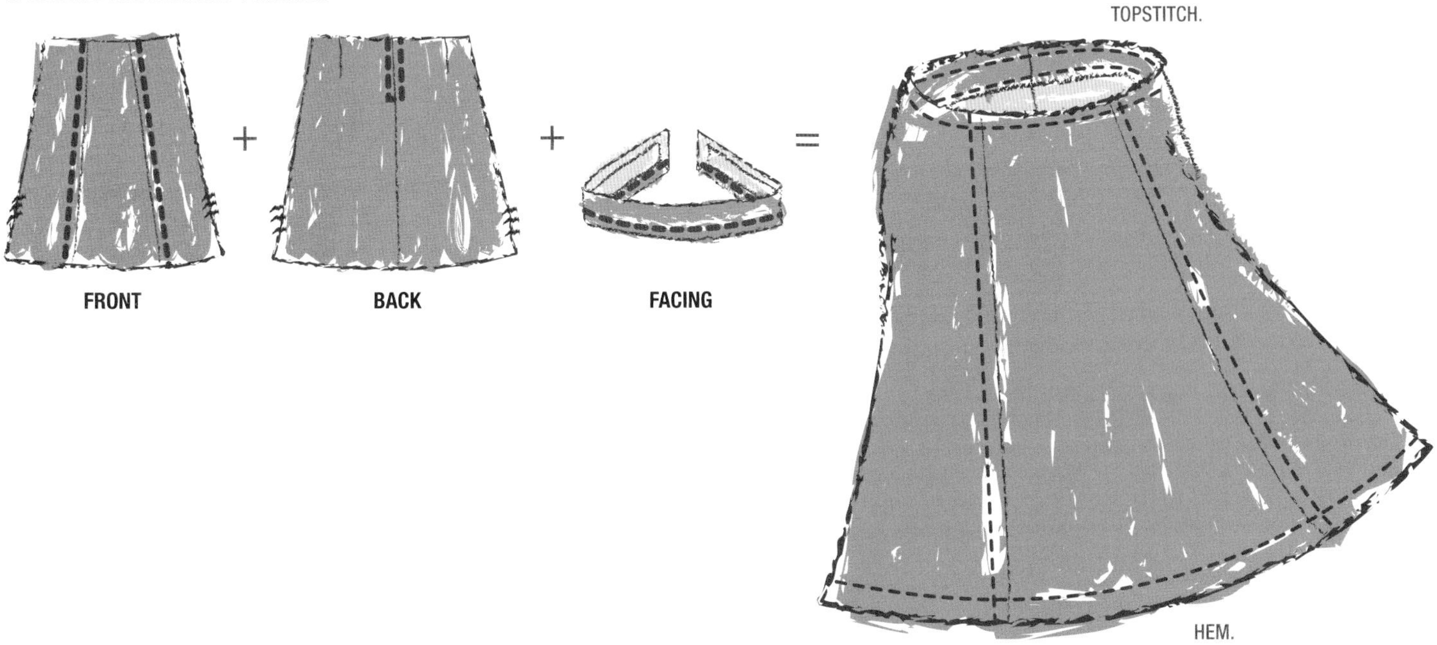

FRONT

BACK

FACING

TOPSTITCH.

HEM.

Basic Order of Construction continued

BLOUSES

1. GET THE SMALL PIECES READY

INTERFACE.   **Cuff**   +   **Cuff facing**   PRESS THE EDGE UP.   =   **CUFF**

Under collar PRESS THE EDGE UP.   +   **Upper collar** INTERFACE.   =   **COLLAR** TOPSTITCH.

2. COMPLETE EACH SECTION IN ITS ENTIRETY

STAYSTITCH.   **Front yoke**   +   TOPSTITCH.   **Front body**   =   STAYSTITCH.   +   INTERFACE.   **Band**   =   **FRONT × 2**   TOPSTITCH.

EASESTITCH.   **Sleeve**   SEW UNDERARM SEAM.   +   **Cuff**   =   **SLEEVE × 2**

STAYSTITCH.   **Back yoke**   +   **Back body**   =   TOPSTITCH.   **BACK**

3. JOIN ALL THE SECTIONS TOGETHER

FRONT × 2   +   **BACK**   +   **COLLAR**   +   **SLEEVE × 2**   =

MAKE THE BUTTONHOLES, AND ATTACH THE BUTTONS.

HEM.

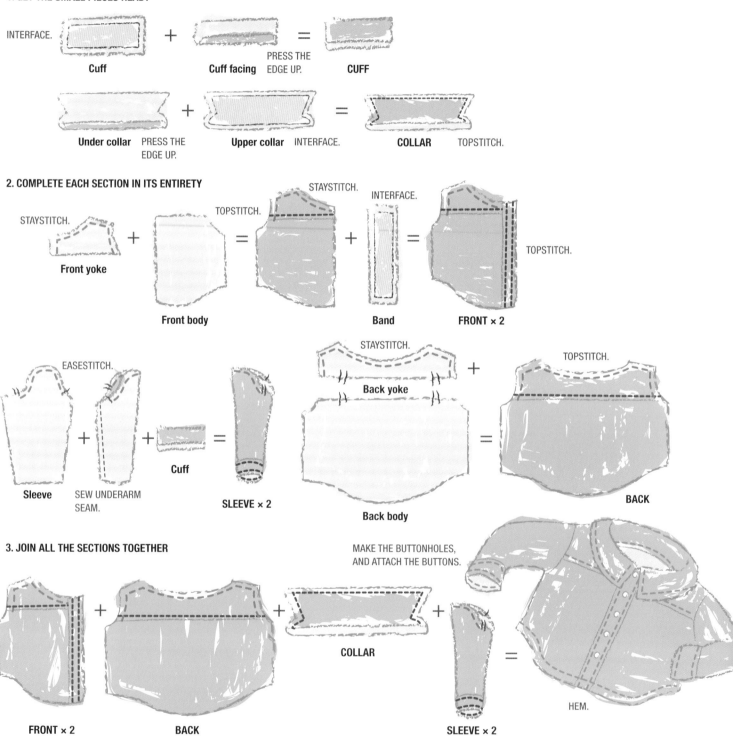

PANTS

1. GET THE SMALL PIECES READY

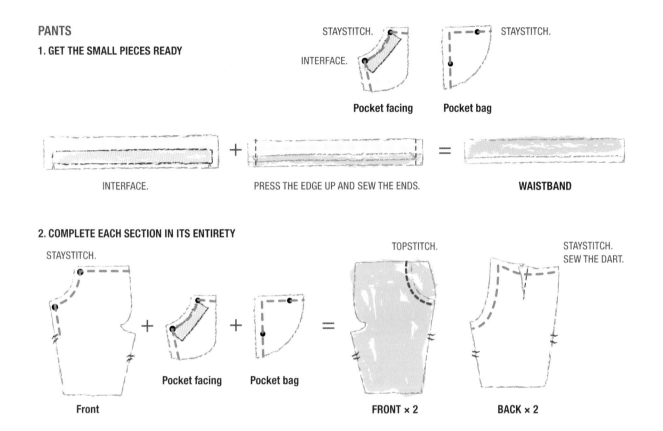

STAYSTITCH.

INTERFACE.

STAYSTITCH.

Pocket facing **Pocket bag**

INTERFACE.

PRESS THE EDGE UP AND SEW THE ENDS.

WAISTBAND

2. COMPLETE EACH SECTION IN ITS ENTIRETY

STAYSTITCH.

TOPSTITCH.

STAYSTITCH.
SEW THE DART.

Pocket facing **Pocket bag**

Front

FRONT × 2 **BACK × 2**

3. JOIN ALL THE SECTIONS TOGETHER

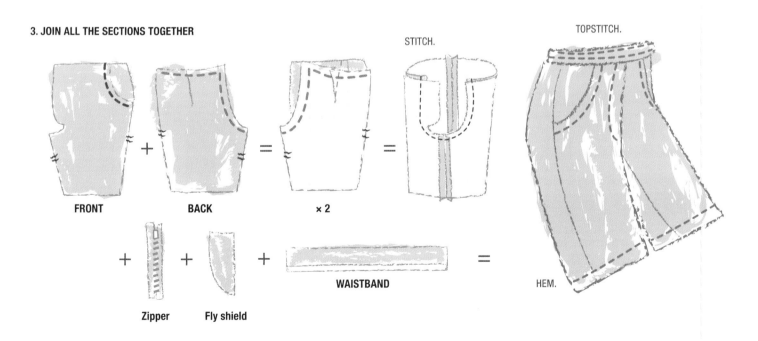

STITCH.

TOPSTITCH.

FRONT **BACK** **× 2**

Zipper **Fly shield** **WAISTBAND**

HEM.

VI
SHAPING
THE GARMENT

Darts

To turn flat fabric into a three-dimensional garment that conforms to the various curves of the body, designers use a number of shaping techniques. Darts are among the most common, and are found in tops as well as pants and skirts. These simple, wedge-shaped tucks remove excess fabric where it's not needed, and direct fullness where the body requires it. Sew and press darts carefully for the smoothest, least obtrusive shaping.

HOW DARTS WORK

A dart is a stitched, wedge-shaped tuck that forms a point at one end (classic) or both ends (contour) to build shape into a flat piece of fabric. It's easy to create perfect darts that shape the bust, hips, waist, and back of a garment as long as you mark accurately, stitch carefully, and press gently.

See "Marking the Fabric," on page 109, and "Pressing Techniques," on pages 146–148.

Darts that fit well should point to, and end slightly before, the fullest part of the body. You can check for placement and fit by pin fitting the pattern tissue before cutting the fabric.

See "Tissue-Fit the Pattern," on page 98.

To match your body's shape, you may need to lengthen or shorten the darts that are marked on the pattern. Typically, round and/or short body

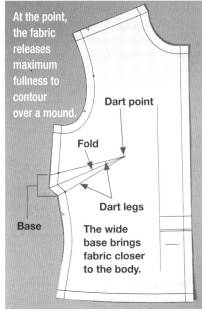

At the point, the fabric releases maximum fullness to contour over a mound.

Dart point

Fold

Dart legs

Base

The wide base brings fabric closer to the body.

types benefit from shorter, curved darts. Tall or slim figures do best with straight, tapered darts.

SEWING A CLASSIC DART

The main goal in sewing darts is to stitch the points as smoothly as possible, with no bumps or bubbles where the dart ends. Correct pressing further flattens the stitching and shapes the dart. Choose from these two approaches.

Starting at the Edge

1. Mark the dart by clipping at the dart leg ends within the seam allowance, and inserting pins vertically into the dots on the sewing lines and point. Remove the pattern, then fold the dart right sides together, matching the clips and appropriate pin marks; be sure the pins remain at the dot placement to indicate the slant of the dart legs.

2. Position the needle at the garment edge, just beside the clips. Following the line indicated by the pins, sew with a 2.5-mm to 3-mm stitch length until about ½ in. from the dart point.

3. Shorten the stitch length to about 1 mm near the point and then sew off the fabric fold at the point. Lift the presser foot, grasp the dart point, and pull the threads out about 1½ in. Do not cut.

4. Reposition the needle 1½ in. from the point on the original stitching line. Sew for 1 in.—do not back-tack—then clip your thread ends close to the fabric.

5. Press the dart open for a flat, no-bulk dart. For a supersharp point, insert a tiny crochet hook as you press.

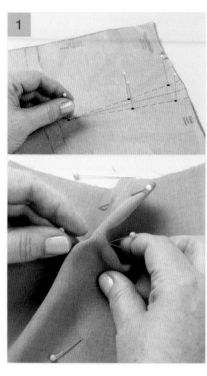
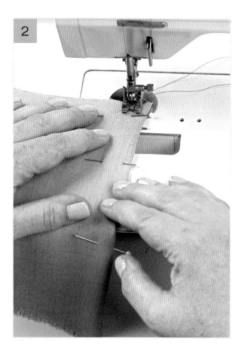

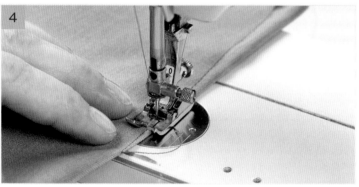
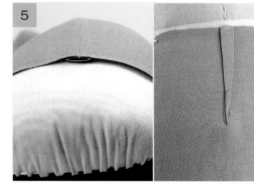

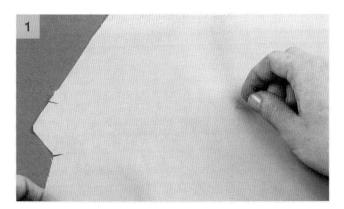

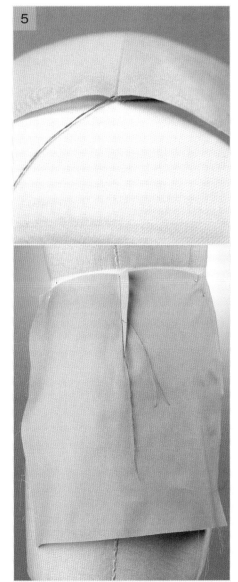

Starting at the Point

1. Clip the fabric at the dart leg ends within the seam allowance, then insert one pin at the dart tip. Remove the pattern.

2. Fold the dart with the right sides together, match the clips, and finger-press the fold to the pin. (If desired, mark a line joining the clips and the pin as a stitching guide.)

3. Position the needle at the dart point, and—without back tacking first—sew from the point to the clips on the fabric edge. Follow the marked line, or simply guide the stitching by eye. Use a 3-mm stitch length or longer. There's no need to back-tack at the seam allowance end, as the stitching will be crossed with another seam.

4. To reinforce the stitching, stitch from halfway along the dart stitching line to the point. Again, don't back-tack. Leave the thread ends a couple of inches long; they'll create their own knot by tangling around each other.

5. If the dart is wide at the garment edge, trim away some of the allowance.

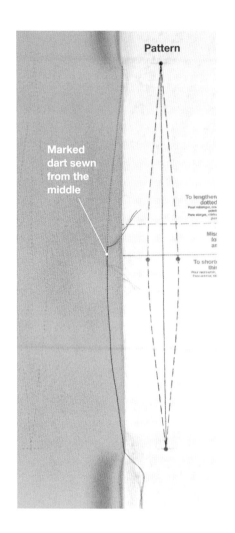

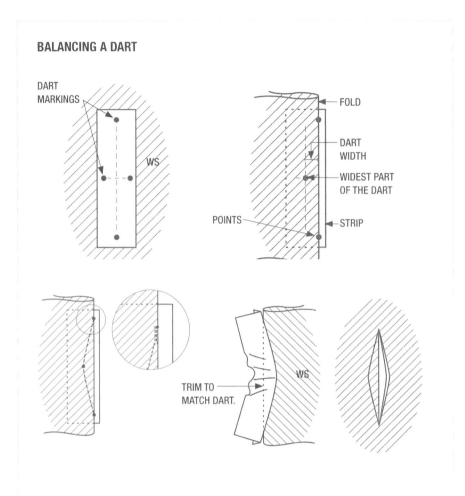

SEWING CONTOUR DARTS

The contour dart has two points, one that points toward the bust or back and the other that points toward the hip. Mark these darts with dressmaker's carbon and a tracing wheel, or using thread tracing. Fold the dart along the center line. Stitch from the center out toward each point, overlapping the stitches by ½ in. at the dart's widest point, and finish the points as for a classic dart. Clip the dart in the center and above and below as necessary, depending on the curvature. Press the darts toward the garment center.

BALANCING DARTS IN BULKY FABRICS

Darts sewn in heavy fabrics can create lumps, ridges, or uneven areas in the garment, especially when the dart is pressed to one side, as is common in most garments. To avoid this, add a small piece of fabric to balance the dart.

A contour dart is shown, but this technique works for classic darts as well. Cut a strip of self-fabric about 2 in. longer and 1 in. wider than the dart markings. Fold the dart in half, right sides together, as if to stitch. Position the fabric strip beneath the fold, with the widest part of the dart at the center of the strip.

Sew the dart as normal, catching the fabric strip in the stitching. Fold and press the strip together along the dart stitching line, and trim the edges to match the dart shape. Press the dart to one side and the fabric strip to the other.

Gathering & Shirring

2

Gathering involves reducing a large area of fabric into a smaller area to add fullness or shape, through small fabric folds, to a garment or other project. You'll find gathering at waistlines, yokes, sleeve caps, and cuffs, and occasionally at the center front of a blouse to replace the use of bust darts. Shirring is a form of gathering, using several parallel rows of stitching to produce a decorative effect that also shapes the garment, typically at areas such as the waist, wrist, or chest.

GATHERING

When gathering, you can choose among several techniques. The type of project you're sewing, and the fabric itself, should determine the best method of gathering to use. Whether it's a casual garment, an heirloom piece, or a home decorating project, the goal is to create small, evenly distributed folds of fabric along the gathered area.

Determining Fullness

The ratio of flat area to finished gathers is often dictated by the pattern (which typically takes into account the weight of the recommended fabrics and the length of the area to be gathered), but there are general guidelines you can follow when planning gathering on your own. A 2:1 or 2½:1 ratio gives an attractive amount of fullness in most fabrics that are suitable for gathering. This means that 40 in. to 50 in. of fabric would be gathered into a 20-in. length.

The fabric thickness, hand (soft or crisp), and the length of the gathered area affect how full the gathering can and should be. Soft, lightweight fabrics are the easiest to gather, and with featherweight types, like chiffon or voile, you may increase the ratio somewhat. When gathering thick or stiff fabrics, like wool coating or corduroy, the ratio should be lowered considerably, and the length of the gathered area reduced.

How to Gather

Gather the fabric using one of the following methods. For casual, quick-to-sew clothing, stitch over transparent elastic. For long stretches of gathering, as in tiered skirts, ruffles, and some home decorating projects, zigzag over cord, or use a ruffler attachment or gathering presser foot. For the most precise and even gathering, suitable for most clothing, pulling up multiple rows of basting stitches is the best option.

ROWS OF BASTING STITCHES

1. Machine-sew two or three rows of long basting stitches on the fabric being gathered and leave long thread tails at each end. If you are sewing two rows, stitch one on each side of the seamline. Three rows of basting make it easier to gather the fabric evenly; position them ⅞ in., ⅜ in., and ¼ in. from the edge of the fabric. If you are working with challenging fabrics, a fourth row of gathers makes for smoother gathers. Start and stop stitching ⅝ in. from the ends of the area to be gathered. Tie the top thread tails together and the bobbin thread tails together at each end so you don't inadvertently pull a thread too far. Pull the bobbin threads firmly but gently to gather the fabric.

MACHINE-COUCH A CORD

2. Use this method for tulle or other loosely woven fabrics; with heavy, stiff fabrics (which can break basting stitches when gathering); or for very long stretches of gathering. Cut a cord or heavy thread (dental floss is strong and slippery enough for this purpose) about 10 in. longer than the fabric length. Secure the cord to the wrong side of the strip with a pin, leaving a 5-in. thread tail. Zigzag (set the stitch length and width to 4 mm to 5 mm) over the cord, being careful not to catch it. Pull the cord to gather the fabric, then pin or

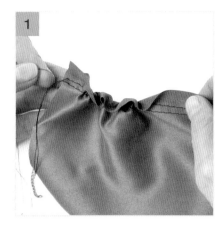

stitch the cord to the fabric at each end to secure the gathers until the fabric is secured in a seam.

USING A RUFFLER ATTACH-MENT OR GATHERING FOOT

3. Both a ruffler attachment and a gathering foot create nonadjustable (fixed) gathers. A ruffler attachment enables you to make a perfectly pleated fabric strip. You can adjust the depth and spacing of the pleats, so that they give the effect of gathering. A gathering foot simply sews soft gathers, often less full than those you can create by other methods. In both cases, you should make a sample strip or two to find out what settings produce the gathered effect you like. To learn to use the attachments, refer to the instructions that came with the ruffler or gathering foot.

ZIGZAGGING OVER CLEAR ELASTIC

4. For stretchy gathers, cut narrow, clear elastic to the desired gathered length. Divide the area that is to be gathered in quarters and mark; do the same with the elastic strip. Pin the elastic to the fabric wrong side, matching the marks. Zigzag along the elastic, stretching it to fit as you sew.

Attaching the Gathered Fabric

Gathered edges must be inserted in a seam or attached to an unfinished edge. To insert gathered edges into a seam, begin by marking both the base fabric and the gathered section with pins at key match points, such as the center front and side seams.

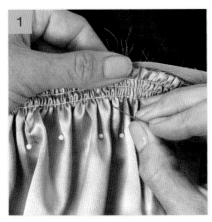

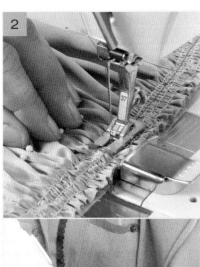

1. Pin the gathered layer to the flat layer with right sides together, matching markings. Or, wait to gather the layer until it is pinned to the flat layer at the markings. In this case, anchor the bobbin threads at one end by wrapping them in a figure eight around a straight pin and pull the bobbin threads from the opposite end to gather the fabric. Pin the layers together and use a pin to distribute the gathers evenly.

2. With the gathered layer on top, stitch slowly, adjusting the fabric folds and removing the pins as you stitch. Check the evenness of the gathers from the right side. Remove the basting stitches and then press the seam over a ham toward the ungathered side. Use steam to set the gathers evenly, then gently pull them lengthwise to create parallel folds. Be careful not to flatten them.

SHIRRING

Shirring is formed by multiple rows of gathering and is best suited for soft, lightweight fabrics. Typically, the stitching lines are straight, parallel, and evenly spaced. As with gathering, there are three easy shirring techniques. Note that in all these techniques, stitching is visible on the right side of the fabric, so choose a thread that matches the fabric closely. Once the shirring is complete, you can stay the area by catching the sides in a seam, enclosing the thread ends/knots in a small pintuck, or by slipstitching a strip of self-fabric over the wrong side of the area.

Basting Stitches

Mark the placement for the rows of gathering stitches. With a long basting stitch, machine-sew along each row, leaving long thread tails. Pull the bobbin thread of each row individually, gathering each row to exactly the same

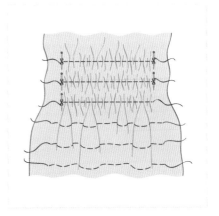

length. Knot or wrap the thread ends in a figure eight around a straight pin to anchor the shirring until you secure the thread ends in a seam.

Sewing over Cord

Sewing over multiple rows of cording with a zigzag stitch creates a shirred effect, much like gathering over a cord.

Pull the cord to shirr the area, and knot the cord ends. You can secure the cords by catching them in a seam, or by stitching them to the wrong side of the fabric.

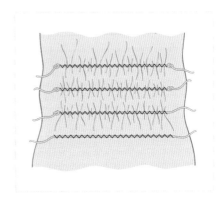

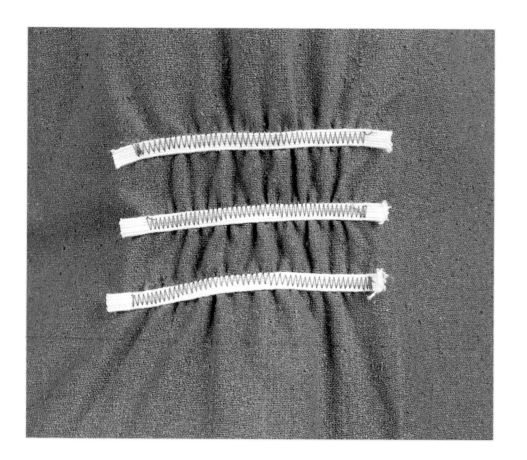

Elasticized Shirring

Work with a sew-through elastic, such as lingerie or swimsuit elastic, or clear elastic. Mark the shirring lines on the wrong side of the fabric. If desired, machine-tack the elastic ends in position. Stitch the elastic to the wrong side of the garment, stretching it between the marks as you sew. You may use a straight or zigzag stitch; test first on scraps to see which looks better. When sewing multiple rows of shirring, be sure to stretch previous rows fully as you sew.

Tucks

A tuck is a stitched fold of fabric that is usually decorative, but can also be used to add shape to a garment. Tucks can be as narrow or wide as you like, and spaced however you want them. Decorative tucks are formed so that the fold and stitching show on the right side, while shaping tucks, often called dart tucks, are stitched with the fold on the inside of the garment.

DECORATIVE TUCKS

Decorative tucks add texture and interest, as well as body, to plain fabric. They may be part of the design of a purchased pattern. If so, their fold and stitching lines should be marked on the pattern tissue. If desired, you can add tucks to a design yourself by tucking the fabric first, then cutting the pattern piece from the tucked fabric. Make some samples to determine the desired width and spacing of the tucks.

In general, the thicker the fabric, the wider and more widely spaced the tucks should be. Very narrow, closely spaced tucks (called pin tucks) are appropriate for lightweight fabrics.

There are two common techniques for sewing tucks. First, you can fold the fabric and sew through both layers, parallel to the fold. This is suitable for nearly all fabric weights and tuck

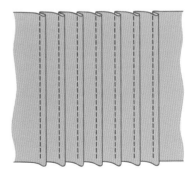

widths. Alternatively, you can work with a pin tuck presser foot, a twin needle, and a single layer of fabric. This method works best on light- to medium-weight fabrics.

Technically, tucks can be sewn at any angle on the fabric, but practically, they're easiest to sew and press—and look most smooth and even—when the tuck fold-line is aligned on the straight grain. Crossgrain tucks are effective around garment hems, but only if the hemline is precisely on the crossgrain, as tucking curved hemlines can result in wavy tucks. If you're in doubt, make a small sample on a swatch of the fashion fabric.

Single-Needle Tucks

Begin by marking all the tuck foldlines on the fabric right side with chalk or a disappearing marker. Transfer the lines from the pattern, if provided. Otherwise, determine the spacing of the lines by adding the desired tuck spacing plus two times the finished tuck width. Add 1/16 in. to 1/8 in., to account for the thickness of the fabric as it folds (called "turn-of-cloth"). Using a ruler as a guide, mark lines this distance apart along the straight grain of the fabric.

1. Fold and press the first tuck with the wrong sides together. Pin perpendicular to the fold at regular intervals to prevent the fabric layers from shifting.

2. Sew parallel to the foldline, using a single needle and standard (or straight-stitch) presser foot. Starting at the top of the garment, sew to the opposite end, with the fabric fold to the right of the foot. The side of the tuck facing out on the garment should face up. To avoid puckers, hold the fabric taut in front and in back of the presser foot to ensure even tension.

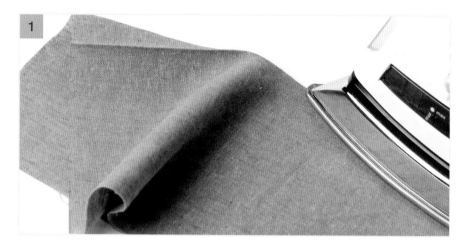

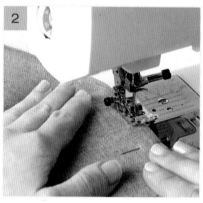

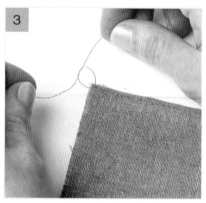

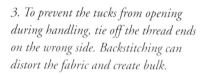

3. To prevent the tucks from opening during handling, tie off the thread ends on the wrong side. Backstitching can distort the fabric and create bulk.

4. Press the tuck flat, as sewn, to set the stitches. Then press it to one side. Use a lift-and-press motion to avoid stretching the fabric.

Twin-Needle Pin Tucks

The easiest way to sew raised pin tucks is with a pin-tucking presser foot and a twin needle. Each pin-tucking foot has grooves on its underside and pairs with a different size double needle to produce pin tucks of varying heights and spacing. The center groove pulls the fabric up into a tuck, while the adjoining grooves ride over previous

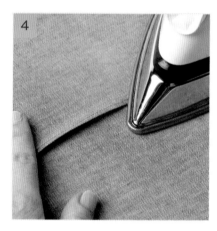

tucks and serve as a guide for making parallel rows of pin tucks. With these pin tucks, which don't require prepressing, you can tuck at any angle, and in curved lines as well.

Mark the first pin tuck foldline on the right side of the fabric. Install a twin needle.

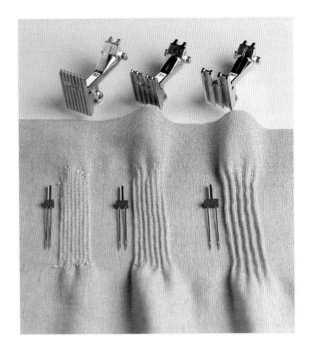

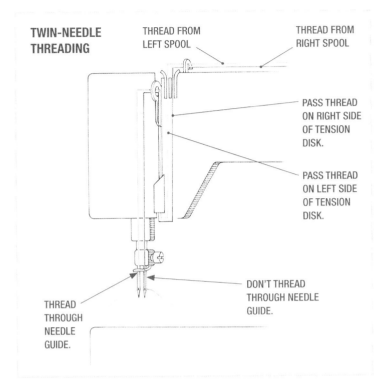

TWIN-NEEDLE THREADING

THREAD FROM LEFT SPOOL

THREAD FROM RIGHT SPOOL

PASS THREAD ON RIGHT SIDE OF TENSION DISK.

PASS THREAD ON LEFT SIDE OF TENSION DISK.

THREAD THROUGH NEEDLE GUIDE.

DON'T THREAD THROUGH NEEDLE GUIDE.

TWIN NEEDLE THREADING

To thread the machine for use with a twin needle, start by mounting two spools of thread, one on the usual spool pin and the other on an auxiliary spool pin (see the machine manual for specific instructions). Bring the right spool's thread around the right side of the thread-tension disk, and leave it outside the needle-thread guide, as shown in the drawing at top right. Bring the left spool's thread around the left side of the tension disk, and thread it through the needle guide. This helps keep the threads from twisting as you sew. Some machines do not have separate tension disks, so check the owner's manual for multiple needle threading instructions. Thread the bobbin as usual.

Set the upper thread tension tighter than normal to increase the pin tuck height. Using a straight stitch, simply sew along the marked line. For subsequent pin tucks, shift the fabric to the left, so that the first tuck rides under the groove in the presser foot. By keeping that tuck in its groove as you

stitch, you create a perfectly parallel pin tuck. Repeat until you've sewn as many pin tucks as desired.

DART TUCKS

Tucks that are used specifically to control fullness are sometimes called dart tucks. These are usually folded to the inside of the garment so they appear only as a short seam or dart on the garment right side. To create shaping, dart tucks are folded and stitched to the desired point, then released. This type of tuck can be used at the shoulder seam or waistline to control fullness, then released to provide space for the bust or hips. Backstitch at the open ends of the tucks, or pull the thread ends to the wrong side and knot them.

DART TUCK VARIATIONS

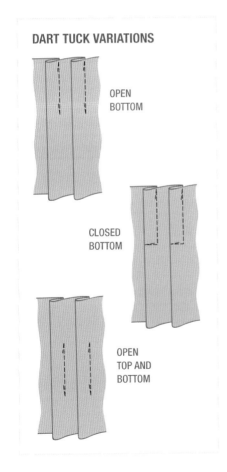

OPEN BOTTOM

CLOSED BOTTOM

OPEN TOP AND BOTTOM

Pleats

Pleats are a distinctive design element, but their main function is to control fullness or ease within a garment. Sharply pressed pleats provide a clean, tailored look; unpressed pleats enable you to add soft fullness to a garment without lots of gathers. When choosing fabrics for pleated garments, consider the fabric's ability to hold a crisp crease, its weight, and its fiber content. Natural-fiber fabrics can usually be pressed into crisp pleats, but the pleats may come out during washing or wearing. Synthetic fabrics can be permanently pleated, but this is best done by a professional pleating service.

TYPES OF PLEATS

All pleats involve folding the fabric, and each folding strategy produces a different type of pleat. A kick pleat or walking pleat is a variation of either the knife pleat (also called straight pleat) or the inverted box pleat; however, it starts approximately mid-thigh and extends to the skirt hem. It allows for walking ease but maintains a slim silhouette.

Knife Pleats

A knife pleat consists of two folds: an outside fold, which forms the visible edges of the pleat, and an inside fold, which is hidden behind the pleat. Knife pleats are usually used in multiples, all facing the same direction, whether continuously around a garment or in small groups. A kick pleat is a variation of a knife pleat.

Box Pleat

A box pleat consists of two knife pleats facing away from each other. The inside folds may or may not meet at the center. A box pleat is most commonly used as a single pleat (for example, at the back of a shirt yoke).

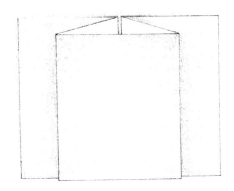

Inverted Pleat

An inverted pleat consists of two knife pleats facing each other—it's the opposite of a box pleat. Like a box pleat, an inverted pleat is commonly used as a single pleat.

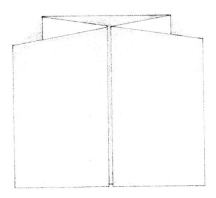

Inverted Pleat with Separate Underlay

You can make an inverted pleat with a separate underlay, using a matching or contrasting fabric to form the underlay.

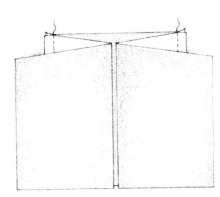

Accordion and Sunray Pleats

A continuous set of very narrow (⅜-in.- to ½-in.-wide) knife pleats are called accordion pleats. Sunray pleats refer to a continuous set of narrow knife pleats that are narrower at the top and wider at the bottom; these are usually worked on fabric cut on the bias. These types of narrow pleats tend to stand away from the body when worn. Because they're so narrow, they're best created by commercial pleating companies or formed on home pleating machines.

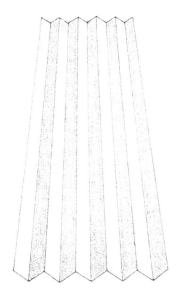

ANATOMY OF A PLEAT

KNIFE PLEATS

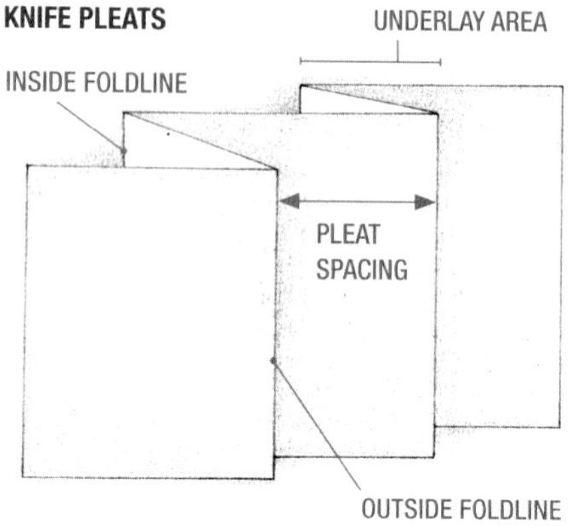

UNDERLAY AREA

INSIDE FOLDLINE

PLEAT SPACING

OUTSIDE FOLDLINE

BOX PLEAT

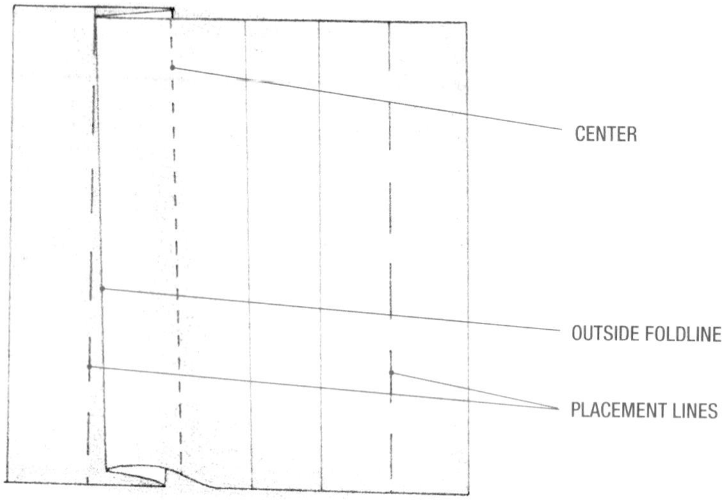

CENTER

OUTSIDE FOLDLINE

PLACEMENT LINES

INVERTED PLEAT

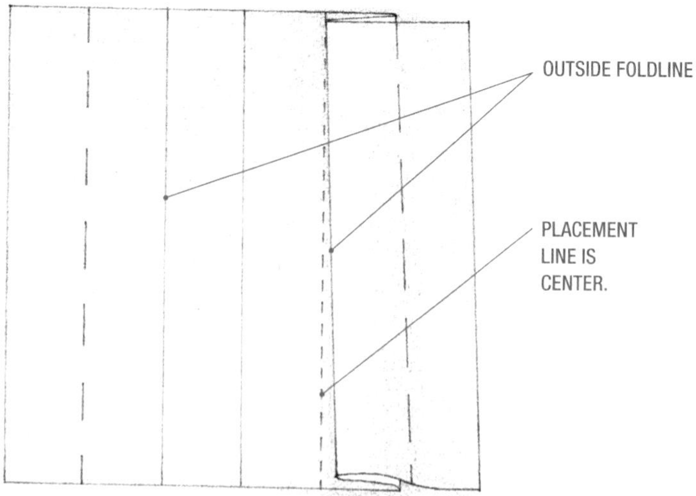

OUTSIDE FOLDLINE

PLACEMENT LINE IS CENTER.

MARKING AND FOLDING PLEATS

To form even, parallel pleats, you must carefully mark a pleat's fold and placement lines on the wrong side of the fabric with chalk, or on the right side with thread basting. Each type of pleat requires different markings, as shown in the drawings at left. Form the pleats by folding along each foldline and bringing it to the placement line. Pin and baste through all the layers, then press in place.

To keep pleats flat and close to the body near the waist, topstitch or edgestitch them in place for several inches. To keep the pleats' edges when pressing doesn't do the trick, edgestitch along the outside or inside pleat folds through the pleat layers. When edgestitching, try to stitch from the bottom up to maintain the direction of the grain and prevent rippling.

PRESSING AND HEMMING PLEATS

To establish a crisp press when forming pleats, use a solution of vinegar and water (one part vinegar to two parts water). Spritz this on the edge of the pleat before pressing. Test the solution on a sample before applying to the garment.

Hemming basic knife, box, and inverted pleats requires careful pressing, but is otherwise the same as making a plain hem. Alternatively, for skirts, you can hem the fabric before pleating, and adjust the length at the waistline.

To hem an inverted box pleat with a separate underlay, clip the underlay seam allowances just above the hem edge. Press the allowances toward the underlay in the hem itself, and away from the underlay above the hem. This reduces bulk within the hem.

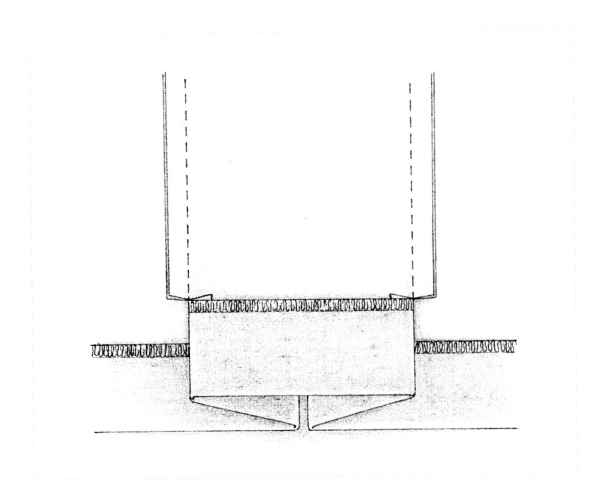

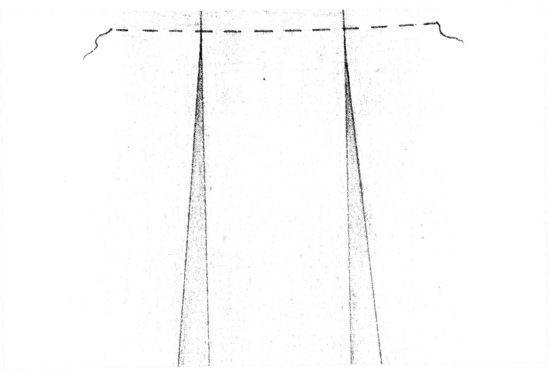

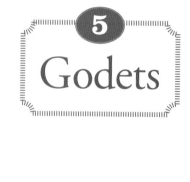

Godets

A godet is a panel of fabric—typically a triangle—inserted into a garment skirt to add fullness and design interest, as well as comfort and ease of movement. Godets create fullness at the hem edge with no bulk at the waist or hip. A godet can be made in any type of fabric, and it doesn't have to be the same fabric as the rest of the skirt. Fabric choice can affect the drape of the godet and the skirt, so sew a sample godet in your fashion fabric(s) to check the way it hangs.

INSERTING A GODET

You can sew a godet into a slit cut perpendicular to a hem edge, but it's more common—and much easier—to insert it into a vertical panel seam, as shown here. Sew in the godet before you complete the upper portion of the skirt seam. To reduce bulk at the top of the godet, don't backstitch—instead pull the threads to one side and tie them off.

1. Mark the top of the seamline on the godet; mark its match point on each adjacent skirt piece.

2. Pin the godet to one adjacent skirt piece. Start sewing at the hem edge, shortening the stitch as you approach the top of the godet. Repeat on the other side.

3. Sew the skirt pieces together above the godet using a short stitch and zipper foot. Fold down the godet top seam allowance and start sewing with the needle

positioned exactly at the match point. You may need to adjust the needle to the left or right for ease of sewing.

4. To ensure that the skirt doesn't bind at the godet top, clip the skirt seam allowances almost to the match point. Press the seam allowances open above the match point and away from the godet below it. Finish the seam allowance edges as desired.

HEMMING GODETS

Because godets are shaped pieces, often with a pronounced curve at the hem edge, they can be tricky to hem. Depending on the weight and hand of the fabric, any of these methods listed below will work when hemming skirt godets.

- If the fabric doesn't ravel, like suede, you can leave the bottom edge unfinished.
- Self-face the hem for a smooth edge. A facing can be added to all but thin or sheer fabrics and is an excellent choice for a large, flared godet or one with a bias hemline.
- Stitch-turn-and-stitch, then turn and stitch again for a fast, strong machine finish that's suitable for sheer or silky fabric. This technique works especially well on bias hemlines.
- Serge a narrow rolled hem when most of the hemline follows the straight grain—this finish doesn't work well for bias edges. Use texturized nylon thread in the upper looper for the best coverage.
- Bind the edge with a bias strip of fabric for subtle or bold contrast. A bound hem looks great on full godets, where the wrong side is visible as you move.

VII
SEWING SEAMS

The Perfect Seam

1

eams are what hold a garment together. A perfect seam is strong, supple, as bulk-free as possible, and smooth, so that it doesn't disrupt the overall drape of the garment. Although a seam is, fundamentally, a row of stitches, there's more to creating a good seam than simply sewing in a straight line. It's also important to trim and grade, press, and finish seam allowances neatly. Make at least one test seam to ensure that you've chosen the right thread, needle, stitch, and thread tension combination to produce a strong, smooth seam.

BASTING

Basting, either by hand or machine, is an important step that takes just a few minutes, but ultimately makes your sewing easier and more accurate. The purpose of basting is to temporarily hold or mark fabric before it's permanently stitched in place, to prevent layers from shifting, or to attach underlining or interfacing to the fabric, so the two layers can be handled as one. Basting seams also enables you to fit a garment during the construction process.

You don't need to baste every seam before sewing it permanently, but take the time to do so when the fabric is slippery, when you want to match a pattern such as a plaid or stripe, or when you need to ease one pattern piece to another exactly.

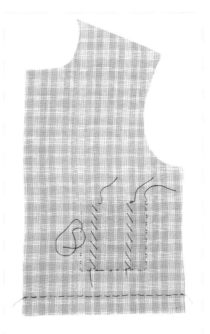

Hand Basting

Hand-baste fine or tightly woven fabrics, where a machine needle would leave a hole, and slippery fabrics, where distortion might be caused by the presser foot and feed dogs. Basting by hand is also helpful when you want to build shape into a seam, as at an armscye or collar. Use a fine hand needle and, for most projects, a single strand of fine thread.

Silk thread works best for most fabrics, because it resists tangling and is smoother than other threads, so it slides easily out of fabric when you're ready to remove it. Silk thread can also be pressed over without leaving a mark, and it leaves no lint behind. Special basting thread, usually in white cotton, is suitable for basting heavier fabrics.

If you want the basting to be quite visible, choose a contrasting color basting thread, but note that some threads leave lint or dye residue. Opt for white basting on white fabrics, to ensure that no color is left behind.

Baste seams with a long, evenly spaced running stitch, close to, but not on, the seamline. To hold layers together, as when attaching underlining to fashion fabric or positioning a pocket, use diagonal or slip stitches. Don't knot basting thread, and start with a new length of thread each time you turn a corner, to facilitate removing the stitches.

> See "Essential Hand Stitches," on page 284.

Machine Basting

Machine-baste when you're sure the machine needle won't leave a mark. Use regular sewing thread in a color that's visible but doesn't leave traces in the fabric. Set the machine for the longest

stitch possible, and sew with a straight or zigzag stitch. You may need to loosen the thread tension to avoid puckering when basting lightweight fabrics. Baste within the seam allowance, close to but not on the seamline. Don't backstitch at the beginning or end of seams.

Pin Basting

Pin-basting is quick and easy, and is the ideal method when there's little concern about fabric slippage. Pin into the seamline, with pin heads facing you as you sew, or place pins perpendicular to the seam, so they're easy to remove as you sew. Place a pin at each end of the seam, and at each notch or match point. Use pins every 6 in. to 8 in. to anchor long, straight seams; place pins closer together when basting curved seams or smaller garment sections, or when the fabric is especially slippery. Don't sew over pins.

If you want to try the garment on before sewing, pin-baste along the seamline, with the fabric wrong sides

together. Put on the garment and adjust the pins to refine the fit. Mark the changes along the seamline, and sew.

Glue Basting

Adhesive products make basting fast and accurate, but should be used with care. Choose a temporary adhesive, such as narrow, wash-away basting tape or glue stick, for jobs where you don't want the adhesive to stay in the finished project. It's fine to apply lightweight fusible tape to baste trim, zippers, and pockets in place. Test the adhesive on the fabric before using to ensure that it adheres well and is, indeed, removable (if you want it to be), and that it doesn't show through the fabric.

SEWING SEAMS

Seams, whether straight or curved, should be smooth and pucker free (unless you're inserting a gathered section), with seam allowances of a consistent width. Even subtle changes in the width

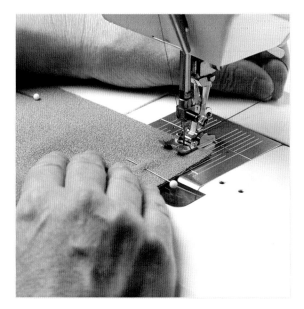
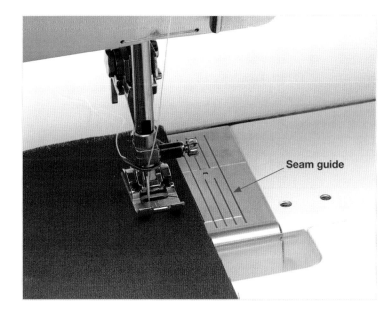

Seam guide

Hold the thread tails while you commence stitching to get a clean start.

of multiple seam allowances around a garment can significantly change the garment's size. To maintain an accurate, even seam allowance, use the seamline guides embossed on the right side of the sewing machine's throat plate. Align the cut edges of the fabric along the desired mark, and keep it aligned there as you guide the fabric.

If the guideline you need isn't marked on the throat plate, you can mark it with a pen directly on the throat plate, or attach strips of masking tape. Simply cut across the roll of tape in two places an inch apart to a depth of three or four layers of tape. Peel off all the layers in one unit, and affix the tape to your machine at the appropriate seam allowance. The depth of the tape unit is a helpful guide that prevents your seam allowance from wavering as you sew.

You can also purchase a magnetic seam guide that attaches to your machine stitch plate. The magnet is strong enough to stay securely in place, but it's easy to move when you need to stitch wider or narrower seams. Before using a magnetic guide

on a computerized machine, read the manual or consult with the machine dealer to be sure that the magnet won't destroy the machine's electronics.

Beginning a Seam

To begin a seam, place the fabric under the presser foot with the thread tails behind the presser foot, and turn the handwheel to anchor the thread in the fabric. Use one hand to guide the fabric in front of the presser foot and the other hand to hold the thread tails behind the presser foot, just until you've started sewing. This keeps the tails from

knotting on the wrong side. Backstitch a short distance or use the machine's "fix" function (if your machine has this feature) to lock the stitches at the beginning of the seam. Stitch forward and allow the feed dogs to move the fabric ahead.

To begin a seam on lightweight or slippery fabrics, place a 3-in. square of lightweight muslin, folded in half, under the presser foot, aligning its long raw edges with the correct seam guideline on the throat plate. Start stitching, and as you come to the strip's end, stop and line up the beginning of the garment seam with the strip.

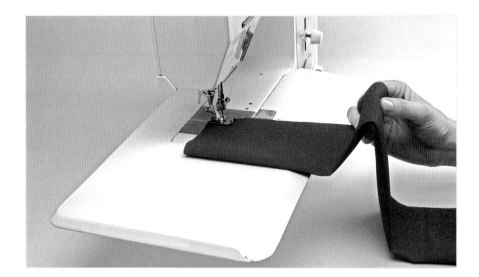

Sew onto the fabric, backstitch, then complete the seam. This gives the machine's feed dogs something to grip as you begin the seam. After you complete the seam, simply cut away the muslin.

When you're sewing through two or more layers of fabric, the bottom layer moves under the needle slightly faster than the top one. This happens because the feed dogs grip and pull the lower fabric under the presser foot, while the presser foot creates a slight resistance on the top fabric. Over the length of a seam, the layers become offset, with the lower layer shorter than the upper layer at the end of the seam. To keep both layers moving through the sewing machine at the same rate, drape a loop of fabric over your hand as shown in the top right photo.

As you sew, make sure the cut edge is constantly aligned with the right seam guide. If it starts to move out of alignment, pivot the fabric from in front of the needle to the correct position.

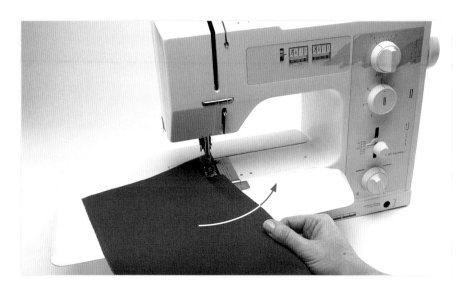

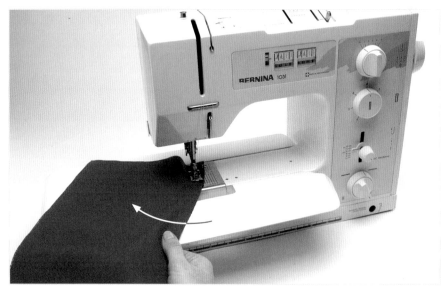

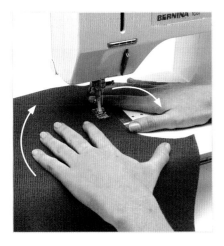

Handling Curves

When sewing curves (whether you're staystitching or seaming), it's important to avoid stretching the fabric along the edges as you stitch. You can distort the fabric enough to change the length or shape of the seamline. Use your whole hand with fingers extended to maneuver the fabric under the needle.

To stitch a concave curve, use your right-hand fingers to maneuver the fabric around the curve and to the right from behind the needle. Use your left hand to control the feed toward the needle. Don't stretch the fabric.

To sew a convex curve, use your hands and fingers to move and direct the fabric through the curve, following the original shape.

Handling Bumps

When seams intersect with a waistband or hem, or you otherwise come to a point with a many-layered bump to sew over, it's easy for your machine to jam and end up with a snarled mess of threads. There are two ways to jump the bumps. Both require that you keep the sole of your presser foot parallel with the feed dogs. This will enable you to sew over bumps without skipping a stitch.

Purchased shims fit under the presser foot and help it remain horizontal.

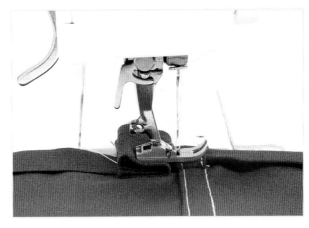

Use a folded scrap of fabric to raise the low end of the foot. Slide the folded scrap under the heel of the presser foot, and stitch until the toe of the foot drops.

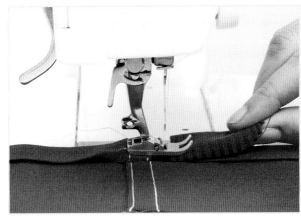

Then position the scrap under the toe. Drag it along as you sew until the heel drops.

TAUT SEWING AND EASED SEAMS

Depending on the weight, texture, and stretch of your fabric, you might need to hold the fabric taut as it feeds through the machine. Conversely, you may need to work fullness or ease into a seam (for example, when sewing a sleeve to a bodice, where the sleeve cap seamline is usually longer than the armscye seamline).

Taut Sewing

Taut sewing is the practice of manually creating a slight tension in the fabric as you sew it, without disturbing the tension or pace of the machine. In front of and behind the needle, gently pull the fabric to tighten it. Maintain an equal amount of pressure from the front and back as the fabric passes under the needle, and the feed dogs control the movement of the fabric as they should. This enables you to sew perfectly smooth seams on lightweight or slippery fabrics and sew uniform topstitch-ing on woven fabrics. This technique is not for knits. Note, too, that if you pull too hard from either side, you can break the needle, so exercise caution when taut sewing.

Eased Seams

If one seamline was intentionally cut longer than the adjacent seamline, and they're supposed to go together without gathers, pleats, or darts, you need to ease the longer seamline to match the shorter one. Patterns are usually marked to show where to position ease along the seam. Typically, you ease a seamline when setting in a sleeve; when joining shoulder seams where the back shoulder is longer than the front; when seaming the longer upper collar to the under-collar; and when shaping a jacket lapel.

There are three ways to work ease into a seam: prepare the seam by gathering before sewing; stretch the shorter seam as you sew the unequal layers together; or let the machine ease the longer edge as the layers move under the presser foot.

GATHERING TO EASE

For the most precise placement of fullness when working with delicate or otherwise difficult fabrics, set the machine for six stitches per inch, and sew two (or more) rows of machine basting just inside the seamline that needs easing. Pull the bobbin threads to draw in the fabric until the seamline is the same length as the shorter edge to which it will be joined. Wrap the thread tails around pins at each end of the eased section to maintain the length you have established. Pin the drawn-up layer to the adjacent seam, and sew the seam with the eased side up to evenly distribute the ease and avoid stitching into the machine basting.

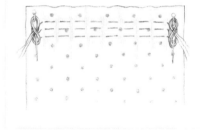

GATHERING TO EASE

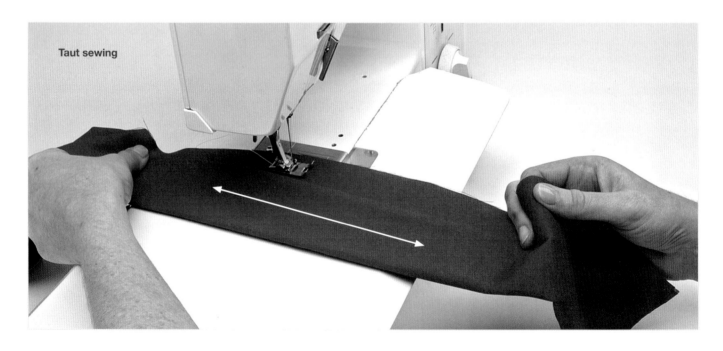

Taut sewing

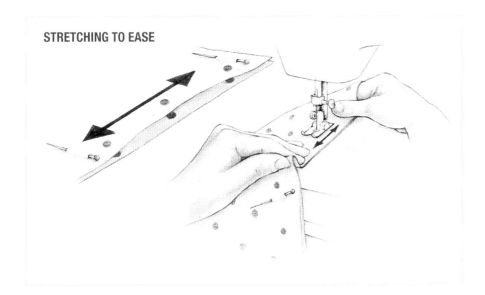

STRETCHING TO EASE

TRIMMING SEAM ALLOWANCES

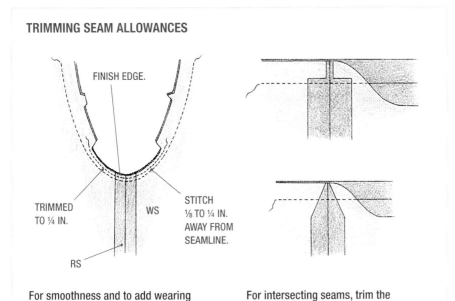

FINISH EDGE.

TRIMMED TO ¼ IN.

WS

STITCH ⅛ TO ¼ IN. AWAY FROM SEAMLINE.

RS

For smoothness and to add wearing ease, stitch the underarm and crotch seams ⅛ in. to ¼ in. from the original seam, and trim as shown. Finish the edge to prevent fraying.

For intersecting seams, trim the ends of the seam allowance diagonally before the intersecting seam is stitched. Or trim corners 1/16 in. to ⅛ in. from the stitching after the seam is stitched.

flattens and lies evenly on the shorter seamline. Hold the layers this way as you sew. As when taut sewing, let the feed dogs actually move the fabric, or you may bend or break the needle. Either layer may be faceup when you use this technique. When the stretched layer relaxes, the other layer will be evenly eased to it.

MACHINE STITCHING TO EASE

The least precise, but still effective, method for easing, especially over long seams, is simply to let the feeding mechanism of your machine ease the seam as it's sewn. Position the longer side against the feed dogs and sew the seam without applying any tension. Use few or no pins to allow the easing to take place evenly, using your hands to keep the edges aligned.

TRIMMING AND GRADING SEAM ALLOWANCES

It's often necessary to cut away some of the seam allowance to reduce bulk and prevent ridges from showing on the right side of the garment. Trimming and grading, the procedures for cutting away these allowances, are explained only briefly, if at all, in commercial pattern instructions. Trimming refers to reducing any seam allowance width. Grading is more specific and is done on enclosed seams where the layered seam allowances create excess bulk.

Trimming

Where and when to trim a seam allowance is determined by the seam location and the fabric type. Always check the fit of your garment before you trim.

Seam allowances on collars, lapels, facings, and underarms always require

STRETCHING TO EASE

In some cases, you can ease one layer to a shorter layer simply by stretching the short one and stitching the two together while both are under tension. This works best on stable, firmly woven fabrics and when neither edge is

primarily on the bias (at the inseam of pants, for example).

Begin by pinning the layers together at the marked start and end of the eased area, with the fullness positioned between. Then stretch the layers until the fullness of the longer seamline

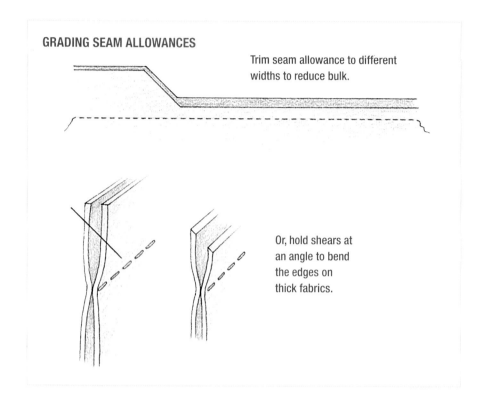

GRADING SEAM ALLOWANCES

Trim seam allowance to different widths to reduce bulk.

Or, hold shears at an angle to bend the edges on thick fabrics.

trimming, regardless of the fabric. As a general rule, trim seam allowances to about ¼ in. For loosely woven fabrics, trim to ⅜ in.

Trim curved underarm and crotch seam allowances to allow for more wearing room and ease, as shown on page 143. Serge, zigzag, pink, or bind these seam edges to prevent raveling.

When using a heavy or bulky fabric, you may need to trim seam allowances in other areas as well, like where seams intersect and on the seam allowances of hems and facings, because the seams are layered and bulky in these areas. For very bulky, nonfraying fabrics, like fleece, you may want to trim all structural seams to reduce bulk.

Grading

To reduce bulk and prevent a ridge on the right side, trim the seam allowances to different widths, leaving the one next to the garment right side the widest.

To grade a seam allowance, trim the side closest to the outer portion of the garment to ⅛ in. to ³⁄₁₆ in. first, then trim the other allowance ¼ in. or ⅜ in. You can also grade the allowances by cutting both seam allowances at the same time, holding the shears at about a 30-degree angle to the fabric while cutting. This bevels the cut edges, and works best on thick fabrics.

CLIPPING AND NOTCHING

Clipping and notching the seam allowances makes them more flexible, so they can be folded back and pressed more smoothly at the seamline. Clipping refers to making small snips into the seam allowance, perpendicular to the seam's stitching line and ending ⅛ in. to ¹⁄₁₆ in. from it. (It is always best to staystitch the garment's edges at curves and corners, as shown on the facing page.) Clipping helps the seam allowance spread. Notching is done

similarly along the seam allowance's edge, but it actually removes small wedge-shaped pieces from the fabric. The purpose of notching is to allow the cut edge to be shortened slightly.

When to Clip, When to Notch

Clip concave (inside) curves, such as necklines and armholes, to allow the cut edge of the seam allowance to spread and lie flat as the allowance is pressed along the seamline. Clipping is also necessary on inside corners that will be turned (as in a faced V-neckline) or need to open so they can be stitched to a straight edge or outside corner (as in an inset corner).

Notch convex (outside) curves where the cut edge is longer than the stitching line to reduce the total length of the cut edge and prevent bulky folds from forming when the seam allowance is turned and encased. Before you notch, fold the seam allowances over at the stitching line to see how much fullness needs to be removed so the allowance can lie flat. Notch the excess fabric where the folds form, staggering them on separate seam allowances for smoother pressing.

Clips or notches should be evenly spaced and made after the seam allowances have been trimmed or graded. Place the clips and notches closer together on tighter curves.

Clip or Notch Curved Seams and Corners to Make Seam Allowances Lie Flat

CLIPPING

Clip a concave (inside) curve to within ⅛ in. to ¹⁄₁₆ in. of the stitching so the seam allowance's outer edge can spread when turned back.

Clip an inside corner so the seam allowance can spread and lie flat when turned or can match the straight edge.

NOTCHING

Notch a convex (outside) curve by clipping away V-shaped wedges from the seam allowance to remove excess fabric.

To determine where and how much to notch along a convex curve, fold back the seam allowance, then cut out excess fabric from the folds that form.

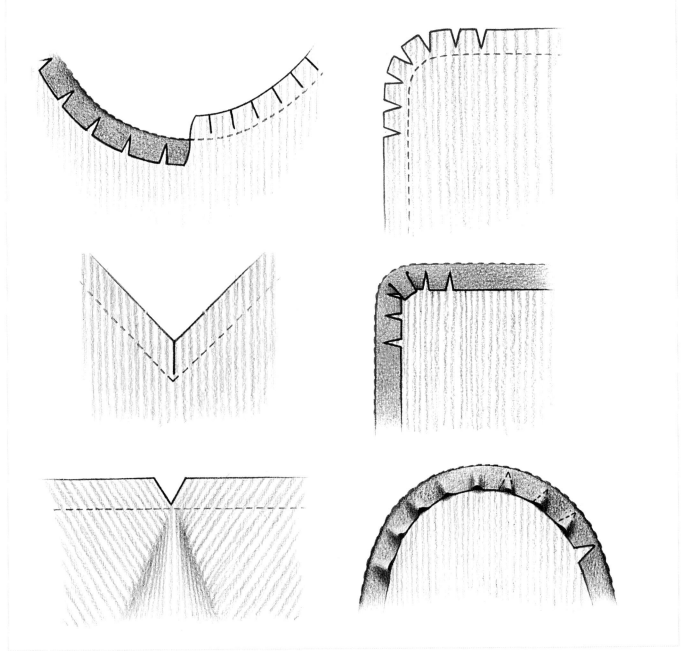

Pressing Techniques

Clothing construction is as much a sculptural as an engineering process. The key to creating professional-looking garments is to work the fabric with an iron, the most effective tool for molding fabric. Pressing gives a garment shape and form, helping to transform a flat piece of fabric into a three-dimensional garment. The combination of heat and steam enables each garment section to fit together correctly and fit the curves and angles of your body. Even if you hate ironing, it is pressing—which isn't the same as ironing—that makes the difference.

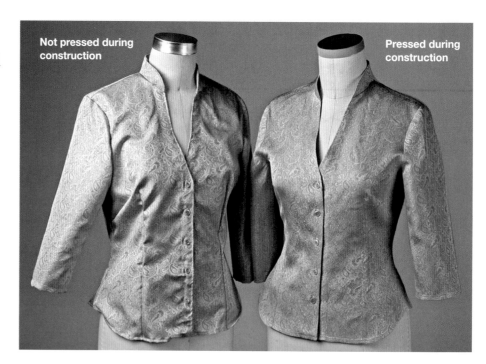

Not pressed during construction

Pressed during construction

IRONING VS. PRESSING

The goal of ironing is to remove wrinkles from fabric or a garment. The back-and-forth motion of ironing smooths and stretches the fabric slightly, encouraging each garment section to lie flat. This is ideal for any broad expanse of fabric in finished garments, as well as for uncut fabric. To get the most accurate fit, iron fabric and pattern pieces flat before cutting out the garment.

The goal of pressing is to shape fabric. Pressing involves an up-and-down motion, with the weight of the iron (along with the pressure you apply) creating sharp folds, soft curves, or smooth seams. This up-and-down motion prevents any distortion of the fabric's grain and helps stitching lines and fabric layers meld together. From pressing seam allowances open to creating a perfectly rounded sleeve cap, you're giving flat fabric a new form.

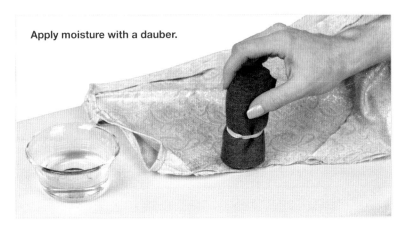

Apply moisture with a dauber.

Spritz to dampen.

HEAT, PRESSURE, AND MOISTURE

Pressing involves applying heat and pressure to the fabric. However, moisture is the key to shaping the fabric. Water, whether delivered as liquid or vapor, is critical for pressing natural-fiber fabrics. Apply moisture to the fabric using one of the methods described below, then press with a dry iron. Finally, leave the fabric in place until it's completely dry. If you move it while it's still damp, the shape you've pressed in won't hold.

Use a damp press cloth.

Applying Moisture

You can apply moisture precisely to small areas with a dauber. Make your own dauber by tightly rolling up a length of woolen fabric and securing it with an elastic band, string, or thread. Dip the dauber into water and dab only on the seam. Press with a dry iron.

To apply steam, use the steam feature on your iron. Check that the iron is fully heated before pressing to avoid water drips that may discolor your garment. Another option is to spritz the fabric with a spray bottle. After you spritz, press the fabric with a dry iron. Test the mist on a scrap of fabric to

ensure that it doesn't cause permanent water spots.

If you prefer not to spray the fashion fabric directly, spray-dampen a press cloth instead. Then, position the moist press cloth over the seams or garment and press both layers with a dry iron. This controls the amount of moisture, avoids any potential mineral buildup, and avoids water spotting on fabric. Using a press cloth also protects delicate fabrics from excessive heat.

Where intense, concentrated steam is needed, use the burst of steam feature on your iron. Some irons offer continuous steam as well, above and beyond the normal steam amount.

PRESSING TECHNIQUES

Since pressing is intended to enhance the three-dimensional shape of a garment, you'll find that many pressing tasks can't be accomplished on a flat ironing board. With the proper tools and techniques, you can create a smoothly contoured garment.

See "Pressing Tools," on page 26.

Pressing Straight Seams

To avoid ripples, waves, and deep furrows along seamlines, get in the habit of pressing seams smooth as soon as you sew them. After stitching a straight

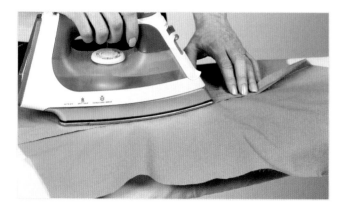

Press curved seams over a tailor's ham.

Use a ham to shape darts.

seam, press it immediately as sewn, then turn it over and press the other side, to embed the stitches in the fabric.

Next, press the seam allowances open from the wrong side (if the pattern instructs you to do so). In some cases, it helps to finger-press the seam allowances open first, to create a clear path for the tip of the iron. Turn the garment over and press again from the right side. If you're pressing a tubular garment section, such as a pant leg or sleeve, insert a tool such as a sleeve board or sleeve roll into the tube so you can press the seams without crushing other layers of the section.

Some designs call for the seam allowances to be pressed together and to one side, then topstitched. In these cases, press the seam allowances flat, as described above, and then to the side, making sure not to press a crease along the seamline.

Pressing Curved Seams

Curved seams, such as armscye, princess, and crotch seams, start the same as straight seams. Press them flat from both sides on the ironing board. Then, if you plan to press the seam allowances open, clip them as needed and press them open over a tailor's ham to accommodate the curvature. Press from the wrong side, then from the right side using a pressing cloth.

Seam allowances in curved areas are not always pressed open. Press armscye seams together and toward the sleeve cap, unless instructed to do otherwise. Press crotch seam allowances open only from the waistline down as far as the seams are actually straight (usually to a notch along the front and back crotch seams). In the U-shaped curved area near the inseam, press the allowances together and trim.

See "Trimming and Grading Seam Allowances," on page 143.

Pressing Darts

When properly pressed, a dart should be almost invisible. Darts usually have one or both ends in the middle of a garment piece; press them only within the area of the dart itself. Using just the tip of the iron, press to, but not beyond, the points of the dart. Press the

dart stitching line flat from both sides. Then, using a ham for shaping, press the dart itself to one side, first from the wrong side and then from the right side.

Vertical darts are usually pressed toward center back or front, and horizontal darts are usually pressed down. In heavier fabrics or with especially wide darts, slash the dart and press it open over a ham.

See "Balancing Darts in Bulky Fabrics," on page 122.

TIP

When you're working on sharp curves or in tight spots, use just the tip of the iron to press. Hold the rest of the soleplate away from the garment; use a tailor board to provide support, if needed.

Stitching for Control & Accuracy

③

Constructing a garment takes more than simply sewing seams. In fact, many techniques that involve stitching are meant to establish or preserve a garment's shape, maintain crisp edges, or control the various layers of fabric that make up a garment section. Some of these lines of stitching show—and even function as design elements— and others are invisible from the outside of the garment. They're all important, though, in fashioning a good-looking, long-wearing piece of clothing.

STAYSTITCHING

Staystitching is a row of permanent, straight stitches sewn on a single layer to prevent stretching in key areas when you're handling the garment section during the construction process. The stitching is done ⅛ in. inside the seam allowance (½ in. from the cut edge if seam allowances are ⅝ in. wide). Staystitch immediately after you've transferred the pattern markings to the cut piece and removed the pattern tissue. There's no need to backstitch when staystitching.

Pattern instructions usually tell you which seamlines to staystitch, but if they don't, follow these guidelines: Staystitch curved and bias edges, such as the neckline, shoulder, princess seams, armscye, waistline, crotch seams in pants, the upper section of a pant back inseam, and the edges of slanted pockets. If the fabric you're working with is quite stable, and you don't intend to do much fitting during construction, you may be able to skip some staystitching steps.

Directional Staystitching

The direction in which you staystitch is important. To prevent distortion while staystitching, staystitch each edge separately. On a bodice, sew each shoulder edge from neckline to armhole, as shown in the photos on the following page. Then sew half of the neckline from the shoulder to center front, flip

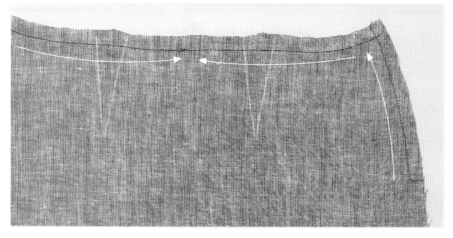

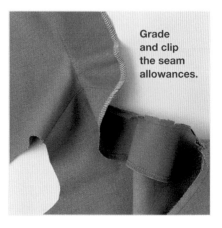

Grade and clip the seam allowances.

Understitch the seam allowances to the facing.

the bodice, and sew the other half from shoulder to center front. Staystitch each armhole from shoulder to side seam.

At the waistline of a skirt, stitch from side seam to center front on one side, then repeat for the other side. To staystitch the upper hip area, start about 9 in. below the waistline and sew up to the waist on each side.

As a general guideline, stitch from the widest part to the narrowest. The only exception is when you're sewing a nap or pile fabric. In this case, you need to sew in the direction of the nap and can't always follow grain direction.

UNDERSTITCHING

Understitching is a technique in which seam allowances are sewn to a fabric layer (usually an inner layer or under-layer, so the understitching is invisible) to help the various garment layers stay in place. Use understitching to keep facings from rolling to the garment right side, to hold undercollars to the underside of a collar, and to maintain clean edges on all manner of garment sections, including pockets.

For most garments, a row of straight machine stitches is ideal for understitching. If the fabric is

very lightweight and sheer, consider understitching by hand, using fine thread and a small running stitch.

Grade and clip the seam allowances before understitching. Press the seam allowances toward the facing.

See "Clipping and Notching," on page 144.

Then, stitch with the facing (or pocket, undercollar, and so on) right side up, through all layers of the facing and seam allowances. Sew about ⅛ in. from the facing seamline, using your fingers to spread and finger-press the seam as you sew. Keep the seamline as flat as possible in the area where you're sewing; allow the facing to flare as needed at its free edge.

Topstitching

shows up best on tightly woven fabrics (such as denim, cotton shirting, linen, or wool suiting) and tends to get lost in napped or loosely woven fabrics.

Step-by-Step Topstitching

1. If you are topstitching along a seam, press the seam allowances to one side, or open the seam allowances to topstitch on both sides of the seam.

2. Trim the seam allowances to ⅜ in. or slightly wider than the desired topstitching margin.

3. Place the garment right side up under the presser foot, with its edge ¼ in. to ⅜ in. (or the desired distance) to the right of the needle. Use the seamline marks on the throat plate or the edge of the presser foot as a guide. Hold the thread tails, and with the needle down, begin sewing (don't backstitch). Allow the fabric to feed evenly through the machine, keeping the garment edge aligned with the seamline marks or foot edge.

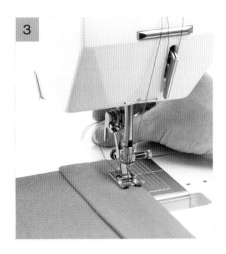

TOPSTITCHING

Topstitching is a row of evenly spaced straight stitches visible on the right side of a garment, typically aligned parallel to an edge or a seam. Its two functions are to anchor layers of fabric together, thus reinforcing a seam or edge and producing a very flat finish, and to accent an edge as a finishing detail. A topstitched seam or edge holds up well to repeated wearing and washing, extending the life of the garment it finishes. It draws the eye to specific areas of a garment, such as a collar or pocket, and thread color ultimately sets the tone.

How far to place a topstitching line from the seam or edge it echoes is a matter of taste. A typical distance is ¼ in. to ⅜ in., but you may increase that distance for thicker fabrics. Pattern instructions usually tell you where to position topstitching so that it looks and functions as it should.

Thread for Topstitching

Topstitch with strong polyester, silk, or silk-finish cotton thread and a top-stitching machine needle that's appropriate for your fashion fabric. Use thicker threads (two strands of polyester or silk, or one strand of topstitching, buttonhole twist, or home décor thread) and a topstitching needle with a large eye. For pucker-free topstitching, use a longer-than-usual stitch, somewhere between 3 mm and 4 mm long.

Topstitching in a color that matches the fashion fabric is tone-on-tone elegant, whereas contrasting thread creates a bold, sporty style. Topstitching

151

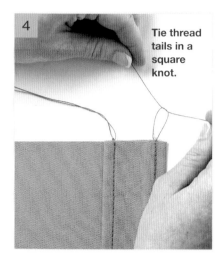

Tie thread
tails in a
square
knot.

**TOPSTITCHING
CORNERS**

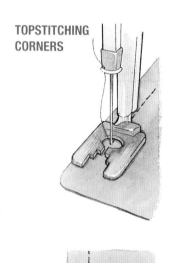

*4. Sew right to the edge of the garment
section (don't backstitch), and tie the
thread ends in a square knot, as shown
in the photo above. To topstitch around a
corner, stitch to the corner, drop the needle
into the fabric, lift the presser foot, then
pivot the fabric.*

Topstitching Corners

To topstitch a corner, keep the bulkier
seam layers from getting stuck under
the needle by creating a thread handle.
Thread a hand needle with a 12-in.
length of thread, but leave it unknotted. Take one stitch through the corner,
leaving the needle dangling.

Topstitch along one side of the piece,
stopping with the needle down at the
exact corner. Lift the presser foot, pivot
your fabric, and gently pull on the
dangling threads to keep the point from
falling into the needle hole on your
throat plate or misfeeding to create
shorter stitches due to the extra bulk.

EDGESTITCHING

Edgestitching is a single line of top-
stitching sewn $\frac{1}{16}$ in. to $\frac{1}{8}$ in. from
the edge or seam to create a very flat
finish that's more functional than
decorative.

To edgestitch around a corner
without having the needle push the
corner in the throat plate, edgestitch
to the corner, handwalking the last few
stitches. At the corner, stop with the
needle in the fabric, while it's on its
way up. Raise the presser foot, pivot
the garment, and tuck under the back
of the presser foot a folded fabric scrap
(or a section of the garment) that is

the same thickness as the corner you're
edgestitching. Lower the presser foot
and stitch.

SEWING CORNERS

When you're sewing corners, no matter
the angle, set the machine for a shorter
stitch length in the seam $\frac{1}{4}$ in. before
and after the turning point. For most
corners, you can simply sew along one
side of the angle to the marked corner
point, position the needle down into
the fabric, lift the presser foot, pivot the
fabric to the desired angle, lower the
presser foot, and recommence sewing. This method works best for inside
corners or inset corners such as the ones
shown on the facing page.

Collar Points

For an outside corner that's crisply
pointed, especially with an acute angle,
such as on a collar, add an extra step.
Mark the stitching lines on each side of
the angle, so that the intersection of the
lines indicates the exact point. Sew one
side of the angle. Stop sewing the seamline a stitch or two before you reach the
turning point of the corner. With the
needle down, pivot the collar, take two
or three stitches across the point, and
pivot again to follow the opposite seam.
Clip and turn the corner right side out.

If you sew straight to the turning point,
as usual, the completed corner is blunt.

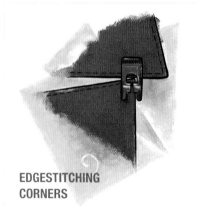

**EDGESTITCHING
CORNERS**

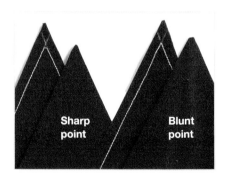

Sharp
point

Blunt
point

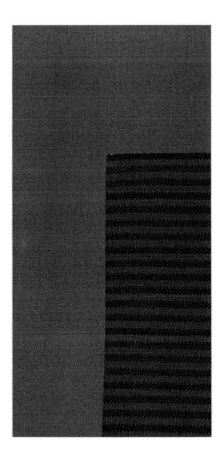

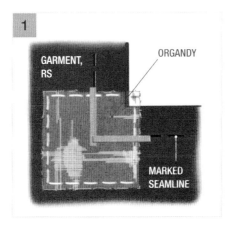

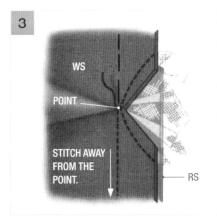

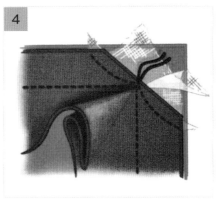

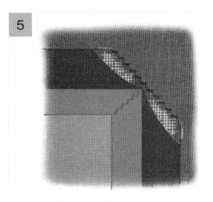

Sewing Inset Corners

An inset corner is one in which an angled piece of fabric is sewn into an angled opening in an adjacent piece of fabric. Sewing an outside corner into an inside corner isn't difficult, but you must clip into the inside corner (as shown in the top left photo), leaving a very small margin of fabric for seaming. For a sturdy and unpuckered inset corner, reinforce the corner with a scrap of cotton organdy or silk organza, as described here.

HOW TO SEW AN INSET CORNER

These diagrams show a 90-degree corner, but the process works for corners of any angle.

1. Lay a small piece of organdy over the corner on the right side of the fabric. Baste or pin the organdy in place and mark the seamlines with tape or pencil.

2. Stitch a rounded V into the corner with short machine stitches, pivoting one thread-width short of the seamline. Clip to the pivot point without nicking the seam. A pin placed diagonally across the point keeps the scissors from overcutting. Remove the tape or basting from step 1 and press the organdy toward the seam allowance of the clip so it is out of the way and lies flat.

3. Mark the seamlines on the corner to be inset (shown in blue), and place the piece with the right side up. With the organdy toward the raw edges and out of the way, place the reinforced corner wrong side up on top of the corner to be inset, aligning the pivot points and seamlines on the right-hand edge. Insert the machine needle exactly at the pivot point and, leaving long thread tails, sew the seam on the right-hand edge. Remove the fabric from the machine.

4. Pivot the reinforced fabric at the corner to align the left-hand edge of the inset and, starting at the pivot point again, sew the seam. Pull all the thread tails to the inset side and tie them off.

5. Press the seam allowances open. Trim the corner seam allowance on the inset piece to form a miter, and then whipstitch the edges together. Trim the organdy flush with the edges of the clip and overcast by hand. If the fabric ravels, fold the organdy over the clip edge and then trim and overcast.

Removing Stitches

4

Ripping out stitches is a necessary part of sewing. Any time you baste or use any other temporary stitching, or if you want to adjust the fit of a garment, or have simply made a mistake in construction, you need to remove stitches. The right tools make the job quick and easy, while eliminating damage to the fabric. The most basic tools are a conventional seam ripper and a pair of small, sharp scissors. Also helpful are tweezers and masking tape (for removing loosened thread fragments), and a scalpel-style seam ripper. Experiment with these tools to find the most effective method for the stitches and fabric you're using.

STRAIGHT STITCHES

Use a conventional seam ripper to remove straight stitches. Pick out back-stitching at both ends of the seam with the ripper's point. Working from the fabric right side, slip the seam ripper's point under every fifth or sixth stitch and cut. Turn the fabric over, and use the ripper's point to pick out 1 in. or so of bobbin thread. Lift the bobbin thread, and pull it away from the fabric.

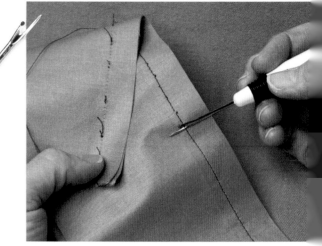

ZIGZAG STITCHES

Use a scalpel-style seam ripper to easily rip out zigzag stitches. Working from the fabric right side, slide the ripper blade through the zigzags, cutting the stitches' diagonal threads. Turn to the wrong side, and lift the bobbin thread away from the fabric.

BLIND-HEM STITCHES

Use a combination of techniques for straight and zigzag stitches. Gently pull the hem away from the garment. Using the point of either the conventional or scalpel-style seam ripper, carefully cut through the large zigzag stitches holding the hem in place. Remove the straight stitches in the hem allowance as for straight stitches.

Seam Finishes & Specialty Seams

Beautifully finished seams are the trademark of a well-made garment. They prevent the fabric from fraying and make the garment both neat on the inside and long wearing. You can clean-finish the raw edges of seam allowances using one of the methods described below, or opt to use a seaming technique that fully encloses the raw edge. Choose a technique that's suitable for the fabric you're using, as well as the garment type. For hard-wearing work clothes, try flat-fell seams. For lightweight special occasion fabrics that won't be worn more than a time or two, a simple pinked edge is appropriate.

ONE-STEP SEAM FINISHES

Seam finishes don't have to be complex to be neat and prevent fraying. Pinking, serging (see page 164), and zigzag stitching all provide simple, serviceable finishes for appropriate fabrics. Many sewing machines have a built-in overedge stitch that works as a seam finish. Check your owner's manual.

PINKED FINISH

Pinking

Pinking along the edge of the seam allowance is often an adequate seam finish for stable fabric that doesn't fray much. For added security, sew a row of straight stitches ¼ in. from the edge. This finish is especially acceptable in garments that will receive limited wear, like taffeta evening gowns or wedding dresses.

After stitching the seam, use a pair of sharp pinking shears and trim along the very edge of the fabric. Pinking also helps buffer a fabric's hard edge, so it's a good way to eliminate a ridge that can form on the right side of the garment after pressing the seam, especially in a heavy fabric.

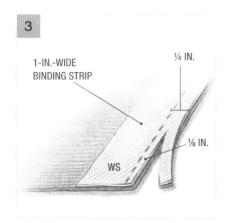

Zigzag Stitch

If the fabric is very loosely woven and tends to fray, finish the seam allowances by zigzagging or serging their edges. As you serge, trim only the slightest amount from the seam allowance edge. If you don't own a serger, sew a row of short-length (1.5 mm to 2 mm), medium-width zigzag stitches. Stitch so the outer point of each zigzag stitch falls just off the edge of the seam allowance. If your machine features an overcasting or overedge stitch, you can use that in place of a zigzag stitch.

BOUND SEAM FINISHES

Binding is a great choice for finishing unlined jackets, and it's especially pretty with a contrasting, lightweight fabric for the binding.

Hong Kong Finish

1. Cut 1-in.-wide bias strips from lining fabrics or silk organza.

2. Sew strips, right sides together, to the raw edge of each seam allowance using a ¼-in. seam allowance.

3. Trim the seam allowances to ⅛ in.

4. Fold and press the binding to the wrong side.

5. Stitch in the ditch of the binding seam through all the layers.

Flat, Bound Seam

This finish encloses and joins seam allowances together with bias binding that can be hand-stitched or edge-stitched in place.

1. Stitch the seam with right sides together, catching a strip of 1½-in.-wide lightweight bias binding in the seam. Trim one of the seam allowances shorter than the other, leaving the one closest to the garment's right side about ⅜ in. wide.

2. Press the binding over the trimmed seam allowances. Press under ¼ in. along the raw edge of the binding. Slipstitch the binding in place or topstitch it along the fold.

ENCLOSED SEAMS

French and flat-fell seams enclose the raw edges of the seam allowances. French seams leave a narrow ridge of seam allowances on the wrong side, and so are best used on sheer and lightweight fabrics, as is the hairline seam.

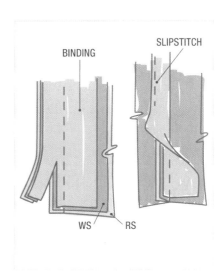

A flat-fell seam encloses and anchors the seam allowances to the garment, and is both strong and low-profile; use it for garments that will be worn and washed a lot.

Both the French and flat-fell seams require trimming one or both of the seam allowances, so always check the fit of your garment before you start to sew using these seam finishes.

Bias Strips

Bias strips can cover, trim, embellish, finish, or reinforce many facets of your sewing. Use them as facings, as trim bands, and to bind seam allowances or edges, or to make spaghetti straps, button loops, and piping. Strips cut on the bias curve easily and don't ravel, making it easy to shape them along curved seam allowances.

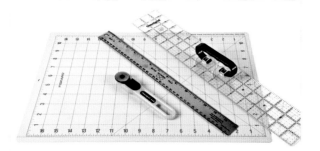

CUTTING AND MAKING BIAS STRIPS

Bias strips must be cut on the true bias—that is, 45 degrees from the selvage. First, mark the bias lines on the fabric, then cut along them with scissors or a rotary cutter, and finally join the strips to make one strip as long as needed for your project.

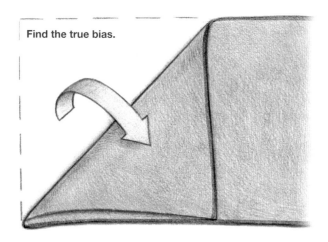

Find the true bias.

1. To make sure the horizontal and vertical grains are at right angles, line up the fabric on a table corner or use a right angle; trim as needed. To find the true bias, pick up the fabric corner and fold it so the selvage is aligned along the cross-grain. Lightly press the fold.

2. Open the fabric, then trace the foldline with chalk and a ruler. Starting at that line, measure and mark parallel lines the desired width of the bias strips. Cut along the lines. A rotary cutter and mat ensure that the fabric lies flat while cutting, and a ruler edge acts as your cutting guide, but you can use scissors if you prefer.

3. To join bias strips to get the length you need, sew them along the straight grain, using a ¼-in.-wide seam allowance. Align the seamlines, not the raw edges. The corners that peek out can be trimmed off later.

Note: The desired strip width depends on the project and fabric weight. For binding seam allowances, cut strips from 1 in. to 1½ in. wide. Remember, bias strips narrow a little once they're cut, so it's better to cut them wide— you'll have better control with generous seam allowances. Trim them later if needed.

French and Mock French Seams

When sewing sheer or very lightweight fabrics, choose a standard French seam for straight seams. It provides a clean finish that's ideal when the seam allowances will show through to the right side of the garment. Keep the finish as narrow as you can—no more than ¼ in. wide.

STANDARD FRENCH SEAM

Follow these instructions for patterns drafted with ⅝-in.-wide seam allowances.

1. With the wrong sides of the fabric together, stitch ⅜ in. from the raw edge. Trim the seam allowances to ⅛ in. and press them open.

2. Fold the layers right sides together on the stitched line, and press. Stitch ¼ in. from the fold. Press the seam allowances to one side.

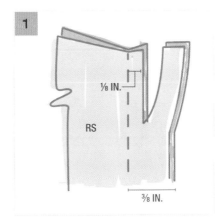

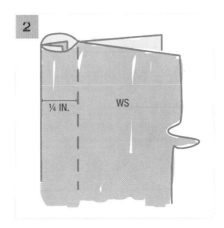

Hairline Seam

This seam is very narrow, fully encloses all raw edges of the seam allowances, and is extremely unobtrusive from the garment right side. Much like a narrow rolled hem, this seam is sewn three times, with each pass further anchoring and enclosing the raw edges. It's most suitable for fine, lightweight fabrics, as the seam allowances are trimmed very narrow and rolled over three times.

Install a straight-stitch foot and/or straight-stitch needle plate if you have one. If you're working with anything but a very lightweight fabric, you may need to adjust the widths given below to accommodate a larger turn-of-cloth. Make test seams to see where to place each line of stitching.

1. With the right sides together, sew the seam, using a ⅜-in. seam allowance (for heavier fabrics, make this seam allowance narrower, so the final stitching pass lands exactly on the ⅝-in. seamline).

2. Fold the seam allowances against the garment just enough to reveal the first line of stitching. Sew a second row of stitching to the left of and very close to the first row.

TIP

SERGED FRENCH SEAM

To avoid having fiber edges poking out of a French seam, use a serger to join the raw edges (with wrong sides together, as below) before you straight-stitch the second seam.

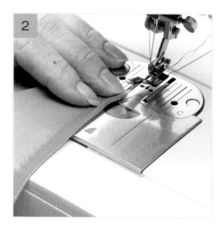

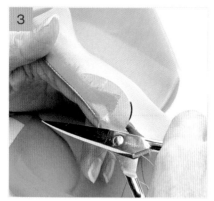

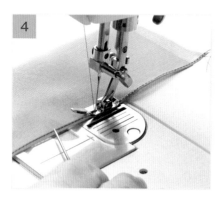

3. Trim the seam allowances as close to the stitching as possible. Duckbill appliqué scissors work well for this step.

4. Fold the seam allowances against the garment again, to reveal the second row of stitching. Sew a third row of stitching to the left of and very close to the second row.

Flat-Fell Seam Variations

In a traditional flat-fell seam, one seam allowance is folded over the other, its raw edge tucked under and anchored to the fabric surface with a line of topstitching. The result is a strong seam with all raw edges completely enclosed. You can form the seam on the right or wrong side of the fabric, so that you see either one or two lines of stitching. These seams are useful for unlined garments that need sturdy seams. You can get the same look from the right side with shortcut methods, as well.

STANDARD FLAT-FELL SEAM

Stitch, trim, wrap, topstitch: This method is straightforward and the one typically used on jeans and active, casual clothing.

1. With right sides together, sew the seam, using a ⅝-in.-wide seam allowance. Press the seam allowances open. Trim one of the seam allowances to ⅛ in. wide.

2. Fold the untrimmed seam allowance over the trimmed one. Fold its raw edge under by ¼ in. Press, then sew through all layers, close to the fold.

MOCK FLAT-FELL SEAM

This quick version uses an overcast edge finish in place of a folded-over seam allowance. You'll see it in mass-produced outerwear and unlined jackets.

1. With right sides together, sew the seam. Serge or zigzag the seam allowance edge together. Press the seam allowances to one side, and turn the garment right side out.

2. Edgestitch ⅛ in. from the fold, and then topstitch in the same direction ⅜ in. from the fold. Or, use a 4-mm twin needle to edgestitch and topstitch in one pass. Press.

FOLD-AND-STITCH SEAM

The fold-and-stitch method works on a wide variety of fabrics and gives consistent, controllable results.

1. Place fabric wrong sides together. Fold the seam allowance of the bottom layer over the top layer by ½ in. Then stitch slightly less than ½ in. from the fold, catching the raw edge.

2. Press the fold toward the fabric, enclosing the raw edge. Edgestitch along the fold. Press.

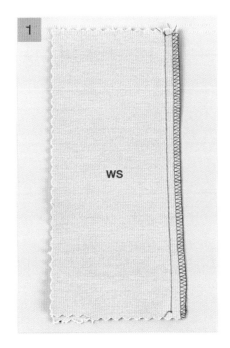

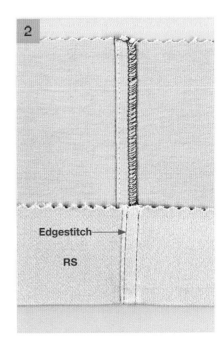

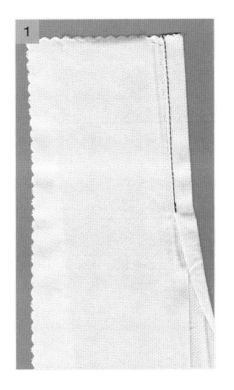

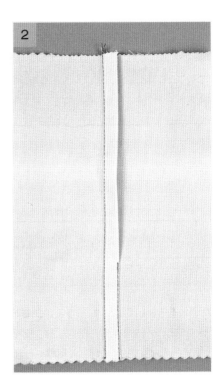

2. *Using a slightly elongated stitch (about 3 mm for heavier fabrics), sew ¹⁄₁₆ in. from the raw edge. Use either an edgestitching foot or the inner edge of the presser foot toe, and adjust the needle position to obtain the placement of the stitching line.*

3. *Stitch again ¼ in. from the first line of stitching. Then, using small, sharp scissors held flat against the fabric, trim the excess seam allowance on the underlap.*

DECORATIVE SEAMS

These seams function as design elements while also holding a garment together. You can add them to designs even if the pattern doesn't include them. Plan ahead so you can adjust the seam allowance width or the construction sequence as needed.

Lapped Seams

A lapped seam is formed when one fabric layer is lapped over the other, and a topstitched seam is sewn to secure the two layers together. Because the raw edges aren't finished and are exposed on both the right and wrong sides of

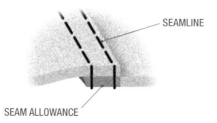

SEAMLINE

SEAM ALLOWANCE

the seam, you must use a nonraveling fabric with some body, such as felt, boiled wool, melton, double-knit, or Ultrasuede.

1. *Mark the seamlines on the pieces to be joined. Trim away the seam allowance on the overlapping edge only, then position the raw edge of the overlap on the stitching line of the underlap, pinning or basting to hold the layers in place.*

Slot Seams

A slot seam is a partially open, top-stitched seam with a facing behind the "lips" or flanges that creates a dimensional striped effect. The underlay can be made in self-fabric or, for greater visual effect, in contrasting fabric. Since the construction of slot seams includes several layers of fabric, choose fairly thin, firm fabrics that can be crisply pressed. Wool flannel and crepe, as well as cotton denim and poplin, are suitable. The slots are typically topstitched ¼ in. to 1 in. from the center opening. The instructions here are for a slot seam that's 1 in. wide, with topstitching ½ in. from the slot opening.

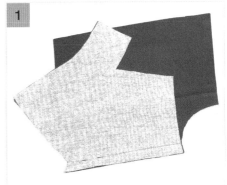

CREATING A SLOT SEAM

ANATOMY OF A SLOT SEAM

SLOT LIPS

TOPSTITCHING

UNDERLAY

PREPARING A PATTERN

PATTERN IS SLASHED ON THIS LINE.

FRONT TOP

¾-IN. SLOT FACINGS ADDED.

FRONT CENTER

FRONT BOTTOM

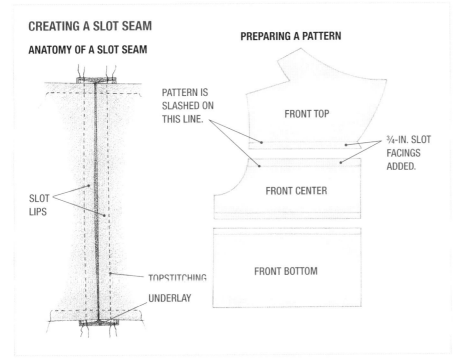

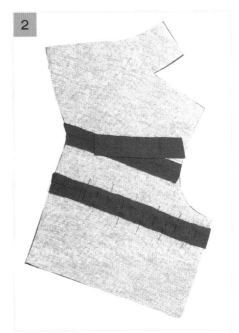

Few patterns include slot seams, but you can easily adapt your pattern. Draw a line to mark the placement of the slot seam, cut along the line, and add ¾-in. slot facings to each cut edge for a 1-in.-wide finished slot.

1. Using the adapted pattern, cut out the garment sections and interface the slot areas. Cut underlay strips 1½ in. wide and as long as each slot seam. Baste each slot seam closed, using a ¾-in.-wide seam allowance. Press the seam open.

2. Pin an underlay strip to the seam allowances on each slot seam. From the inside, sew each side of the underlay to the self-facing with a scant ¼-in.-wide seam allowance.

3. On the garment right side, mark and topstitch ½ in. from each side of the slot opening. Remove the basting stitches and sew across the slot along the seamline at each end.

VIII
SERGER SEWING

Understanding the Serger

A serger can trim excess fabric, overcast raw edges, and sew a seam all in one pass—at twice the speed of a regular sewing machine. Sergers offer a variety of stitches, from the wide, stable safety stitches you find on jeans, to stretchy overlocks that are perfect for activewear, to narrow rolled hems, ideal for delicate fabrics. Some machines are able to sew a chain stitch and a cover stitch, both of which provide the look of topstitching. A serger can't replace a sewing machine, but it does make your sewing neater, faster, and more efficient. Whether you want to construct garments of slithery knits or simply finish the seam allowances on woven fabrics, consider adding a serger to your sewing room.

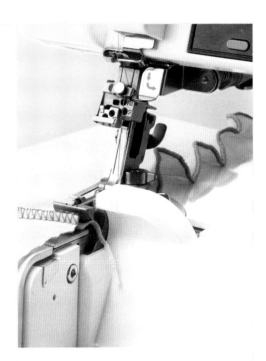

SERGER FUNCTIONS AND FEATURES

The basic operation of a serger is to overcast a raw edge while also trimming off excess seam allowance. But this is just the beginning.

Today's sergers offer a range of alternative stitch functions that make your sewing look more professional while giving you the chance to experiment creatively.

What a Serger Does

All sergers have at least one needle and two loopers. The loopers are moving metal arms with an eye that carries thread over and under (but not through) the fabric edge. All sergers produce a three-thread overlock stitch, which is suitable for finishing raw edges and for sewing seams in knits and wovens. Before the stitch is formed, the fabric is drawn under the presser foot by the feed dogs, where a moving knife parallel to the presser foot trims the seam allowance edge an instant before the stitches are formed. Two loopers then overcast the edge, combining their threads around a metal stitch finger (which keeps the fabric edge flat), to create an overcast edge that is immediately secured as the needle sews what looks like a straight stitch through the fabric. Use this stitch to seam stretch knits, or to overcast single-layer raw edges.

A four-thread overlock stitch has a second reinforcing "straight" stitch, which is added simultaneously by using a second needle. This stitch produces a stronger seam than the three-thread overlock stitch. When you sew a seam, the allowances are overcast together. You can then press them to one side

SERGER STITCH FORMATION

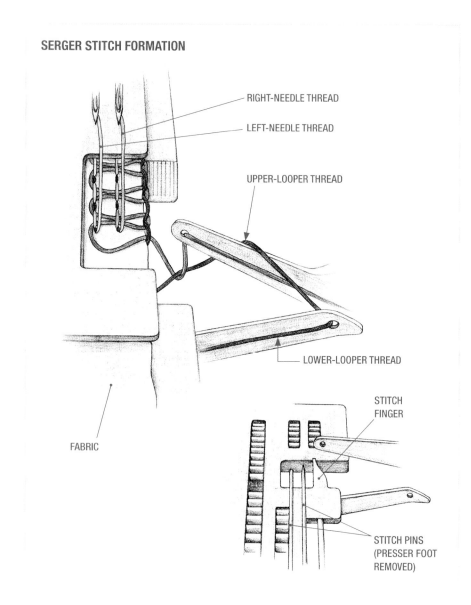

RIGHT-NEEDLE THREAD

LEFT-NEEDLE THREAD

UPPER-LOOPER THREAD

LOWER-LOOPER THREAD

FABRIC

STITCH FINGER

STITCH PINS (PRESSER FOOT REMOVED)

the most essential serger stitches. A 5/ indicates that the machine sews a chain stitch, which is a two-thread seaming stitch that can be used alone or combined with a three-thread overlock to form a five-thread safety stitch (ideal for sewing heavy fabrics).

Stitch Length and Width Adjustments

You can adjust the length of the serger stitch to suit the fabric you're stitching or to create decorative effects. For most fabrics, a stitch length of 2.5 mm to 3 mm works well. Thicker fabrics may require longer stitches. Note that stitch length affects thread tensions in a predictable way. Short stitches need less thread (tighter tensions), and long stitches need more thread (looser tensions).

Most sergers have an adjustable cutting width for specialty work such as rolled hems (which use a narrow setting), and to accommodate very thick fabrics (which use a wider width than normal). The cutting width adjustment controls the position of the cutting blade, which in turn establishes how wide a seam allowance is left within the overcast edge. For most serging, set the blade so it leaves the widest seam allowance within the stitch. This reduces the need for increasing the thread and looper tensions.

and, if desired, topstitch to anchor them in a false flat-fell seam.

Most sergers today sew a variety of stitches, depending on how many threads the serger can handle, what type of accessory presser feet are available, and what options are available for adjusting needle and knife positions, looper function, feed dog speed, thread tension, and threading paths. Instructions for each stitch configuration are shown in the owner's manual. Subtle adjustments

to the setup of the basic stitches produce a variety of seam, hem, and embellishment options.

Sergers are often described with a string of numbers, indicating the type of stitches the serger is capable of forming. A 2/3/4/5 machine can make all the basic stitches calling for two through five threads. If a machine is identified as a 3/4/5 machine, it can't make a two-thread stitch. A 3/4 signifies that the machine sews three- and four-thread overlock stitches,

Differential Feed

Once an optional feature, differential feed is now seen on the majority of machines at every price level. Its function is to adjust the way fabric is fed under the needle and thus ensure a smooth, pucker-free seam on various fabrics. This is accomplished with two sets of feed dogs, one in front of the other, which move independently. By changing the speed of the front feed dogs, you can produce a stitch that's slightly gathered or eased, or slightly stretched. This feature can be used to intentionally stretch or gather fabric for decorative purposes, or simply to control slippery or difficult fabrics when seaming them.

THREADING

A serger must be properly threaded to form any stitches, so follow the proper thread paths, as well as the manufacturer's recommended threading sequence. Some sergers call for threading the upper looper first, then the lower looper, and last, the needles. Others start with the lower looper. Each threading path is unique and not as simple as a conventional sewing machine. To help you with the process, a color-coded threading diagram is often printed inside the front cover of the serger. If you're replacing or adding only one thread, the sequence still must be maintained to prevent the threads from crossing incorrectly.

TIP

Since serging uses so much thread, especially in the loopers, purchase serger thread, which is sold in 1,000-yd. to 3,000-yd. cones.

If you are having a problem with a stitch, always check that the serger is properly threaded. Improper threading can cause tension problems. The most common threading problems occur when a thread isn't properly seated between the tension disks, when it gets incorrectly wrapped around a thread guide, or when a thread guide has been skipped.

When you are changing looper threads, always clear the needle threads from the lower looper first. You can pull the needle threads free of the lower looper with serger tweezers, but unthreading and rethreading the needle eyes is the best way. Also, if you are serging with only one needle, remove the second one, otherwise the stitch may have loose loops where the unused needle has caught the looper threads, preventing them from pulling the stitch tight.

Threading Tips

- Always thread your serger in the recommended sequence.

- When rethreading loopers, clear needle threads from the lower looper by gently pulling the threads toward the back of the machine, so they're not wrapped around the looper.

- To change looper threads quickly, cut the old thread near the top of the thread tree, tie the new thread to the old one, and trim the thread tails to ½ in. Now you have two choices for pulling the new threads through the threading sequence: (1) serge a scrap of fabric slowly as the old looper threads pull the new ones through the threading sequence, or (2) loosen the looper tensions to 0, raise the presser foot, grasp the old thread chain, and

pull it until the new looper threads pass the presser foot, then reset the tensions.

- To change the needle threads, start at the beginning of the threading sequence, or tie on the new thread color, but manually thread the needle eye. Trying to pull a knot through the needle eye will damage it.

Setting Thread Tensions

Setting multiple thread tensions to achieve a balanced serger stitch is more complex than setting the single tension on a standard sewing machine. Additionally, tension adjustments can produce different stitches. Surprisingly, the fabric's fiber content, weave, and weight have little effect on tension. Thread weight and texture has the greatest effect. You'll need to adjust tensions more often for novelty and decorative threads. When you change the stitch length or width, you may have to adjust the tension as well.

For basic serger stitches, like the three- and four-thread overlock stitches, balanced tension is desirable. This means that the threads lie close to the fabric surface, with neither loose loops nor fabric puckers. To achieve balanced tension in a four-thread stitch, follow these guidelines. Your owner's manual will give instructions for adjusting the thread tension to create specialty stitches.

Begin with a properly threaded machine. Serge the edge of a two-layer test swatch, trimming off at least a sliver of the edge. Now, evaluate each component of the stitch individually, and adjust as needed. Make each tension adjustment separately, then serge a few inches on your swatch to assess the results.

BALANCED FOUR-THREAD OVERLOCK STITCH

WS

LEFT NEEDLE THREAD
RIGHT NEEDLE THREAD
UPPER LOOPER THREAD
LOWER LOOPER THREAD

Common Tension Problems

Take a good, close look at your serged stitches to diagnose problems with tension and related settings (such as cutting width).

CUTTING WIDTH TOO NARROW

Loops extend beyond the fabric edge when too much fabric is trimmed from the seam allowance.

NEEDLE THREAD TENSIONS

Puckers: Loosen needle tensions. "Ladders" along the seamline: Tighten needle tensions.

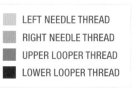

LEFT NEEDLE THREAD
RIGHT NEEDLE THREAD
UPPER LOOPER THREAD
LOWER LOOPER THREAD

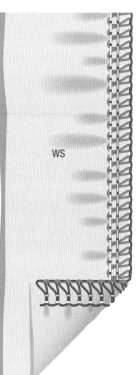

WS

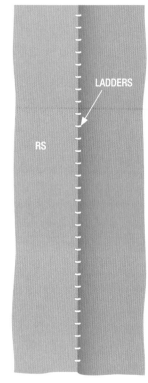

WS

RS

LADDERS

Start with the left needle thread. If the fabric is puckered along the seam, loosen the needle tension, one setting at a time, until the puckers disappear. When no puckers are apparent, open the fabric, pulling firmly, and look at the seam from the right side. If you see "ladder" stitches in the seam, tighten the tension, one setting at a time. The

left needle thread is the one that holds the seam together, so its tension must be correct.

Next, set the right needle tension. This is the easiest one: Set the dial to the same setting as the left needle tension dial, or one unit lower. Once you've determined the difference between the left and right needle tensions for

one fabric, that difference will remain consistent for all two-needle serging.

Finally, observe where the looper threads interlock. They should link precisely on the edge of the fabric, with the seam allowance lying smooth and flat within the stitches. If loops of thread extend beyond the edge of the fabric, you'll need to tighten the looper

LOOPER THREAD TENSIONS

Loops roll to one side: Loosen the looper tension on that side. (In this case, the loops are pulling toward the upper side, so the upper looper tension should be lowered.)

THREADING ERRORS

Irregular loops on fabric edge: Check that each thread is properly seated in the tension disks, or no amount of adjustment will be able to create a balanced stitch.

tensions. If the extending loops seem to be formed by just one of the loopers, tighten the tension on that looper only.

If the looper stitches are rolling to one side of the fabric, the tension is probably too high on that side. Loosen it in increments until the loops connect on the fabric edge. You may need to increase tension on one side and decrease it on the other, but begin by loosening rather than tightening whenever possible. If you make your adjustments in this order, you shouldn't have trouble getting your serger to work on any fabric that can fit under the presser foot.

Serger Stitches

To execute most sewing/serging tasks, six stitches are all you need. These utility stitches—overlock, overedge, flatlock, chain, safety, and cover stitches—make a variety of seam types, as well as finish raw edges. By adjusting thread tension and stitch length and width, you can create additional stitch effects. When you purchase a serger, practice adjusting it from stitch to stitch, and experiment with these stitches on an assortment of fabric types. The more familiar you become with the machine, the more useful it will be for a wide range of sewing jobs.

BASIC UTILITY STITCHES

Each of the six stitches shown here makes a different kind of seam, and together, they form the basis of all enhanced serger sewing. Not all sergers can sew all six—and some can sew several variations of the six. Refer to your owner's manual for the specifics of your serger.

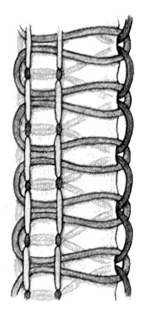

Overlock Stitch

The three-thread overlock is the basic serger stitch. It is made with a single needle thread and two looper threads. It is used to sew seams and simultaneously overcast the seam allowance, and it has moderate strength and stretch, ideal for T-shirts or loose-fitting garments and those made from lightweight woven fabrics. It is also used to overcast the raw edge of a single layer of fabric. If the tension settings are adjusted, this

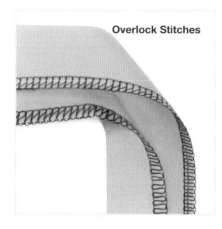

Overlock Stitches

Two-thread Overedge Stitch

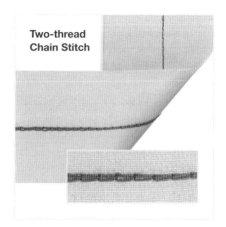

Two-thread Chain Stitch

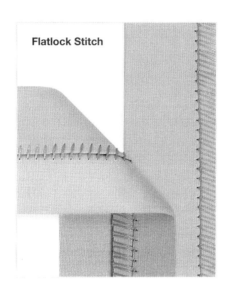

Flatlock Stitch

stitch creates a narrow rolled edge or a flatlock seam.

A second needle and fourth thread add a second row of straight stitches to create the four-thread overlock, which produces a stronger seam appropriate for heavy fabrics, like denim, or garments that receive stress, like children's wear.

Two-Thread Overedge Stitch

When the machine is set to this stitch, the upper looper is converted to a hook that pulls the needle thread into an interlocking pattern with the lower looper thread. Too stretchy to make a good seam, a two-thread overedge binds the edges of lightweight fabrics beautifully, can be used to sew a stretch blind hem for knits, and will create a fine rolled edge.

Flatlock Stitch

Used on sporty clothes where you want the seam allowance felled (stitched flat to the garment instead of hanging loose from it), a flatlock stitch is achieved by loosening the needle tension of a two-thread overedge or three-thread overlock stitch.

To make a flatlocked seam, sew two layers of fabric, wrong sides together, and then lift one away from the other. The seam allowance folds against the fabric on one side, inside the threads, and a thread ladder forms across the seam on the other side. This stitch makes an interesting embellishment when sewn on a folded edge with decorative threads in the looper. When you unfold the fabric, the stitching forms a ladder on one side, and a series of intertwined loops on the other.

Two-Thread Chain Stitch

This stitch looks like a straight stitch on the top of the fabric, and a thicker straight stitch on the bottom. On closer examination, the thickness on the bottom comes from the thread looping back three times for each stitch. Rarely used for knits because it has little or no stretch, it is often used on woven fabrics for seams (often in combination with an overlock stitch). By disengaging the knife, you can sew a chain stitch away from the fabric edge, with the fabric wrong side up for decorative topstitching. When elastic thread is used in the looper, the stitch creates shirring. If the lower thread is pulled, the stitch unravels instantly, so it makes a good basting stitch. If you use a chain stitch for seaming, be sure to knot the thread ends, or enclose them in an intersecting seam.

Five-Thread Safety Stitch

A five-thread serger can be set to simultaneously sew a two-thread chain stitch and a three-thread overlock stitch. This combination is commonly called a five-thread safety stitch: The chain stitch functions as the seam, and the overlock finishes the raw edges while providing

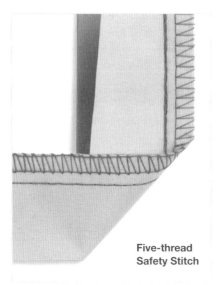

Five-thread Safety Stitch

Coverstitch

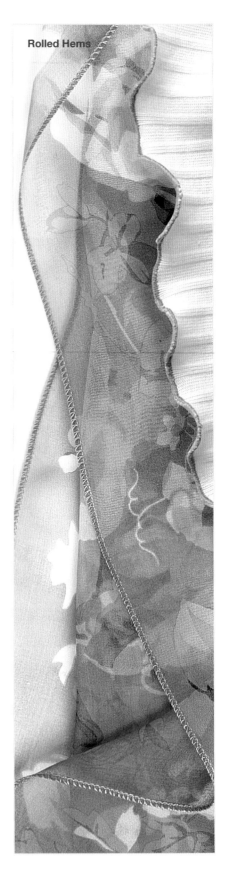

Rolled Hems

an additional backup seam. It is stable, nonstretching, and appropriate for use on woven fabrics.

Coverstitch

The coverstitch is often seen on ready-to-wear. When made with the knife disengaged, this stitch can be used to secure a hem of any depth. The two needle threads form parallel lines on the top of the fabric, and the threads in one or more loopers form a looped pattern on the underside, covering the raw edge of the folded-back hem allowance.

For an attractive embellishment, place decorative thread or yarn in the loopers and sew with the fabric wrong side up. Sophisticated machines offer more coverstitch options with various stitch patterns. Some sergers accept a twin needle, which adds a third row of topstitching.

You can purchase a single-purpose coverstitch machine, which is a cousin to a serger. These machines are useful if you sew knits, as they create an attractive hem that doesn't interfere with the fabric's stretch.

DECORATIVE SERGER EFFECTS

With their multiple threads, adjustable thread tension and stitch length, and differential feed, sergers are ideal for working with slippery or stretchy fabrics, and for fashioning decorative edges. A serger can replace some hand-sewing techniques, and even produce delicate, heirloom effects on fine fabrics. Add to this the ability of sergers to accept decorative threads in the loopers, and you'll find this machine as much a creative inspiration as a utilitarian tool.

ROLLED HEM

A rolled hem is created with a three-thread overlock stitch, formed over a rolled hem stitch finger. To set the machine for a rolled hem, consult the owner's manual. Some machines require a change of presser foot or stitch plate, while on others (including most recent models), you need only slide a lever. In this stitch, the serger trims the seam allowance, then rolls it into a narrow tube that is then secured by the overlock stitch. The rolled hem is suitable for most light- to medium-weight fabrics, but make a test swatch first. (Some stiff fabrics don't roll well and are better finished with a two-thread overedge stitch set to a short stitch length.)

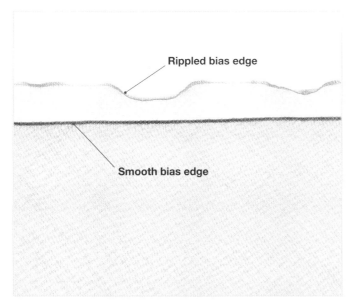

Rippled bias edge

Smooth bias edge

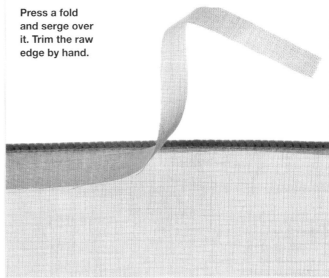

Press a fold and serge over it. Trim the raw edge by hand.

No matter what fabric you're using, your goal is a supple, smooth, and even stitch. Serging a rolled hem is the fastest way to make a neat, uniform edge and can be used on hems, necklines, armholes, and ruffles. It's easiest on the straight grain but can also be done on the crossgrain or bias. When serging on straight- or crossgrain fabric, especially fine or lightweight materials, the most common problem you'll encounter is puckering. To reduce this, loosen the needle thread tension until the rolled hem forms along the edge without any visible puckers.

Serging can stretch the edge of bias-cut or stretch fabrics, resulting in a wavy "lettuce leaf" look. To enhance this rippling for decorative effect, decrease the differential feed and gently tug on the hem after serging. To eliminate the waves, increase the differential feed. This compresses the fabric and maintains its original shape.

Single layers of sheer fabrics and knits don't provide much of a foundation for the serger stitch to grab. For professional results, press up a small hem allowance, then serge the edge with the fold running next to the cutting blade. Don't trim the fold. When the serging is complete, trim off the excess hem allowance close to the stitching (appliqué scissors make it easy). See the right photo above. Another option is to roll-hem over water-soluble stabilizer, then remove it after stitching.

SETTINGS

Using the settings listed here, serge single- and double-layer test swatches, adjusting the settings if necessary. If your fabric is soft, starch it lightly before serging. Make a note of the successful settings, and attach it to a swatch of fabric for future reference.

- **STITCH TYPE** Three-thread rolled-hem stitch.
- **STITCH LENGTH** 2.0 to 2.5 mm; you should be able to see a little bit of the fabric edge between the stitches, but the stitch column should be flexible and smooth, not bumpy.
- **NEEDLE SIZE** 70/10 or 75/11.
- **DIFFERENTIAL FEED** Normal; adjust as needed to increase or eliminate ripples.
- **CUTTING WIDTH** Wide setting; adjust to a narrower setting as needed to make the finished hem 1/16 in. to 1/8 in. wide.
- **THREAD** High-quality serger thread or 60-weight machine embroidery thread.
- **NEEDLE THREAD TENSION** 2 to 4; loosen tension to prevent puckering.
- **UPPER LOOPER TENSION** 2 to 4; loosen as needed to increase the roll of the hem.
- **LOWER LOOPER TENSION** 7; tighten as needed to increase the roll of the hem.

PIN TUCKS

Conventionally sewn pin tucks are a test of your stitching accuracy. The rolled-hem stitch guarantees even, equal-size tucks because the stitch width determines the tuck width.

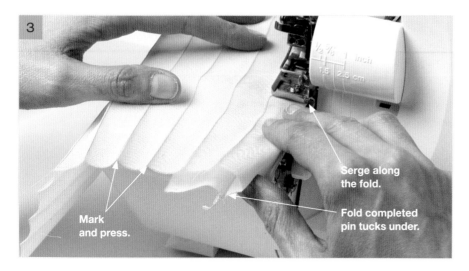

Mark
and press.

Serge along
the fold.

Fold completed
pin tucks under.

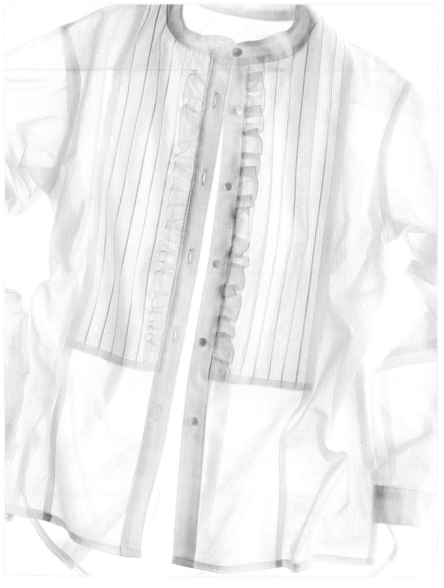

1. Mark the pin tuck placement lines on the fabric, at least ¾ in. apart. Keep the lines on the straight grain as much as possible.

2. Fold the fabric along the lines, wrong sides together, and press.

3. Serge along each pressed fold, guiding the fold next to, but not touching, the serger blade. If your serger allows it, inactivate the cutting blade to avoid clipping the fold. Fold the fabric section with completed pin tucks under, and watch the edge you're serging to avoid shaving off fabric with the serger knife. Always serge a series of pin tucks in the same direction, as there is a definite right and wrong side to the pin tuck.

4. Press the pin tucks gently to one side without crushing them. If the tucks end in the middle of the fabric rather than at an edge, leave a thread tail and weave it back into the tuck on the wrong side with a needle.

Attaching Lace Trims

Serging lace trims offers a strong, clean-finished attachment seam with no fuss. You can position lace either along an edge or within the body of a garment.

CHOOSE AND PREPARE THE LACE

Lace edging has one straight edge (called a heading) and one scalloped edge. It's used as an edge finish, with the heading sewn to the garment. Lace insertion has straight edges on both sides and is inserted between two pieces of fabric, as shown in the photo on the facing page. Opt for high-quality lace, preferably 100 percent cotton. Starch it lightly before serging.

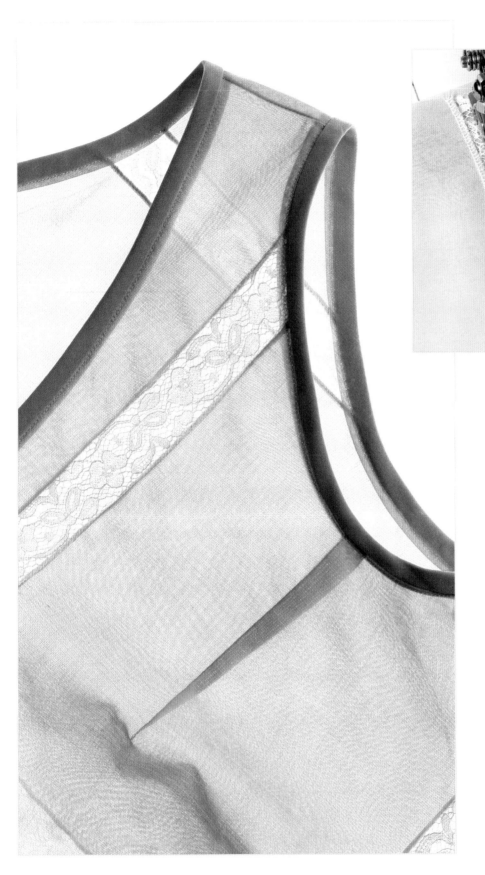

SERGE CAREFULLY TO ATTACH LACE

Lay the lace on top of the fabric, right sides together, with the heading edge of the lace parallel to and about ¼ in. to the left of the fabric's raw edge. Lower the needle just inside the heading of the lace, and begin to serge. To guide the fabric, keep your eye on the needle as it stitches through the lace heading. As the layers are serged together, some of the fabric to the right of the lace heading is rolled into the seam, and the rest is trimmed off. In the photo above, one edge of a lace insertion has already been attached. The second edge is being stitched and trimmed.

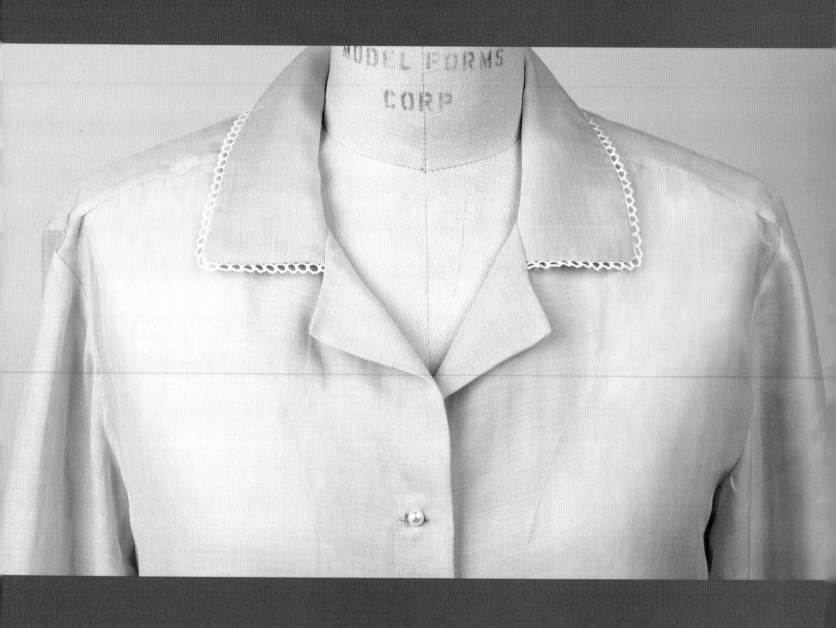

IX
CONSTRUCTION
TECHNIQUES

Sleeves

Most sleeve styles fall into three basic categories: set-in, cut-on, and raglan. However, variations at the shoulder seam and at the hem create many other design options. Pattern instructions explain how and when to attach the sleeve, but it's helpful to know some alternative techniques in case you want to make design changes.

SET-IN SLEEVES

Set-in sleeves are joined to the garment bodice at a seam that circles over the shoulder and under the arm—the armscye (or armhole) seam. A well-set-in sleeve meets the shoulder in a pucker-free, smoothly sculpted, curved seam. Perfect sleeve caps boost the appearance of the wearer by making the shoulders proportional to the rest of the body. They create symmetry by squaring up uneven shoulder slopes and heights, and they slenderize the silhouette by hiding roundness at the top of the arm.

Anatomy of a Sleeve Cap

Ease (as a noun) in reference to sleeve construction is the difference between the sleeve cap, seam length, and the armhole circumference. In a traditional set-in sleeve, the difference can be anywhere from ¾ in. to 1½ in., depending on the sleeve silhouette. *Ease* (as a verb) is the act of gathering the longer length to fit the shorter length. Ease lifts the sleeve cap away from the shoulder point and the arm for a proper fit, but it can also be the source of puckers.

Inserting the Sleeve

There are several ways to successfully set a sleeve. You can set a round sleeve into a round armhole, sew a flat sleeve to the bodice before the side/underarm seam is sewn, or sew the sleeve by hand from the outside.

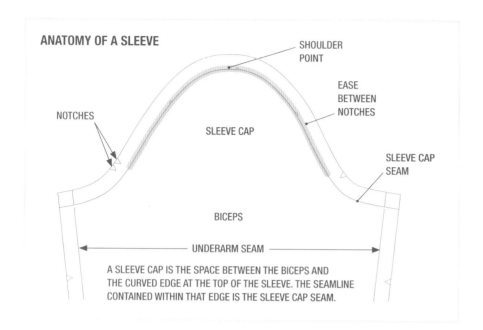

ANATOMY OF A SLEEVE

SHOULDER POINT

EASE BETWEEN NOTCHES

NOTCHES

SLEEVE CAP

SLEEVE CAP SEAM

BICEPS

UNDERARM SEAM

A SLEEVE CAP IS THE SPACE BETWEEN THE BICEPS AND THE CURVED EDGE AT THE TOP OF THE SLEEVE. THE SEAMLINE CONTAINED WITHIN THAT EDGE IS THE SLEEVE CAP SEAM.

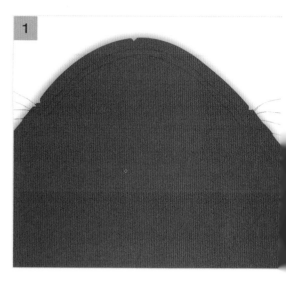

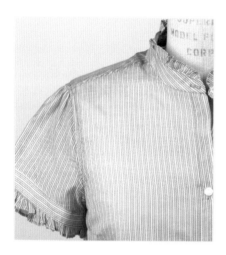

See "Setting in Sleeves by Hand," on page 292.

EASING THE SLEEVE CAP

Proper easing is essential to a well-set sleeve. Since the circumference of a sleeve cap is larger than the circumference of the armhole, to make the two fit, the shoulder part of the sleeve is gathered or eased. Different sleeve styles contain different amounts of ease. Puffed sleeves need a fully gathered sleeve-cap seam, but dropped or extended shoulders need less ease, or may have none at all.

1. Sew two rows of basting stitches within the seam allowance, one just outside the armscye seamline and the other ¼ in. away. Stitch between the sleeve notches.

2. Gently draw up the bobbin threads. You don't want gathers to form, but you do want to ease the sleeve cap just enough so that it cups inward.

For a gathered sleeve cap, sew a line of machine basting on each side of the seamline. Pull the bobbin threads to form even gathers, then slip the sleeve into the garment armscye as above. Adjust the gathers and baste the sleeve in place on the seamline. When the gathers are evenly distributed, machine-sew the seam.

SETTING A ROUND SLEEVE INTO A ROUND ARMHOLE

When sewing a close-fitting set-in sleeve, first sew the bodice shoulder and side seams, and then assemble the sleeve. Press all the seam allowances open. Then insert the sleeve as follows.

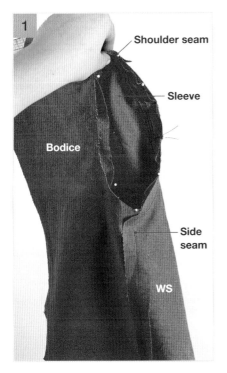

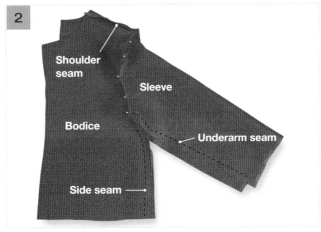

1. Ease the sleeve cap as described on the facing page. Position the wrong-side-out armscye over the right-side-out sleeve. Align the sleeve's front and back notches with the corresponding notches on the armscye and match the underarm seams, if applicable (some designs don't have underarm seams that align). Pin or hand-baste the sleeve into the armscye.

2. Sew with the sleeve side down to allow the feed dogs to gently ease the sleeve cap to the armscye. This helps prevent the tiny tucks that sometimes appear in the seam.

ATTACHING THE SLEEVE FLAT

For a low sleeve cap with little or no ease, set the sleeve in flat, before sewing the garment side seam and sleeve underarm seam. This method works well on dropped-shoulder garments and shirts that have a continuous underarm-to-bodice side seam.

1. Sew the bodice shoulder seams, and press the seam allowances open. Sew all the sleeve seams except the seam that intersects the bodice side seam, and press the seam allowances open. Ease the sleeve cap seam between the notches if needed.

Open the bodice, and with right sides together, pin the sleeve to the bodice, aligning the armscye markings. With the sleeve on the bottom, sew the sleeve to the bodice by machine.

2. Fold the garment right sides together, aligning the underarm sleeve seams and the bodice side seams. Sew from the garment hem up the side and down the sleeve to the wrist, then press the seam allowances open.

179

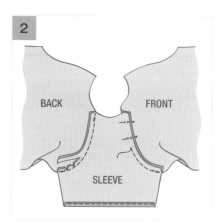

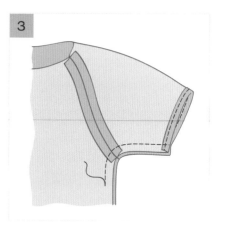

RAGLAN SLEEVES

A raglan sleeve joins the bodice in a diagonal seam that extends from the neckline to the side seam. The two-piece raglan sleeve has a center seam, extending from the shoulder to the wrist, for shaping and to save fabric when cutting. One-piece raglan sleeves may have a dart at the neck end to provide shaping over the shoulder. Each sleeve piece is curved to match the armscye along the bodice front and garment back.

1. Prepare the sleeve: If the sleeve has a center seam, pin the sleeve front to the sleeve back along the center seam, with right sides together, and sew. If the sleeve has a dart at the neckline end, stitch the dart. If desired, finish the sleeve hem.

2. With right sides together, pin the sleeve front to the garment front and sew. Then,

pin the sleeve back to the garment back and sew. Press the seam allowances open.

3. With right sides together, stitch the garment side seams and underarm sleeve seam in one pass. Trim and clip the seam allowance at the underarm area.

A raglan sleeve can also be set in after sewing the center and underarm seam.

CUT-ON SLEEVES

The term *cut-on* is used broadly to designate a sleeve that's cut in one with the bodice, without a separate armscye seam. A cut-on sleeve can be wide and straight, and is sometimes called a kimono sleeve. If it's tapered or gathered at the cuff, it's called a dolman sleeve.

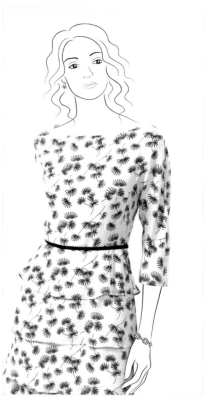

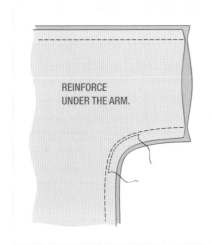

REINFORCE UNDER THE ARM.

With right sides together, pin the garment front and back bodices, matching markings. If there is a shoulder/overarm seam, sew it. Then, sew the side/underarm seamline. Reinforce the underarm curve with a second row of stitching (as shown above), just inside the seam allowance. If desired, add a strip of reinforcing tape in this row of stitching to further strengthen the underarm area. Clip the seam allowance in the curved area and press the seam allowances open.

PLACKETS AND CUFFS

Sleeve hem finishes vary dramatically. You'll find everything from a simply turned-and-topstitched hem to a classic shirt cuff with placket, to facings, bindings, ruffles, flounces, and elasticized casings. Depending on the pattern design you're sewing, you can adapt the sleeve finish to suit your style and skill level. To create a traditional cuff with placket, read on.

Continuous Bound Placket Opening

A continuous bound placket uses a single strip to bind the cut placket opening, creating a narrow overlap when the cuff is applied. For each cuff, cut a binding strip (from self- or contrasting fabric, on the straight grain or the bias) about 1¼ in. wide and twice the length of the slashed opening, plus 1 in. Press each long edge ¼ in. to the wrong side.

1. Mark the slash opening. Stitch just inside the marked slash opening with short stitches. Press the stitches and slash the opening up to the point, but not through the stitching.

2. Unfold one of the pressed edges of the binding and spread the slash open. With right sides together, pin the unfolded edge of the binding to the slashed edge of the opening. Sew the binding to the slash, using a ¼-in.-wide seam allowance. Press the seam flat.

3. Wrap the binding over the seam allowance to the wrong side. Pin the free edge so its fold meets the stitching line, and slipstitch the binding in place.

4. To prevent the binding from twisting, stitch a diagonal line at the top of the fold.

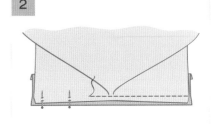

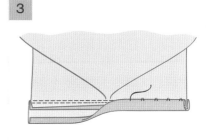

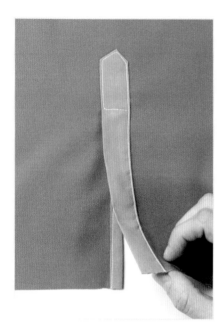

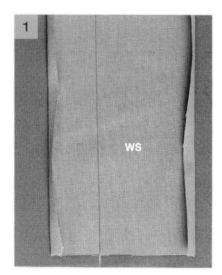

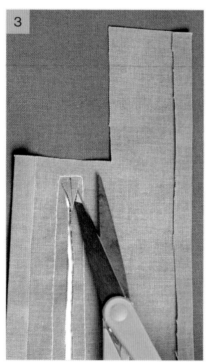

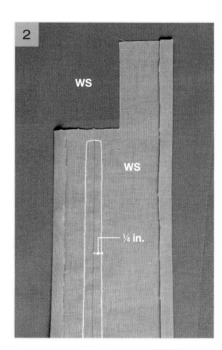

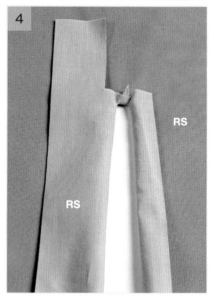

Two-Piece Placket

A two-piece placket—the standard on men's shirts—is composed of two sides: the underlap and the overlap. In most cases, the overlap side is intended to cover the underlap completely. You can vary the fabric, width, length, and position of this placket for design interest, as well as use the same technique to construct neckline plackets.

Mark the slash opening on the wrong side of each sleeve. Cut one fabric placket for each slash using the pattern pieces. Fold under the two outside edges ¼ in., and press in place. Mark the slash on the wrong side of the placket piece.

1. With the right side of the placket against the wrong side of the fabric, align the slash markings. The overlap side of the placket (the side with the taller extension) should be oriented so that it is toward the front half of a sleeve.

2. Mark ¼ in. along either side of the slash line. Stitch precisely along these lines. Stitch from bottom of the slash line to the top, pivot, stitch across the top, and pivot to stitch down the second stitching line.

3. Cut the slash opening along the marked slash line. Clip diagonally into the corners.

4. Turn the placket to the right side of the garment. Press the slash seam allowance toward the placket.

5. Fold the underlap around the seam allowance. Encase the raw edges and pin them in place.

6. Make sure that the folded edge of the underlap covers the visible stitching line. Edgestitch very close to the loose folded edge.

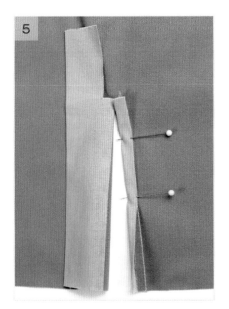

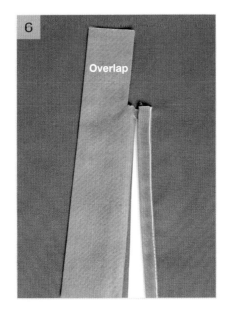

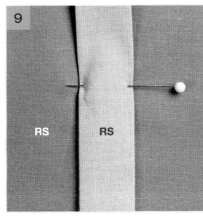

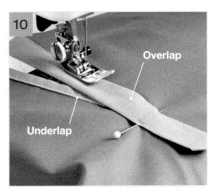

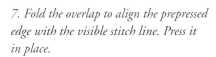

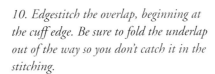

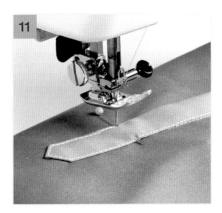

7. Fold the overlap to align the prepressed edge with the visible stitch line. Press it in place.

8. To create the standard arrow-shaped peak at the top of the placket overlap, diagonally fold the underside once and then again.

9. After pressing the peak into shape, insert a pin into the overlap, catching the fabric flap underneath. This pin serves as a marking point for the edgestitching. Insert the point of the pin at the top of the slashed opening.

10. Edgestitch the overlap, beginning at the cuff edge. Be sure to fold the underlap out of the way so you don't catch it in the stitching.

11. Stitch the peak, pivoting at the corners as you sew. Stitch to your pin marking. With the needle in the fabric, pivot at the pin, remove the pin, and stitch straight across to the opposite side of the overlap. Backstitch or pull threads through to the wrong side and knot them.

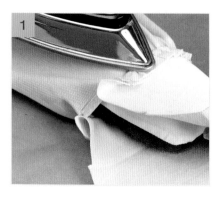

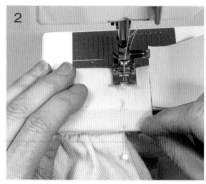

MAKING AND ATTACHING A CUFF

A cuff is simply a faced band that finishes the hem of a sleeve. A barrel cuff can be self-faced, that is, made from a single rectangle, folded to form a facing. Shaped cuffs (including barrel cuffs with rounded corners) must have a separate cuff facing, and thus must be made as two-piece cuffs. Two-piece cuffs curve more smoothly than one-piece cuffs, if you reduce the size of the facing slightly.

One-Piece Cuff

Interface the cuff as instructed in the pattern guide sheet. Mark the foldline on the wrong side of the cuff. Press under ⅝ in. of the unnotched edge (the edge that will be folded to the sleeve wrong side).

1. With the right sides together, pin the notched edge of the cuff to the sleeve edge. Leave a ⅝-in.-wide seam allowance extending at each end of the cuff. Sew the cuff to the sleeve. Trim the allowances of the seam you just stitched, and press them toward the cuff.

2. Fold the cuff right sides together along its foldline; don't press. Pin, then stitch each short edge, catching the folded-back seam allowance, but not the sleeve.

3. Press the seam allowances open and trim them; cut diagonally across the corners. Turn the cuff right side out, pushing out the corners with a point turner. Tuck the sleeve/cuff seam allowances between the cuff layers and press, establishing the finished cuff edge with a crisp crease. Complete the cuff by topstitching through all the thicknesses along the folded-under edge of the cuff. Add a button and buttonhole.

See "Buttons & Buttonholes," on pages 235–242.

Two-Piece Cuff

Interface the cuff and facing as instructed by the pattern. You may interface both the cuff and its facing or just the cuff. On the cuff facing, trim ⅛ in. off the unnotched edges, which include the two short sides and the one long side that forms the lower edge. This makes the facing slightly smaller so the seam rolls to the wrong side, and the cuff curves naturally around the wrist.

1. Turn under and press the notched edge of the cuff ⅝ in. to the wrong side. With right sides together, join the cuff and facing pieces along the short edges and the lower edge; stitch across the cuff's folded edge as pressed. Press and trim the seam allowances. Grade them if the fabric is

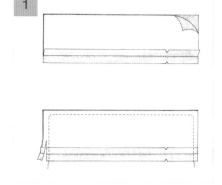

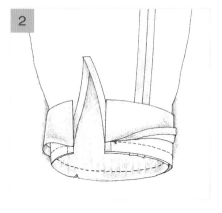

heavy. Turn the cuff/facing unit right side out and press again.

2. With right sides together, pin the facing to the sleeve edge. Sew, pulling the cuff out of the way so that it doesn't get caught in the stitching. Trim and grade the seam allowances as needed.

3. Turn the cuff right side out, tuck the seam allowances between the cuff and facing, and topstitch through all the layers to fasten the cuff piece to the shirt. Add a button and buttonhole.

Shirt Yoke

A traditional shirt or blouse with a yoke can be constructed without any top-, edge-, or hand-stitching. Perform this operation before attaching the sleeves or collar. This technique works with any yoke and yoke facing that are at least 3 in. wide from the front edge to the back at the shoulders. Be sure you cut the yoke and yoke facing exactly the same size so that all their raw edges line up precisely.

1. ATTACH THE YOKE AND FACING TO THE SHIRT BACK

With the right sides together, pin the yoke to the garment back. Pin the right side of the yoke facing to the wrong side of the back. Stitch through all three layers, trim the seam allowances, then press the yoke and yoke facing away from the back.

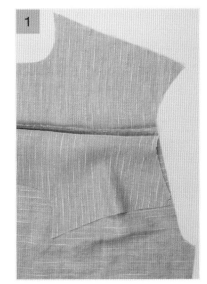

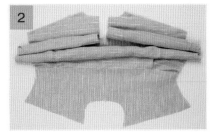

2. ATTACH THE SHIRT FRONTS TO THE YOKE

With the right sides together, pin the garment fronts to the yoke. Spread the yoke and yoke facing apart and roll up the back and fronts between them as shown.

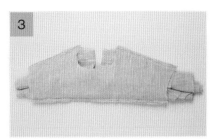

3. JOIN THE YOKE FACING TO THE SHIRT FRONTS

Pin the right side of the yoke facing to the wrong side of the fronts, sandwiching the rolled back and fronts between the yoke layers. Stitch the front yoke seams through all three layers. Trim the seam allowances.

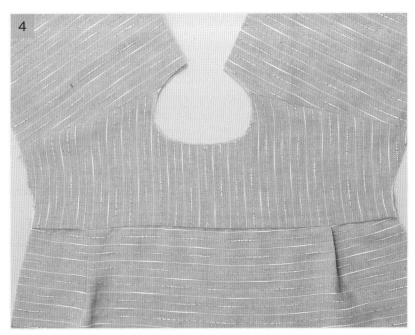

4. TURN THE YOKE RIGHT SIDE OUT

Reach between the yoke layers through the neckline or armhole opening and pull out the fronts and back, turning the yoke right side out. Press, making sure that the rolled fronts and back are pulled taut away from the yoke while pressing.

The yoke is turned and all seams are enclosed.

2
Collars

The collar of a garment frames your face, enhances your overall proportions, and highlights your sense of style. Therefore, collars reward you many times over for precise cutting, stitching, and pressing. With a few basic techniques, you can create smooth collars that have an attractive roll; symmetrical, bulk-free collar points; and an undercollar that stays hidden.

TYPES OF COLLARS

There are many collar styles in the ever-changing world of fashion, but all are variations of three basic types: flat, rolled, and standing. The shape of the collar at the neckline establishes how it fits the garment and the body. By changing the width of the collar and the contour of its outer edge, designers can create unlimited styles. In general, all collars are constructed from two parts: an upper collar and an under-collar (or collar facing).

A flat collar (like a Peter Pan collar) has an inner curve almost identical to the neckline curve of the bodice. This causes it to lie flat when worn. It's found most frequently on dresses, blouses, and children's clothing.

A rolled collar stands up slightly on the neck and then folds over softly along the roll line. It can be constructed from one piece (with a fold along the outer edge), or two pieces (with separate upper and undercollars). Convertible collars, shawl collars, and notched collars are common versions of a rolled collar.

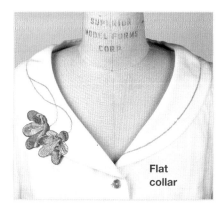

Flat collar

Rolled collar

Standing collar

A standing collar, often referred to as a Mandarin collar, stands straight up away from the neckline and can be straight and stiff, or soft and drapey. It can be cut on the straight grain or on the bias. The most common example of a standing collar is a men's shirt, which has a separate collar mounted on top of a standing collar.

For most collar styles, you construct the collar first, then apply it to the neckline. Patterns provide the necessary pattern pieces and sewing instructions, but a basic understanding of the construction techniques is helpful.

PREPARING A COLLAR

Many pattern companies purposely draft the undercollar slightly smaller than the upper collar, so that the collar's outer seamline rolls to the underside of the collar and the collar itself folds smoothly on the roll line. Mark the collar pieces carefully so you don't mix them up during construction. If the upper and undercollars are the same size, try the shaping method described on page 188.

Interfacing the Collar

The type of interfacing you choose and the application method depends on the fabric weight and collar style.

See "Interfacing," on page 34.

Usually, the interfacing is applied to the wrong side of the upper collar of a rolled or flat collar and to the outer half of a standing collar, to support the shape and hide the seam allowances.

See "Applying Interfacing," on page 111.

As a general rule, trim the seam allowance from medium- to heavyweight interfacing and trim corners diagonally to reduce bulk. Lightweight fusible interfacing doesn't require trimming since it adds little bulk. Machine- or hand-baste sew-in interfacing to the collar, just inside

the seamline. Fuse fusible interfacings following the manufacturer's instructions.

Basic Collar Construction

With the right sides of the under and uppercollar together, start stitching at the center back, stitch the collar edge to the corner or curve, and continue stitching to finish one side.

See "Collar Points," on page 152.

Repeat for the other half, starting again at the center back. This ensures that both collar points(or curves) are sewn with the grain, and the ease is distributed evenly on both sides of the collar. Trim and grade the seam allowances.

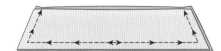

TIP

Shorten the stitch length to 15 to 20 stitches per in. for about 1 in. on each side of the point or curve so you can trim close to the stitching.

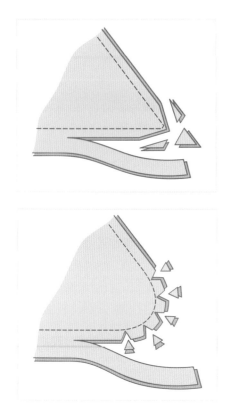

To make points easier to turn right side out, trim off the point and then grade each seam allowance diagonally.

Cut small notches out of the curved collar sections so the curves are smooth when pressed.

Shaping a Rolled Collar

With some fabrics and some collar shapes, you may need to take a few extra construction steps to produce a rolled collar that folds over smoothly, without ripples or puckers. This is especially helpful when you're working with heavy or stiff fabrics. This method works for collars in which the upper and undercollar pieces are cut to the same size. It builds ease in so that the seamlines roll to the underside.

1. With right sides together, pin the upper and undercollars on the seamline at the center back. Then, instead of aligning the short ends of the collar pieces exactly, offset

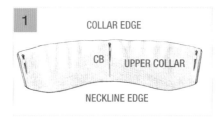

the cut edge of the upper collar by ⅟₁₆ in. to ¼ in. (less for lightweight fabrics, more for heavier fabrics) from the undercollar ends. This creates some ease in the upper collar. Pin along the outer edge of the collar pieces, distributing the ease evenly. Pin and stretch the collar between the center back and each pin to distribute the ease.

2. Stitch the long, outer collar edge with the upper collar down so the feed dogs help ease in the fullness. Start sewing at the center back and stitch out to one end. Remove the collar from the machine, rotate it, overlap stitches at the center back, and sew to the opposite end. Grade

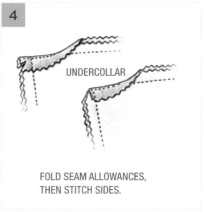

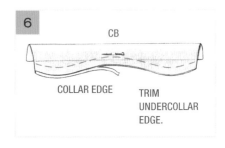

the seam allowances, turn the collar right side out, and press.

3. Refold the collar with right sides together, with the seam allowance extended, and ease the upper collar up from the neckline edge the same amount originally offset at the ends (⅟₁₆ in. to ¼ in.). Distribute the ease evenly along the seamline, and pin if necessary.

4. Fold and pin the seam allowances with the seam rolled slightly to the undercollar. Place the upper collar down against the feed dogs, and stitch from the neckline to the collar edge. Trim diagonally at the collar point to eliminate bulk. Press the seam flat, and grade the seam allowances.

5. Press allowances open, then hold them toward the undercollar and turn the collar right side out. Finger-press and steam the collar, encouraging the seam to roll toward the undercollar.

6. Fold the collar on the roll line as it would sit on the finished garment. Pin through all the layers to secure the collar at the center back, then trim the undercollar neckline edge flush with the neckline edge of the upper collar. Keep the raw edges aligned at the neckline edge (baste if necessary), then pin and sew the collar to the garment, following the pattern instructions.

APPLYING A FLAT OR ROLLED COLLAR WITH A FACING

Most flat and rolled collars are sandwiched between the garment and a neck facing. This facing usually comprises shaped back-neck and front facing pieces that are joined at the shoulder, as shown here, but variations occur as well. The facing may be a simple bias strip (this method is used most often for children's clothing). Some patterns instruct you to apply a rolled collar without a back-neck facing; in this case, the upper collar's neck edge is folded under and hand- or machine-stitched in place.

1. Prepare the collar. Join the bodice fronts to the back at the shoulder seams.

2. Staystitch the bodice neck edge.

3. Pin the collar to the garment with the undercollar against the right side of the garment, matching center front or center back notches and other construction markings. Clip the garment neck edge if necessary to ease the collar and eliminate any puckers. Baste in place. Note: A rolled collar appears to bubble when

When sewing with natural-fiber fabrics, it helps to mold and steam a rolled collar into shape before attaching it to the garment. Position it on the curve of a tailor's ham to steam and shape. Once it is dry, pin and baste the neck edges together as they fall.

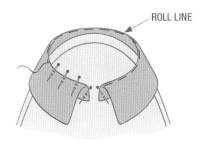

ROLL LINE

opened out because of the rolled shape that you steamed in place. The unevenness disappears when the garment is worn.

4. Sew the back and front facings together at the shoulder seam and finish the unnotched edge.

5. With right sides together and the collar sandwiched between them, pin the facing to the garment at the neckline. Stitch along the neckline and, if the front/back opening has a separate (not fold-back) facing, sew the facing to the bodice at the front or back opening as well. Grade, clip, or notch the seam allowances as needed so the facing can be smoothly turned to the garment inside.

6. Press the seam allowances toward the facing. Understitch with the facing side up, close to the seamline, through all the seam allowances. Press the facing to the inside of the garment and tack the facing to the garment at the shoulder seams.

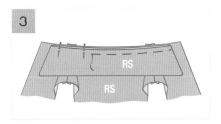

RS
RS

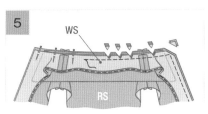

WS
RS

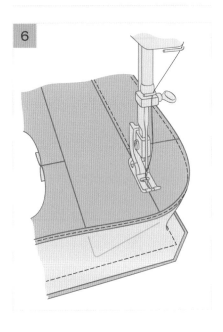

APPLYING A ONE-PIECE STANDING COLLAR

A one-piece standing collar is cut as a long rectangle, which is folded lengthwise to create an outer collar and collar facing.

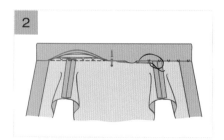

TWO-PIECE STANDING COLLAR

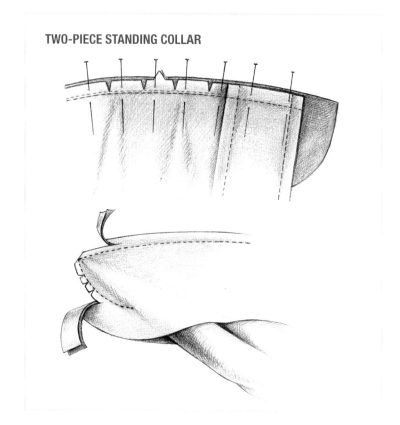

1. Prepare the collar by applying interfacing (page 111). Mark the facing foldline carefully, preferably with thread tracing so you can see it from both the right and wrong sides. Press under the raw facing edge ⅝ in. With right sides together, fold the collar along the foldline and stitch the ends. Grade and clip the seam allowances as needed, and turn the collar right side out. Push the corners out and press.

2. With the collar outer side against the garment right side, pin the collar to the neck edge, matching centers and any other notches. Sew the collar to the garment, leaving the collar facing edge free. Trim and grade the seam allowances. Press the seam allowances up, between the collar and its facing. Slipstitch the facing edge to the garment along the seamline.

APPLYING A TWO-PIECE STAND-ING COLLAR

Standing collars, particularly traditional shirt collars that have a curved edge at center front, are usually constructed with two separate pieces: an outer collar and a collar facing. The standing part of a shirt collar is called either the collar band or the collar stand. Here, we'll

refer to it as the collar stand. A common concern when applying the two-piece collar stand is excess bulk at the center front corner, where the stand meets the neckline/center front corner of the shirt. To avoid this, follow this sequence to apply the stand, then add the collar itself afterward.

1. Trim the stand and shirt neckline seam allowances to ¼ in. Pin the stand layers to the neckline seam, with the outer collar right side against the shirt right side, and the facing right side against the shirt wrong side. A ⅝-in.-wide seam allowance extends beyond the ends of the neckline. Sew the neckline seam, starting and stopping exactly at the outer edges of the shirt placket or opening.

2. Roll the shirt front edge into a tight twist away from the collar stand end, to keep it out of the way for the next step.

3. Stitch the front edge of the stand, starting at the last stitch on the neckline seam, and stopping at the collar placement dot (just around the curved end of the stand). Trim the seam allowances to ⅛ in., then turn the collar stand right side out.

4. Construct the collar, and add it in either of two ways: Press the open edges of the collar stand in by ⅝ in., slip the collar between the layers, and edgestitch through all layers, sandwiching the collar neck edge in the stand. Or, sew the collar to the stand, with the undercollar against the right side of the stand. Don't catch the stand facing in this line of stitching. Trim the seam allowances and press them toward the stand. Press the stand facing raw edge in ⅝ in., and edgestitch to close the stand, sandwiching the collar neck edge.

3

Pockets

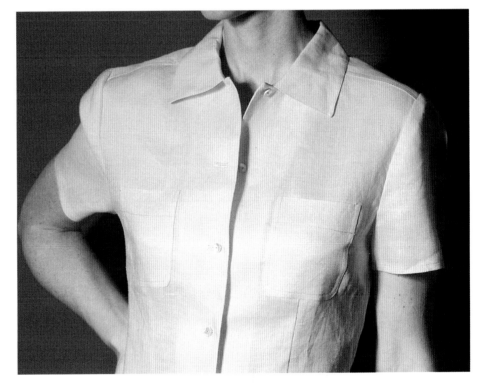

Pockets, while not essential for good fit or garment function, add design interest to any garment, and they make your life easier. You can add a pocket to almost any garment, whether it's something you already own or something you're getting ready to sew. Because pockets are typically at least as much about function as form, take the time to make them sturdy, so they look great throughout the life of the garment. And if you're adding a pocket where there wasn't one, plan the construction and application sequence ahead of time to make the process easy and the finished result strong and attractive.

PATCH POCKETS

A patch pocket is just that: a piece of fabric, usually rectangular, sewn to a garment on three sides. The unattached, finished upper edge becomes the pocket opening. Patch pockets can be lined or left unlined, depending on the weight of the fabric and the desired finish of the opening edge.

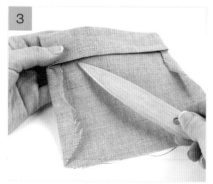

Constructing an Unlined Patch Pocket

An unlined patch pocket is finished along its opening edge with a fold-over facing. Mark the foldline after cutting out the pocket.

POCKETS WITH ROUNDED CORNERS

A tagboard template makes it easy to accurately press rounded corners into shape.

1. Finish the raw edge of the facing by pressing ¼ in. to the wrong side and topstitch along the inside fold to secure. Alternatively, if the fabric is bulky, or you want a very lightweight edge that won't create a ridge on the outside of the pocket, finish the raw edge with an overlock or zigzag stitch.

2. Fold and pin the facing toward the right side of the pocket, along the foldline. Measure to ensure accuracy.

3. Stitch both side edges in the facing area. Trim the seam allowances and clip corners to eliminate bulk. Turn the pocket right side out, and gently push out the corners with a point turner. Press. If desired, topstitch along facing edge to anchor the fabric.

4. Trace the finished pocket pattern (without seam allowances or fold-back facing) onto a manila file folder, then cut it out to form a pressing template. Place a large piece of white tissue paper on your ironing board, then place the sewn pocket right side down on top. Slip the template under the facing, and tightly pull the edges of the tissue paper toward the template's center, drawing the seam

allowances tight around the template. Press along all the edges to set the shape. Allow to cool, then remove the tissue and template.

POCKETS WITH SQUARE CORNERS

Square corners on pockets should be mitered for uniformity.

1. Sew along the stitching line of the sides and bottom of the pocket. Prepare the facing as described for a pocket with rounded corners, but don't turn it right side out. Fold each bottom corner diagonally to the pocket right side.

2. Open the fold and, with the right sides together, stitch on the crease from the raw edge to the corner. Trim and press open the corner seam allowances.

3. Turn the pocket edges and facing to the wrong side. Press. Hand-stitch or topstitch the facing edge in place, and baste the sides and bottom.

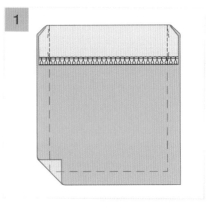

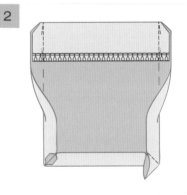

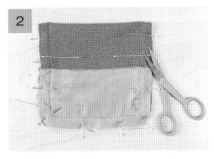

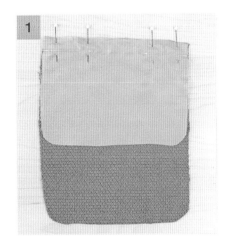

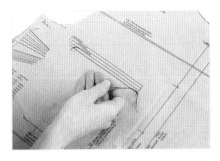

Constructing a Lined Patch Pocket

Line pockets made of lightweight material, or those that will endure a lot of use. If desired, reinforce the pocket fabric further by fusing a layer of lightweight interfacing to the wrong side.

Lining a pocket to the edge is straightforward and is the best method to use if the pocket is an unusual shape. Use the pocket pattern piece to cut both the fashion fabric and lining. With right sides together, sew the lining to the pocket. Trim, clip, and notch the seam allowances as needed. Then, cut a diagonal opening in the middle of the lining, about 2 in. long. Gently turn the pocket right side out through this opening, press the pocket flat, and hand-sew the opening closed. Alternatively, fuse the opening closed by tucking a patch of fusible interfacing between the layers, with the fusible side against the lining wrong side. Press to secure.

Many lined pockets are designed with a fold-over facing, so the pocket lining piece is smaller than the pocket piece.

1. With the right sides together, align the pocket and lining at the top edges. Stitch, leaving a 2-in.-wide opening in the middle. Press the seam allowance toward the lining piece.

2. Pull the pocket lining, and align its lower edge with the lower edge of the

pocket. Pin in place, then sew around the side and bottom edges.

3. Trim the seam allowances to ¼ in. and clip the corners. Turn the pocket right side out through the opening and press. Hand-stitch the opening closed.

Marking the Pocket Placement

Transfer the pocket placement marks from the pattern to the right side of the flat, unsewn garment piece. Tailor's tacks are the simplest method because they don't leave marks on the fabric, are easily removed, and can be seen from both sides.

See "Tailor's Tacks and Thread Tracing," on page 110.

If you're not sure where you want the pockets, complete the garment just as

far as necessary so you can try it on and test various pocket positions. Pin the pocket in place, remove the garment, and mark the position. If the garment has symmetrical pockets, position one pocket while trying on the garment, then use that side to mark the placement on the opposite side.

Attaching the Pocket

With the garment facing right side up, align the upper corners of the pocket with the tailor's tacks. Pin, then baste it in place.

With the garment right side up, edge-stitch around the pocket, starting at the top right and continuing around the pocket to the top left edge. Because the top corners take the most stress, reinforce them with a small triangle of stitches.

If desired, turn the pocket inside out and trim ⅜ in. from the seam allowance to reduce bulk and release tension around the curved bottom edges. Be careful not to cut the garment fabric with your scissors.

If you don't want visible stitching on the pocket, hand-sew it, using a slipstitch to attach it.

IN-SEAM POCKETS

In-seam pockets, usually in a side seam of pants, jackets, coats, skirts, or dresses, are made by attaching the pocket bags to the front and back garment pieces, sewing the side seams above and below the pocket, then sewing around the pocket bag. Prepare the garment by stabilizing the pocket's front opening with a strip of fusible knit interfacing, fused over the seamline in the pocket opening position and extending ½ in. at each end. The pocket pieces extend above and below these marks.

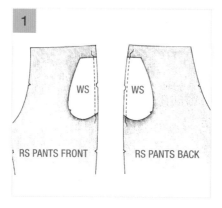

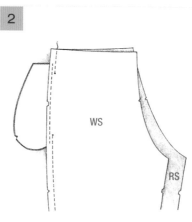

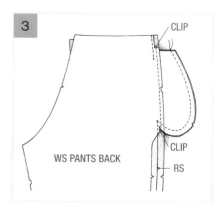

1. With the right sides together and using the notches as your guide, position and pin one of the pocket pieces to the garment front piece, and one of the pocket pieces to the garment back piece. Sew the pocket pieces to the garment pieces using a ⅜-in.-wide seam allowance. (A ⅝-in.-wide seam allowance would be right along the garment side and would add bulk and potentially allow the pocket bag to be visible during wearing.)

2. Press each pocket piece and the seam allowances away from the garment. With the right sides together, pin the garment front to the garment back, aligning the pocket pieces and any notches or other marks. Stitch the side seams, working from the hem to the bottom of the pocket opening, then backstitch. Reposition the needle at the top of the pocket opening. Backstitch again and sew the rest of the seam.

3. Press open the side seam allowances. Before stitching the pocket halves together, clip the back side seam allowance on the diagonal and press the back of the pocket toward the front of the garment. Sew the pocket together, beginning and ending at the pocket opening. Serge or pink the edges of the pocket. Press the finished pocket toward the front of the garment.

SLANT-FRONT POCKET

Although this pocket is called "slant-front," it can be any shape from straight to curved to L-shaped, as long as the top of the opening originates at the waist in front of the side seam, and the bottom ends at the side seam. This is a typical jeans-front pocket, but it is also found in many other styles of pants and skirts. Pattern pieces include the garment front, garment side front (or pocket), and underlay (or facing).

1. Cut a length of stay tape equal to the length of the pocket opening to prevent stretching. With right sides together, pin the pocket underlay to the garment front, matching the notches, and then pin the

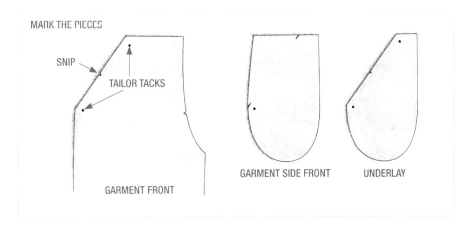

MARK THE PIECES

SNIP

TAILOR TACKS

GARMENT FRONT

GARMENT SIDE FRONT

UNDERLAY

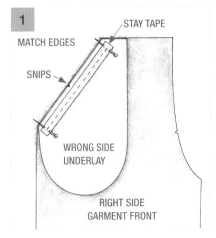

1

MATCH EDGES

STAY TAPE

SNIPS

WRONG SIDE UNDERLAY

RIGHT SIDE GARMENT FRONT

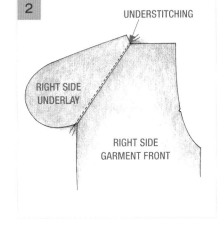

2

UNDERSTITCHING

RIGHT SIDE UNDERLAY

RIGHT SIDE GARMENT FRONT

WELT POCKET

Welt pockets are a hallmark of tailored and couture garments. Essentially, a welt pocket is a slit cut in the garment fabric, then bound with strips of fabric, leather, or even flat trim. You can make a version of a welt pocket using narrow piping to bind the edges. The pocket bag is attached on the inside of the garment.

A double-welt pocket has two visible bands of equal width at the pocket opening. This style is commonly used on the back of trousers, as well as on jackets. A single-welt pocket has one wider band that covers the entire pocket

stay tape along the seamline. Baste, then stitch through all the layers using a ⅝-in.-wide seam allowance.

2. Press the pocket underlay away from the garment, then press both seam allowances toward the pocket underlay. Understitch the seam allowances approximately ⅛ in. from the seam.

3. Trim and grade the seam allowances so that the seam allowance closest to the garment is the widest. Press the pocket underlay to the inside. Topstitch the slanted edge, if desired.

4. Pin the garment side front under the garment front at the waist and side seams, matching notches. Fold the garment front out of the way and sew the free edge of the underlay to the corresponding edges of the garment side front, forming the pocket

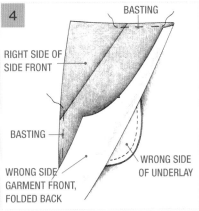

4

BASTING

RIGHT SIDE OF SIDE FRONT

BASTING

WRONG SIDE GARMENT FRONT, FOLDED BACK

WRONG SIDE OF UNDERLAY

bag. Bind, zigzag, or serge the raw edges of the pocket bag. Baste the garment side front to the garment front at the waist and side seam. The side of the pocket will be caught in the side seam when it's sewn, and the top of the pocket will be caught in the waistline seam or waistband.

opening, and which conceals a narrower band. You'll find single-welt pockets on coats and jackets, often oriented vertically or diagonally.

For the best results, work with medium- to heavyweight fabrics that can be crisply pressed. When first making welt pockets, avoid fabrics that ravel excessively. Welt pockets in stretch fabrics require thorough stabilization of the pocket pieces as well as the garment area.

Double-Welt Pocket

These instructions are for a pocket opening that is 1 in. by 6 in. with ½-in.-wide welts, and a pocket that's 8 in. deep. If your pattern includes pieces that are a different size, simply use those, following these guidelines.

1. Cut two welt strips, 2 in. wide and 7 in. long, on any fabric grain.

2. Cut two strips of fusible, nonstretch interfacing, parallel to the stable grain, 1 in. wide by 7 in. long. Fuse in the center of the wrong side of each welt strip. Press the welt strips in half lengthwise, with wrong sides together.

3. Interface the garment wrong side in the pocket placement area with a 2-in. by 7-in. strip of interfacing cut on the most stable grain. Mark the approximate position of the opening with pins or chalk. Position the interfacing parallel to the opening and centered over it, so that all construction stitching will be on the interfacing. With a long machine-basting stitch, mark the pocket opening line and ends on the garment.

4. Stitch through the folded welt strips along the exact center of each piece.

5. On the garment right side, position the welt strips, cut edges on each side of the opening line, with right sides down and

raw edges together, and centered between the end markings. Pin in place, then transfer the end markings to the strips with chalk.

6. With a long stitch length, sew along the center line of each welt, starting and stopping exactly at each end marking. Backstitch at the ends, then turn the work over to check the wrong side. The stitching should be exactly at the end markings, centered on the opening marking and parallel. Correct if necessary.

7. Cut a one-piece rectangle of pocket lining, 8 in. wide by 20 in. long. Position the lining right side down over the welts, starting about 1 in. above the opening line and pinning at each end, as shown.

8. Set the machine to a regular stitch length. From the wrong side, stitch exactly on top of the stitching from step 6, from end to end, anchoring the pocket lining to the garment.

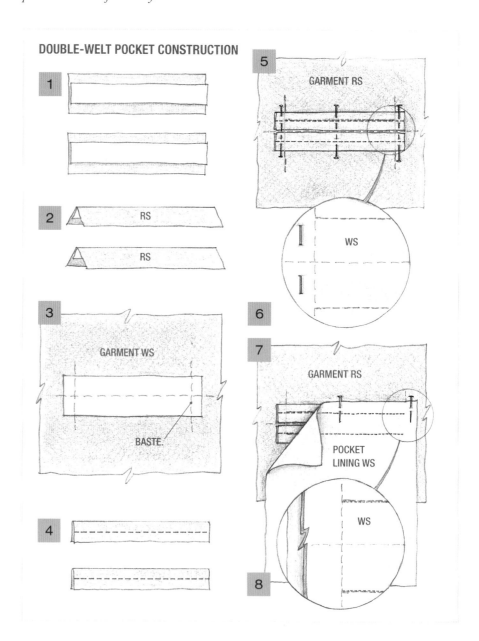

DOUBLE-WELT POCKET CONSTRUCTION

9. *Slash through all layers along the center marking, starting and stopping 1 in. from each end of the stitching line. Cutting through only the lining on the right side, and only the garment on the wrong side (don't cut the welts), snip from the slash ends to each end of the stitching line from step 8, forming triangles.*

10. *Trim away the seam allowance on the garment layer to grade the seam, leaving a ¼-in.-wide allowance.*

11. *Turn the pocket lining to the wrong side through the opening, tucking the welt ends through the openings at each end, between the lining and the garment triangles. Don't handle the triangles more than necessary. Arrange the welts in the center of the open garment and lining seams along the welts. From the right side, hand-baste the welt edges together at the opening. Leave the basting in place until the garment is complete.*

12. *Fold the pocket lining and the garment layers back from each end, exposing the triangles and welt ends. Sew through the triangles just outside the end mark stitching to close the ends of the pocket opening. Press the welt seam allowances open using a point presser.*

13. *Fold up the other end of the pocket lining to align with the upper end. Sew around all the open edges, closing the pocket all around. Trim and overcast the raw edges. If the pocket seems likely to sag, stitch the top of the pocket back to the upper welt seam, close to the opening seamline. Remove all basting marks.*

COMPLETING THE WELT POCKET

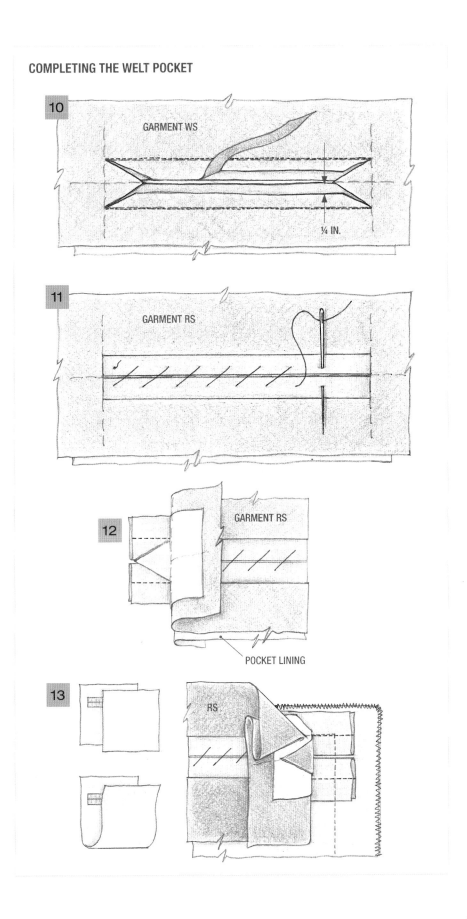

10 · GARMENT WS · ¼ IN.

11 · GARMENT RS

12 · GARMENT RS · POCKET LINING

13 · RS

Single-Welt Pocket

This pocket finishes with a single visible welt 6 in. long and 1 in. wide.

1. Cut one upper welt strip 2 in. wide by 7 in. long. Interface, press in half lengthwise, and mark-stitch the center.

2. Cut a lower welt strip 3 in. wide by 7 in. long. On the wrong side, interface one half of the strip to ½ in. beyond the fold line. Fold in half with wrong sides together and mark-stitch ½ in. from the raw edges.

3. Interface the garment wrong side in the pocket area. Mark-stitch the pocket ends. Determine and mark-stitch the opening line ½ in. below the desired position of the wider welt's top edge.

4. Arrange the welt strips on the garment right side. Place the upper welt with its raw edges aligned on the pocket opening line. Place the lower welt with its raw edges ½ in. below the pocket opening line.

5. Construct the pocket from this point exactly as for the double-welt pocket (see page 196), overlapping the welts when turning them to the wrong side. Baste the welts together before stitching the triangles, pressing, and completing the pocket.

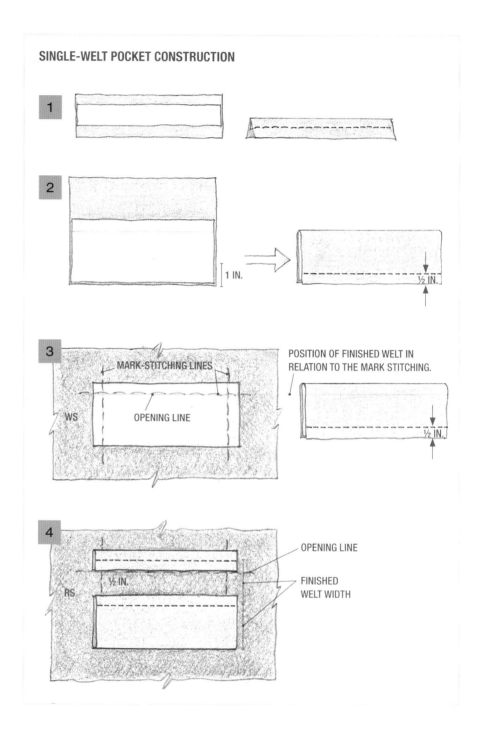

SINGLE-WELT POCKET CONSTRUCTION

1

2

1 IN.   ½ IN.

3   MARK-STITCHING LINES

WS

OPENING LINE

POSITION OF FINISHED WELT IN RELATION TO THE MARK STITCHING.

½ IN.

4   OPENING LINE

RS   ½ IN.

FINISHED WELT WIDTH

Waistline Finishes

4

Waistline finishes include the seam joining the bodice and skirt of a dress, and the top edge of pants and skirts. A waistline seam creates shape in dresses and coats. Facings, casings, and bands provide an anchor for pants and skirts, which hang from the waistline treatment. Note that the waistline of a garment may not fall at the body's natural waist; many garment styles are designed with the waist treatment below or above the natural waist. It's important to fit the waistline of the garment carefully, no matter where it falls, so that it can support the weight of the garment properly.

WAISTLINE SEAMS

The seam that joins the bodice and skirt of a garment can be positioned above, below, or at the actual waist. Sew the bodice and skirt separately, including any shaping details such as darts or pleats, and all vertical seams. Only a center back or front opening, such as a zipper, is inserted after the bodice and skirt are seamed.

Fitted Skirt

1. Staystitch both the bodice and skirt waistline edges and easestitch (page 142) the skirt from the right side if needed. With right sides together, pin the waist edges of the bodice to the skirt, with the bodice inside the skirt. Align the side seams, center front and back, and all markings.

1

BODICE, WS

SKIRT, WS

2. Pull the bobbin thread of the ease stitching so the skirt fits the bodice. Distribute the ease evenly, without forming tucks. Baste the layers together.

3. Try on the garment to make sure the seam is smooth and fits properly. Stitch the seam with the bodice right side up. Press the seam flat and then toward the bodice. Clean-finish the seam allowance edges and, if necessary, apply a waistline stay to prevent stretching (see "Tip" at right).

Gathered Skirt

Depending on the garment design, a skirt may be gathered all the way around the waist, or just in select areas. Stitch two or three rows of basting (page 123) along the waist edge where indicated on the pattern, and pull the bobbin threads to reduce the skirt waistline to the same size as the bodice waistline. With right sides together, pin the skirt to the bodice, and adjust the gathers so they're evenly distributed. With the skirt side up, stitch the seam. Remove the basting stitches. Clean-finish the seam allowances and press them up.

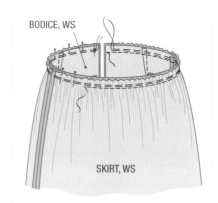

BODICE, WS

SKIRT, WS

Use a firmly woven tape or grosgrain ribbon to stay a waistline seam. Hand- or machine-stitch it over the entire waistline seam allowance.

ELASTICIZED WAISTS

All elastic waistbands fall into two categories—those in which the elastic is inserted into a stitched casing and those in which the elastic is sewn directly to the fabric. Select the method that provides the most comfort with the least bulk.

Stitched Casings

A waist casing is like a tunnel that houses either elastic or a drawstring. You can stitch a casing at the upper edge of a skirt or pants, or add a casing in the body of a garment by sewing on a strip of fabric. The elastic width is up to you. Determine the length by pinning the elastic around your waist, stretching as needed so that it's comfortable but won't slip down. For a casing application, use firm, nonroll elastic. If you plan to sew through the elastic, make sure you choose a type that can be stitched (see "A Guide to Elastics" on page 37).

FOLD-DOWN CASING

1. Finish the garment's raw upper edge by pressing under ¼ in., zigzagging, or serging. Fold the finished edge to the wrong side to make a casing that is ¼ in. wider than the elastic. Sew close to the lower casing edge, leaving a small break in the stitching. Working with a safety pin or bodkin, feed the elastic through the casing.

2. Join the elastic ends by butting them together (to reduce bulk), centering the join over a piece of muslin or other thin, stable fabric. Zigzag the ends together and trim away the excess muslin.

3. Insert the ends of the elastic into the casing and sew the opening closed. Stretch

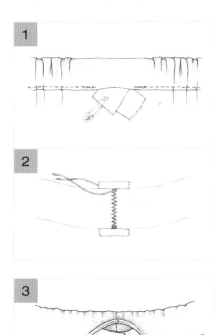

TIP

If the elastic isn't too heavy, simply overlap the ends and sew back and forth or zigzag to join the two layers.

the elastic to distribute the fabric ease evenly, then stitch in the ditch through the elastic at the vertical garment seams to prevent the elastic from twisting.

APPLIED CASING

An applied casing can be made from lightweight grosgrain ribbon, premade bias tape, a strip of self- or contrast fabric, or any trim that's wider than the elastic. The casing is topstitched to either the right or wrong side of the garment, depending on the desired effect. It can be applied at the top edge of skirts or pants, or within the body of a dress, top, or tunic.

Casing applied to an edge

1. To make the casing from self-fabric, cut a strip the length of the garment's waist circumference, plus ½ in. for seam allowances. The finished width needs to be ¾ in. wider than the elastic to provide ¼ in. ease for the elastic and a turn-under allowance to finish the raw edges. Press the short ends and the casing's raw edges ¼ in. to the wrong side and press.

2. Trim the garment's waist edge seam allowance to ¼ in. Unfold one long edge of the casing and, with right sides together, pin it to the garment waistline so that one short end is aligned on the side or back seam. Stitch along the crease, ¼ in. from the cut edge.

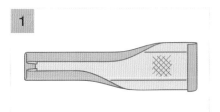

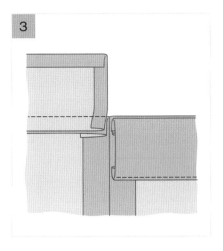

3. Turn the casing to the garment wrong side, allowing the seamline to roll slightly to the inside. Pin and edgestitch the casing along the lower edge. The short ends remain open so you can insert the elastic.

4. Working with a bodkin or safety pin, insert the elastic. Sew the ends by hand securely to the casing at each end, keeping the garment free.

Casing Options

The elasticized casing can be treated in several ways for decorative effect, and to stabilize the elastic within the casing.

1. Sew several parallel rows of topstitching through the casing and the elastic, stretching the elastic as you sew. Be sure to use sew-through elastic and pull it tightly from both sides while topstitching.

2. To create a ruffle or header at the top edge, plan so that the fold-over casing is wider than the elastic. Add twice the desired ruffle width to the fold-over casing. Then, sew an additional row of stitches below the upper fold to form the top of the casing.

3. For multiple pieces of narrow elastic, topstitch parallel lines of stitching with enough room between them for the elastic to fit through smoothly. Attach a safety pin to each of the pieces of elastic and feed all of them through at the same time, working each piece several inches at a time.

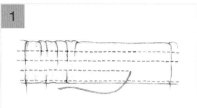

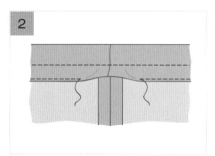

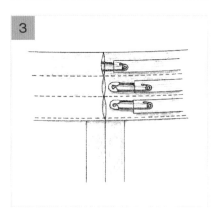

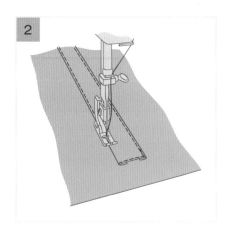

Casing applied within the garment body

1. Cut and prepare the casing and elastic the same as for a casing applied to a top edge. Press the short ends of the casing to the inside and edgestitch them. Mark the casing placement line on the garment. Note that casings can be applied on the right or wrong side of a garment.

2. Pin or baste the casing to the garment, with its lower edge aligned on the placement line. Edgestitch on both long sides. Backstitch at the beginning and end of the stitching. Press the casing.

3. Working with a bodkin or safety pin, insert the elastic. Machine- or hand-stitch the ends of the elastic to the ends of the casing.

TIP

A drawstring waistband is made much the same way as an elastic-cased waist. Simply make the casing narrower and make buttonholes in the outer fabric layer for the cording to exit through. Stitch through the drawstring and casing at the center back so the cording doesn't pull through.

Sewn-on Elastic

For a sporty finish, stitch the elastic directly to the garment waistline, then fold it under and topstitch it. This finish works well with stretch fabrics.

1. Cut the elastic to fit the waist snugly, then join the ends by overlapping and zigzag-stitching them. Divide and mark the elastic ring and the garment waist edge in even quarters. Pin the elastic to the garment waist on the wrong side, matching quarter marks and aligning one edge of the elastic with the garment raw edge.

2. Serge or zigzag the elastic to the garment edge, stretching the elastic as you stitch so that it equals the circumference of the garment.

3. Fold the elastic to the garment wrong side, and topstitch along the lower edge of the elastic to anchor it to the garment. Stretch the elastic while stitching as before.

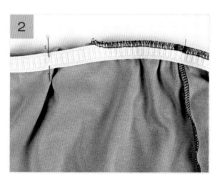

FACED WAIST FINISHES

A faced waist is smooth, comfortable, and elegant. Its only horizontal seam is right on the waist edge, so there's little bulk, making this treatment ideal for shortwaisted figures and for garments that will be worn under tops and jackets. A facing can be applied to garments that sit directly at the waist or above it, as in a Hollywood waistline.

Prepare the garment by sewing the vertical seams and inserting a zipper or other closure, if the garment includes one. Staystitch the edge to be faced in order to prevent stretching during handling.

Shaped Waist Facing

1. Interface the waistline facing pieces and stitch them with right sides together at the seams. Clean-finish the unnotched edge. With the right sides together, stitch the facing to the waistline. Trim and grade the seam allowance, and clip if necessary. Press the seam allowance toward the facing, and understitch along the facing, close to the waistline seam.

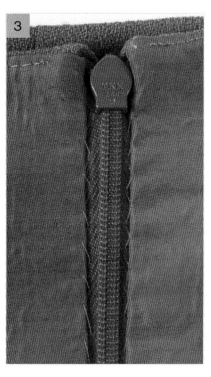

2. Turn the facing to the garment wrong side and press it in place, rolling the seamline slightly to the interior of the garment.

3. Fold the raw short ends of the facing under and slipstitch them to the zipper tape for side or back zipper openings.

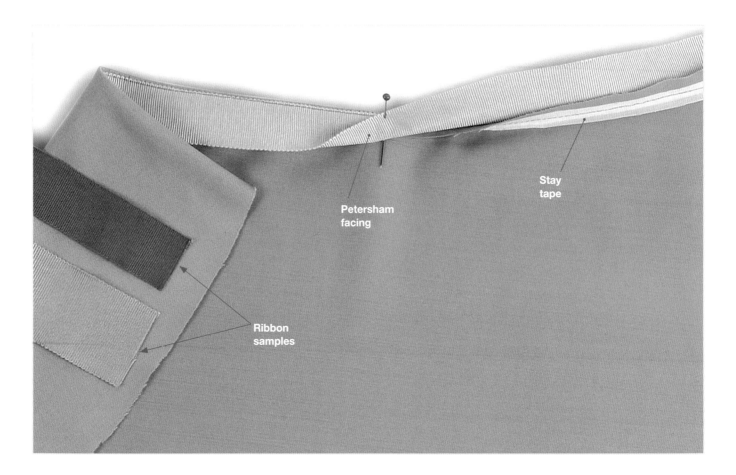

Stay tape

Petersham facing

Ribbon samples

Petersham Facing

Petersham ribbon is a sturdy cotton or cotton/rayon ribbon with a flexible, scalloped edge that can be shaped with a steam iron to conform to the body curves. It's a perfect substitute for a waist facing on medium-weight skirts or pants. Petersham shrinks, so before using it, soak it in warm water, then air-dry.

Begin by staystitching the garment waist seamline, or, for greater stability, sew a strip of ¼-in.- to ⅜-in.-wide stay tape over the seamline. Cut a strip of Petersham the length of the garment waistline plus 1 in. to 2 in. to fold under and finish at the closure. Lay it on your ironing board, spray lightly with water, then press, stretching and shaping one scalloped edge along the entire length.

Place the ribbon over the waistline seam allowance on the right side of the garment, aligning the unstretched edge with the waist seamline, and having the stretched edge extending beyond the upper edge of the garment. Sew close to the ribbon's edge. Fold the seam allowance and ribbon to the inside of the garment, rolling the seamline slightly to the inside of the garment. Press the waistline over a tailor's ham, and tack the Petersham's lower edge to the garment's vertical seam allowances and darts to keep it from folding up and out.

WAISTBANDS

The fitted waistband is simply a band of fabric, straight or shaped, that fits closely and supports the garment from the top. A classic waistband is typically

TIP

For a waistline that has a little give, use 1-in.-wide nonroll elastic in place of Petersham ribbon. There's no need to stretch or shape the elastic; simply apply it as you would a Petersham facing, using a zigzag stitch instead of a straight stitch.

straight (cut from a rectangle), and 1 in. to 2 in. wide. It sits above the waistline edge of a skirt or pants. Straight waistbands are usually cut twice the width of the finished band, plus seam allowances, and folded. A contoured waistband is curved, so that it follows the shape of the body closely. Because

STRAIGHT WAISTBAND

CONTOUR WAISTBAND

it's shaped, it must have a separate, identically shaped facing.

Garments designed to have a waistband typically include a waistband pattern piece. You just need to make any necessary size adjustments and transfer the pattern markings. The waistband includes an extension (overlap or underlap) at the garment opening. An overlap extends beyond the garment opening on the garment right side. An underlap is hidden beneath the waistband at the garment opening. Complete the body of the skirt or pants, including inserting the lining, before you construct and attach the waistband.

Waistband Support

A properly constructed waistband is comfortable and stable, and appears smooth and unwrinkled during wear. The interfacing you choose for the waistband determines how the band looks, wears, and feels.

You can use fusible or sew-in interfacing (see pages 34–35 for types and application methods) on most waistbands. You'll find precut fusible interfacing strips, with perforated foldlines made specifically for waistbands, but you can cut your own from a favorite interfacing. Always fuse a swatch first to make sure the interfacing and the fabric are compatible.

To hold their shape, straight waistbands need firm, sturdy interfacings to prevent the band from rolling or curling when worn.

Contoured waistbands don't require the same firm structure as a straight waistband, but they do need reinforcement that is crisper and stiffer than the fabric to prevent stretching, ensure a smooth fit, and provide top-down support for the garment.

Prepare and Attach a Straight Waistband

1. Cut interfacing the full width and length of the waistband. Fuse or sew it onto the wrong side of the waistband. Staystitch the waist edge of the garment.

2. With right sides together, match and pin the notched edge of the waistband to the garment waistline. Ease the staystitching as needed. Stitch.

3. Press the waistband and both seam allowances away from the garment. Trim and grade the seam allowances and finish the unnotched edge with one of the techniques listed (page 207).

4. Fold the waistband along the foldline with right sides together. Stitch across both short ends. One will be even with the garment opening, and the other

will extend beyond the garment to form the overlap or underlap. Trim both end seam allowances and corners. Turn the waistband right side out. Press the foldline.

5. From the right side, pin or hand-baste the waistband in place through the seam. Then, also from the garment right side, stitch in the ditch of the seam, catching the waistband free edge in the stitching. Turn in the seam allowances on the under- or overlap, and hand-sew them together with a slipstitch. If the waistband has an underlap, you can zigzag the opening instead.

6. Attach a hook(s) to the wrong side of the waistband overlap, even with the garment opening, and sew an eye(s) to the underlap (page 42).

Contour Waistband

This shaped waist finish follows the body curve and can sit at, below, or above the natural waist. Attaching the outer waistband is very much like applying a straight waistband, but the inner waistband (facing) is attached as you would a waist facing. Start by constructing the garment, including zipper closures if present. Sew any darts or seams to assemble the waistband and/or waistband facing. Interface the waistband and, if desired, its facing as well. For waistbands that contour above the waist, you need firm support to keep the band up. Join the waistband pieces to form the full band, and press open the seam allowances. Join the facing pieces to form the full facing,

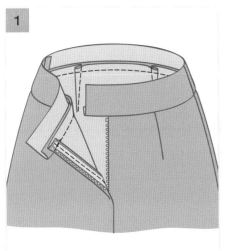

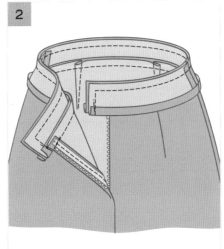

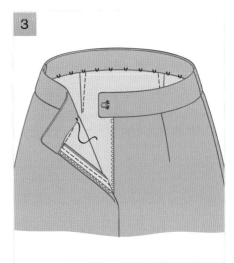

press open the seam allowances, and either press the lower edge to the wrong side ¼ in., or clean-finish it by serging, binding, or zigzagging.

1. With right sides together, raw edges aligned, and seams and notches matching, pin the waistband to the waistline of the garment. Sew the seam, then press the seam allowances up toward the band.

2. With right sides together, raw edges aligned, and seams and notches matching, pin the waistband facing to the waistband. Sew the facing to the band, up one short end, around the top of the band, and down the other end, keeping the facing's free edge folded if you pressed it under.

3. Trim, grade, and clip the seam allowances as needed, and press the waistband seam open over a pressing tool. Turn the facing to the garment inside, pushing out the corners. Press the band and facing, and pin the facing free edge along the waistline seam. Either slipstitch the edge to the waist seam allowances by hand, or stitch in the ditch of the waist seam from the garment right side, catching the facing edge. At the under- or

overlap end, press the seam allowances between the band and facing layers, and slipstitch the opening.

FINISH THE INSIDE WAISTBAND EDGE

The waistband's inside edge can be finished with any one of these four techniques. However, make sure the inside of the band extends beyond the waist seam by ¼ in. to ½ in. so you can

stitch in the ditch along the waistband/garment seam.

- Serge the edge.
- Bind the edge with a bias strip of lining or lightweight cotton fabric.
- Press ¼ in. of the seam allowance under.
- Cut the waistband (if it's a straight band) with the inside edge on the fabric selvage.

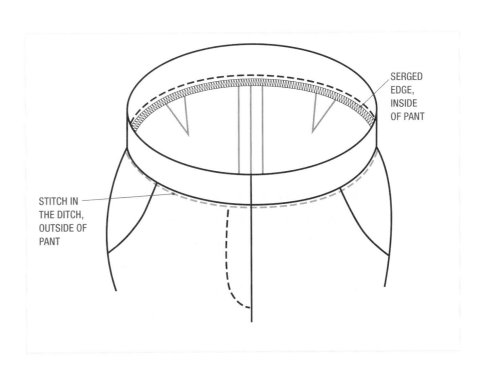

SERGED EDGE, INSIDE OF PANT

STITCH IN THE DITCH, OUTSIDE OF PANT

X
EDGE FINISHES
& HEMS

Edge Finishes

Necklines, armholes, and front and back opening edges all need some sort of finish. Depending on the look you want and the demands of the garment, you can use a facing, a band (woven or knit), binding, piping, ruffles, or even a deliberately "raw" edge like self-fabric fringe. Consider appearance, comfort, and longevity when choosing an edge finish, and don't hesitate to adapt pattern instructions by changing the suggested finish.

FACINGS

Facings are a classic element in garment construction used to finish edges at necklines, armholes, front and back openings, hems, vents, and slits. Whether a facing is a separate pattern piece that echoes the shape of the opening it finishes, made from a fold-over fabric extension (called a self-facing), or cut from a strip of bias fabric, its role is to create a crisp edge while also providing stability and support.

A perfectly attached facing finishes the garment raw edge, of course, but just as important, it adds support, prevents the edge from stretching, and ensures a flat, crisp outer edge. When you need an edge finish that performs all these functions, try a facing.

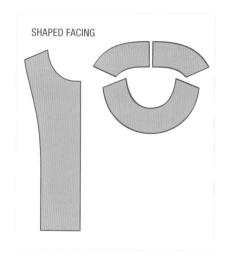

SHAPED FACING

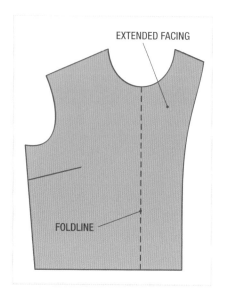

EXTENDED FACING

FOLDLINE

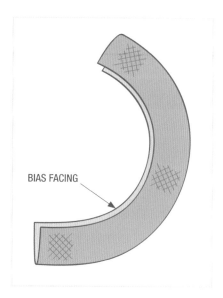

BIAS FACING

Facing Fabrics and Interfacings

The first step in constructing a perfect facing is deciding what type of fabric to use. Cutting facings from the garment fabric is usually the obvious choice. However, if the fashion fabric is especially thick or rough (and hence uncomfortable against the skin), substitute a lighter-weight or smoother fabric for the facing. Cotton shirting and flannel facings are soft and sturdy, and silk dupioni and silk taffeta both make crisp yet lightweight facings.

Preshrink the facing fabric in the same manner as the fashion fabric. This way, you'll be confident they'll be care–compatible. When you cut, be sure to follow the grainline marked on each facing pattern piece. It's important that each facing have the same grainline as the corresponding portion of the garment so the facing and the garment drape in the same way when worn.

Shaped facings must be interfaced so that they provide support. Some extended facings, such as those at the front or back openings of shirts or blouses, don't require interfacing, but consider adding a very lightweight interfacing if you intend to sew buttons or buttonholes in the faced area. Don't interface bias-strip facings. When choosing an interfacing, consider the garment style and fabric and decide if you want soft or crisp support.

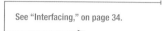

See "Interfacing," on page 34.

Making and Applying a Shaped Facing

1. Interface the individual facing pieces. Then, with the right sides together, sew any corresponding facing pieces to each other as instructed in the pattern (for example, join the front and back neck facings at the shoulder seams), and press the seam allowances open. Finish the edge of the facing that won't be seamed to the garment, using one of the methods shown on page 213.

2. With the right sides together, pin the facing to the garment, aligning seamlines and notches. Stitch. Trim and grade the seam allowances. Trim the seam allowances at corners and clip along the curves. The tighter the curve, the more clips will be needed.

3. From the wrong side of the garment, use the iron to push and press the seam allowances toward the facing. This prevents a "valley" from forming in the seam. Press any curved areas over a dressmaker's ham, further clipping the seam allowances as needed. Check the right side of the garment to make sure the seam is pressed flat, without any lumps or ridges. Lightly press again.

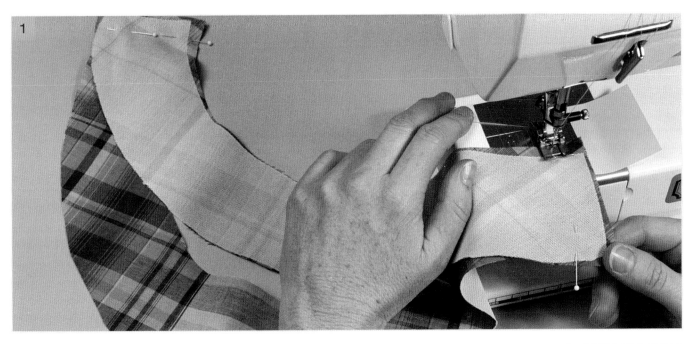

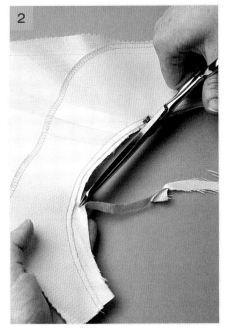

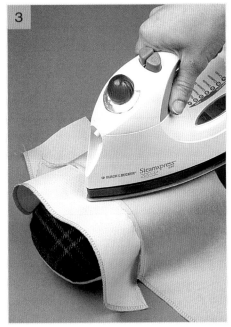

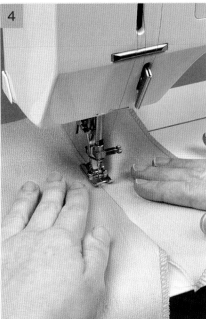

4. Understitch to ensure that the facing won't roll to the outside of your garment (see page 150). Press the facing toward the wrong side of the garment, supporting it on a ham or sleeve board so the rest of the garment falls out of the way. Then press lightly from the right side of the garment, using a pressing cloth if the garment fabric is delicate.

Variations of Shaped Facings

No matter what the shape of the facing, the basic technique for applying it is as described here. Corners, openings, or adjoining facings require a few additional steps.

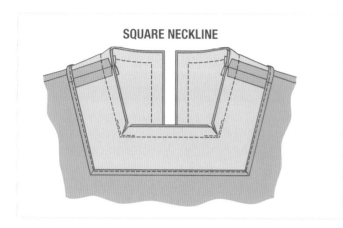

SQUARE NECKLINE

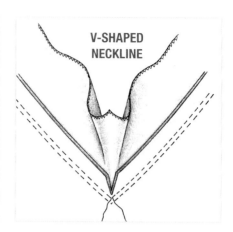

V-SHAPED NECKLINE

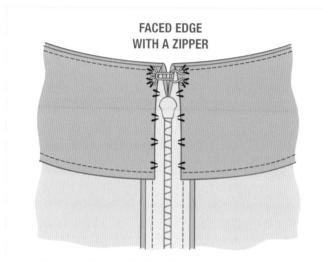

FACED EDGE WITH A ZIPPER

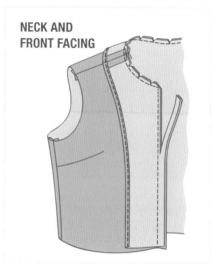

NECK AND FRONT FACING

SQUARE NECKLINE

Reinforce the corners of the facing by staystitching ⅛ in. from the seamline within the seam allowance, pivoting at the exact marked corners. As you attach a square facing, shorten the machine stitch for 1 in. on both sides of the corner to reinforce the stitching. Then clip diagonally into each corner, up to but not through the stitching. Turn and press the facing carefully to preserve the square shape.

V-SHAPED NECKLINE

Sew the facing and neck edge with right sides together, but shorten the stitch length for 1 in. on each side of the V. Clip to but not through the V. Press the facing toward the seam allowances and understitch the facing to the seam allowances, one side at a time (don't try to turn the corner at the point of the V). Trim, grade, and press the facing to the wrong side of the garment.

FACED EDGE WITH A ZIPPER

This treatment may occur at a neckline or the waistline of a skirt or pants. Insert the zipper first (see page 243). Attach the facing as above, with the short ends of the facing extending beyond the neckline. Fold the short ends to the wrong side, and pin them to the zipper tape. Open the zipper and hand-stitch the facing to the zipper tape. Close the zipper and, if desired, sew a hook and eye (page 42) above the zipper pull.

COMBINED NECK AND FRONT FACING

Sometimes, facing pieces are joined and then attached to the garment as one, particularly neck and front/back facings. First, join the facing pieces, press the seam allowances open, and finish the unattached edge as shown at right.

Pin and stitch the facing to the garment edge, and shorten the stitch length for 1 in. on each side of any corners. Follow the pattern instructions for handling the lower ends of the front/back facing (these might be left unstitched until a later construction stage). Trim, grade, and clip the seam allowances, making the garment seam allowance the widest. Press, under-stitch, and turn the facing to the garment inside.

Edge Finishes for Facings

Choose one of these methods for clean finishing the free edge of a facing.

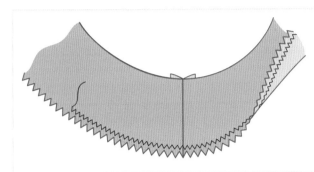

PINKED OR STITCHED EDGES

TRIM THE EDGE WITH PINKING SHEARS, OR STITCH ALONG IT WITH A ZIGZAG OR SERGER STITCH TO PREVENT RAVELING. THIS METHOD IS SUITABLE FOR MOST FABRICS.

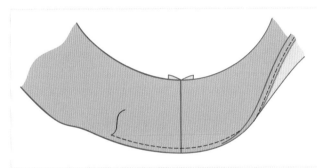

TURN AND STITCH

FOR LIGHTWEIGHT FABRICS, FOLD THE EDGE TO THE WRONG SIDE AND STITCH IT IN PLACE.

FACE THE FACING

Give the free edge of a facing a beautiful finish when using sew-in interfacing. Sew the facing's joining seams before applying the interfacing. Pin the facing and interfacing pieces right sides together along the edge that won't be sewn to the garment, and sew, using a ¼-in.-wide seam allowance.

Press the seam allowances toward the interfacing. Turn the facing right side out, slightly rolling the seam toward the interfacing. Press again to keep the interfacing from showing. Understitch if desired, baste the open edges, and then sew the interfaced facing to your garment.

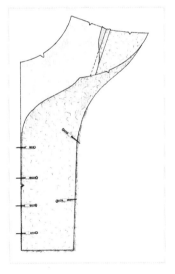

Applying an Extended Facing

Often the center front or center back of a garment has an extended facing, which is cut in one with the garment and simply folded to the wrong side on a marked foldline. A cut-on facing eliminates the vertical seam found on a sewn-on facing and works only when the front or back is cut on the straight grain.

1. Apply interfacing either to the facing area, or to the garment itself (as shown), using the interfacing pattern piece when cutting. (Sometimes, it is a good idea to support the garment further by applying the interfacing to the actual garment as well, as long as the interfacing doesn't change the hand of the fabric.) Position the inner edge of the interfacing at the foldline. If you prefer a softer edge, cut the interfacing ½ in. wider than the pattern, and position it ½ in. beyond the foldline, as shown.

2. If there is a back neck facing, sew it to the extended facing at the shoulder and finish the raw edge of the facing (page 213). Turn the facing to the garment right side along the foldline, and pin and baste it in place along the neck edge. Stitch the neck seam. Trim, grade, and clip the seam allowance.

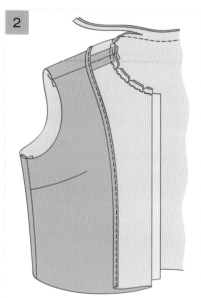

3. Turn the facing to the garment wrong side and understitch close to the seam through the facings and seam allowance.

See "Understitching," on page 150. ⟶

Secure the facing to the garment at the shoulder seam with several loose hand stitches.

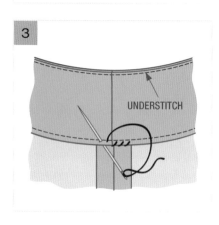

Making and Applying a Bias Facing

A bias facing is typically used when the garment fabric is scratchy, bulky, or sheer. The facing can be made from any lightweight fabric. Lining fabric or smooth cotton is appropriate. The finished width of the facing can vary from ½ in. for lightweight garments to 1 in. for thicker fabrics. Cut the strip twice the desired finished width, plus two seam allowances.

1. Cut a bias strip the length of the seamline of the edge being faced, plus 2 in. for shaping and finishing. Fold the strip in half lengthwise with wrong sides together and press it, shaping it gently with a steam iron to match the edge you're facing.

2. Insert the zipper, if there is one, before attaching the facing. Pin and baste the bias facing to the garment right side, with raw edges aligned and the strip ends extending 1 in. beyond the garment at both ends. Stitch the seam.

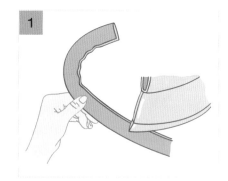

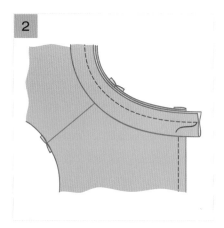

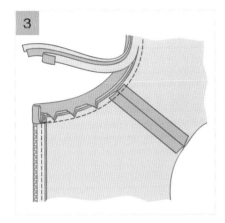

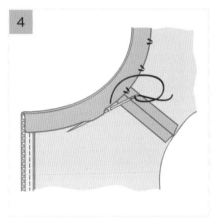

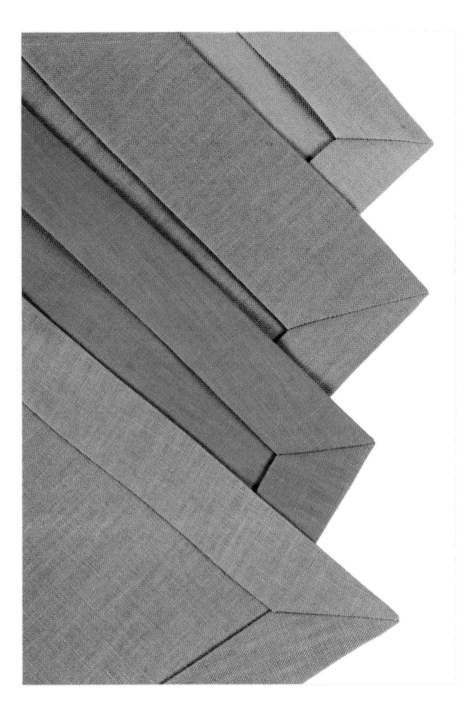

3. Trim, grade, and clip the seam allowance. Trim the facing at both ends to ¼ in. beyond the garment. Press the facing up and away from the garment, and press the ends of the facing to the inside.

4. Press the facing to the inside of the garment so the seam rolls slightly to the wrong side. Slipstitch the folded edge and ends of the facing to the garment. For a sportier finish, topstitch to secure the facing.

MITERED CORNERS

Most corners in garments occur at the intersection of two hems or a hem and a facing. They are usually right angles, but many designers include obtuse and acute angles, too. When you fold all the layers of these intersecting garment sections, there's often a lot of bulk and stiffness. Mitering the corners removes that bulk and establishes a sharp, precise corner. Whatever the angle of the corner, the same steps for mitering apply.

Accuracy in pinning, marking, and sewing is crucial for a perfect miter.

Begin by finishing the raw edges as desired; here, they've been folded under ½ in., but you could serge or zigzag them if you prefer.

1. Press the adjacent edges to the wrong side, and place pins exactly where the two edges intersect. Place the first pin perpendicular to one folded edge, pinning

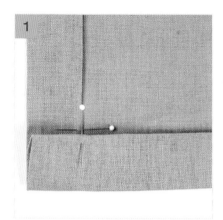

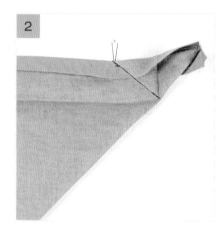

through the allowance layer only. Place a second pin in the opposite fold, also perpendicular to the folded edge, forming an X with the pins.

2. Open out the edges at the fold (keep the raw edges turned under if you've pressed them that way). Fold the corner with right sides together, and match the pins at the edges. Pin the layers together to prevent the fabric from shifting, then draw a line from the pins to the intersection of the two pressed folds. (If the corner isn't a right angle, or the two edges are of different widths, the overhanging point won't be symmetrical—don't worry about that.) Stitch along this line from the pins to the corner.

3. Trim the excess corner fabric, leaving a ¼-in. seam allowance. You don't need to clip or trim the corner point any further.

Press the seam allowances open over the tapered end of a point presser. To turn the corner right side out, place your thumb inside the corner pocket, pinch the seam allowance open between your thumb and forefinger, and turn the fabric over. If the corner isn't as sharp as you'd like it to be, shape it gently with a point turner.

BANDS

Bands are either shaped or straight pieces (depending on the shape of the garment edge) cut from woven fabric or knit. Bands extend beyond the garment edges, adding length at hems or width across a garment. If you choose to add a band to a garment that doesn't include one, be sure to account for the band's width by trimming the garment edges. Rib-knit bands appear on T-shirts at the neckline, sleeve, and/or garment hem. Woven bands are found on necklines, center front garment openings (kimono-style robes and jackets), sleeve openings, and hems.

Woven Bands

Woven bands are finished with a fold-back or separate facing. These instructions show how to attach a woven fabric band with a fold-back facing to the front and back neck of a robe. Cut a strip of fabric on the straight grain,

the length of the edge to be finished, by twice the desired finished width, plus two seam allowances. Press one edge of the band to the wrong side ⅝ in.

1. To attach the band, pin the right side of the band to the wrong side of the garment, aligning the unpressed edge of the band with the front edge of the garment. Sew, then press the band and the seam allowances away from the garment.

2. At the short ends of the band, fold the band in half with the right sides together. Unfold the pressed edge and align the pressed crease just over the seam. Sew across the narrow ends of the band, in a continuous line with the garment hem (or perpendicular edge), from the fold to the seam. Trim the seam allowance, refold the pressed edge, and turn the band right side out.

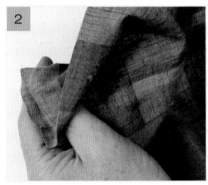

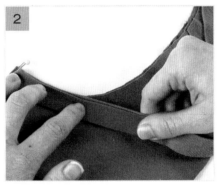

3. Fold the band with right sides together, and press. Pin the folded edge of the band so that it covers the original seamline. Topstitch the band in place, taking care that one layer of fabric doesn't creep ahead of the other, and don't stretch or pull, just hold the fabric taut.

Knit Bands

Knit bands are ideal finishes for edges that need to stretch, such as T-shirt necklines and the hems of knit tops. Cut a band twice the desired finished width, plus ½ in. for seam allowances; make the length equal to the seamline at the garment opening. Press the strip in half lengthwise, with wrong sides together.

1. Trim the garment seam allowance to ¼ in. Divide and mark the garment edge into four equal sections. Fold the band strip in half and pin-mark the center to indicate center front.

2. Fold the garment in half on the center-front/center-back lines. Pin the center of the band to the garment center front, aligning all raw edges. Gently stretch the

band as you guide it around the edge toward center back, pinning as needed. When you reach the center back, mark it on the band. Add a seam allowance, and trim off the excess. Unpin the band and, with it folded at center front, trim the other end to match.

3. Open out the band and sew the short ends, with right sides together, to form a circle. Refold the band, aligning the long raw edges. Divide and pin-mark the band in quarters, using the seam as center back. With right sides together and raw edges aligned, pin the band to the garment, matching quarter marks.

4. Sew or serge the band to the garment edge, using a ¼-in.-wide seam allowance. If sewing, use a narrow zigzag stitch to build some stretch into the seam. Press the seam allowances toward the garment.

BINDING

To bind an edge, fold a strip of fabric (or trim) over the raw edge, and sew it in place. This covers the raw edge, adds stability, and can provide a decorative element as well. You can purchase premade trim for binding, but for the widest range of design options, make your own binding strips from fabric.

Most bindings are cut on the bias to allow for shaping around curves. If you're binding a straight edge, however, you can cut the binding strips on the straight or cross-grain. Choose a binding fabric that's compatible with the project's fabric in weight, hand, and care requirements.

See "Bias Strips," on page 158.

Types of Bias Tape

Bias tape is simply a bias strip that's been folded and pressed lengthwise, in one of several manners. The different folds are used for different purposes:

- **HALF-FOLD TAPE** has one lengthwise fold down the center. The raw edges are exposed.

- **SINGLE-FOLD TAPE** has two folds. Each long edge is folded ¼ in. to the center on the bias wrong side.

- **DOUBLE-FOLD TAPE** starts as a single-fold strip, then it's folded in half again, either exactly down the center, or with one side slightly wider (to be placed on the underside when it's stitched, so the topstitching is sure to catch it).

Bias tape maker

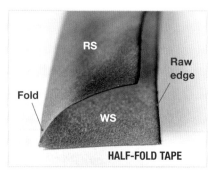

HALF-FOLD TAPE

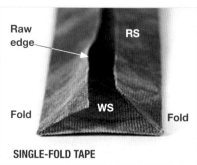

SINGLE-FOLD TAPE

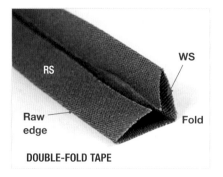

DOUBLE-FOLD TAPE

To make your own bias tape, cut bias fabric strips (see page 158) four times the desired finished width of the binding, plus a little extra for turn of cloth. If you are working with a soft or unstable fabric that stretches and narrows when pulled, cut the strip six times the finished width. Make a test sample with the project fabric before cutting strips. The finished binding width is a matter of taste, but a good standard is ½ in. wide. Anything narrower than ¼ in. or wider than 1 in. can be challenging to handle.

Although it's possible to press a bias strip by hand to form folded tape, a bias-tape tool makes the job faster and easier. With a bias-tape maker (see photo above), you pull the strip through the tapered metal collar, which folds the strip evenly. You then press it flat as it exits the folder. You can also purchase a special bias-binding presser foot, which folds, wraps, and stitches the binding to an edge in one step.

Binding a Raw Edge

To simplify the binding application, trim any angles on your pattern edges into rounded corners. If the pattern was designed for binding, cut the binding as instructed by the pattern, and use the seam allowances indicated. If you're replacing a different edge finish with a binding, trim off the original seam allowance so that the seamline now lies on the cut edge of the garment. The bias tape's fold configuration determines the method you use to sew the binding.

HALF-FOLD TAPE FOR A FRENCH BINDING

1. Align the two bias tape raw edges on the garment right side. Stitch one-third of the folded tape width away from the raw edges.

2. Wrap the folded edge of the tape to the wrong side. Cover the previous stitch line, and slipstitch along the fold.

SINGLE-FOLD TAPE

1. With right sides together, unfold one pressed bias edge and align the cut edge with the edge to be bound. Stitch along the pressed foldline.

2. Wrap the tape to the wrong side. Slipstitch the folded bias edge over the previous stitching line.

DOUBLE-FOLD TAPE

1. With the garment right side up, slide the garment raw edge all the way into the double-fold tape.

2. Machine-stitch along the inside folded edge of the binding. This catches the underlayer at the same time, and stitches are visible.

HALF-FOLD TAPE

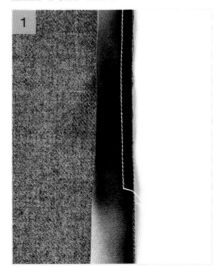 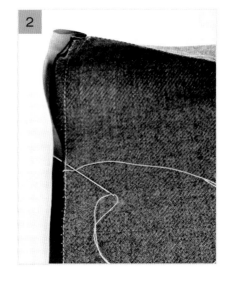

SINGLE-FOLD TAPE

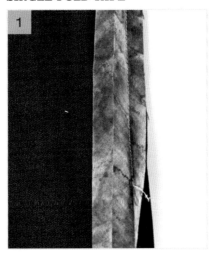 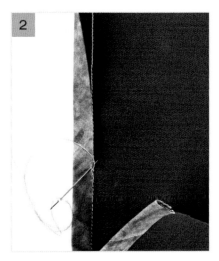

DOUBLE-FOLD TAPE

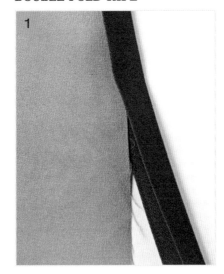 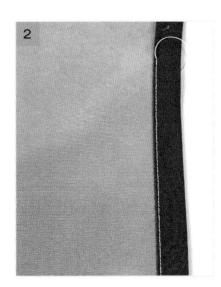

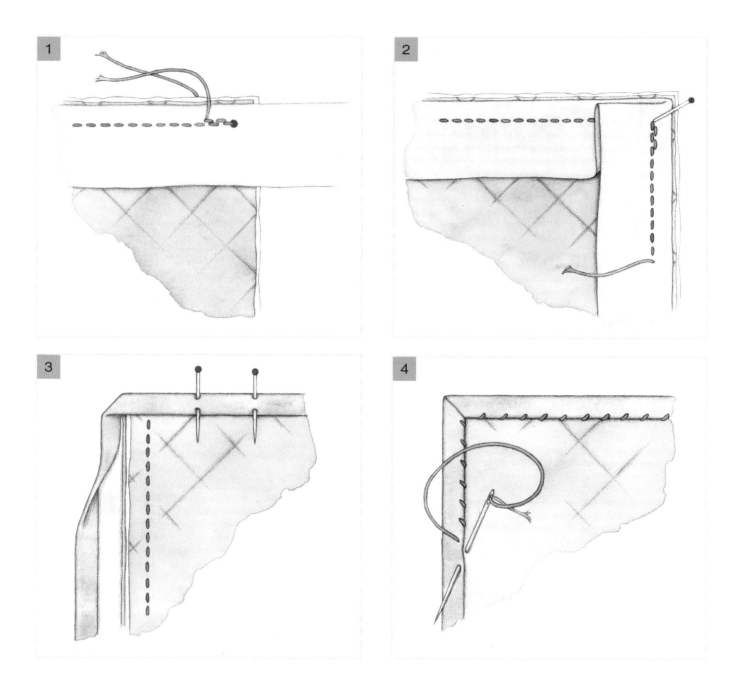

How to Form a Neat Corner

If you're binding a garment that has an angled corner, and you don't want to adjust it to a rounded corner, follow these directions for mitering the corners. Start with a plain bias strip, or a half-fold tape.

1. Mark the intersection of the seamlines at the corner. Stitch the binding along one edge to the mark. Backstitch, and remove it from the machine.

2. Miter the corner by pressing the strip away from the edge diagonally, then back over to form a triangular tuck, as shown. Align the edge of the binding with the adjacent edge of the garment, and mark the seamline intersection through the

binding with a pin. Begin stitching the adjacent edge at the mark.

3. On the reverse side, wrap the binding over one edge, fold the binding raw edge under, and pin it in place.

4. Wrap the binding on the adjacent edge over, fold the raw edge under, forming a miter at the corner. Slipstitch the folded binding edge in place.

PIPING

In addition to being decorative, piping (with or without filler cord) can provide added strength along a seamline or edge and create definition between connecting sections, as on the lapel edge of a jacket. Piping is made with strips of fabric wrapped around a filler cord and applied to a garment at a seamline or edge. The strips are usually cut on the bias, to facilitate bending the piping around curves and corners, but for perfectly straight applications, you can cut the strips on the straight grain.

TIP

PIPING OR CORDING

The terms *piping* and *cording* are often used interchangeably. However, piping always has a flange that is inserted within a seam; cording doesn't. Decorative cording may have a flange added so it can be inserted into a seam like piping; nondecorative cording is intended to be covered to make piping.

Choosing Fabric

The best fabrics for making piping are flexible, relatively thin, and opaque. Stiff, thick fabrics like corduroy or denim are difficult to manipulate around a filler cord, and they produce bulky seam allowances. Sheer fabrics may allow the texture of the cord to show. Make sure your garment and piping fabrics are compatible in terms of weight, drape, texture, and care requirements. To avoid a piping mismatch, test fabrics in a little piped sample before you commit to using them in an entire garment. Be sure to pretreat the piping fabric to avoid shrinkage or dye transfer.

Filler Choices

Although filler cord is completely covered by the piping fabric, its thickness and surface does affect the final result. You can use a product that's specifically for making piping, or any filler that's the right size. Pretreat the filler cord before making the piping.

Note that you can make piping that has no filler at all; instead, the piping is simply a narrow, flat flange used as an accent along a seamline. When you want a very supple, bulk-free effect, this is the piping type to use.

- White or off-white twisted cording is sold at home-decorating centers and larger fabric stores and is available in a range of diameters. It was created for heavier home-decorating fabrics. Nylon cords made for stringing window shades make a fine, shrink-proof narrow cording.

- Yarn is readily available at sewing and craft stores. Choose a synthetic fiber content that won't shrink when washed and has a smooth surface—stray fibers can get caught

in your stitching. Use pearl cotton for very fine piping. Match the yarn color to the piping fabric when possible.

- Rattail (and its thinner cousin, mousetail), a narrow, shiny rayon cord, is firm, smooth, and consistently thick so it never gets caught in machine stitching.

Making and Applying Piping

To determine how wide to cut the bias covering strips, make a sample. Cut a strip that's at least 3 in. wide. Wrap and pin it around the filler cord, and baste it in place. Trim the seam allowances to the same width as those on the seam where the piping will be inserted. Remove the basting stitches, and measure the width of the strip. Add ½ in. to 1 in. to this width, to account for the narrowing that can occur when bias fabric stretches. Cut strips this width, and as long as needed to cover the cord, plus several inches for joining ends.

HOW TO MAKE CORDED PIPING

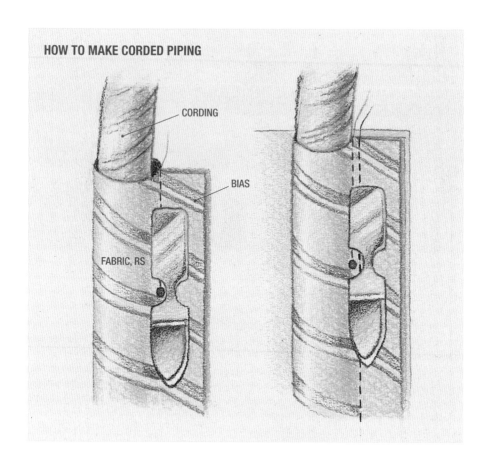

CORDING

BIAS

FABRIC, RS

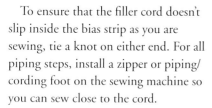

Clip seam allowances on inside curves.

Notch seam allowances on outside curves.

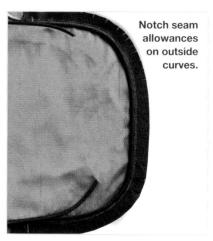

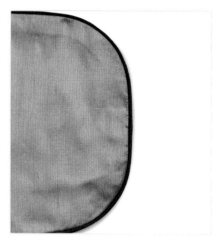

To ensure that the filler cord doesn't slip inside the bias strip as you are sewing, tie a knot on either end. For all piping steps, install a zipper or piping/cording foot on the sewing machine so you can sew close to the cord.

1. With its right side out, wrap the bias strip around the cord, aligning the raw edges. Set the needle position to stitch close to the zipper foot, and sew about ³⁄₁₆ in. from the filler cord.

2. Trim the seam allowances to match those of the garment seam. Place the piping on the garment right side, aligning all cut edges. Clip the piping seam allowances as needed to curve around the edge (see top photo at right). Move the needle slightly to the left, and sew ⅛ in. from the filler cord.

3. Place the adjoining fabric on top of the piped fabric, right sides together and *with raw edges aligned. Pin in the seam allowance. Turn the work over so you can see the line of stitching from step 2. With the cording now to the right of the presser foot, sew just to the right of the visible stitching line to complete the seam.*

Piping Curves

To sew piping along anything but the straight and narrow, you need to clip or notch the piping seam allowances before you sew on the piping. For the allowances to lie flat, you must snip right up to the stitching line, but not through it.

For an inside curve, such as a neckline or armscye edge, clip the seam allowances. Clip every ¼ in. to ½ in. until the piping lies flat. After you stitch and turn the piping, the seam allowances fan out, without puckering.

For an outside curve or corner, notch the seam allowances. Notch out a triangle every ¼ in. to ½ in. After you stitch and turn the piping, the resulting seam allowance segments can overlap without bulk.

Piping a Corner

It's nearly impossible to form a truly pointed angle with piping, but you can come close. Start with filler cord that's flexible and not too thick. For a slightly rounded square corner, clip the seam allowances in three places. Pin the piping, bending it into a rounded shape. Sew.

For a sharper square corner, sew to the exact corner point, stop with the needle down, and make one clip to the stitching. Pivot the work, and continue

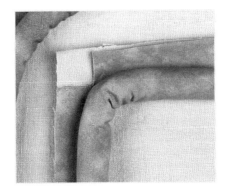

sewing the adjacent edge. You can also add a second line of stitching very close to the piping to tighten where it turns the corner.

Joining the Ends

If piping is inserted in a single straight seam, the ends will be sewn into an adjoining seam. But if the piping is to completely encircle a project, as on the outer edge of a jacket, you'll need to join the ends together.

ABUT THE CORD ENDS

To abut the ends of the piping when you apply it, begin sewing about 1 in. from the starting end (start the piping at an inconspicuous point on a long edge, not at a corner). When you reach the other end, lap it over the first free inch by ¾ in., and leave the overlap unsewn. Remove the basting from the overlapping end, open out the bias, and cut off ¾ in. of the filler cord. Then turn ¼ in. to the wrong side across the end of the bias strip. Lay the other end of the piping on top, abutting the cord ends, and wrap the bias back over the cord. Sew the overlapped section in place.

OVERLAP THE PIPING ENDS

For a quick finish, overlap the ends of the piping when you apply it. Begin sewing 2 in. from the starting end.

Abutting Ends

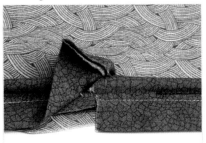

Overlapped ends

When you reach the other end, lap it over the first end by 2 in., leaving both ends unsewn. At each end, push the bias back to expose the cording, and cut off 1 in. of cording. Let the bias relax, then angle the cordless ends into the seam allowance. Finish attaching the piping, sewing across the empty piped sections where they angle over the seamline.

RUFFLES

Ruffles come in three configurations: strip, header, and double. All three types can be cut on the straight or cross-grain or on the bias. The fabric strips for ruffles are commonly anywhere from two to three times the length of the edge they will be applied to, and as deep as desired. The exact ratio depends on the thickness and drape of the fabric (lightweight or sheer fabrics generally look better gathered more tightly than heavy ones). Test the ruffle-to-garment-edge ratio with a few scraps of your fabric until you're pleased with the results, then cut the ruffle accordingly.

You may need to piece fabric strips together to get the needed ruffle length(s). Join lengths with narrow, finished seams and hem the strips before gathering. Hand-rolled, serged, or narrow machine hems are ideal for most ruffles, but a very deep ruffle can handle a larger hem. (If the fabric is lightweight, you can cut the strips double the needed width and fold them lengthwise, using the fold as the finished edge.) After hemming, gather the fabric and apply the ruffle to your project.

See "Gathering," on page 123.

Types of Ruffles

Ruffles can have one or two free edges, and are either inserted into a seam or along an edge, or applied to the surface of a garment.

STRIP RUFFLE

A narrow strip of fabric with one finished edge, and which is gathered along the opposite, unfinished edge. The gathered edge is sewn into a seam or to an unfinished garment edge.

Strip ruffle

Ruffle with header

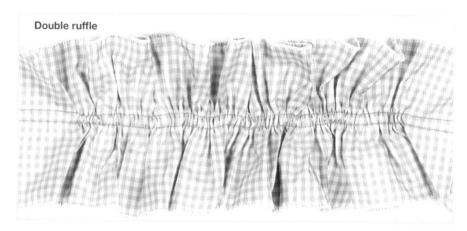

Double ruffle

RUFFLE WITH HEADER

A narrow strip of fabric finished on both edges, and gathered at a determined distance below the upper edge. The ruffle is then topstitched to a garment along the gathering line.

DOUBLE RUFFLE

A narrow length of fabric finished on both edges and gathered along its center. The ruffle is then topstitched to a garment along the gathering line.

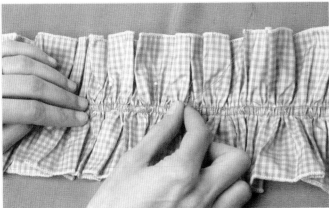
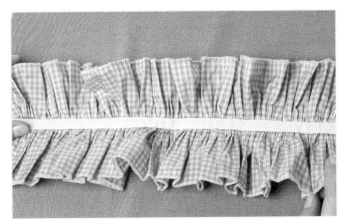

Attaching Ruffles

To attach a strip ruffle to an edge, follow the instructions for attaching a gathered edge to a flat edge (see page 125).

If you are inserting a ruffle in a seam or between the garment and its facing, baste the ruffle to one edge first. Then, pin the second garment section to the piece with the attached ruffle, right sides together, and sew just inside the ruffle basting line. For both edge and seam applications, lightly press the gathered piece away from the garment, and press the seam allowances toward the garment. Trim the seam allowances to ¼ in., and topstitch if desired. If appropriate, bind or serge the seam allowances.

To topstitch a header or double ruffle to a base fabric, pin the ruffle to the garment, aligning match points. Make sure the gathers are evenly spaced. Machine- or hand-baste in place.

Topstitch along both sides of the basting line. If desired, cover the top-stitching with a piece of ribbon or trim, and hand- or machine-stitch to secure.

FRINGED EDGES

If you like a textured effect at the edges of a garment, you can leave them raw, and purposely fray them to create self-fringe. The effect is unique and perfectly coordinated to the fabric. Loosely woven fabrics are the easiest to fray, such as linens, raw silks, many woolens, and coarse cottons. Crisp and fine or sheer fabrics can be fringed as well, but unraveling delicate yarns takes more time, and these fringes tend to tangle more easily.

Patterned and textured fabrics, as well as fabrics woven with different colored yarns in the lengthwise and crosswise grains, all yield interesting results when fringed. You can fringe fabric on the straight or cross-grain, but test first to see which effect is most pleasing.

For a lightweight, supple, and bulk-free edge, simply fringe the raw edge of the garment. This works best along straight edges, such as hems, front openings, or pocket and collar edges. If the edge you want to fringe lies along a grain that can't be fringed effectively, or if it calls for support or stabilization (for example, if you plan to sew buttons or buttonholes adjacent to the fringe), consider adding a facing on the edge and inserting a separate fringed strip in the facing seam, just as you would add a ruffle or piping.

Making Proper Fringe

Always test the fringing process on a swatch of the garment fabric to be sure you like the effect. Pin-fit and try on the pattern to decide where you'd like the fringe to start. Modify the seam or hem allowance if necessary to include the fringe depth, then cut the fabric. Mark the fringe stopping point on the fabric's wrong side.

Stabilize the fringe stopping point by fusing a strip of interfacing to the wrong side along the marked line. Sew along the line with a narrow zigzag stitch. Tug the stitching to make sure the fabric yarns are anchored securely. Adjust the stitch proportions if necessary.

Starting at the cut edge, remove the yarns parallel to the stitched line one at a time, using a pin to gently separate each yarn from the fabric, if necessary. If the yarns are long and resist unraveling, cut into the fabric, perpendicular to the fabric edge, at intervals of several inches. Stop pulling yarns when you reach the line of zigzag stitching.

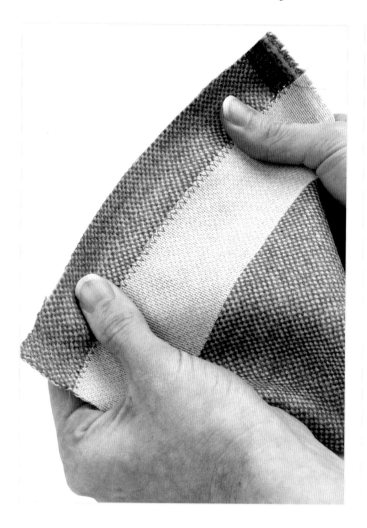

2

Hemming

A hem demands as much attention as the rest of your garment details. It finishes the bottom edge and helps the garment hang properly. Although hems are generally easy to stitch, there are common preparatory steps to follow for best results. Hemline choices depend on your fabric and garment.

Hem Preparation

Prepare to hem a garment by marking the desired hemline and finishing the edge of the hem allowance as desired.

Mark the Hemline

Decide on your garment's finished length, and mark the hem evenly from the floor to ensure accuracy. Wear the undergarments and shoes you intend to wear with the garment (especially for pants), and have someone else do the marking. For skirts and dresses, you can use a chalk hem marker. Pin up the hem allowance on the marked line, and try the garment on again to make sure you are happy with the length.

To mark a pants hem quickly and easily, measure 12 in. up from the floor and make a horizontal mark on the crease line at the calf of each leg. Then pin up the actual hem length on one leg only.

Have the wearer remove the pants. Lay them out, folded along the center creases, one leg on top of the other, and align the calf

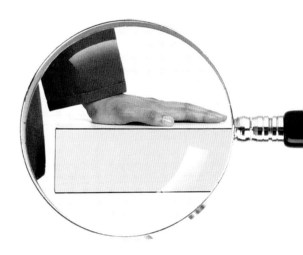

marks. Use the pinned hem as a guide to mark the other leg.

To mark the jacket and sleeve hem of a traditional, blazer-style jacket, try these traditional tailor's tricks. To determine the correct location of the sleeve hem, have the wearer stand by a table and place her palm flat on the surface. The end of the finished sleeve should just touch the back of her hand.

To establish the hemline on a traditional tailored jacket, use the length of the wearer's arm as a gauge. When she stands with her arms straight at her sides, the bottom of the finished jacket should touch the palm of her cupped hands, and her fingers should be able to wrap around the hem as shown in the top right photo.

Pressing and Finishing the Hem Allowance

For any style or depth of hem, prepare as follows:

1. Use pins, chalk, or basting to mark the hemline.

2. Fold up the hem allowance along the marked line and press. Trim the allowance evenly to ensure the hem hangs properly.

3. When the raw edge of the hem is fuller than the garment, machine-baste a line ½ in. from the raw edge. Pull up one thread to ease in the fabric fullness. Gently press the gathers to flatten.

4. To prevent fraying on hand-sewn hems, clean-finish the raw edge before sewing the hem in place.

Determining the Hem Depth

In addition to the fabric type, the hem depth also depends on the hemline's shape. The more curved the shape, the narrower the hem should be, so there's less fullness to ease in. Follow these guidelines for common hem depths.

BASIC STRAIGHT SKIRT	A-LINE SKIRT OR TAILORED TROUSERS	FULL, GATHERED SKIRT	CIRCULAR, CURVED, OR BIAS-CUT SKIRT
2 in.–2½ in.	1½ in.–2 in.	½ in.–1½ in.	⅜ in.–⅝ in.

1 Hem allowance · Hemline · Ease in fullness

4

The type of hem and fabric weight determines the best way to clean-finish the cut edge for a hand-sewn hem.

- For most fabrics, serge the edge using a two- or three-thread overlock, or zigzag the edge. Alternatively, stitch ¼ in. from the cut edge and then either hand-overcast the edge or cut the edge with pinking scissors.

- For lightweight fabric, turn under the edge ¼ in. and press.

- For heavier fabrics or those that fray, bind the edge with a narrow strip of bias-cut tricot or lining fabric.

- For loosely woven fabrics or those that fray, machine-stitch hem tape over the cut edge.

- For a couture look, use a Hong Kong finish (see page 157).

- When you don't have enough fabric, consider a faced hem.

HAND-STITCHED HEMS

Hand-sewn hems have long been the standard on well-made garments because the stitching is less visible on the garment's right side. The most common hand-hemming stitches are the blind-hem stitch, the catchstitch, and the slipstitch.

Keep the stitches somewhat loose to avoid puckering on the garment right side, and to build a slight amount of flexibility between the hem allowance and the body of the garment. Work with a small hand-sewing needle to get the smallest possible stitch. A size 7 or 8 sharps needle works best with regular-weight thread. Use a size 10 sharps needle and fine silk thread for the most invisible hem. Cut the thread about 18 in. long and apply beeswax (pressing the waxed thread to melt the wax) to smooth the fibers and prevent knots. Use a single strand of thread.

A blind hem, though nearly invisible, is quite sturdy. It works best on medium to thick fabrics, such as wool and fleece. Fold the fabric as shown in the top right photo. Sew from right to left under the hem allowance, ¼ in. from the finished edge of the hem allowance. Pick up just one thread with each stitch of the garment; take a larger stitch on the hem allowance if desired.

Catchstitching is also invisible but stretches slightly, an advantage in stretch fabrics. Sew from left to right in a crosshatch pattern, as shown in the center photo.

See "Catchstitch," on page 284.

To hand-sew a very narrow, rolled hem on extremely lightweight fabrics, choose the slipstitch. Prepare the hemming area by machine sewing a row of straight stitches ½ in. from the raw edge. Trim the allowance to ⅛ in. Fold the fabric to the wrong side just enough to reveal the machine stitches. Sew from right to left using a slipstitch. Stitch in the fold, then stitch again about ⅛ in. to ¼ in. over and below the previous stitch, rolling the fabric over as you go.

See "Slipstitch," on page 285.

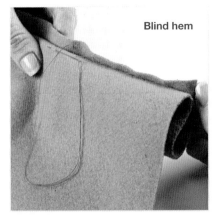

Blind hem

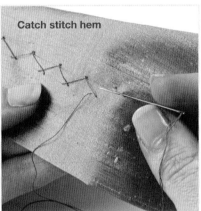

Catch stitch hem

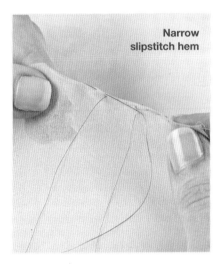

Narrow slipstitch hem

MACHINE-SEWN HEMS

Machine-sewn hems are suitable for a wide range of fabric and garment types. Because they usually include more stitches per inch, they're generally a little stronger than a hand-sewn hem, so choose a machine-stitched hem for garments that need durability.

A topstitched hem is a functional edge that works with most fabrics. Press up the allowance on the marked hemline. Open out this fold, and press the raw edge under as far as desired (all the way to the fold, for a sturdy, opaque hem; just ¼ in. for a lightweight, supple hem). Alternatively, serge or zigzag-finish the raw edge and omit this folding step. Fold the hem back into position, and pin in place. Using a 3-mm to 3.5-mm stitch length, sew along the folded edge.

Narrow hemming is the perfect solution for sheer and lightweight fabrics as shown in the top left photo. Press up the hem on the fold line, and straight-stitch ⅛ in. from the fold. Trim the allowance close to the stitching.

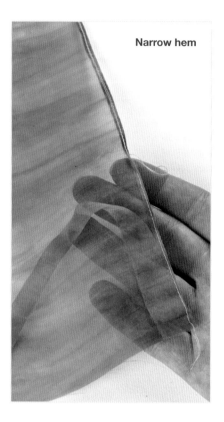

Narrow hem

Narrow hem presser foot

Blind hemming

Topstitch hem

Turn up the edge again, just bringing the row of stitches to the wrong side. Stitch over previous stitching from the wrong side.

A narrow-hem presser foot enables you to turn under and stitch a narrow hem in one pass (see top right photo). It folds the fabric edge under as the machine stitches the edge. A rolled-hem foot works similarly, but comes in different sizes to make hems of different widths, from ¼ in. to ⅞ in. wide. Your machine dealer can tell you if one is available for your machine.

Blind hemming is appropriate for nearly all fabrics. It requires the blind-hem stitch on your machine, which looks like a series of several straight stitches, followed by one zigzag stitch to the left. A special presser foot (see page 10) is helpful for guiding the fabric edge. Folding the fabric correctly is the key to a virtually invisible blind hem: Fold up on the hemline, then fold under as shown in the bottom right photo above, forming a second crease with ¼ in. of hem allowance extending.

Follow the sewing instructions in your machine manual, and test the stitch to make sure the zigzag stitch takes just a very small "bite" along the garment fold-back.

Most machines also have a stretch version of the blind hem that's more suitable for knits—it offers a zigzag stitch between the bites into the foldline, adding flexibility.

INTERFACED HEM

To prevent a hem from stretching out of shape or rippling, or to support lightweight embellishment, apply interfacing within the hem area. On jackets, a hem interfacing creates a smoother line over the hip area and reduces wrinkling when the wearer is sitting. It also eliminates shapeless, limp, and undefined sleeve hems.

Select interfacing that's lighter than the fashion fabric and cut it on the bias, if it has a grain. On unlined garments, cut the interfacing narrower than the hem allowance. On lined garments, it's usual to cut the interfacing so it extends at least ½ in. above the hem allowance to prevent any impression from the hem edge from showing through on the right side of the garment.

For soft support in lightweight and medium-weight fabrics, apply the interfacing to the hem allowance, and also fuse a strip to the garment itself right above the hem foldline. This prevents a seam allowance ridge from showing on the right side of the fabric when you press. For a soft-fold effect, extend the interfacing into the fold of the hem to keep the edges looking smoothly unpressed (no matter how firmly pressed they are), rather than crisply creased.

For a stiffer, sharper hem, apply horsehair braid, twill tape, or Petersham ribbon (listed in order of firmness, with horsehair being the stiffest) between the hem allowance and the garment. These products provide greater support and help the hem stand away from the body.

Horsehair braid is actually made from polyester and comes in different widths and weights. Choose the lightest weight that effectively supports the garment hem. One edge of the braid includes a pull string, which enables you to shape the braid to follow a curve.

HEMMING TIPS

- When hemming by hand, pin the hem allowance in place from the right side to prevent the thread from catching on the pins.
- Press hems only along the fold and not at the sewn edge, to avoid a visible ridge on the garment right side.
- Use a serger to ease in excess fullness by increasing the differential feed setting.
- A light spritz of spray starch and a pressing make it easier to hand-sew a rolled hem on lightweight fabrics.
- For an extra-secure hand-sewn hem, take a tiny backstitch in the hem allowance every few inches of stitching.

INTERFACING

HORSEHAIR BRAID

PETERSHAM RIBBON

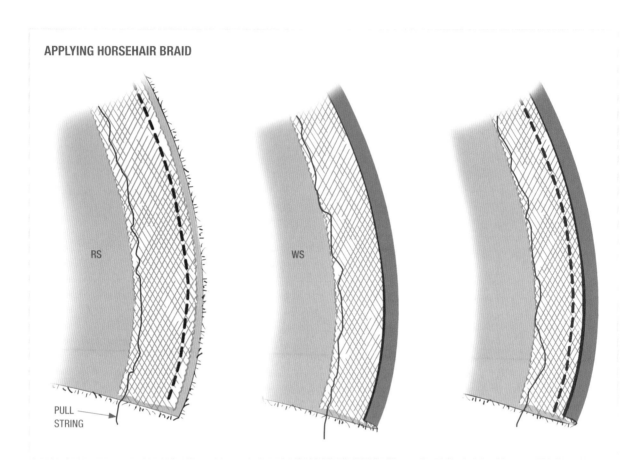

APPLYING HORSEHAIR BRAID

RS

PULL
STRING

WS

To use horsehair braid, lay it on the right side of the garment, aligning the raw edge of the skirt with the edge of the horsehair that doesn't have the pull string. With the horsehair on top, sew ⅛ in. from the garment edge. Turn the horsehair to the wrong side of the garment, folding the fabric so it wraps the edge of the horsehair. Topstitch from the right side, ¼ in. from the turned edge. Draw up the pull string as needed so the horsehair hugs the inside of the skirt. The stiffness of the braid keeps it upright, without need for further stitching along the upper edge.

Cotton or wool twill tape helps create a sharp edge. Because it stretches only slightly and can't be shaped, use a narrow ¼-in. width to topstitch it in place on the hem allowance, with its lower edge along the hem foldline.

Petersham ribbon can be shaped to match a curved hemline. Spritz it with water, then press with a dry iron, stretching and shaping one edge to match the hemline curve. Tack it to the hem allowance, with the stretched edge at the hemline.

FUSED HEMS

There are times when it may be appropriate to simply fuse a hem in place, with or without additional stitching. To determine if this is workable for your fabric, make a test sample and evaluate the appearance. On some fabrics, any added stiffness may be undesirable. On knit fabrics, using a lightweight fusible to hold the hem in place, then topstitching from the right side, enables you to stitch a flat, professional finish that doesn't stretch during sewing.

Remember, fusible webs come in different weights, so experiment with several to find a product compatible with your particular fabric.

For a basic fused hem, start by preparing the hem as usual. Then, fuse a strip of paper-backed fusible web on the wrong side of the fabric, along the edge of the finished hem allowance, and press in place. Remove the backing paper, fold the hem up, and press to secure.

The basic fused hem glues the hem allowance to the garment wrong side. In some garments and fabrics, this may cause the garment to wear and hang unattractively, as the two layers have no give between them. To solve this problem, try the method described on the facing page, a hybrid interfaced/fused hem. It's ideal for tailored, lined

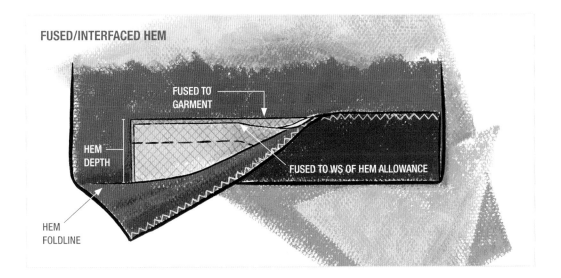

FUSED/INTERFACED HEM

FUSED TO GARMENT

HEM DEPTH

FUSED TO WS OF HEM ALLOWANCE

HEM FOLDLINE

jackets as it supports the hem and eliminates the need for stitching the jacket hem.

1. Cut two layers of lightweight, woven fusible interfacing on the bias, 1 in. wider than the finished hem depth. Stitch the strips tighter along one long edge, with adhesive sides out. For lined garments, use a ¾-in.-wide seam allowance (this allows you to fold down the upper edge of the hem later to attach the lining). For unlined garments, use a ¼-in.-wide seam allowance.

2. Trim the unstitched long edges to match the hem depth.

3. Place the joined strips between the garment and the hem allowance, with the stitches toward the top of the hem. Press from the wrong side to fuse the strips to the fabric. Then, press from the right side, using a press cloth, to complete the fusing.

FACED HEMS

If you're short on fabric, or the fabric is bulky or heavy, consider facing the hemline with a separate piece of fabric in a similar or lighter weight. Cut a 2½-in.-wide bias strip equal to the finished hem circumference, plus 1 in. Depending on the hem size, it may be

necessary to allow extra length for piecing bias strips together. Fold under ¼ in. along one long edge of the bias strip, then pin its unfolded edge to the garment's lower edge, right sides together, and sew the facing to the hem with a ¼-in. seam allowance. Grade the seam, press the seam allowance toward the facing, and understitch. Then press the facing to the inside just below the understitching, and press under and hand-stitch the edge.

If the hemline is dramatically curved or unusually shaped (so that a bias strip won't follow its curve smoothly), you can cut a shaped facing to fit perfectly by tracing the lower 2½ in. of the garment's front and back pieces, minus any hem allowance included in the pattern. Cut these pieces, join them to match the garment hem, and attach as described above.

XI
CLOSURES

Buttons & Buttonholes

Buttons are among the oldest of fasteners, but that makes them classic. There's such a huge range of button styles to choose from that you can find a button to suit nearly any project, both in function and in form. Select the correct button and sew it on sturdily, and you'll never have to worry about losing it. To partner the perfect button, you need to stitch the perfect buttonhole: Place it properly, sew it correctly, and it will stand up to years of use.

BUTTONS

Button size, weight, and durability contribute to a garment's aesthetic, hang, and fit. The pattern envelope lists a recommended button size, which corresponds to the amount of overlap at the garment's opening, and assumes the thickness of a ⅛-in. flat button. You may use buttons that vary up to ¼ in. in diameter and/or thickness, but deviating any more than that can adversely affect the garment's fit, drape, and over-all proportion. (If you use a different button size, you must also adjust the length of the buttonhole.)

Always make sure that the button weight is compatible with the fabric weight. Lightweight buttons on a heavy fabric don't pose a functional problem (though they may be unsuitable aesthetically), but when the garment fabric is lightweight, use only lightweight buttons to avoid fabric distortion. The buttons you choose should have care requirements compatible with the garment fabric.

Button Types

Although there are many sizes, weights, and shapes of buttons, they all fall into two basic styles: sew-through and shank. Sew-through buttons usually feature two or four holes in the center, and you attach them by sewing through the holes. On thin fabrics, you can stitch flat buttons directly to the fabric, but with thicker fabrics, you need to create a thread shank to ensure that the buttons clear the buttonhole thickness. Shank buttons have a metal, plastic, or wooden loop on the back that raises them above the fabric and allows them to comfortably clear buttonholes, even in thick fabric. Stitches used to secure these buttons are looped through the shank and hidden from view.

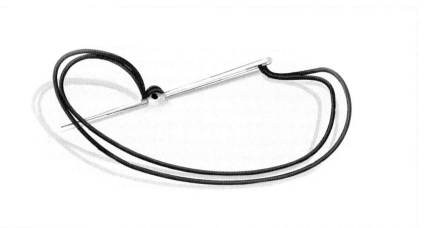

Sewing on Buttons

Before sewing on buttons, be sure that the area is properly interfaced. For both shank and sew-on buttons, it's a good idea to first sew one onto a project fabric scrap, then slip it through a buttonhole to make sure all the fabric layers lie smoothly, and that the button doesn't press down into the upper fabric layers and create puckers. If puckers occur,

you need to increase the shank length, or add a thread shank to a flat button.

When sewing buttons onto light- to medium-weight fabrics, use a double strand of the same all-purpose thread you used to sew the garment. For heavyweight fabric, use a single strand of heavy-duty buttonhole twist or carpet thread. To prevent tangling and to give extra strength, coat the thread with beeswax, then press it lightly with the tip of your iron.

ANCHORING THE THREAD

Thread the needle and knot the ends together, if using a double strand. At the button mark, insert the needle between the garment and the facing to hide the knot (if there isn't a facing, insert your needle on the right side of the fabric to hide the knot between the fabric and the button).

Take one or two tiny stitches through all the fabric layers to anchor the thread, then position the button over the stitches.

ATTACHING A SEW-THROUGH BUTTON BY HAND

Bring the needle up through one hole and down through another, sewing through all the fabric layers. Repeat.

For a two-hole button, sew five times. For a four-hole button, sew three times

through each pair of holes. Secure the thread between the garment and facing (or under the button on the fabric's right side).

ATTACHING A SEW-THROUGH BUTTON BY MACHINE

Fit your machine with a special button foot or a standard or open-toe embroidery foot. Adjust the machine to zigzag-stitch in place by setting the stitch length to zero or by disengaging the feed dogs. (Some machines offer a button-sewing setting that makes these adjustments automatically.) Place the button under the presser foot (hold the button in place with a bit of transparent tape, if necessary), and set the stitch width to equal the space between the holes. Slowly turn the fly wheel to determine the correct stitch width. Once you've found the right setting, and the needle doesn't hit the button,

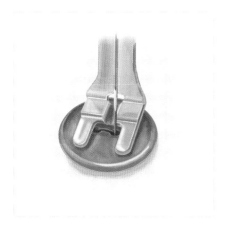

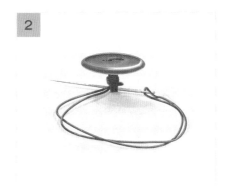

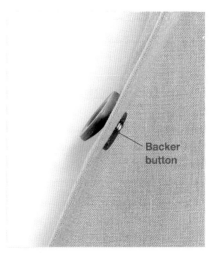

Backer button

hand-crank the flywheel to take several stitches. Finish by locking the thread in one hole: Sew in place (using a stitch length of zero) with a straight stitch.

CREATING A THREAD SHANK FOR A SEW-THROUGH BUTTON

A thread shank ensures that the buttons clear their holes without puckering or indenting the fabric. The shank length should be ⅛ in. longer than the thickness of the fabric opening.

1. Place a straight pin or toothpick over the button to act as a spacer. Sew on the button by hand or machine, pulling the thread tightly over the spacer. Leave a long thread tail.

2. Remove the spacer and hold the button away from the fabric. Bring a threaded needle up through the fabric to the base of the stitches, wind the thread around them three or four times, then knot the thread at the base.

ADDING A BACKER BUTTON

For extra security (especially on knits or loosely woven fabrics), to help support very large buttons, and as a nice finish, align a small, flat button on the inside of the garment, underneath the main button. Choose a button with the same number of holes as the main button, and with the holes similarly spaced. Stitch through the main button and

backer button, making a thread shank if necessary, then secure the stitches behind the backer button.

If the fabric is lightweight but you still want to reinforce the button area, add a small piece of interfacing, ribbon, or other stabilizing material on the wrong side, in place of the backer button.

ATTACHING A SHANK BUTTON BY HAND

Make sure the shank is parallel to the buttonhole opening. Bring the needle up on the button mark and pass it through the shank and then all the fabric layers. Repeat five times. Secure the thread between the garment and facing or at the base of the shank.

BUTTONHOLES

Unless they're a design feature, machine-sewn buttonholes should be discreet, uniform in length, an equal distance from the garment edge and each other, and, of course, perfectly stitched.

Buttonhole Support

Buttonholes always look better, and are easier to sew, when the fashion fabric is properly supported with interfacing. In most cases, the fusible or sew-in interfacing required for the garment facings will adequately support the buttonholes. With some lightweight or loosely woven fabrics, however, you may need to add another strip of thin interfacing or organza in the buttonhole area. Because sewing buttonholes falls at the end of the construction process, plan your interfacing needs in advance.

Sew a test buttonhole (layer two fabric scraps with interfacing to simulate the faced garment front) and scrutinize the results. If the hole stretches out of shape even slightly, you'll need to add an extra strip of interfacing. Slip the button through it to make sure it's snug enough to be secure, but loose enough for the button to pass through easily.

BUTTONHOLE PLACEMENT

The button/buttonhole placement is printed on the pattern piece or on a separate guide that comes with the pattern. These marks are just a suggestion, however. You should adjust the button/buttonhole placement if you alter the pattern, if you use a button size other than that recommended, or if the given placement doesn't correspond to your particular figure needs.

Hold the pattern up to your body to make sure the buttons are positioned in the key areas shown on the facing page. Place a pin at all relevant key areas. Set the pattern on a flat surface and space the additional buttons at even intervals from the pins, along the center front. Place the revised pattern on the right side of the garment, folding it back as shown in the top photo, and place a pin through the fabric at each mark. Remove the pattern.

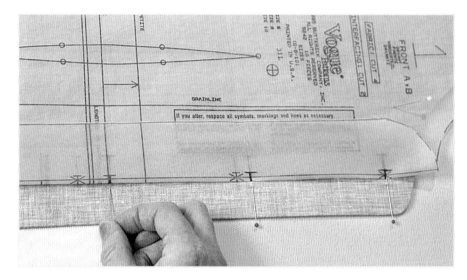

Using a fabric marker, make a small dot on the center-front or -back line at each pin mark on the right side of the fabric. Using a ruler as a guide, draw a line at each dot, the desired length of the buttonhole. Then draw a short perpendicular line at each end.

BUTTONHOLE ORIENTATION

Buttonholes are usually oriented vertically or horizontally; occasionally, a diagonal orientation is chosen for design effect. Before you decide how to align a buttonhole, consider how much stress will be placed on the button and buttonhole during wear. Horizontal buttonholes can take the most strain

without stretching out of shape. Always place the stress-bearing end of the buttonhole ⅛ in. beyond or above the desired button position (see page 240).

Horizontal buttonholes provide a secure closure, staying closed even when they are large (to accommodate a large button). Use this orientation on jackets, coats, fitted dresses, and on waistbands. Place them perpendicular to and ⅛ in. beyond the center front.

Vertical buttonholes provide a secure closure as long as they are not too large. Orient buttonholes vertically on shirts and blouses that aren't close-fitting. Position them directly on the center front line. When spacing, measure the

Determining Buttonhole Size and Position

Buttonholes must be large enough for the button to fit through, without stretching the buttonhole out of shape. They should be snug enough that buttons won't come undone during wear. And they should be placed so that they keep a garment closed without strain or gaps.

BUTTONHOLE SIZE

Buttonholes must accommodate not just the diameter of the button, but also its thickness. These three formulas help you calculate the correct buttonhole size for buttons of different proportions.

SEW-THROUGH BUTTONS, LESS THAN 1/8 IN. THICK

MEASURE THE DIAMETER.

DIAMETER + 1/8 IN. = BUTTONHOLE LENGTH.

SEW-THROUGH BUTTONS, MORE THAN 1/8 IN. THICK

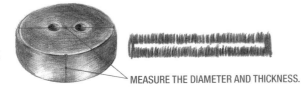

MEASURE THE DIAMETER AND THICKNESS.

DIAMETER + THICKNESS + 1/8 IN. = BUTTONHOLE LENGTH.

DISTANCE FROM FOLD TO PIN + 1/8 IN. = BUTTONHOLE LENGTH.

DOMED BUTTONS

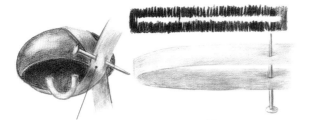

WRAP TWILL TAPE AROUND THE BUTTON AND PIN WHERE THE TAPE ENDS OVERLAP.

BUTTONHOLE POSITION

For a good fit, without gaps, be sure to place a button and buttonhole at these key garment locations. Then space additional buttons evenly between these buttons.

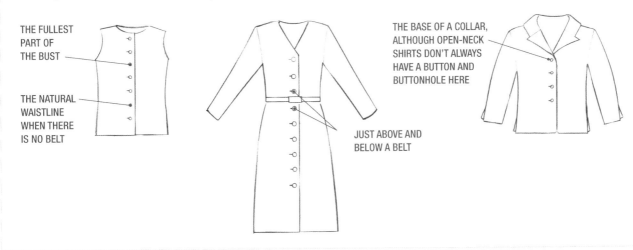

THE FULLEST PART OF THE BUST

THE NATURAL WAISTLINE WHEN THERE IS NO BELT

JUST ABOVE AND BELOW A BELT

THE BASE OF A COLLAR, ALTHOUGH OPEN-NECK SHIRTS DON'T ALWAYS HAVE A BUTTON AND BUTTONHOLE HERE

BUTTONHOLE ORIENTATION

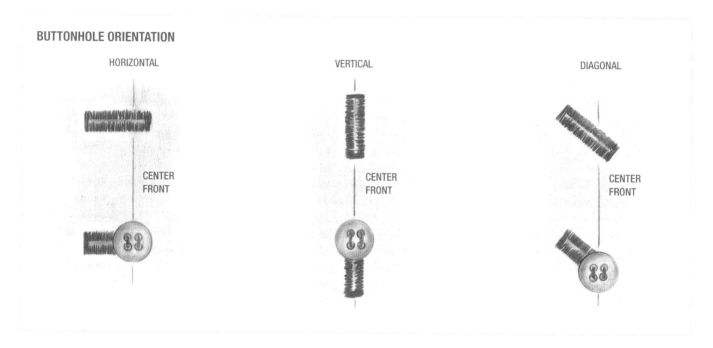

HORIZONTAL   VERTICAL   DIAGONAL

CENTER FRONT   CENTER FRONT   CENTER FRONT

desired interval between buttons, not buttonholes, and use that measurement to mark the top of each buttonhole.

Diagonal buttonholes provide a whimsical touch. Place them at an angle to and ⅛ in. beyond the center front. Add extra interfacing to inhibit stretch along the bias.

Machine-Made Buttonholes

A machine-made buttonhole is really nothing more than a slit bound by two parallel rows of narrow satin stitches, with a bar tack at each end. Most sewing machines today include an automatic buttonhole feature, which stitches the buttonhole in one step, or in multiple steps (each side and bar tack is sewn separately and in succession). Refer to your owner's manual for specific machine settings and instructions.

AUTOMATIC BUTTONHOLES

If your machine has an automatic, one-step buttonhole function, it's likely that it also comes with a special buttonhole

presser foot, which works with the machine to sew a buttonhole the precise size you want. Often, you set the size by inserting the button into the foot and sliding a gauge to grasp it. Make a test buttonhole first, to ascertain in which direction the machine stitches the buttonhole (from front to back, or back to front), and mark the appropriate end of the buttonhole.

Center the buttonhole foot over the marked position on your fabric and stitch the buttonhole as described in your owner's manual, either in a single step or in four successive steps.

Cut the buttonhole open by slicing carefully between the rows of satin stitching, taking care not to cut the stitches themselves. Before cutting open the buttonhole, protect the bar tacks by inserting a pin across the buttonhole, just inside the bar tacks. Use a fine, sharp seam ripper, a single-edge razor blade, a buttonhole chisel, or small, sharp scissors to cut the buttonhole open. If desired, apply a light bead of seam sealant, such as Fray Check™, along the cut edges.

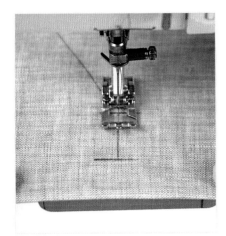

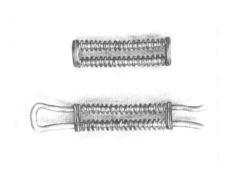

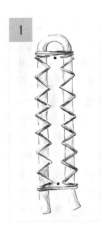

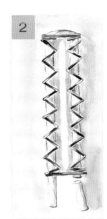

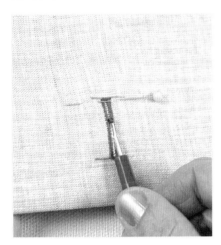

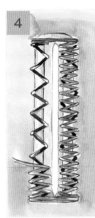

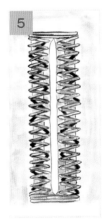

CORDED BUTTONHOLE

For a truly professional-looking buttonhole, and to strengthen and enhance its appearance, add pearl cotton or buttonhole twist under the stitching. Place the cording under the presser foot, and cover it with the buttonhole side stitches as you sew. After you've stitched, pull the cord tails to hide the loop. Thread the tails into a hand needle with a large eye (use a needle threader), take them to the underside, and knot them together. Bury a small amount on the wrong side, and cut off the excess.

On some buttonhole presser feet, there's a small hook at one end, where you can attach the cording material so that it's held in just the right place during stitching. Consult the machine manual for instructions on using this feature.

TWICE-STITCHED BUTTONHOLES

For an extremely strong buttonhole with a smooth, raised appearance, consider stitching over the basic buttonhole a second time, using the manual settings on your sewing machine.

1. Set up the machine for a corded buttonhole, and stitch the buttonhole, using a long zigzag on the sides and lightly stitched bar tacks.

2. Pull the cord tight, trim the ends, then cut open the buttonhole. Trim the raw edges as close as possible to the stitches.

3. Continue with manual settings from here on. Adjust the width and length of the zigzag to create a smooth, dense satin stitch, and stitch over one side of the buttonhole.

4. Stitch over the bar tack at one end, then satin-stitch over the second side of the buttonhole. Either pivot the garment, or return to the starting end, to avoid stitching backward.

5. End with a second, lightly stitched bar tack and lock the stitches by sewing in place. Clip the threads or pull them to the wrong side and tie them.

Stitching Button Loops

If you don't want to make an actual buttonhole in a garment, you can instead hand-sew a small, unobtrusive thread loop on the edge.

Thread a needle with one strand of buttonhole twist (thinner sewing thread yields a skimpy loop). Use a pencil

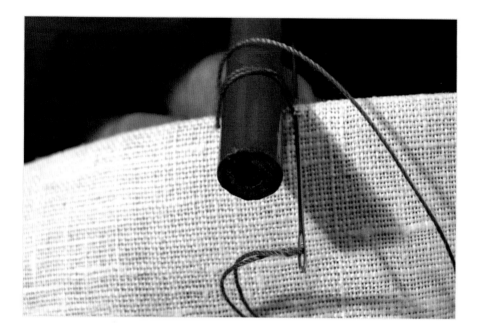

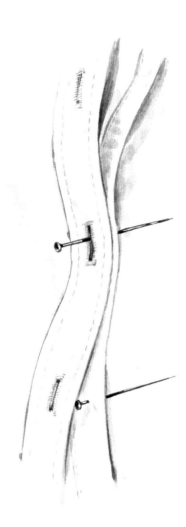

or dowel as a spacing device. First, secure the thread to the edge of the piece where you want the loop. Loop the thread over the dowel, and stitch through the edge on the other side.

Repeat this step in reverse and back to get three threads forming loops over the dowel, then knot them.

Next, cover the threads with blanket stitches.

See "Blanket Stitch," on page 286.

Bring the needle up through the loops of thread, and loop the working thread under the needle point. Pull the stitch closed.

Continue to sew blanket stitches until the entire thread loop is covered. Press the finished loop with steam to "set" the stitches.

MARKING THE FINAL BUTTON POSITION

If you have used the pattern's buttonhole placement guide, and chosen buttons exactly as instructed on the pattern, you can use the button placement marks as well. If not, use the buttonholes as a guide for positioning the buttons.

Stitch and cut open all the buttonholes. With the garment wrong sides together, line up the closure edges and align the neckline and hem. Pin the layers together. Insert a pin through each hole ⅛ in. from the end closest to the garment edge for a horizontal buttonhole, or ⅛ in. below the upper end for a vertical buttonhole. Mark a dot where the pin emerges on the under layer with a disappearing fabric marker. Then sew the buttons in place.

See "Sewing on Buttons," on page 236.

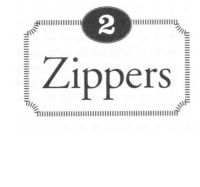

Zippers

Zippers fall into two basic categories: separating (opening at both ends) or closed (opening at one end), but there are many variations. Their interlocking teeth come as plastic coils, metal or plastic teeth, and decorative interlocking rhinestones, giving you plenty of design options. With strategic pressing and pinning, inserting zippers is easy. Consider zippers design features as well as closures.

PREPARING THE ZIPPER AND THE GARMENT

Take the time to stabilize the zipper opening area and to prep the zipper for the easiest, smoothest application.

Preparing the Zipper

Press any wrinkles out of the zipper tape, using only the tip of the iron to avoid melting synthetic zipper teeth. If the zipper is too long for the opening, shorten it.

To shorten a zipper, mark the desired finished length across the zipper tape. Then straight-stitch, with a hand needle and thread, several times over the zipper teeth ¾ in. below the desired length to form a new thread zipper stop. Alternatively, you can bar-tack by machine, instead of hand stitching.

If the garment has a waistband or facing treatment at the top of the zipper, you can wait and shorten the zipper after inserting it. Align the zipper bottom stop at the marked end of the zipper opening area, and insert the zipper, allowing the extra length to hang over the edge of the garment. Later, open the zipper, and attach the waistband or facing to the

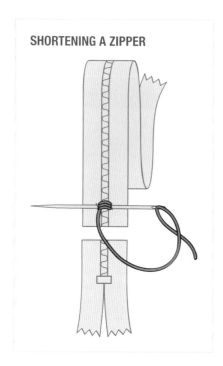

SHORTENING A ZIPPER

garment, catching the zipper tape in the seamline. This seam acts as a top stop for the zipper. Trim off the excess length to about ½ in., and enclose the new zipper end within the waistband or between the facing and garment.

Preparing the Garment

The following steps are completed on flat garment pieces. Instead of using standard ⅝-in. seam allowances, cut wider ¾-in. seam allowances. This ensures that you'll have enough fabric for the zipper overlap. If the location is curved, staystitch within the seam allowances.

1. To prevent stretching as you sew and to create crisp edges on the zipper laps, stabilize the zipper area with fusible interfacing in a weight appropriate for the fabric. Cut two strips on the straight grain and 1 in. longer than the zipper. Cut the strip for an overlap 1½ in. wide and the strip for an underlap ¾ in. wide. Fuse the strips to the fabric's wrong sides,

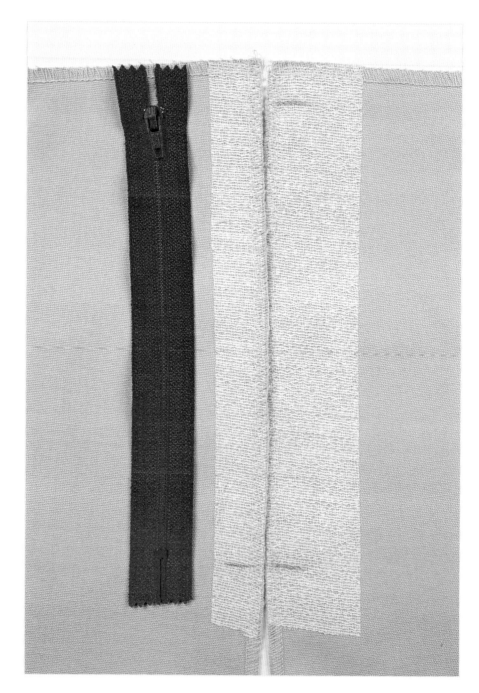

aligning one edge with the cut edge of the zipper opening location.

2. Serge or zigzag-stitch the fabric's raw edges at the zipper location to prevent them from raveling.

3. Mark the top and bottom of the zipper opening on the garment.

CENTERED ZIPPER

Centered zippers are found on a variety of garments, including dresses, skirts, and pants. With a centered zipper, the teeth are aligned along a seam and covered with symmetrical overlaps on each side. Parallel lines of topstitching flank the seam.

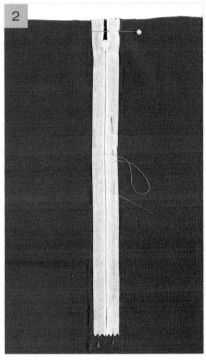

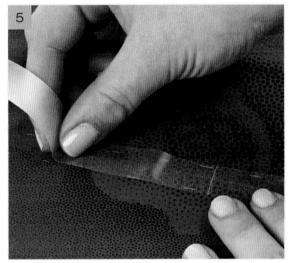

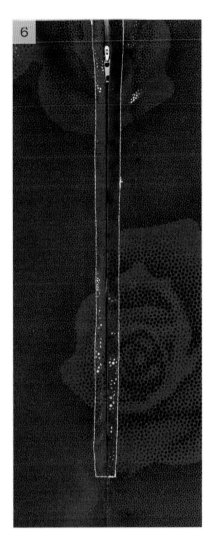

1. With right sides together, machine-sew the seam below the zipper opening. Baste the seam shut along the zipper opening. Press open the seam allowances.

2. Lay the garment face down on a flat surface. Lay the zipper right side down on top of the seam allowance, centering the teeth over the seamline and aligning the upper edge of the tape with the top edge of the garment. You know the zipper is centered if there are equal amounts of the seam allowances showing on either side of the zipper tape.

3. Baste to secure. Hand-baste the zipper through all layers. Keep the zipper centered over the seam. (Alternatively, use wash-away basting tape or narrow fusible tape to keep the zipper in place before sewing.)

4. Turn the garment right side up. Locate the zipper pull by the bump it forms in the basted seam. Release a few basting stitches directly over the zipper pull, so the zipper pull can peek out while you're stitching.

5. For a perfect topstitch line, center a strip of ½-in.-wide cellophane tape over the seam as a stitch guide.

6. Install a zipper foot, and machine-sew along the tape edge. Sew both sides from top to bottom. When you reach the bottom of the second side, sew across the zipper bottom. Do not overlap or backstitch. Instead, pull all of the threads to the back, and hand-knot. Remove the basting and the tape.

SEPARATING ZIPPER

A separating zipper opens at the top and bottom and is usually inserted in a centered application. Insert the zipper before sewing the hem or applying facings or bands.

1. Baste the seam closed. Follow steps 2 through 5 for a centered zipper (page 245).

2. Install a zipper foot. Topstitch each side of the zipper along the edge of the tape,

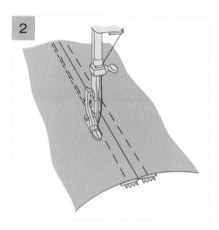

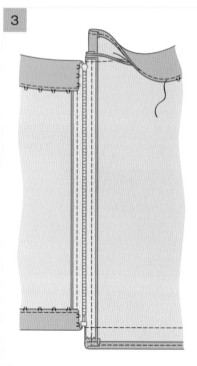

starting at the lower edge of each side. Keep the facing and hem edges free.

3. Turn the facing and/or hems to the wrong side, and fold the ends under to clear the zipper teeth. Slipstitch them to the zipper tape.

INVISIBLE ZIPPER

Invisible zippers, when properly inserted, are indeed undetectable, aside from the zipper pull. There's no visible topstitching in an invisible zipper application, so the finished closure looks like a continuation of the garment's seam. These zippers are especially flexible and soft, making them ideal on fine fabrics. Because you must sew very close to the zipper coil, the fabric can get caught in the zipper during use; therefore, reserve this type of zipper for use with fabrics that are light- to medium-weight, with a relatively smooth surface and supple hand.

You can follow the directions that come with the zipper. They advise you to leave the seam completely open until the zipper is installed, and they call for use of a specialized invisible-zipper foot. Alternatively, the industry method shown below is a quick and easy way to a streamlined, lightweight, and hidden zipper. It goes into a seam that's already partially sewn and uses a basic zipper foot.

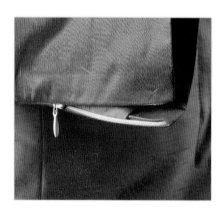

1. Prepare the zipper opening by sewing the garment seam from the hem up to about 4 in. below the zipper opening. On the wrong side, fuse a ⅝-in.-wide strip of lightweight tricot interfacing to the seam allowances. Make sure that it covers the seamline.

2. Mark the desired finished length on the zipper tape, with the zipper closed, measuring from the top of the coil (teeth) toward the bottom. Unzip the zipper, uncurl the zipper teeth, and extend the mark from the tape across the teeth to the other side of the tape.

3. Position and stitch the first side of the zipper tape. With the garment right side up and the zipper open and facedown, lay one side of the zipper tape along the opening. Align the coil on the seamline. With your zipper foot set to the right of the needle, machine-stitch along the tape, from the top of the zipper to ¼ in. beyond the mark at the lower end.

4. Sew a second row of stitches close to the coil, starting at the top. Use your index fingers to uncurl the coil in front of the presser foot, and sew in the groove to the right of the coil. Stop at the mark and make several stitches in place. The coil will spring back to conceal these stitches. Then close the zipper.

5. Position and sew the second side of the zipper tape. With the garment wrong side up, pin the zipper tape to the seam allowance, right sides together, with the zipper coil aligned with the seamline. Check that the unsewn section of the seam below the lower end of the zipper is equal.

If not (as can happen with unstable or slippery fabrics), reposition the zipper so the seam matches perfectly below it. Open the zipper to stitch the tape in position, sewing from bottom to top.

6. Sew another row of stitches along the coil of the second side of the zipper as

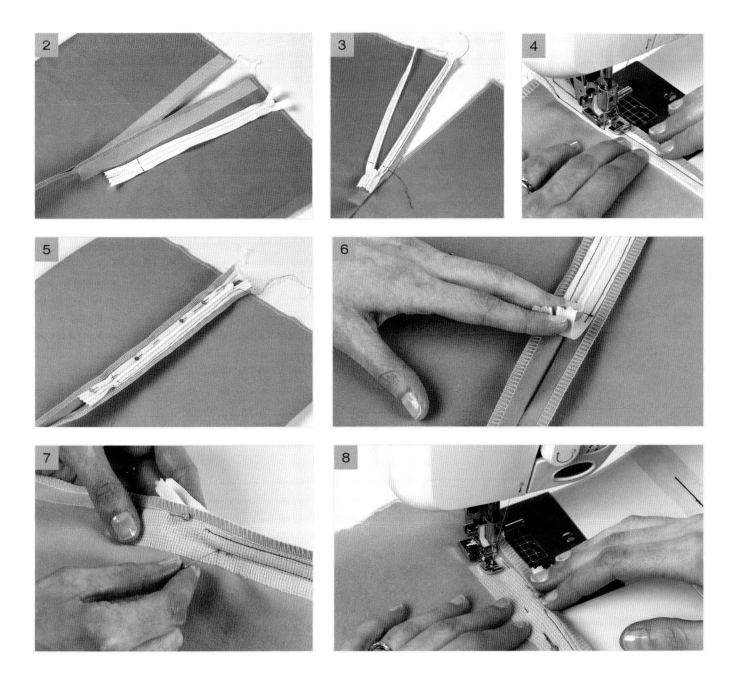

you did the first, but start at the bottom mark. Take several stitches in place, then stitch toward the top. Close the zipper and check that it is, indeed, invisible from the garment's right side, and that the opening in the seam below the zipper is even on both sides.

7. Pull the free zipper tape at the lower end of the zipper away from the seam allowances, align the edges of the seam

allowances, and pin them together. Spear a pin through the two ends of the stitching lines that attach the zipper to anchor them together. This ensures a smooth transition from seam to zipper.

8. Move the zipper foot to the left of the needle. Start with several stitches in place at the top of the unfinished seam and proceed upward, toward the bottom of the zipper, stopping at the pin and stitching

in place several times. Then anchor the free zipper ends to the seam allowances with a few hand stitches, if desired. Press the seam lightly from the right side, using a press cloth if needed.

TIPS FOR INVISIBLE ZIPPERS

• Quick fix for visible zipper teeth: If you haven't stitched close enough to the zipper coil, the teeth will show when the zipper is closed. Simply unzip the zipper, uncurl the coil, and restitch closer to the coil without removing any of the earlier stitches.

- Quickly customize the zipper pull: If you can't find a zipper in a color that matches your fabric, paint the zipper pull. Nail polish works well and is available in a wide range of colors. You can also use model paints.

- Perfect alignment at seam inter- sections: To ensure the alignment of a horizontal seam intersecting the zipper, sew the first side of the zipper and close it. Align the seam and make sure the seam opening below the zipper is undistorted. Pin the zipper above and below the seam, unzip it, stitch the tape, and stitch close to the coil for about 1 in. across the seam.

EXPOSED ZIPPER

An exposed zipper is sewn directly on the outside of the garment, with the zipper tapes used as a decorative feature. When installing an exposed zipper, you turn the seam allowances to the right side, topstitch the zipper over them to conceal the fabric edges, and let the zipper tape show on the outside of the garment.

1. Prepare the zipper location by fusing a 1-in.-wide interfacing strip to the right side of both zipper seam allowances. Staystitch ¾ in. from the edge on the interfaced section. Pivot at the point the zipper will end, and sew off the edge. Then position both layers right sides together, and use a ⅝-in. seam allowance to sew the seam below the zipper opening.

2. Clip diagonally into the seam allowances at the zipper base. Press the triangles formed at the zipper base to the

wrong side under the seam allowance. Press the seam allowance open below the zipper. Turn the zipper seam allowance to the right side along the staystitching, and press.

3. Position the zipper, right side up, on the garment right side, so it's centered over the seam. Hand-baste the zipper tape to the seam allowances close to the teeth.

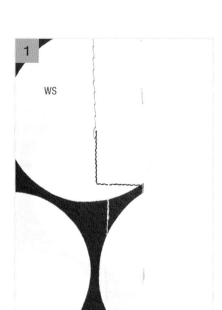

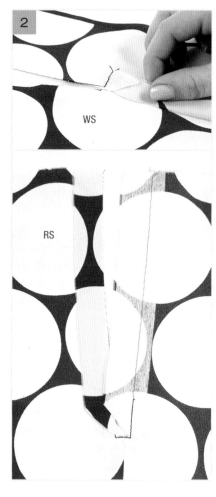

Turn under the bottom ends of the zipper tape.

4. Install a zipper foot on the machine, and sew the zipper tape to the seam allowance as basted, close to the zipper teeth.

5. Trim away the seam allowance that extends beyond the zipper tape.

6. Working with a zipper foot, edgestitch the zipper in place from top to bottom along each side. Sew across the zipper base to secure.

LAPPED ZIPPER

A lapped zipper is sewn so that the zipper is completely hidden beneath a lap of fabric. It's often found in the side seam of skirts and pants and in the center backs of skirts and dresses. When you want to conceal the zipper completely, but don't have or can't use an invisible zipper (for example, with very bulky or textured fabrics), use a lapped application.

1. Mark each side of the seam opening along the ⅝-in. seamline for the length of the zipper (here, basting was used). Then, with right sides together, sew the seam below the zipper opening.

2. Turn the garment right side up. Along the zipper opening, press the right seam allowance under ½ in. (the fold doesn't fall on the basted line). Press the left seam allowance under ⅝ in., along the thread mark.

3. Place the zipper right side up under the ½-in. seam allowance. Position the folded edge next to the teeth. Baste or pin it in place. Use a zipper foot to sew from the zipper top to the bottom through all layers, stitching just to the left of the basting line and ending slightly below the top of the sewn seam.

4. From the right side, with the garment flat, position the fabric so that the thread marks on each side are aligned. Fold the left (lap) side over the right side, exposing the seam allowance and the free zipper tape. Baste through the seam allowance and zipper tape.

5. With a fabric-marking tool, draw a topstitching line parallel to the zipper, ⅜ in. from the fold and across the zipper base.

6. Topstitch through all layers down the lap, along the marked line, until you reach the zipper base. Pivot and sew across the zipper base to the seam. Pull the threads to the wrong side and knot. Remove the basting stitches.

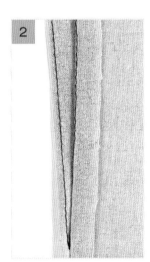

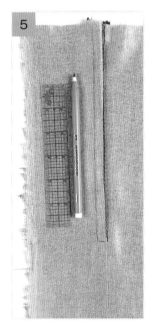
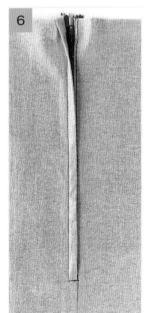

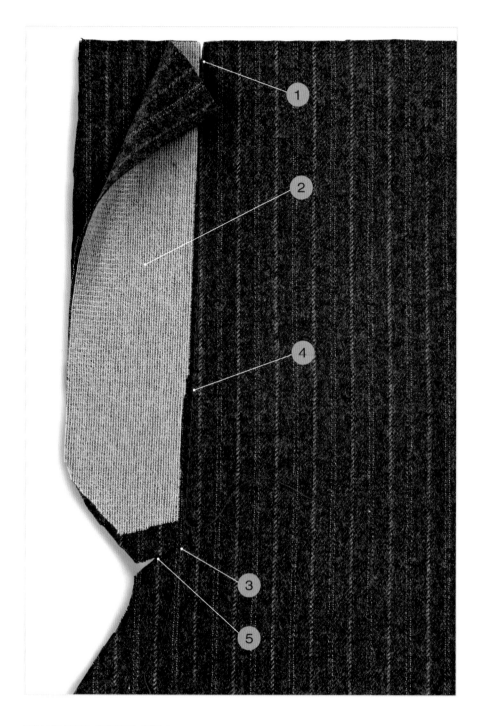

FLY-FRONT ZIPPER

Accurate marking and interfacing are fundamental to smooth, straight fly-front zippers. The zipper shown here includes a zipper guard (fly shield). If your pattern doesn't include a pattern for a zipper guard and you want to include one, cut a rectangle of fabric 4 in. wide by the length of the zipper opening. This zipper laps right over left for a woman's garment. If you prefer the zipper to lap left over right, as in men's trousers, simply reverse these instructions. Start with a zipper that's an inch or two longer than the zipper opening.

Preparing the Zipper Area

1. Snip the seam allowances at the center-front waist. Also mark the zipper end point.

2. Interface the wrong side of the right extension. The left front isn't interfaced.

3. With right sides together, stitch the crotch curve from the inseam to the zipper end point. Backstitch to secure.

4. Machine-baste the center front from the zipper end point to the waistline.

5. Clip both seam allowances to the stitching line at the zipper end point.

Attaching the Zipper

When the zipper-opening area is prepared, clean-finish the raw edges of the fly extensions.

1. Press back the right extension. Keep the left front extension flat on the ironing board as you do so. Place the zipper facedown on the left front extension, with the zipper stop at the zipper end point on the garment and the edge of the right tape butted against the center-front seam. Pin as shown. Move the machine needle to the far-left position, and stitch from bottom to top on the left tape edge. Remove the pins. Note: Excess zipper tape will extend at the top, but don't cut it off just yet.

2. Fold the left extension back, so the zipper is faceup, with its teeth exposed. With the needle still in the far-left position, topstitch from the waist down, as close to the fold as possible.

3. Open the right extension away from the pants, and fold the free zipper tape over the extension, as shown. Stitch the tape in place.

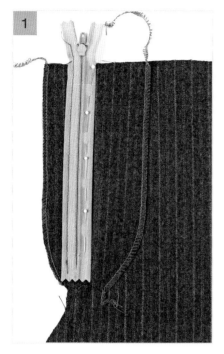

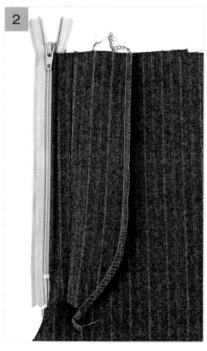

Making a Zipper Guard

A zipper guard protects your undergarments and skin from the zipper teeth.

5. Fold the zipper guard down the center with wrong sides together. Press. Serge or zigzag the cut edges.

6. Open the zipper and lay the garment facedown. Align the extension edge with the finished edge of the guard. The guard bottom should align with the zipper tape and extend to or beyond the waist.

7. From the right side, hold back the overlap. Stitch through all layers of the pant, extension, zipper tape, and zipper guard. Sew from the waist down, with the presser foot edge against the zipper teeth; adjust the needle position to stitch ⅛ in. from the first row of stitching. Note: You don't need to stitch all the way to the zipper bottom.

8. Close the zipper, then bar-tack (use a narrow, short zigzag stitch to make a bar tack) through all layers at the end of the topstitching. Put a second bar tack on the inside to hold the zipper guard in place, through the folded edge of the zipper guard and the left-front extension.

4. Lay the garment faceup, and smooth the layers over the zipper area. Mark the topstitching line on the fly overlap. Set the needle in the center position, and topstitch from the waistline to the bottom of the zipper. Remove the machine basting.

Other Fasteners

Style and function dictate the type of closure you need for a garment. Whether you want the closure to be invisible or decorative (as shown at right), it's important that it be secure. Choose closures that are compatible with the fabric's weight and care requirements, and assess the type of strain that may be present when the garment is worn. Consider the wearer's ability to manipulate closures, too.

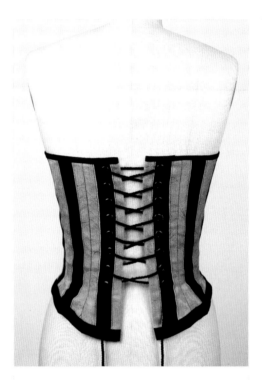

SEWING HOOKS AND EYES

Typically, you'll find hooks and eyes at the top of a zipper closure on dresses or tops, inside fur coats, and on waistbands. To stay closed, most hook-and-eye sets need to be under a small amount of tension, so that the hook is pulled against the eye. If you use a hook on a loose-fitting garment, it's likely to unfasten eventually.

The best way to sew on hooks and eyes properly is with a blanket stitch (see page 286). It doesn't take any more time than other ways, but it is stronger and looks professionally finished. When sewing delicate hooks or snaps, use a single strand of thread. For heavier hooks and eyes, buttonhole-twist-weight thread works well.

Attaching the Hook

Position the hook ⅛ in. or more from the edge for a lapped edge; for waistbands, place it ¼ in. from the edge. For abutted edges, set the hook just far enough from the edge to conceal the eye when the closure is fastened (1/16 in. to ⅛ in.). Check the placement of the hook by sliding the eye through it and gently pulling. If you see the hook, move it farther in from the edge.

Holding the hook in place, take several stitches through the hook end to anchor it. Tug the hook's eyelets gently to seat the hook securely in the stitches. Then, sew both eyelets in position using a blanket stitch.

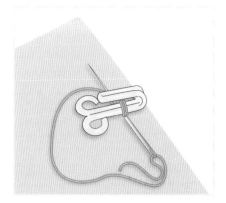

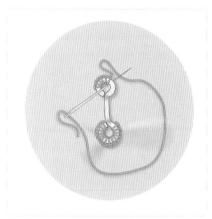

Attaching the Eye

The shape of the eye depends on the configuration of the closure: For an overlapping edge, use a straight eye; for abutting edges, use a round eye.

OVERLAPPING EDGES

Arrange the garment overlap as desired. Insert a pin in the wrong side of the underlap, and slide its point through the hook and back through to the underlap wrong side, to form a temporary "eye." Unhook the hook from the pin, and use the pin as a marker for the placement of the loop (bar). Most loops are slightly curved to receive the hook more securely. Identify which way yours curves, and position it so that the hook goes through the inward-curving side.

Sew the loop (bar) with a blanket stitch.

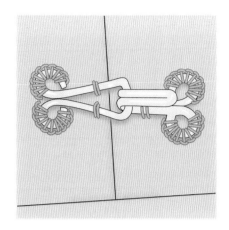

ABUTTING EDGES

To position the eye, align the garment edges evenly and mark with a pin where the center of the hook abuts the opposite edge. Sew the eye on so that it projects very slightly beyond the edge, using a blanket stitch to attach the eyelets. Finally, anchor the sides of the eye, as shown, with a few stitches.

Marking and Sewing Waistband Hooks

For a waistband, take two stitches on the wrong side of the overlap, ¼ in. from the opening edge. Bring the needle up through the hook's upper eyelet and work a blanket stitch. Sew the remaining eyelets in the same way. Zip the garment closed and arrange the overlap as desired. Mark the position of the bar on the underlap with pins and stitch the bar in place.

APPLYING SNAPS

Snaps take many forms, including standard functional snaps that are meant to be hidden, decorative snaps that come in many colors, and snap tape.

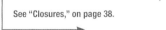

See "Closures," on page 38.

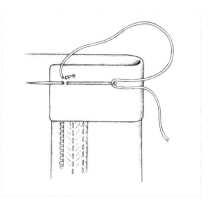

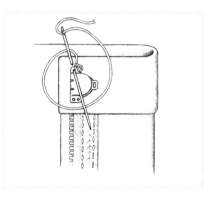

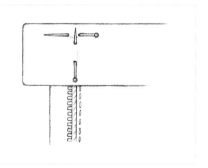

TIP

You can purchase hook-and-eye tape by the yard: This fastener comprises two strips of cotton twill tape, with hooks on one strip and eyes on the other. It's intended for use in garments with abutting edges, and is useful as a closure for inner structures, such as corselets. Fold the raw edges of the opening to the wrong side, and edgestitch the tape to the garment opening.

Snaps are easy to use as a garment fastener—they close and open with a pinch or a tug. However, they can't take the tension that hooks and eyes need, so they're best for use on loose-fitting garments, or in low-stress areas, such as the inside of a coat or jacket, pocket openings, or to attach a removable trim.

As with hooks and eyes, snaps look better and stay on longer when sewn with a blanket stitch. Choose a thread weight that's compatible with the size of the snap, and work with a single strand of thread.

Attaching Sew-on Snaps

1. Bring the needle up from the fabric's wrong side, and through one snap hole. Stitch into the fabric and through the hole again, making a loop. Don't pull the loop tight yet.

2. Bring the needle up through the loop from the back, and draw the thread away from the snap to pull the loop closed.

3. Make three or more stitches per hole. When you've finished one hole, run the needle to the next one, as shown at right. Make a stitch to create a loop, and then repeat the blanket stitches as before.

TIP

To make sure the socket part of the snap is properly positioned to meet the stud part, position and install the stud first. Then, apply chalk to the stud. Arrange the garment layers as desired, and press the chalked stud against the garment where the socket will go. The chalk will transfer to the fabric, indicating exactly where to place the socket.

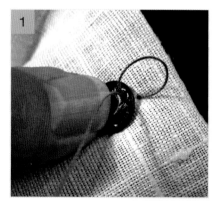

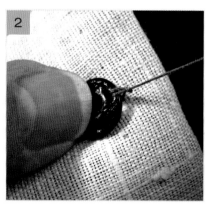

Decorative Snaps

Also called gripper snaps, these decorative snaps (page 42) are hardware that's meant to be permanent. They're applied with a hammer or setting tool, the pressure from which forces the metal components of the snap together. Because the post or prongs penetrate through all the fabric layers, the snaps are visible on both sides of the garment; choose decorative styles and make them a design feature. Be sure to interface the garment in the snap location.

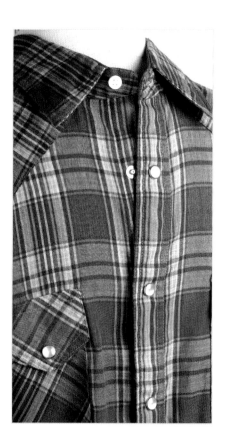

GRIPPER SNAPS

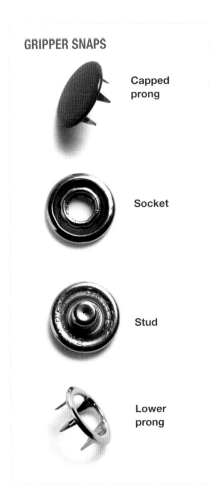

Capped prong

Socket

Stud

Lower prong

Gripper snaps come in two basic types: those with a post, and those with prongs. The snap found most often on ready-to-wear, medium- to heavyweight garments is a post snap, which has a shaft, or post, requiring a hole in the fabric for insertion. You'll find prong snaps on light- to medium-weight items like infants' and children's clothing, cotton shirts, and knit fabrics. These snaps, when removed, leave teeth marks or holes in the fabric.

To attach gripper snaps, use a snap-setting tool (usually the one you purchased with your snaps), and follow the included instructions. Tools vary from heavy-duty pliers to a setting device that you pound with a hammer. For post snaps, you'll first need to punch a small hole using an awl or

another tool, then push the cap's post through the hole, add the socket piece, and crush the post as instructed.

Snap Tape

Snap tape features snaps attached to cotton tape. It is often found on the inseam of infants' and toddlers' clothing, but it sometimes occurs in edgy designer garments. Use it when you need to apply several evenly spaced snaps in a row. Snap tape is sold in white and black; if desired, you can dye the tape to match your fabric.

Snap tape requires a lapped application and is edgestitched to the garment edges, which have been folded back (the fold-back should be wider than the snap tape for greater strength), or faced. A zipper foot makes it easier to stitch around the snap sections.

HOOK-AND-LOOP TAPE

Hook-and-loop tape requires a lapped opening, like snap tape. You can apply it as tape or as precut squares or dots, depending on the location and the amount of security needed. Avoid using it on lightweight or sheer fabrics, as it stiffens the closure area and can show through even multiple fabric layers.

For sew-on tape, fold back the garment edges so they are slightly wider than the tape (or use a facing). Position the hook section of the tape on the underlap and stitch around the perimeter, through all the layers. Align the loop section over the hook section and pin it in place. Stitch as for the first piece. If you don't want the machine stitches to show on the garment overlap, attach the loop section by hand, anchoring it to the facing or fold-back. To apply fusible tape, follow

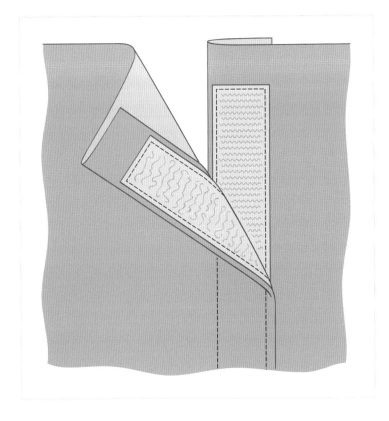

TIP

If you are sewing individual squares or dots, don't try to sew around the perimeter. Instead, stitch a square, an X, or a star pattern through the fastener center.

the package instructions; make a test swatch first to see if the tape alters the hand of the fabric unacceptably.

BUCKLES

Buckles are simple to attach to a garment or accessory. There must be a strap to wrap around the bar; this can be made of fabric, leather, or trim. If there's also a prong, punch a hole, or sew or install an eyelet in the strap. Fold the strap over the bar, and topstitch across through all layers to anchor the buckle.

GROMMETS/EYELETS AND LACING

Holes, whether reinforced by a metal grommet or not, and lacings were one of the earliest closure methods, dating back to the time of primitive society. Today, eyelets and grommets are used to create reinforced holes for lacings and can be used for casual and specialty closures.

See "Grommets, Eyelets, and Lacing," on page 43.

To create lacing, use purchased cording, or make your own fabric-covered cording and thread it through the grommets to close the garment.

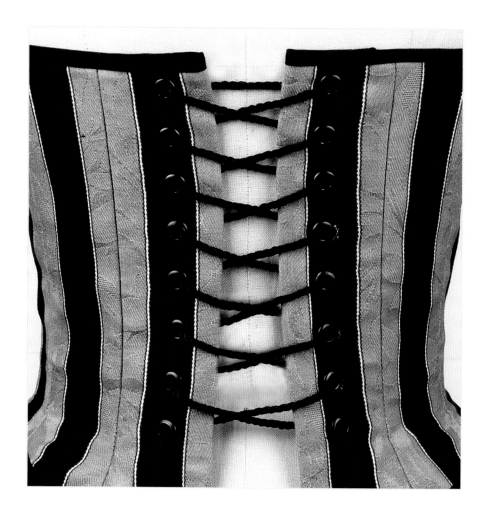

Setting Grommets/Eyelets

Consider purchasing setting pliers or a setting press if you'll be setting a lot of grommets or eyelets. Otherwise the setting tool that usually comes in the package and a rubber mallet are all you need. Prepare the garment by interfacing the area where the grommets will be set, and punching holes (setting tools and grommets often come with a hole-punching tool as well).

SETTING A TWO-PIECE GROMMET/EYELET

A two-piece grommet has a washer on the wrong side, so the fabric is sandwiched between two metal rings for a strong, smooth-edged opening.

Place the grommet in the cradle with the barrel facing up, so that it can pass through the precut hole in the fabric. Slide the washer over the barrel, sandwiching the fabric between them. Insert the setting device through the washer. It will spread and curl the barrel end over the washer, compressing and attaching the grommet and washer when you apply pressure with the mallet.

SETTING A ONE-PIECE GROMMET/EYELET

A one-piece eyelet doesn't have a washer on the reverse side. Its barrel is split into several sections, so that when the eyelet is set, the sections flare out around the hole on the wrong side,

SETTING A TWO-PIECE GROMMET

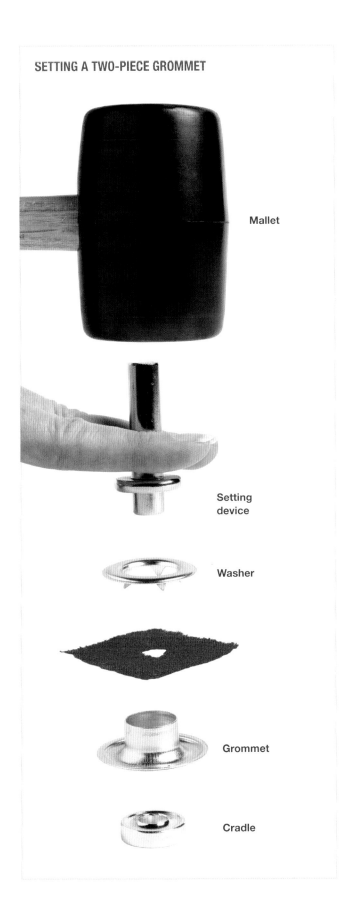

Mallet

Setting
device

Washer

Grommet

Cradle

like the petals of a flower. These eyelets appear less finished than a two-piece grommet, and can abrade the lacings as well as the wearer's skin. The setting tool spreads the barrel over the cut edge of the fabric (and not over a washer). Again, you need to precut a small hole.

Tailoring

ailoring is an approach to garment sewing that relies on special materials and techniques to mold the fabric into a three-dimensional garment. Inner materials support and stabilize the fabric, while pad stitching and steam pressing shape it. A well-tailored garment fits and flatters, and can last for years without sagging, bagging, drooping, or hanging limply. As you'll see in this chapter, support fabrics, stabilizing with interfacing and tape, pad stitching properly, and more all come into play when you take a tailored approach to garment sewing.

CHARACTERISTICS OF A TAILORED GARMENT

Tailored garments are typically made of high-quality, natural-fiber fabrics, especially wool; these materials are easy to shape with the application of steam. Garments with notched collars and lapels are usually fully tailored because these design elements are best constructed using tailoring methods.

Interfacing—often several different types at different locations on the garment—is a necessity in tailoring. Under- and interlinings may be applied in addition to interfacing to add body or warmth to the fashion fabric. Finally, every tailored garment is finished with a full lining. The lining conceals all the inner workings that help the garment keep its shape, and prolongs the life of the garment while also making it more comfortable to wear.

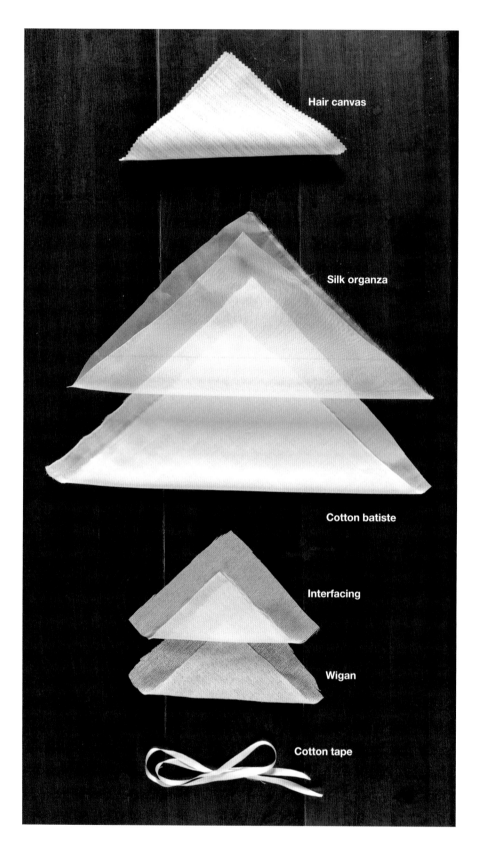

Hair canvas

Silk organza

Cotton batiste

Interfacing

Wigan

Cotton tape

SUPPORT FABRICS

Tailoring techniques build shape by using malleable natural fibers with interfacing, pad stitching (by hand or machine), and pressing to control the fabric. The process starts with the application of support and stabilizing materials, in the form of interfacing and tapes.

A tailored garment usually calls for several types of interfacing, which performs different functions. There's a wide variety of both fusible and sew-in interfacings that are suited to tailoring, so you can choose products in a weight and color that's compatible with the fashion fabric.

Hair Canvas

Also called tailor's canvas or Hymo, this sew-in product is the sturdiest interfacing available. It comes in many fiber blends, including wool/goat hair, which is well-suited to using in wool garments. It can be used in the front of a jacket or at the hem.

Silk Organza

This fabric is the sheerest and lightest fabric used for interfacing and stabilization. It can be torn easily into strips. In tailoring, organza and batiste can be used interchangeably.

Cotton Batiste

As light as organza but more stable, this fabric provides virtually invisible support. Be sure to preshrink it before use.

Interfacing

The fusible and sew-in interfacings you use for any sewing project are appropriate for tailoring as well. Knit interfacings are best for soft tailoring applications, while wovens are a better choice when more stability is needed.

Wigan

A stiff, loosely woven, lightweight fabric made of cotton or a cotton blend, wigan is typically sold as a 2-in.- to 4-in.-wide bias-cut tape, and comes in fusible and sew-in varieties. It's used for stabilizing armscyes, necklines, and hemlines.

Cotton Tape

This sturdy, thin, straight-grain tape (also sold in a twill version) is good for

concentrated support and bulk-free stability along roll lines, foldlines, or seamlines.

STABILIZING WITH INTERFACING

Garments tend to wear out in high-stress areas. Plan ahead and reinforce these areas during construction so you won't have to mend them later.

Buttons and Buttonholes

Apply a patch of fusible interfacing or organza at the button and buttonhole locations on the fabric's wrong side. You'll have to determine where you want the buttons very early in the construction process; use a muslin test garment or tissue-fit the pattern to place the buttons.

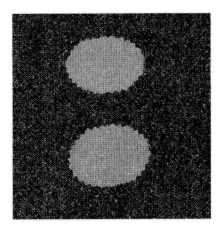

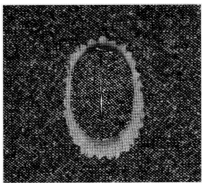

Pockets

Stabilize pockets anywhere you'll be sewing them or cutting an opening. Use a strip of fusible interfacing, silk organza, or cotton batiste that is 1 in. larger on all sides than the cutting or stitching line. Fuse it at the pocket location on the fabric's wrong side, or hand-baste it in place.

Sleeve Caps

Interface the cap with a piece of bias-cut interfacing. Begin at the notches and extend the strip 2 in. to 3 in. down from the top of the sleeve in a curved shape. This prevents the sleeve cap from collapsing and smooths out any puckers in the armscye seam. Depending on the garment fabric, choose a fusible or sew-in woven for this purpose.

TIP

WHAT EXACTLY IS HAIR CANVAS?

This woven interfacing (sew-in or fusible), sometimes referred to as Hymo or tailor's canvas, is traditionally used by tailors to shape and support jacket fronts, lapels, and collars. Preshrink the canvas by soaking it in hot water for 20 minutes, let the water cool, then air- or machine-dry. It's available in black, white, natural, or gray and in a variety of weights and widths.

Zippers

Cut two strips of fusible interfacing, silk organza, or cotton batiste 1 in. wide by the length of the zipper plus 2 in. Fuse or hand-baste them at each side of the zipper opening on the fabric's wrong side.

Hems

Use a strip of bias fusible interfacing between the hem allowance or facing and the body of the garment. For heavy wool garments, use hair canvas.

Jacket Front and Back Shoulder Area

A piece of cotton batiste or interfacing applied to a jacket back supports the fabric over the shoulder blades. A piece of hair canvas (as shown on page 261) for interfacing ensures a smooth line from shoulder to bust.

STABILIZING WITH TAPE

Stabilizing tapes are used to prevent stretching along edges, foldlines, and seamlines, sometimes alone and sometimes in conjunction with other interfacings. With lightweight fabrics in particular, test the tape to be sure that it doesn't stiffen seams and foldlines excessively.

To support with tape, cut cotton tape to the length of the seam, or slightly shorter if indicated, and include it as you sew the seam. Ease the fabric onto the tape as necessary to ensure that the final seam is exactly the correct length and won't stretch out over time.

V-Neckline in a Blouse or Jacket

To keep the bias edge of a V-neckline from stretching during handling and wear, cut the tape about ¼ in. shorter than the seamline as measured on the pattern. You can cut the tape even shorter if the neckline tends to gape over the bust. Ease the neckline onto the tape so that the garment hugs the body.

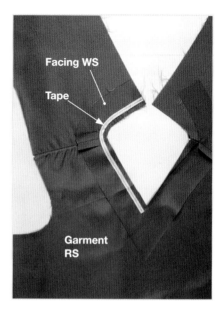

Underarm Curve

Once you've set the sleeve, add tape to the underarm curve, between the notches, to stabilize this bias section as shown above. In a sleeveless garment with facing, once you've sewn the shoulder seam and side seam, add tape around the entire armhole in the seam that joins the facing to the armscye.

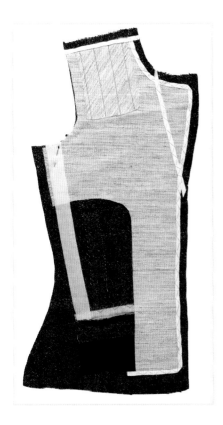

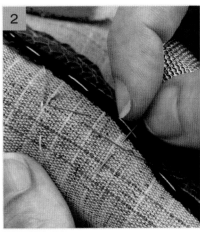

Jacket Neck, Front Seam, Shoulders, and Roll Line

Add tape to a jacket front and back neck seamlines if the neck is finished with a facing rather than a collar. Reinforce the shoulder seams with a strip of tape. Tape the center-front seam if the fabric is lightweight; you can apply tape just below the lapel or to the entire seam. Use tape to stabilize the roll line on a jacket with lapels, as this fold is on the bias and can stretch out of shape. Cut the tape ¼ in. to ½ in. shorter than the roll line on the pattern, and ease the garment front to match.

PAD STITCHING

Pad stitching consists of rows of short, even, diagonal stitches arranged in chevron rows, used to fasten canvas interfacing to the lapel, undercollar, and front shoulder area of a coat or jacket,

giving these garment components three-dimensional shape. It enables the fashion fabric and canvas interfacing to behave as one while maintaining their individual characteristics.

For pad stitching to effectively create a curved shape, you must softly drape the fabric and interfacing layers together over your hand as you stitch. This accommodates the shift in alignment of the two layers that occurs when the lapel is folded back.

The orientation of the stitching rows and the sequence in which you work is dictated by the piece you are shaping. Generally, the rows run parallel to the collar or lapel roll line, and you work from the roll line out.

Sewing Pad Stitching

Work with fine cotton or silk thread in a color that matches the garment fabric. Select a short, size 6 sharps needle. Cut the thread into 36-in. lengths (longer lengths snarl). Draw each length through beeswax three times, then iron it lightly, or pull it between your thumb and index finger to set the wax. Thread the needle.

1. Lay canvas interfacing on the wrong side of the garment section, and pin- or thread-baste along the seamlines. Mark the roll line by basting a piece of temporary stay tape to it (shown here in black). To reduce bulk, trim the canvas seam allowances to ¼ in.

2. Insert the threaded needle into the interfacing to anchor the knot, then take a loose diagonal stitch. Pick up only a thread or two of the fashion fabric, and come up below the first stitch, as shown.

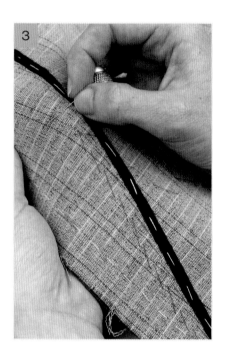

Continue to make diagonal stitches in a vertical row until you reach the bottom of the fabric section (don't pad-stitch into the seam allowance). As you work, curl the garment piece over your left hand to create a softly rolled shape.

3. Without turning the fabric, make diagonal stitches up along the left side of the row, placing each directly opposite a stitch in the previous row, to create a chevron pattern. Continue stitching parallel rows up and down in this manner, spacing the rows about ¼ in. apart, until you cover the entire area. Remove the basting stitches.

When you finish pad stitching, place the garment section on a dress form (or drape it over a tailor's ham) to analyze how the stitched area falls into shape. It may take a few tries to master the trick of molding the garment piece over your hand as you pad-stitch, but you'll soon be skilled at producing a fully supported, softly rolled shape.

NOTCHED LAPELS

The key to making a perfect notch for notched lapels is mastering the pivot point on the lapel's inside corner where all of the collar and body pieces join. In classic tailoring, you cut an undercollar piece to join to the body of the jacket, and an upper collar piece to join to the facing. These four pieces (under- and

Pad-Stitch Direction Matters

The direction of the pad-stitch rows helps determine the way the garment section folds or curves. Follow the guidelines below for standard jacket construction.

LAPEL FOLLOWS ITS ROLL LINE

Create a softly rolled lapel by pad stitching in rows that run parallel to the roll line. Begin at the roll line and work toward the front edge.

THE UNDERCOLLAR FOLLOWS ITS ROLL LINE

Maintain the stretch of an undercollar bias grain, and allow for easy molding with an iron by pad stitching the undercollar in two parts. First, use smaller stitches (about ½ in.) and work in parallel rows from the roll line to the neckline edge. Then use slightly larger stitches and work in parallel rows from the roll line to the collar's outer edge. Work the chevrons in opposite directions above and below the roll line.

THE SHOULDER FOLLOWS THE CROSS-GRAIN

Support the front shoulder/armhole area with a pad-stitched interfacing that follows the body's curve. Pad-stitch parallel rows along the cross-grain of the canvas. Begin at the shoulder and work to the lower edge of the interfacing, extending each row to the armscye or side seam.

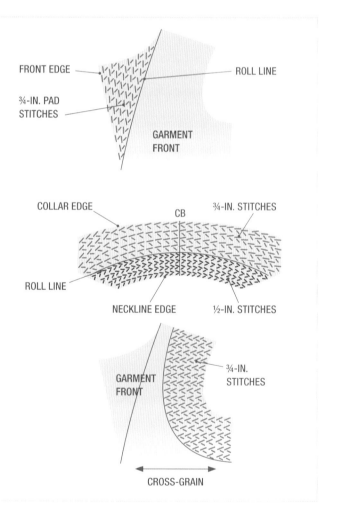

FRONT EDGE — ROLL LINE
¾-IN. PAD STITCHES
GARMENT FRONT

COLLAR EDGE — CB — ¾-IN. STITCHES
ROLL LINE
NECKLINE EDGE — ½-IN. STITCHES

GARMENT FRONT — ¾-IN. STITCHES
CROSS-GRAIN

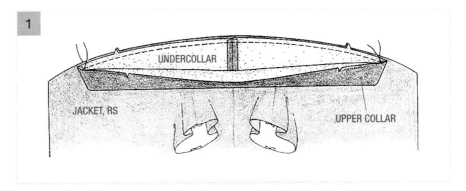

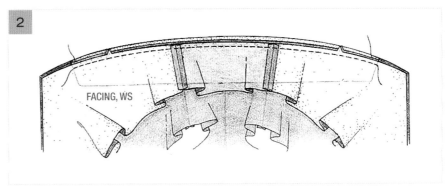

upper collars, jacket body, and facing) are sewn together, so there are several seam allowances crowded together at that inner corner. To perfect that inner corner, trim, clip, and press the seam allowances carefully throughout the construction process.

The notched-lapel technique shown here is based on a method used in the garment industry, and is suitable for use with all fabric weights. Begin by interfacing the upper and undercollars, and the facings. Join the upper and undercollar pieces, shaping the finished piece as described for a rolled collar (see page 188), then grade, clip, and press open the seam allowances.

1. Attach the undercollar to the neck edge of the jacket, matching notches and marks. Stitch as close as possible to each end of the collar, within at least ¼ in.

2. Attach the upper collar to the facing neck edge, matching notches and marks.

3. Attach the front edges of the facing to the jacket, from the hem to the lapel corner. Clip into the seam allowances at the bottom end of the roll line. Grade the seam allowances, with the wider allowance on the garment below the clip, and on the facing above the clip.

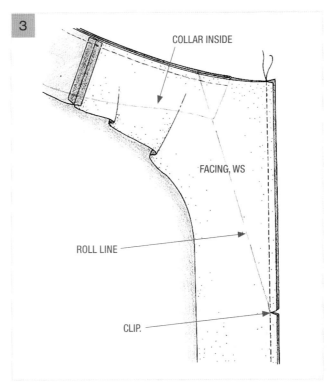

Understitch the seam allowances to the facing below the clip, and to the garment front above the clip.

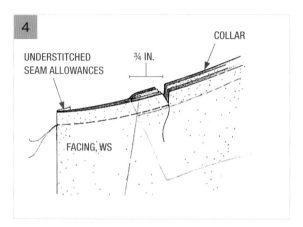

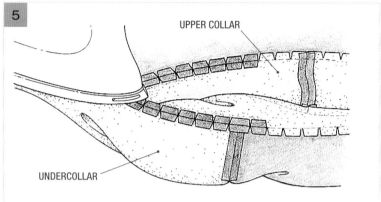

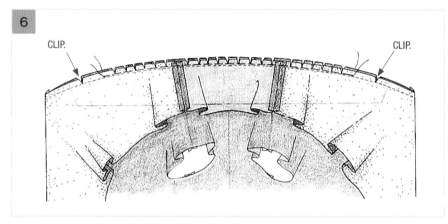

4. Sew across the top edge of the lapel from the corner to the end of the collar, stitching over the collar/neckline seam about ¾ in. on each end. Clip through all the layers to the seamline, exactly where you stopped stitching.

5. Working over a point presser, press open the collar/facing and collar/jacket seam allowances, between the clips you made in step 4. Clip the seam allowances as needed so you can press them flat.

6. Join the lower seam allowances of the jacket and facing necklines across the back, leaving about 1½ in. free at each end between the clips you made in step 4.

TAILORED HEMS

A tailored hem is supported by two separate layers of interfacing to make an edge that's firm, yet flexible, and curves around the body without any dips, folds, or puckers. To create a tailored hem, you need a strip of wigan (or bias-cut hair canvas), some lightweight, fusible interfacing, a hand needle, and thread. You can use this technique in closely woven medium- or heavyweight fabrics, such as wool suiting or coating, as well as lightweight fabrics with body, such as linen, silk, or tweed.

Before you cut out and construct the garment, make sure a 2-in. hem allowance is included. If it isn't, adjust the pattern as necessary. Construct the garment as usual, then follow the hemming steps that follow.

1. Cut lightweight, fusible interfacing the length of the hem and 3 in. wide. Place it on the garment's wrong side, with the bottom edge 1½ in. above the raw edge, and fuse.

2. Mark the hem foldline with running basting stitches. Press up the hem along the basted line.

3. Cut a 2½-in.-wide strip of wigan, or a bias strip of tailor's canvas the length of the hem. Slip the canvas between the hem allowance and garment, with the edge butted up against the hem fold. Use a diagonal basting stitch to baste the canvas only to the hem allowance.

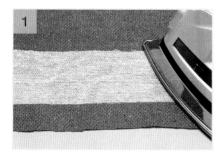

4. Fold the hem allowance and wigan strip back, and catchstitch these two layers to the garment, stitching only through the fusible interfacing on the garment.

Place the row of catchstitching at least ½ in. below the raw edge of the hem allowance, so that you can attach the lining later to the free edge. Remove the basting stitches.

See "Catchstitch," on page 284.

The hem allowance edge is left unfinished to ensure a flat finish. The canvas and interfacing show ½ in. above the hem allowance, which provides a buffer between the top of the hem and the body of the garment so you don't see a ridge on the outside. These edges will be hidden by the lining.

UNDERLINING AND INTERLINING

Underlining and interlining are both interior layers of fabric placed beneath the fashion fabric. The terms are sometimes used interchangeably, but the functions of interlining and underlining are different.

Underlining is layered behind the fashion fabric to improve the look, feel, and functionality of the fabric. It provides body, opacity, and support for longer wear and a more professional appearance. Construction details can be attached to the underlining without evidence of them showing on the garment outside. Typical underlining fabrics include cotton batiste, cotton flannelette, wool flannel or felt, rayon challis, or, for nearly weightless support, silk organza.

Interlining is a layer of fabric added to the garment lining for warmth and insulation. Cotton flannel is a favorite

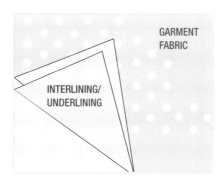

for interlining, but you can use wool or synthetic batting that's made specifically for this purpose; these add more warmth with less weight.

Securing the Interlining or Underlining

Interlinings and underlinings are applied to the wrong side of the fabric, and then the two layers are treated as one. Underlining is applied to the fashion fabric, while interlining is usually applied to the lining. These instructions refer to underlining but the process is the same for attaching interlining to the lining fabric.

1. Cut out an inter- or underlining piece for each pattern piece needed. Then transfer the markings, including the grainline, onto the underlining. Baste the underlining to the fashion or lining fabric. Lay the fabric right side down on a table in a single thickness. Lay the underlining pieces on the fabric's wrong side with the markings facing up, aligning the grainlines properly along the fabric's grain. Smooth the layers, and pin them together in the seam allowances. Working with a fine silk thread or a rayon machine-embroidery thread, baste the underlining pieces to the fashion fabric about ¾ in. inside the stitching lines.

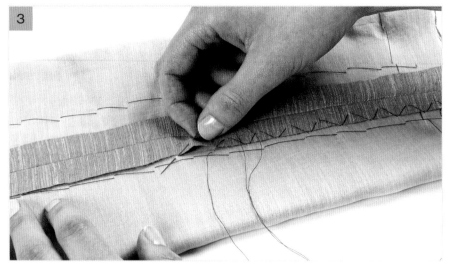

2. Once all of the under- or interlining pieces are basted to the fabric, cut the fabric, using the underlining pieces as a cutting guide. The fashion fabric pieces now match the underlining pieces perfectly.

Construct the garment following the pattern instructions, and treating each underlined piece as a single unit. To prevent the fabric and underlining layers from creeping or shifting as you machine-sew the seams, attach a walking foot to your sewing machine.

See "Presser Feet," on page 10.

3. After you've pressed the seam allowances open, use a catchstitch to tack the seam allowances to the underlining layer only.

UNDERLINING A GARMENT WITH SILK ORGANZA

Underlining a garment with organza adds support, crispness, or slight weight to a fabric. It supports lightweight or limp fabrics for tailored styles, stabilizes loosely woven fabrics to prevent sagging or stretching, and adds opaqueness to sheer or light-colored fabrics.

Underlining linen with organza helps reduce wrinkling. It allows construction details like hem stitches to be concealed from the outside of a garment, because you stitch only to the organza and not through to the fashion fabric.

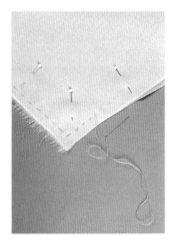

Shoulder Pads

The main role of shoulder pads is to support a garment and prevent sagging at the shoulders and through the upper torso. They are important for adding shape and structure, and they affect the way that a garment fits, hangs, and looks on the body. Even a small pad can make a difference. Tailored jackets and coats usually require set-in tailor's shoulder pads to hold their structure. In some cases, a firmly shaped raglan pad can be used, even if the garment has set-in sleeves.

SELECTING SHOULDER PADS

Shoulder pads come in many shapes and sizes. Firmer, larger pads are best for jackets and coats made of heavy fabrics. Small, lightweight, soft pads are better suited to knits, blouses, and dresses. If the garment is designed to have shoulder pads, the pattern envelope indicates the type and thickness of the pad. However, you can adjust the size if desired. Thicker shoulder pads can solve a fitting issue if your shoulders slope more than the pattern does, for example.

The two basic types of shoulder pads, set-in and raglan, are available either covered or uncovered and in sizes and thicknesses from ¼ in. to 1½ in.

Set-in Shoulder Pads

A set-in shoulder pad has one straight edge, which corresponds to a garment's armscye seam, and a curved edge, which arcs toward the neck. Its thickest part is at the armscye. Set-in pads that are specifically designed for jackets and coats (commonly called tailor's shoulder pads) are generally larger in front than

used in blouses, dresses, and less-tailored jackets are usually symmetrically balanced front and back.

Raglan Shoulder Pads

Raglan shoulder pads are more oval in shape, rounded at the armscye edge, and slightly molded to fit over the shoulder point. Thus, the thickest part of a raglan pad is in the center. Although raglan pads are designed for garments in which there's no armscye seam (raglan, dolman, or kimono styles) or the armscye seam is dropped below the shoulder point, they're versatile and can

be used with a set-in sleeve as well, to smooth out the top of the sleeve.

Shoulder Pad Materials

Most shoulder pads are made from cotton or polyester batting, needlepunched felt, or foam, and they're usually covered in lightweight lining fabric or tricot knit. You can also purchase an uncovered pad and cover it with fabric to coordinate with your garment, if the garment is unlined.

Tailor's pads have an additional layer of hair canvas or buckram covering the padding and aren't covered with fabric because the garment's lining will cover the pad.

in back, in order to fill in the hollow of the chest below the shoulder, while the sleeve edge of a tailor's pad is crescent-shaped to follow the shape of the top of the armhole. Smaller pads typically

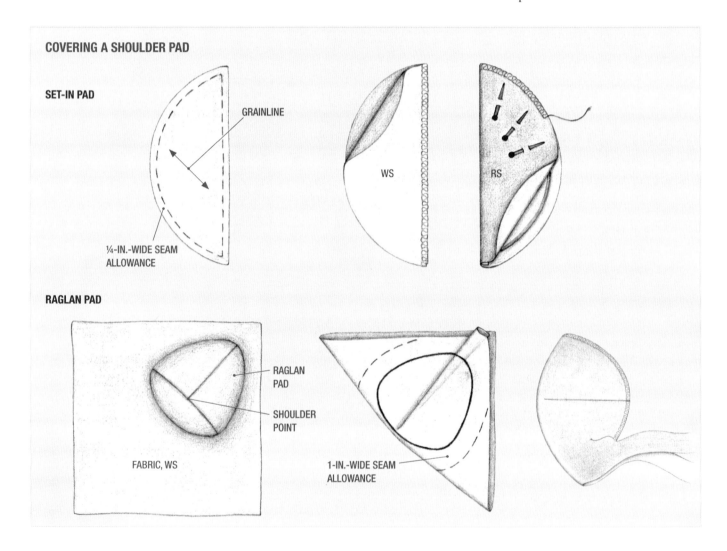

COVERING A SHOULDER PAD

SET-IN PAD

GRAINLINE

¼-IN.-WIDE SEAM ALLOWANCE

WS

RS

RAGLAN PAD

RAGLAN PAD

SHOULDER POINT

FABRIC, WS

1-IN.-WIDE SEAM ALLOWANCE

COVERING SHOULDER PADS

If the garment is unlined, cover the shoulder pads with a lightweight fabric to coordinate with your garment or, for a sheer garment, choose a lining or tricot knit fabric in a color that blends with the wearer's skin tone.

Covering Set-in Pads

To cover a pair of shoulder pads, cut four bias lining pieces the size of the pad, plus ¼-in. seam allowances. With right sides together, sew or serge two pieces along the straight edge.

  With right sides out, fold the cover around the shoulder pad. Pin in place and serge around the curved edge, bottom side up, to maintain shaping.

Covering Raglan Pads

Cut a square of fabric large enough to fold over each pad. Place the pad on the fabric's wrong side and fold the fabric over. Trace around the edge of the pad, allowing a 1-in. margin, and cut out. To shape the cover, form and stitch a dart from the excess fabric on the underside of the cover. Refold the cover over the pad with right sides out, pin in place, and serge around the raw edges.

POSITIONING SHOULDER PADS

Position shoulder pads before sewing them into the garment so they feel comfortable and have no ridges show-ing. If you have narrow shoulders or are working with a wide-necked pattern, trim the thin end of the pad to prevent it from showing at the neck opening.

  For a tailored garment, position set-in pads at least ½ in. from the neck edge and extending ½ in. beyond the armscye seams into the sleeve cap.

Making Set-in Shoulder Pads

When you can't find ready-made shoulder pads that are just right for your garment, it's easy to custom-make your own. Follow these guidelines, using your garment pattern as a guide, or try a commercial shoulder pad pattern. Use bonded, low-loft quilt batting.

1. For a pattern, start with a semicircular shape, approximately 8 in. in diameter, or trace a pattern from the garment pattern as shown, following the shape of the front and back armscye.

8 IN.

BACK

FRONT

2. Cut graduated layers of batting as shown: five for a thick pad, three to four for a thinner pad, eliminating the smallest semicircles. Stack the layers with straight edges even. The largest layer will form the top of the pad, the smallest will be on the bottom.

GRADUATED LAYERS OF BATTING

3. Stitch the layers together by hand, using large stitches and a double strand of thread. Hold the pad over your hand to begin shaping the curve.

4. Pin the pad over a pressing ham or the shoulder of a dress form and steam generously to set the shape. Let the pad dry completely before removing. Cover the pad if desired.

SET-IN PAD

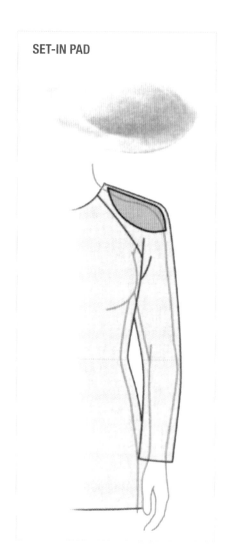

RAGLAN PAD

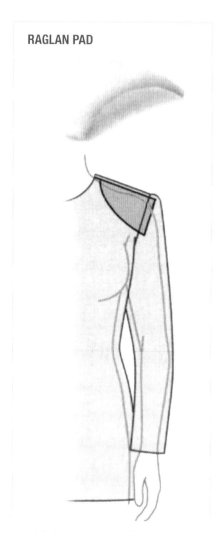

This supports the eased fabric in the sleeve cap. For a dress or blouse, the edge of the pad usually aligns with the armscye seam. Pin the pads in place, then try on the garment and adjust the pads as needed.

Position raglan-style shoulder pads so that they cup around your shoulders and extend slightly onto your arms.

SEWING SHOULDER PADS IN PLACE

Once the pads are correctly positioned, pin them in place from the garment right side along the shoulder seam, and remove the garment. Then stitch each pad in place along the shoulder seam allowance using a cross-stitch or catch-stitch. Don't tack them to the armscye seam allowance because the sleeve may pull up and pucker.

Alternatively, stitch from the outside of the garment, in the ditch of the shoulder seam and through the pad. Small stitches are all but invisible on the garment's right side, and the pad won't budge. Leave the stitching somewhat loose to avoid dimpling the seam.

STITCHING A SHOULDER PAD IN PLACE

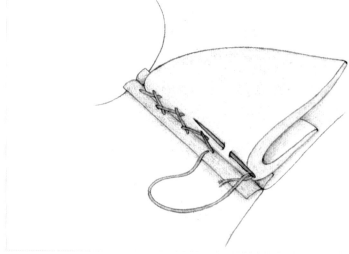

3
Linings

Lining is a functional and luxurious finishing touch to a garment. It covers construction details, makes the garment easy to slip on and off, provides added insulation, prevents wear on the fashion fabric, and generally lends a professional finish. Although it's not always visible, a lining improves the overall quality of anything you sew.

LINING TECHNIQUES

If you are making a tailored garment, lining instructions and pattern pieces are provided in the pattern envelope. However, you can also use a quick and easy ready-to-wear lining method, called bagging, with professional-looking results. Bagging the lining means applying it almost 100 percent by machine (including the sleeves), with minimal or no handwork.

Although bagged jacket and vest linings are most popular, it's possible to bag linings in tops, dresses, skirts, and pants, which more commonly have free-hanging linings. Bagged linings creep less, conceal interior construction and unfinished seam allowances completely, and are quick to apply.

The principles used to bag linings are the same for creating fully reversible garments. In both, the lining is sewn, right sides together, to the outer garment around all the edges, with an opening left for turning the garment right side out. The two crucial points to consider are the location of the opening and the sewing sequence for joining the lining and fashion fabric garment. Whether you're bagging an edge-to-edge lining (as shown in these examples), or one that attaches to facings, the basic sew-and-turn process is the same.

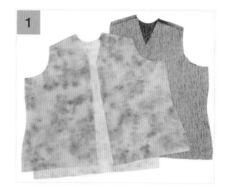

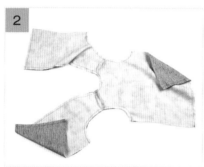

TIP

EASY TURNING

When you leave an opening in a seam to turn the lining through, shorten the stitch length at the beginning of the seam and pivot and sew perpendicular to the seamline and off the raw edge. Repeat at the other end. This helps prevent tearing during the turning process.

Lining a Vest

When lining sleeveless garments, it's easiest to turn them through open side seams. After the layers are joined, you can machine-sew the side seams of the fashion fabric layer and then close the lining side seams by hand or by machine (fold in the seam allowances and sew through all layers close to the folds).

1. Construct the fabric vest and the lining independently, leaving the side seams unsewn on both.

2. With the right sides together, sew the vest to the lining around the neckline, along the center front opening edges, along

the front and back hems, and around the armholes. Trim, grade, clip, and press the seam allowances as needed.

3. Pull the fronts through the shoulders and out one of the open back side seams.

4. With the right sides together, sew the side seams of the fashion fabric layer, keeping the lining free. Turn the garment right side out, press, and hand- or topstitch the lining side seams closed.

Lining a Sleeveless Garment

To line a sleeveless garment without a front or back opening, join the front and back to their linings, attach them at the shoulders and hem, and finish by sewing the side seams.

1. With right sides together, sew the fashion fabric front to the lining front at the armholes, neckline, and hem, leaving the side and shoulder seams open. Repeat for the backs. Trim, grade, clip, and press the seam allowances open. Turn the front section right side out and press the edges.

2. Slip the front section inside the back section, placing the fashion fabric layers and the lining layers right sides together. Push the shoulder straps of the front inside the back straps, and align the shoulder seam allowances. Sew the shoulder seams between the neck seamline and armscye seamline only, turn the garment right side out, and press.

3. With right sides together, sew the side seams of the fashion fabric layer, keeping the lining free. Turn the garment right side out, press, and sew the lining side seams closed by hand or machine.

Lining a Jacket

Bagging a lining for a jacket (or any garment with a front or back opening and sleeves) requires some odd twists and turns to access all the edges. The sleeve hems must be pulled through an opening, to be joined after the bodies are attached at the edges.

1. Assemble the jacket fashion fabric pieces, including any pockets. Assemble the lining, leaving a 6-in. opening in either a side or underarm seam.

2. With the right sides together, stitch the lining to the jacket around the neckline, center front opening, and bottom hem, but leave the sleeve layers separate at the wrist. Trim, grade, clip, and press seam allowances open as needed.

3. Turn the entire garment right side out through the side or underarm opening. Tuck each sleeve lining inside the corresponding fashion fabric sleeve, aligning the underarm seams and pinning them together at the wrist.

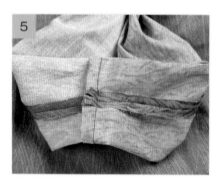

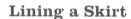

sides pinned together. Remove the pins, taking care not to twist the sleeves out of alignment. Position the sleeve hem openings so they face each other. Keeping the raw edges aligned and the sleeve seams matched, pin the lining and sleeve with right sides together (you may need to fold one edge into a temporary cuff to align them).

Sew the layers together along the wrist hemline (the sleeves will twist as you sew through the doughnut formed by the fashion fabric and lining, but they'll twist back into position when removed from the machine).

Trim, grade, and press the seam allowances open, and pull the sleeve back through the lining and armscye. Repeat these steps for the second sleeve.

5. Sew the opening in the lining closed by hand or by machine (fold in the seam allowances and sew through all the layers close to the folds).

Lining a Skirt

Attach the lining for a basic straight or A-line skirt at the hem, turn the lining to the inside, and finish the garment by adding a waistband, facing, or bias binding.

1. Assemble the skirt fashion fabric pieces according to the pattern instructions, including any zippers or pockets, but don't sew the waist finish or hem. Assemble the lining at all vertical seams, forming unstitched pleats in place of any darts, and leaving an opening corresponding to the length and location of the zipper.

2. With the right sides together, insert the skirt into the lining, aligning the hem edges. Sew around the hem. Press the seam allowances open, then turn the skirt right side out, with the lining inside. Press the hemline flat.

4. Pull one sleeve through the opening in the lining, keeping the layers pinned at the wrist.

The lining and fashion fabric sleeves will emerge side by side, with their wrong

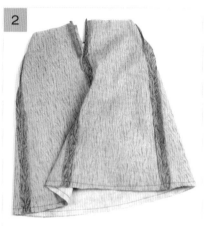

3. On the lining, fold under the zipper opening seam allowance and hand-sew it to the zipper tape. Align the waist edges, baste the layers together if desired, and complete the waistband or facing finish.

Lining and Underlining in One Step

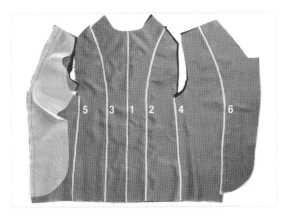

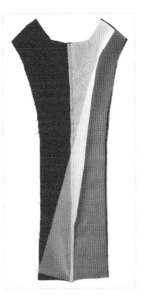

This quick method enables you to incorporate an underlining as you sew the garment's seams, and in such a way that it hides the seam allowances.

Traditional silky linings, organza, flannel, and batiste are suitable lining fabrics for this technique. For both lining and fashion fabric, avoid heavy or lofty fabrics; the seam allowances are pressed together and to one side, so heavier fabrics can create bulk.

Clean-finish facing edges, armscye, and sleeve cap seam allowances. Collars, facings, plackets, and cuffs should be interfaced as usual. Consider using a slightly lighter interfacing than normal for facings, since the underlining on the body of the garment adds a layer of fabric in faced areas.

Once you've underlined the garment body following the directions here, set in the sleeves, and attach any collars, facings, or cuffs, then sew the hems.

PREPARE THE PATTERN PIECES

Cut the fashion fabric and underlining fabric, using the major pattern pieces for both. You don't need underlining fabric for facings, collars, pockets, or cuffs. Interface the fashion fabric as needed, and complete any surface details such as darts, pockets, or embellishments before lining.

BEGIN AT THE CENTER BACK SEAM

Stack the back pieces of fashion fabric, right sides together, with center back seam allowances aligned. Do the same with the underlining pieces, then lay these on top of the fashion fabric. Pin, then sew all four layers together along the center back seamline. Trim all the seam allowances to a scant ¼ in. and press them flat, as sewn. Open out the fashion fabric and press the seam allowances to one side as shown at top right.

TOPSTITCH TO ANCHOR THE UNDERLINING

Open out the underlining fabric so that one layer covers the seam allowances, and press in place. From the garment right side, topstitch the underlining to secure it to the fashion fabric, and to enclose and cover the center back seam allowances as shown above.

COMPLETE THE REMAINING SEAMS

Working from the center back toward the front, sew subsequent seams in the same way, in the sequence shown top left (adjust as needed to the number of seams in the garment). Then sew the shoulder seams conventionally and clean-finish the seam allowances.

Bust Support & Boning

itting a bodice that is strapless, is off-the-shoulder, or has only the skinniest of straps involves engineering support that works from the waist up, rather than the shoulder down. A snugly fitted waist stay, in combination with vertical boning in the bodice, provides a structure that stays up on its own. The extra steps you take to sew a special occasion dress are well worth the time for a gown that reflects your taste exactly and fits your figure perfectly.

SUPPORT FOR STRAPLESS GOWNS

A strapless dress is supported from the waist, not the top of the bosom. A waist stay, combined with boning and a snug bodice, holds up a strapless gown.

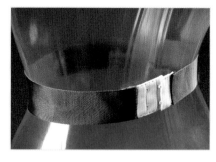

Making a Waist Stay

A waist stay is a firm band of ribbon or elastic attached to the interior of a dress. It provides support and stability, and anchors boning or tension systems to hold a dress in place. Even dresses that don't have boning can sometimes benefit from a waist stay. It can support the weight of a skirt on a light bodice, and can prevent the bodice from being pulled down.

To make a waist stay, cut 1-in.- to 1½-in.-wide grosgrain ribbon or nonroll elastic to fit snugly around the waist. Sew bra extenders (multi-hook fasteners that you can purchase in the notions department of a fabric store) to each end for an adjustable closure. Sew the waist stay inside the gown, tacking it at the side seams through the lining to the fashion fabric seam allowance or to the boning, if present. Fasten the stay before the dress is zipped.

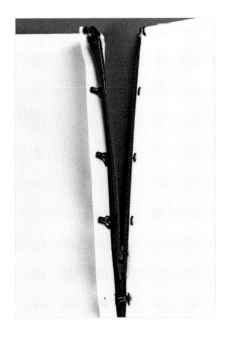

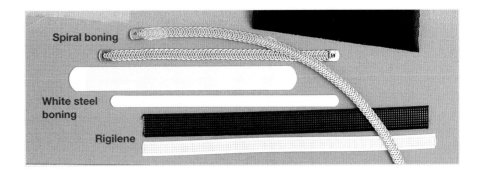

Reinforcing a Zipper

Because it's tightly fitted, a strapless dress places extra stress on the zipper. Sometimes, if the bodice is really tight, you can see the teeth, or, even worse, the tension can cause the zipper to separate. As a precautionary measure, sew hooks and thread eyes every 1½ in. down the zipper and under the flap. If the zipper separates, the dress will always be secure.

BONING

Boning is a stiff yet pliable band that comes in various materials, and in widths of ¼ in. or ½ in. Boning is usually sold in ½-in. increments or by the yard, and is inserted between the structural layers of a strapless bodice, or to an internal corselet (a separate but attached foundation piece that supports a strapless dress). Even a single piece of boning placed on each side seam can make a world of difference in the fit of a dress.

Depending on the type of boning you use, you simply need to sew a casing (purchased or self-made bias tape makes great casings) or a channel of fabric in the underlining for the bone to slide into. Rigilene® (see above) is a sew-through boning that doesn't require a casing. You can apply the casings through all the fabric layers, resulting in visible topstitching on the garment exterior, or to the inner layers only, for invisible support.

Ideally, boning is inserted during construction, but you can add boning afterward as well. When inserting a bone, check that it doesn't extend into the intersecting seam allowances. If it does, trim it to fit. The boning should fit snugly, but not tightly, into the channel.

Types of Boning

Spiral boning is the most expensive. Made of coiled metal wire, it curves easily from side to side or front to back, so it can be inserted into seams that curve in any direction. It must be inserted into a casing. It's sold by the piece in ½-in. increments ranging from 2 in. to 20 in. long. Use wire cutters to cut it to the right length for the garment, and purchase steel boning tips to cover the sharp ends.

White steel boning offers strong, inflexible support, requires a casing, and can only be used on straight seams. It is sold by the piece in ½-in. increments ranging from 2 in. to 20 in. long. Cut it with wire cutters, and cover the sharp ends with tipping fluid, which is purchased separately, is brushed over the cut edges, and quickly dries into a smooth cap.

Rigilene, a flexible, lightweight, woven polyester boning, can be sewn directly to bodice or bustier seam allowances. However, it is not rigid enough to lie flat or support a garment between seams. It is inexpensive and sold by the yard. Cut it with scissors, and cover the ends with boning tips (rounded polyester caps you can purchase separately) or lightweight fabric.

TIP

Straight, precise sewing is absolutely necessary when applying boning, especially when the stitches are visible on the outside of the bodice.

For tubular tape casing, use a regular machine foot and sew 1⁄16 in. from each edge. Don't use the edge seams woven on the tape as a guide, because they're often unevenly spaced.

For Rigilene, use a zipper foot and sew along the outside groove on each side.

APPLYING BONING WITH VISIBLE STITCHES

When you apply casings or boning with visible stitches, you sew through all the garment layers. This adds sturdily anchored support and a topstitched design element at the same time.

Sewing a Straight Casing

For a flat finish and the most secure seam, press the seam allowances open, then center and sew a boning casing or Rigilene through all the layers. This technique works best with straight seams, and produces a line of topstitching on each side of the seam.

1. Press the seam allowances open. Draw a line lengthwise on the center of the casing (top photo below). Align the casing line or the center ridge of the Rigilene over the seam. Pin or hand-baste in place.

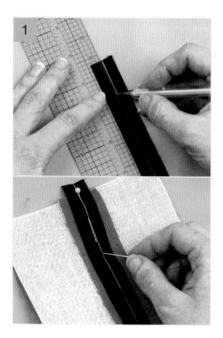

2. Sew each edge of the casing or Rigilene through all the layers. Insert the boning into the casing.

Sewing a Casing to the Seam Allowances

For a curved seam, or to enclose the seam allowances within the casing, press the seam allowances to one side, then sew one edge of a boning casing or Rigilene to the seam allowance, and the other edge through all the layers. A single line of topstitching that parallels the seam is all that shows in this method.

1. Press the seam allowances to one side. Fold the bodice out of the way. Butt one edge of the casing or Rigilene against the seamline. Sew the edge of the casing or Rigilene (not shown) to the seam allowances, stitching through both layers.

2. Grade the seam allowances, with the wider seam allowance against the garment to ensure that a ridge doesn't show through on the outside.

3. Fold the seam allowances and the applied casing onto the bodice. Sew the free edge of the casing or Rigilene through all the layers. Insert the boning into the casing.

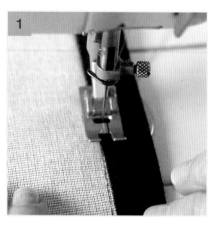

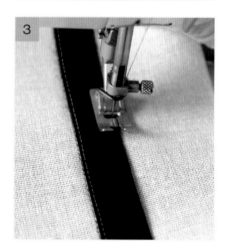

Sewing a Channel between Seams

For very flat support in an area between seams, sew two parallel rows of stitches through all the fabric layers, then slip the boning between the layers into the resulting channel. For this technique, the garment must have at least one layer of inner fabric, such as an underlining, that's sturdy enough to serve as a channel. You can make straight channels for white steel or spiral boning, or curved channels to use with spiral bones.

1. Draw a straight line on the inner fabric on one side of the desired channel location, then sew on the line through all layers. Place the boning under the fabric

against the stitches. Pin the fabric layers snugly, then remove the boning and draw a line parallel to the first seam.

2. Sew on the marked line, and insert the boning in the channel. For extra support where the boning might show through or damage fabric, use two layers of support fabric to create a channel.

APPLYING BONING INVISIBLY

If you don't want visible topstitching, apply the casings or boning to the inner fabric layers.

Sewing a Casing to the Seam Allowances

For a secure seam, but not an absolutely flat finish, press the seam allowances open and secure a boning casing or Rigilene only to them. This technique is the sturdiest invisible-stitching method, and because the seam allowances are loose (unlike the double-row visible-stitching method), it works well on moderately curved and straight seams.

1. Press the seam allowances open. Mark a line down the center of the casing. Center the casing (or Rigilene, not shown) over the seam. Pin or hand-baste to secure.

2. Fold the bodice out of the way, and sew one edge of the casing or Rigilene to one allowance. Repeat for the other edge.

3. Insert the boning into the casing.

Sewing a Hidden Casing between Seams

For invisible support in an area between seams, sew a boning casing to the underlining fabric. Plan ahead, as you must sew on each section of the bodice in sequence, adding a casing before sewing on the next section.

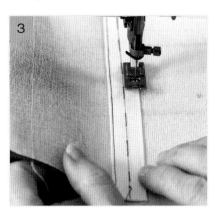

1. Draw a line lengthwise on the center of the casing. Draw a straight line on the underlining fabric, at the desired casing location.

2. Fold the fashion fabric out of the way, and align the center line of the casing with the line on the support fabric. Pin or hand-baste in place.

3. Sew on the casing.

4. Insert the boning.

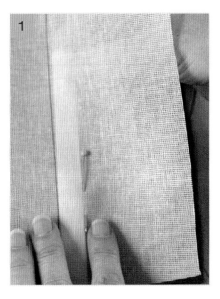

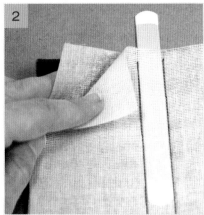

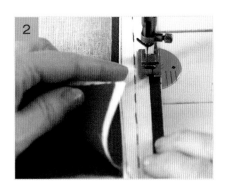

XIII
COUTURE
TECHNIQUES

Fundamentals of Couture Sewing

The term *couture* evokes the highest quality of high-fashion garments, sewn by hand and created from the finest of fabrics. With patience and some easily mastered sewing skills, anyone can achieve couture results at home. The beginning steps of couture sewing include learning a few hand stitches, which are used throughout construction, and adopting a new approach to fitting and cutting.

HAND SEWING

Sewing by hand is an essential skill in garment construction, even though you can make plenty of garments entirely by machine. For reaching into tight spaces, stitching an ultra-fine seam finish, sewing an invisible hem, attaching buttons, and adding small finishing touches throughout a garment, a hand needle and thread (plus beeswax or thread conditioner and, if desired, a thimble) are the best tools to use.

Whether you're creating couture pieces or everyday garments, a few basic stitches are all you need to know. By adjusting the size and spacing of the stitches, you've got nearly every hand-sewing task covered.

The stitches shown here are used for hemming and fine garment construction. Practice for smooth, even, and consistently sized stitches. Use a short length of thread to prevent tangles. The length of your forearm is a good measure. To further prevent tangles, coat the thread with beeswax.

Basic Knots

Always anchor the thread at the beginning and end of your stitching. The only exception is the basting stitch, which is temporary. All securing knots should be hidden between fabric layers or on the wrong side of the fabric. In most cases, you should begin stitching with a slide, or wrap, knot and complete a row of stitching with a finishing knot. In some cases, a "finishing" knot can be used at the beginning as well as at the end.

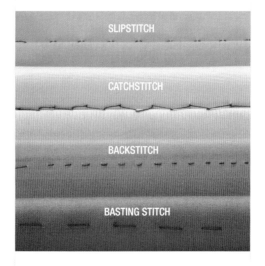

SLIPSTITCH

CATCHSTITCH

BACKSTITCH

BASTING STITCH

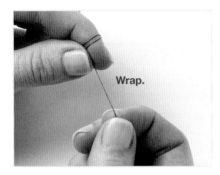

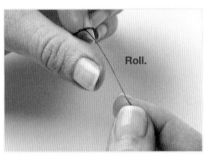

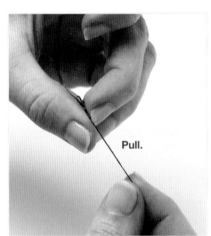

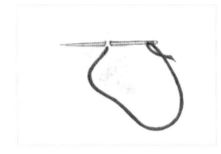

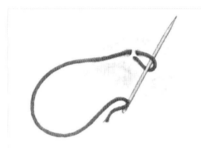

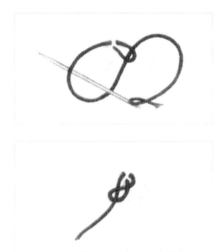

ESSENTIAL HAND STITCHES

Unless you're embellishing with hand stitching, choose the easiest, most invisible stitch for your hand-sewing tasks. All of the following stitches require a single length of thread and are demonstrated for the right hand. If you're a lefty, reverse the directions.

1. Running stitch

Uses: Seaming, visible hemming, mending, and craft work

How to sew: Sewing from right to left, bring the needle up through the fabric from the wrong side, and take as many stitches as fit on the needle, while maintaining desired spacing and stitch length. Slide the needle out of the fabric and pull the thread to create even tension. Repeat.

2. Basting stitch

Uses: To temporarily hold fabric layers together and to gather

How to sew: Sew as for a running stitch, but take stitches ¼ in. to ½ in. long. For gathering, leave thread ends 4 in. long to pull up later.

3. Backstitch

Use: To stitch permanent seams

How to sew: Bring the needle up to the right side of the fabric. Sink the needle ¼ in. to the right of the point where the thread emerges. Bring it back up ½ in. to the left. Repeat.

4. Catchstitch

Uses: To secure a hem, seam edge, or facing to a garment

How to sew: Working from left to right but with the needle point facing to the left, catch a few threads of the garment fabric. Then move ½ in. to the right and catch the hem, facing or seam edge. Move

SLIDE KNOT

Hold one thread end between the index finger and thumb of one hand, and the other end in the other hand. Wrap the thread end two or three times around your finger (not too tightly). Keeping the thread taut with your other hand, use your thumb to roll the loops down off your index finger. Secure the entangled loops onto your thumb with your index finger, then use your nail to pull the tangles into a small knot.

FINISHING KNOT

To finish a row of stitching, end with the needle on the fabric wrong side. Catch one or two yarns of the fabric under the needle, then pull the needle and thread through until a small loop forms. Pass the needle through the loop forming a second loop. Put the needle through the second loop, and pull gently to tighten.

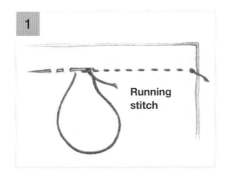

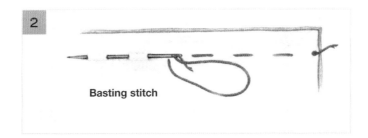

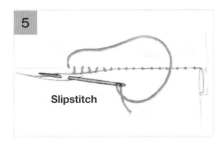

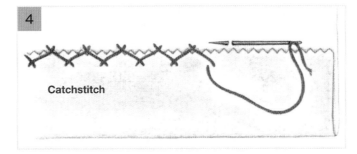

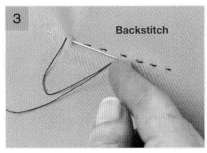

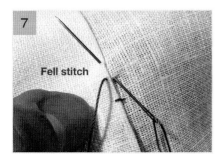

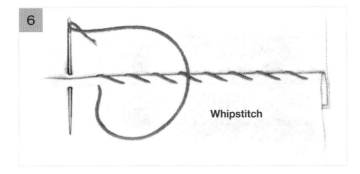

½ in. to the right and repeat, catching the garment fabric.

5. Slipstitch

Uses: To firmly and invisibly secure a folded edge for hemming, also for applying trims and mending

How to sew: To attach a folded edge to flat fabric, come up through the folded edge, and catch a yarn or two of the flat fabric. Then slide the needle inside the fold for ½ in. to ¾ in. The carrying thread is hidden inside the fold. Repeat.

To join two folded edges, come up through the lower fabric. Sew into the upper fabric exactly where the fabric edges meet. Pull the thread lightly through. Continue to sew, alternating from edge to edge until ladders form, then pull the thread lightly until the fabric edges meet. Repeat.

6. Whipstitch

Uses: To close openings, overcast edges, and hem; for a decorative finish, use heavier thread

How to sew: Sewing from right to left, come up through the lower fabric. Then, a short distance away, and with the needle pointing down, sew a vertical stitch through the upper fabric and lower fabric. Pull the thread to the desired tension after each stitch, which, when sewn correctly, will slant.

7. Fell stitch (also called appliqué stitch)

Uses: To attach one fabric layer on top of another, as in hemming, binding, and closing openings, and attaching appliqués

How to sew: Work from right to left. Bring the needle up through the edge of the top fabric layer, very close to the edge. Insert the needle into the bottom fabric layer, directly above where you started. Then, run the needle diagonally (on the wrong side of the fabric) to the left, and bring it up ⅛ in. to ¼ in. beyond the first stitch, through the edge of the top fabric layer. Pull the thread gently to tighten the

Blanket stitch

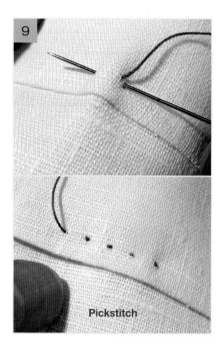

Pickstitch

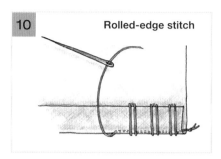

Rolled-edge stitch

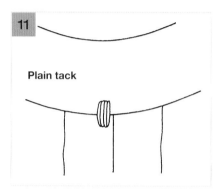

Plain tack

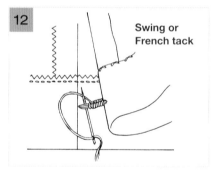

Swing or French tack

stitch. The tiny visible stitch should be perpendicular to the fabric edge. Repeat.

8. Blanket stitch

Uses: To decoratively finish an edge

How to sew: Secure the thread at the edge of the fabric. Bring the needle one stitch-length to the left, insert it into the fabric from the right side, ⅛ in. to ⅜ in. from the edge, and hook the thread behind the needle point. Pull the needle up to close the stitch, making sure the thread lies on the edge of the fabric. Bring the needle one stitch-length to the left, and repeat.

9. Pickstitch (sometimes called prickstitch)

Uses: To topstitch and insert zippers by hand or trim lapel edges

How to sew: The pickstitch is simply a very small backstitch. Insert the needle about ⅛ in. to the right of the point where the thread emerges. In the same action, bring the point of the needle up through the fabric for the next stitch, about ⅜ in. to the left of where you inserted the needle. Pull the thread to close the stitch. Repeat. For decorative stitches, use a single or double strand of buttonhole twist.

10. Rolled-edge stitch

Uses: To hem silk, lace, sheer, and slippery fabrics

How to sew: Fold the raw edge of the fabric up a scant ⅛ in. Insert the threaded needle between the layers and bring it out at the fold. Take a small stitch just above the raw edge, picking up one or two threads from the fabric. Bring the needle back down and insert it into the fold, a thread or two from where it emerged. Glide it between the layers for about ⅜-in. and then bring it out at the fold. Repeat the sequence, keeping the thread relaxed as you work, to create a "picket fence" pattern with nice, straight posts.

Stop after you've sewn 3 in. or 4 in., and gently pull on the thread to roll the edge.

11. Plain tack

Uses: To anchor shoulder pads and neckline facings to shoulder seams

How to sew: Take three to four ¼-in. stitches through the shoulder seam allowance and the facing or shoulder pad. Align the stitches horizontally so they're just touching (don't bunch or cross them).

12. Swing or French tack

Uses: To hold layers loosely in place inside a garment, to anchor linings to garments, usually at a side seam

How to sew: Take a small stitch in one layer, then one in the other layer, leaving about 1 in. of thread between the two layers. Repeat, forming a "bridge" of several threads between the layers. Starting at one end of the bridge, cover the threads with a blanket stitch.

MAKING A MUSLIN

One defining feature of a couture garment is a custom fit. To obtain a perfect fit, it's essential to make a test garment, or muslin. The couture muslin is a bit different from a standard test garment, as it relies on marked seamlines rather than cutting lines.

See "Working with a Muslin Test Garment," on page 100.

Since couture sewing doesn't rely on ⅝-in. seam allowances, don't cut the muslin based on the pattern with its included seam allowances. Instead, transfer the stitching lines and other pertinent information, such as darts and button and buttonhole placement, to the muslin, using a tracing wheel and waxed tracing paper. Cut the muslin, leaving wide (at least 1-in.-wide) seam allowances, so there's room for fitting adjustments. Make a full set of muslin pieces, with both right and left sides. This makes fitting more accurate, and enables you later to cut the fashion fabric in a single layer, using the muslin as a pattern.

See "Marking the Fabric," on page 109.

Stitch over the traced marks with long machine stitches, so the traced information now appears on both sides of the muslin. Having the marks on the inside simplifies the construction

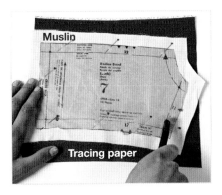

Muslin

Tracing paper

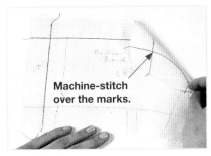

Machine-stitch over the marks.

process while clearly indicating the placement of design elements and seamlines. The machine stitches also strengthen the muslin for fitting.

Sew the test garment together with long machine stitches. They'll be easy to undo when it's time to use the muslin as the pattern. Check and correct the fit and style lines. You can pin it, cut into it, pare it down, and adjust, mark, and annotate it endlessly. Note the changes directly on the muslin, then take it apart and press it flat.

CUTTING AND MARKING FABRICS

Couture garments are almost always underlined. The underlining not only improves the drape and wear of the garment, but serves the purpose of carrying construction marks and guidelines, so you don't have to mark the fashion fabric. Use the fitted muslin as a pattern for cutting the underlining, lining, and fashion fabrics, each in a single layer.

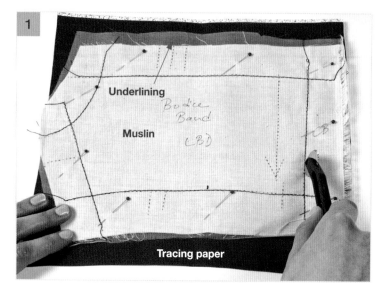

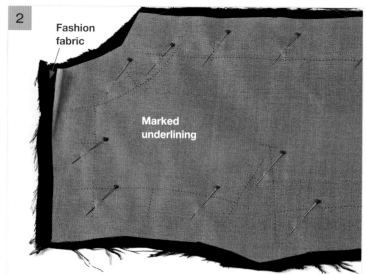

1. Cut the underlining first, with wide seam allowances (at least 1 in. wide). Transfer important marks from the muslin to the underlining, working with a tracing wheel and waxed tracing paper. With dark fabrics, you can use any color tracing paper. For white and mid-value fabrics, use a light application of color.

2. Lay out the fashion fabric in a single layer, with the right side down. Place the marked underlining face up, on top. Be sure the grainlines are perfectly aligned. Pin the underlining to the fashion fabric, placing the pins within the wide seam allowances and taking care not to shift the fabric layers. If the underlining is particularly slippery, silk chiffon or silk crepe de Chine, for example, keep the muslin pinned to the underlining for the sake of stability, and pin them to the fashion fabric as a unit. Remove the muslin pattern before you baste the fashion fabric and underlining together.

3. Working with lightweight basting thread (silk is a good choice), hand-baste the marked underlining and the fashion fabric together along the seamlines with a running stitch. Hand-baste darts, button and buttonhole placement, and any other design details that need to be visible from the right side of the garment. Control the layers, keeping the grainlines aligned and smoothing out bubbles or irregularities; turn the work over occasionally to check that the fashion fabric is perfectly smooth. Knot each thread as you begin, and finish by repeating a stitch or two in place, beginning and ending before the cross points of each seam.

ASSEMBLING THE GARMENT

To guarantee that the garment fits, baste it together, check the fit, and then machine-sew.

Baste the Garment for Fitting

Using a running stitch, hand-baste the entire garment together for fitting. Make sure the hand stitches are secure, but not too tight, and anchor them firmly at the ends of seams so they don't pull out during fitting. Because you fit-

TIP

For long, uninterrupted lines of hand stitching, cut a thread twice the usual length, and start it in the center of the stitching line. Then, work one thread end right to left, and the other end left to right.

ted the garment carefully at the muslin stage, any adjustments now should be minor and easy to execute; the wide seam allowances enable you to let the garment out slightly.

Check the seamline placement, the neck edge position, armscyes, dart fullness, hemline, how the fabric/garment is hanging, and the overall appearance. At the fitting, mark any changes with pins, then re-baste and check again. And of course, mark any changes onto the muslin because you'll be using it to cut the lining as well.

Machine Stitching the Garment

Before machine stitching the garment, experiment with the stitch length and tension on scrap fabric, using the same layering used with the garment. Then press the seam carefully to make sure you're happy with the result.

Stitch the darts without back tacking (instead, tie a secure knot with the threads). Sew the seams from raw edge to raw edge, without back tacking (except for the top of a slit on a skirt

seam or the vent on a jacket sleeve). Whenever possible, sew from the widest to the narrowest points of a garment. Fit the garment again, and once all is well, remove the basting threads. Then trim, clip, and press the seam allowances. Cut and apply the lining as described on page 290.

Managing the Seam Allowances

Couture garments are usually lined, so the seam allowances are spared heavy use and abrasion. However, the wide seam allowances that were useful during the initial stages of the garment's construction are no longer needed, so they can be trimmed down. In certain areas, such as a princess seam over the bust, the seam allowance needs to be clipped, carefully pressed, and sewn with the catchstitch to the underlining to keep it flat.

For an unlined garment, hand overcasting with a whipstitch is a traditional couture seam allowance treatment.

See "Whipstitch," on page 285.

This technique gently controls the raw edge without the application of a great deal of thread. Further, it causes no distortion to the seam allowances (a tendency with long, off-grain seams), and is undetectable from the right side of the garment.

Another technique used on unlined garments is a Hong Kong seam finish, using a lining fabric to bind the seam allowance edges.

See "Hong Kong Finish," on page 157.

Special Couture Techniques

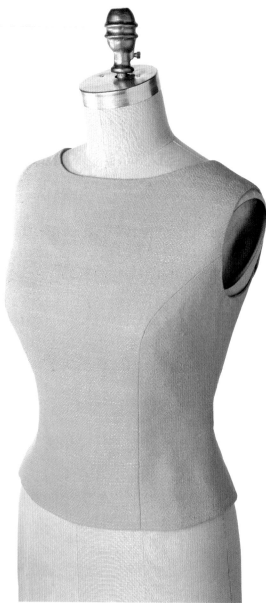

Some of the hallmarks of couture garments include bulk-free edges and seams, perfectly smooth sleeve caps, and refined closures. Each one of these details improves the appearance of a garment, and while you don't have to incorporate every one of them in all your garments, you may find that the look of beautiful buttonholes or a hand-sewn zipper appeals so much you begin adding these to your noncouture pieces as well.

EDGES AND LININGS

A couture edge is lightweight and flat, but stable. This refined look is achieved by eliminating facings at the neckline and armholes, along with their seam-allowance bulk. Replace them with generous seam allowances to serve as built-in (or "cut-on") facings. Sew the lining by hand, right up to the garment's edge, using the underlining as a base for the hand stitches. The finished look is smooth and clean both inside and out.

290

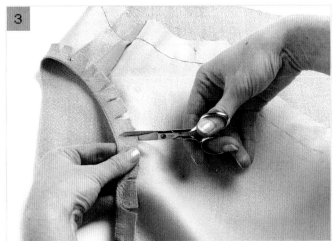

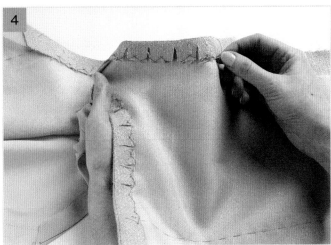

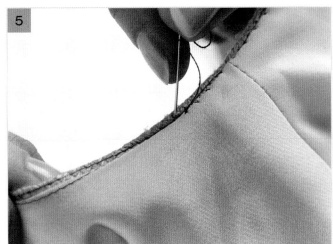

1. Assemble the garment as described on pages 288–289, so that it's fully sewn, but not yet lined. Staystitch around the curved openings at the neckline and, if applicable, the armholes. Cut the lining, using the muslin as a pattern, and assemble it. Press its seam allowances open and staystitch the openings that correspond to those on the garment.

2. Press the garment seam allowances on the curved edges to the wrong side, using just the tip of the iron so you're pressing just along the staystitching line, rolling it to the inside and not pressing creases in the allowance.

3. Clip the seam allowances as needed to establish a smooth, undimpled, curved

edge. Trim the seam allowance to ¼ in., and repress.

4. Catchstitch the seam allowances to the underlining, making sure not to stitch through the fashion fabric.

5. On the lining, press the seam allowances of the curved edges under, as you did for the garment, and clip them. Position the lining inside the garment, aligning the side seams, shoulder seams, and pressed edges. Bring the lining slightly to the inside of the fashion fabric edge. Sew the lining to the opening edges with small, firm fell stitches (see page 285), placing them right at the fashion fabric's line of staystitches.

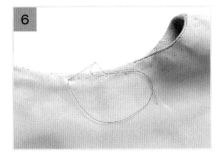

6. Understitch the lining to the under-lining with a pickstitch (see page 286). Stitch about ½ in. below the finished garment edge. Sew each stitch to just catch the underlining and lining layers, but don't catch the fashion fabric. The linking thread between stitches should tunnel between the fabric layers.

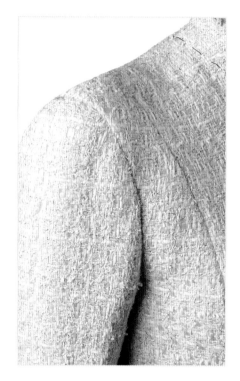

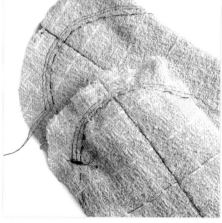

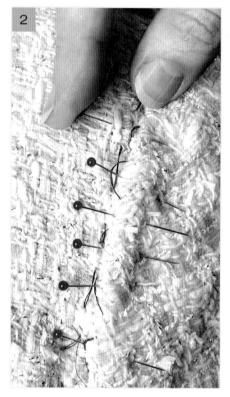

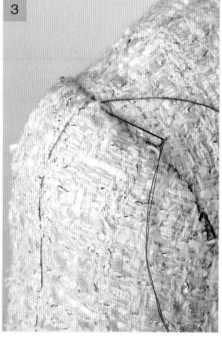

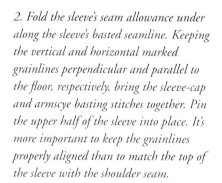

SETTING IN SLEEVES BY HAND

For a perfectly smooth sleeve cap, sew the armscye seam by hand. Hand sewing gives you maximum control over the ease and the position of the grainlines. This method works best with a fabric that can be shaped with steam and that's lofty enough to hide hand stitches. Begin with a well-fitted muslin, in which there's 1¼ in. to 1½ in. of ease in the sleeve cap seamline. Baste-mark the seamlines, cut the sleeve, leaving wide seam allowances, and mark the lengthwise and crosswise grains with basting stitches. Sew the sleeve seams.

1. Ease the sleeve cap seamline between the notches by steam shrinking the sleeve cap over a ham or tailor board, or by sewing two or three rows of easestitching, and pulling the threads to gather. Place the jacket bodice on a dress form, and pin it closed.

2. Fold the sleeve's seam allowance under along the sleeve's basted seamline. Keeping the vertical and horizontal marked grainlines perpendicular and parallel to the floor, respectively, bring the sleeve-cap and armscye basting stitches together. Pin the upper half of the sleeve into place. It's more important to keep the grainlines properly aligned than to match the top of the sleeve with the shoulder seam.

3. Sew the pinned section of the sleeve to the garment from the right side, using firm, small fell stitches and a double strand of waxed thread.

4. Remove the jacket from the dress form. From the inside of the garment, align the sleeve and bodice seamlines along the underarm, and pin. Sew this portion of the seam with small backstitches.

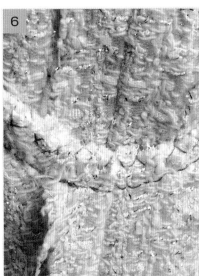

INSERTING A ZIPPER BY HAND

A hand-picked zipper is often found on couture garments (though some now use invisible zippers). The tiny pickstitches used to insert the zipper are unobtrusive, although you can embellish them with beads or embroidery if you prefer to make the zipper a design feature. Hand-sewn zippers are sturdy, and the method is perfect for heavily embellished or delicate fabrics that might be damaged or distorted if sewn by machine.

5. On the upper part of the sleeve, open the seam allowances. Clip the bodice seam allowance as needed to fold it against the garment, and tack the allowance to the shoulder seam allowances. Press the seam allowance toward the sleeve, and trim it to about 1 in.

6. In the underarm area, trim the seam allowances to about ½ in., and overcast the raw edges together.

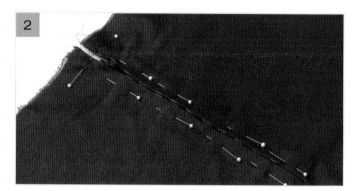

1. Stabilize the zipper area with a strip of silk organza, chiffon, crepe de Chine, or nonstretch fusible interfacing. This prevents distorting and rippling over time. Gently tack the strip in place along the foldline.

2. Pin the closed zipper in place from the garment's right side. Starting at the zipper's upper right-hand side, center the folded edge of the fabric over the zipper pull and teeth and keep the pins or basting at an even distance from the fabric's folded edge.

3. Open the zipper, and, starting at the top of the tape, stitch the zipper in place with a pickstitch on the fabric's right side. Use a doubled strand of thread, space the stitches ¼ in. to ⅜ in. apart, and align the stitching ¼ in. to ⅜ in. from the folded edge.

4. Make a stitch just below the lower end of the zipper and tie a knot on the fabric wrong side. Stitching across the zipper's base is unnecessary and only invites

puckers. Next, stitch the zipper's other side. Start at the bottom left of the zipper and sew to the top. It's not uncommon to find a slight mismatch of the two zipper tape sides at the top edges, but it's easy to mask with the waistband or facing. If the mismatch is more than slight (if the fabric is distorted), take out your stitches and restitch.

5. If desired, add a decorative touch by sewing pearls, beads, or sequins onto your zipper placket. Pick up one or two beads with each stitch as you install the zipper, or go over the original hand-picked stitches once it's in place. Take one or two extra stitches to secure each bead.

HAND-PICKED ZIPPER TIPS

- Overlap the lips to ease tension. If you anticipate strain and tension on the finished zipper, for example, on a tight bodice, overlap the lips of the fabric 1/16 in. when you apply the zipper. The lips will abut when the garment is worn.

- To avoid tangles, coat the thread with beeswax, and press the coated thread to make it smoother, using a press cloth to protect your iron.

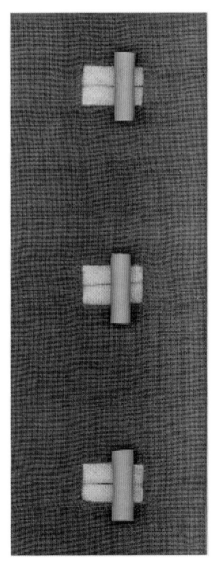

COVERED SNAPS

Covered snaps are a great designer detail. They blend seamlessly into the garment, especially when created from fabric that closely matches the fashion fabric. A lightweight, flexible fabric, such as lining, is the best choice. If the fabric is bulky, it won't wrap well.

1. For each snap, cut two circles of fabric, twice the diameter of the snap. Trace around a coin or use a compass to draw a perfect circle. Create a hole in the center of each fabric circle by gently separating the fibers with an awl. If the fabric frays, dot with Fray Check fray preventer. Hand-baste around the perimeters of the circles, about 3/16 in. to 1/4 in. from the edge.

2. Insert the ball section into the hole in one circle, and pull the basting threads to gather the fabric around the snap. Trim the excess fabric and whipstitch the edges flat. Repeat with the socket section, aligning the hole in the fabric with the opening in the snap.

3. Attach the snaps to the garment as usual, sewing through the fabric cover to reach the snap's holes.

BOUND BUTTONHOLES

Bound buttonholes are finished with strips, or "lips" of fabric, rather than overcast stitches. The look is definitely upscale, and because you can mix and match the fabrics, they can be decorative as well. Most bound buttonholes are positioned horizontally on a garment. Light- to medium-weight fabrics that don't ravel excessively are easiest to use, but you can make bound buttonholes on thicker fabrics—just substitute a thinner fabric for the lips. Begin by interfacing the fabric wrong side in the buttonhole area. Then mark a horizontal line 5/16 in. below the desired buttonhole opening, and mark the ends. Basted lines work well, because you can see them on both sides of the fabric.

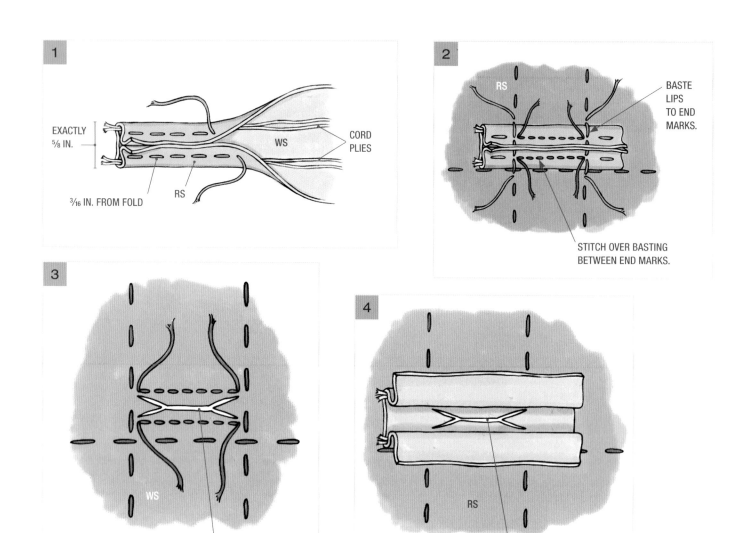

1. To make the buttonhole lips, cut a 2-in.-wide bias strip long enough to make as many buttonholes as you need, plus some extra. (You'll later cut the strips to the proper buttonhole lengths.) Untwist a cotton cord to separate one or two plies. Place the plies on the wrong side of the bias strip, fold over one-third of each long edge to encase the cord, and pin. Baste ³⁄₁₆ in. from the fold. Measure exactly ⁵⁄₈ in. (or ¾ in. if using thick fabric) from the first fold to the opposite fold, and baste the other edge making a ⁵⁄₈-in.-wide strip.

2. On the garment right side, position the lip section, raw edges up. Align the lower folded edge to the marked horizontal line (which is ⁵⁄₁₆ in. below the buttonhole center). Then, hand-baste on the end marks, stabstitching through the lips. Stitch over the horizontal cord basting to attach the lips to the garment, and back-tack at the ends. Sew the lower lip on all buttonholes first and check that the stitching is square, then sew the top lip.

3. On the garment wrong side, snip in the center of the buttonhole outline between the stitching lines, and clip diagonally as shown, being careful to cut only through the garment fabric and the bottom layer of the buttonhole strip. Clip to, but not beyond, the corners.

4. Turn the lips through the opening, straighten, press, and stitch the lips together from the right side until you finish garment construction.

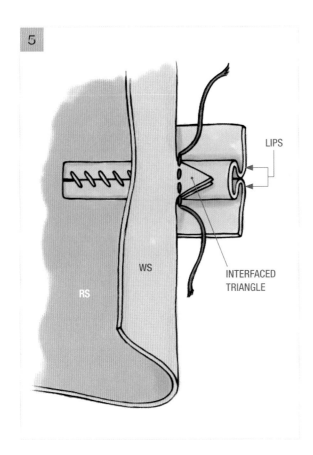

LIPS

WS

RS

INTERFACED
TRIANGLE

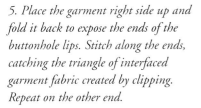

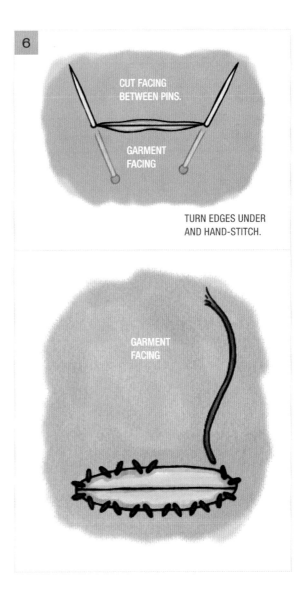

CUT FACING
BETWEEN PINS.

GARMENT
FACING

TURN EDGES UNDER
AND HAND-STITCH.

GARMENT
FACING

5. *Place the garment right side up and fold it back to expose the ends of the buttonhole lips. Stitch along the ends, catching the triangle of interfaced garment fabric created by clipping. Repeat on the other end.*

6. *After sewing the front facing to the garment, mark the ends of the lips with pins, cut a slit in the facing, turn the edges under, and hand-stitch to finish the inside of the garment.*

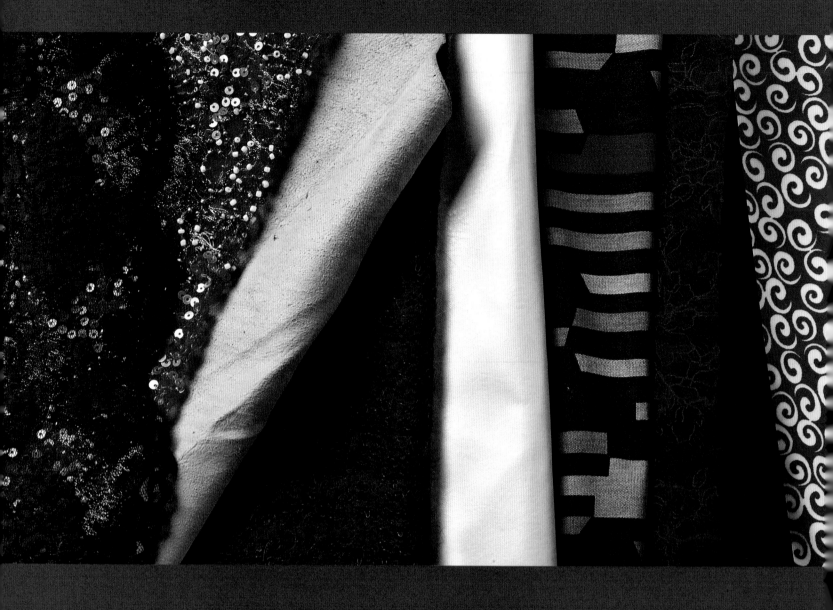

XIV
SEWING SPECIALTY
FABRICS

1

Knits

Knit fabrics come in such a wide variety you could, without too much difficulty, make an entire wardrobe of knits. From light silk jersey and nylon tricot to beefy wool double-knits and lofty sweater knits, knits offer comfort and versatility. Most knits are no more difficult to sew than woven fabrics, but some require special techniques to manage their stretch. Once you've learned to stabilize or build in stretch, you can handle any knit fabric that captures your fancy.

TYPES OF KNITS

Whether made of cotton, wool, linen, synthetics, or a blend, each knit is made in one of two ways. A weft knit (hand knits are one example of a weft knit) is made with a single yarn that's looped to create horizontal rows, with each row built on the previous row. A warp knit is made with multiple parallel yarns that are simultaneously looped vertically to form the fabric. Both types of knits can be made either as flat yardage, or as a tube.

Only four basic stitches are used to make even the most complex-looking knit: a knit, or plain, stitch; a purl, or reverse-knit, stitch; a missed stitch, which produces a float of yarn on the fabric's wrong side; and a tuck stitch, which creates an open space.

All knits stretch to some degree, but due to differences in fiber type, knit tension, and stitch variations, not all knits of similar structures have a predictable amount of stretch. Test the stretch of any knit fabric to be sure it's sufficient for the garment you're planning.

See "Knit Fabrics," on page 58.

It's primarily the structure of a knit that determines how much the fabric can stretch, but the fiber type

contributes as well, both to stretch and recovery. In particular, textiles that incorporate a percentage (usually 2 to 10 percent) of spandex in the yarns have enhanced recovery and resistance to sagging during wear.

Weft Knits

Weft knits fall into three basic categories: rib knits, which are a combination of knit and purl stitches; purl knits, which are made with purl stitches alone; and jersey knits, which are made with knit stitches on the right side and purl stitches on the wrong side.

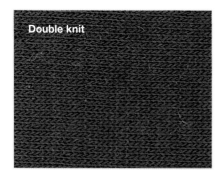

Double knits are made with two sets of yarns; the right and wrong sides usually look the same, with fine ribs running lengthwise. They're heavy, firm, and quite stable; the cut edges don't curl. Use these for tailored garments.

Interlock knits are made of interlocking two simple ribbed fabrics, each made with a single yarn. The right and wrong sides look the same. Interlocks have almost no lengthwise stretch, but are stretchier crosswise than jersey or double knits. The cut edges don't curl. Use interlock knits for T-shirts, tops, and casual wear.

Jersey knits, also called single knits, have a distinct right and wrong side, with smooth, narrow ribs on the right side and purl stitches on the wrong side. There's little lengthwise stretch in jersey knits, and varying amounts of crosswise stretch. You'll find jersey knits in cotton and cotton blends, synthetics, and wool. Stretchier jersey is suitable for active and casual wear. Wool jersey, which tends to have less stretch, can be used for skirts, blouses, and dresses.

Warp Knits

Because of the multiple-needle configuration of warp-knitting machines, warp knits can be very complex and intricate in structure. They don't fall neatly into categories.

Milanese knits are made from two sets of yarns knitted diagonally. The right side has fine vertical ribs; the wrong side has a diagonal structure. These knits are lightweight, drapey, and smooth. Use them for soft blouses, lingerie, or eveningwear.

Raschel knits can be fine and lacy, intricately patterned, or with pile. They range from stable to stretchy, and are either single-faced or reversible. Many novelty knits are raschel knits. You'll find them suitable for just about any type of garment.

Tricot knits have fine, lengthwise ribs on the right side and crosswise ribs on the wrong side. They have some lengthwise stretch, but almost no crosswise stretch. They're usually soft and drapey, with cut edges that tend to curl. Most are made of fine, synthetic fibers, and they are traditionally used for lingerie and lining.

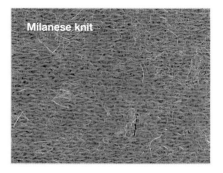

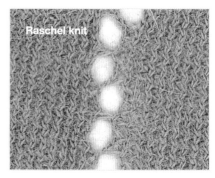

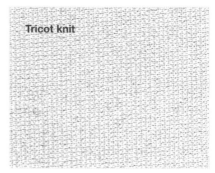

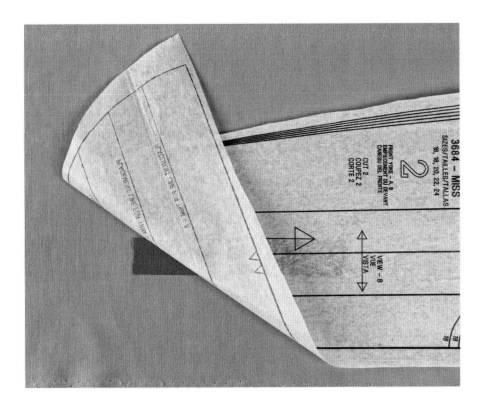

LAYOUT AND CUTTING

For nearly all garments made of knit fabrics, you should lay out the pattern so that the greatest amount of stretch goes around the body. (Exceptions to this rule include some activewear, such as skating dresses.) If the greatest stretch is on the crosswise grain, lay the pattern out that way. For loose-fitting garments, such as drapey or oversized sweaters, you can cut the garment in either grain, as long as the fabric doesn't droop or sag vertically.

Technically, knits don't have a grain, as woven fabrics do, but patterns should still be placed properly on the fabric. To help find the correct "grainline," rely on a visible rib or other vertical pattern, rather than the selvage.

Lay out the fabric in a single layer, and place one pattern piece where you want to cut it out. Note the general area of the placement, remove the pattern, and position a piece of blue

painter's tape or low-tack tape along a lengthwise rib. Reposition the pattern so the grainline aligns with the tape. Position all other pattern pieces with their grainlines parallel to the tape. Cut knits using a "with nap" layout to avoid shading. All pattern piece tops should be placed in one direction.

Knits that stretch easily out of shape, such as jersey, should be handled as little as possible. The cut edges of jersey often curl up due to the way the fabric is knitted. To flatten the edges, spray them with starch and gently press with a steam iron.

CONSTRUCTION TECHNIQUES

When sewing knits, you must either control the fabric's stretch (with interfacing or stabilizing tape), or match the stitch you use to the stretch. You can get successful results with both a basic sewing machine and a serger.

Seams

Install a new ballpoint or stretch needle in your sewing machine or serger. Sew a test swatch on the fabric to perfect the tension settings and eliminate puckering. If the fabric is very stretchy, stabilize high-stress areas and horizontal seams, such as shoulder seams, crotch seams, front edges of a wrap dress, or any other area that can be pulled out of shape during everyday wear. Fuse a strip of interfacing to the seam or edge, and sew through it.

With a regular sewing machine, use a stretch straight stitch if your machine has one; it's usually sewn with a back-and-forth motion that builds stretch into the seam. Alternatively, try an overlock or zigzag stitch. If you don't have these stitches, or they don't work well, sew with long, straight, 3-mm stitches (9 stitches per in.), and gently stretch the seam as you sew it (as much as the fabric stretches easily) to add elasticity. When the seam returns to its normal length, the stitches are closer

Tips for Slinky and Sweater Knits

Super-stretchy knits, like synthetic/spandex "slinky" knits, and highly textured, lofty sweater knits call for some special treatment. Try these techniques to get the best results when working with these stylish and comfortable textiles.

SLINKY KNITS

"Slinky knit" describes many synthetic blends that include acetate, spandex, polyester, and rayon, with or without a ribbed texture. The heavier the fabric is, the better the drape. However, lighter weights are best for tops or for layering.

Slinky knits

- Cut slinky knits with a rotary cutter for accuracy. Scissors can stretch fabric out of place.

- Don't allow the fabric to hang off the table or ironing board during layout, cutting, or pressing. The weight of slinky knits can distort the pieces.

- Sew with a serged overlock stitch, if you have a serger. Experiment with Woolly Nylon™ in the upper looper for added stretch.

- Sew conventional seams (if you're not serging the garment) and topstitching with a narrow zigzag stitch, with a stitch length of 2 mm to 2.5 mm and a stitch width of 0.5 mm to 1 mm.

- Pick the side you want as a right side, and use it throughout your project. Mark the wrong side of all pieces with chalk or removable tape.

- Trim seam allowances to eliminate bulk, especially when attaching facings.

- Choose a stabilizer (fusible tricot) that doesn't reduce softness or drape. Shoulder seams, yokes, and jacket fronts should be stabilized with clear elastic or woven stay tape.

- Choose a firm, nonroll elastic for waistbands to support the weight of the fabric.

- Use a press cloth when pressing, and experiment with scraps to get the heat setting right.

SWEATER KNITS

Sweater knits vary immensely in fiber, structure, and stretch. Test each technique, from laundering to stitching and pressing, on swatches before beginning your project. When working with thick, fluffy, or open-weave knits, try these techniques.

- Cut the pattern pieces with 1-in.-wide seam allowances, and trim later.

- Use ballpoint or stretch needles to avoid snagging or breaking of fibers.

- Sew seams with a zigzag stitch, if you want them to stretch. Use polyester thread, a stitch length of 2 mm, and a stitch width of 3 mm.

- Incorporate a strip of mesh knit or bias-cut organza in the seams of open-weave knits.

- Stabilize horizontal seams with a strip of clear elastic, twill tape, or lightweight woven fabric selvage.

- Finish seam allowances by serging or zigzagging, if desired.

- Interface if needed with stretch mesh.

- Substitute bindings or rib-knit bands for facings, when possible.

- Make hem allowances at least 1 in. wide. Sew with a serger cover stitch, a twin needle, or by hand with a catchstitch.

Sweater knits

together, and the upper and lower thread tensions have loosened.

For seams that will stay pressed open, use a ⅝-in.-wide seam allowance, but this works only on knits that don't curl. For knits that tend to curl, use a ¼-in.-wide seam allowance, which you can finish two ways: Either press it to one side and topstitch with a stretch stitch, or sew a second line of stretch stitching ⅛ in. from the first and then press to one side. The double-sewn seam adds strength and helps keep the seam flat.

If you have a serger, use it for sewing all knits except for very lofty sweater knits. Serged seams have built-in elasticity, so you don't need to stretch the seams as you sew. Make sure the stitch is balanced, adjusting the thread tension so that the stitch doesn't bind or ruffle the seam. If your serger has differential feed, raise the setting if your test seam looks wavy.

Most knits don't ravel, so additional seam finishing isn't needed. If desired, you can serge seam allowances together in sweater knits that you've sewn conventionally, to control the bulk.

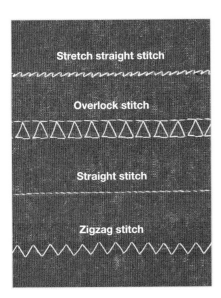

Stretch straight stitch

Overlock stitch

Straight stitch

Zigzag stitch

Hems

To allow the garment to stretch, hang it for 24 hours before you hem it. For most knits, you can simply turn up the hem and topstitch it in place. If desired, you can interface the hem with a lightweight, fusible knit interfacing. This stabilizes the hem and keeps it smooth, but can reduce its stretch. Sew or serge the right side of a strip to the wrong side of the hem edge, with the adhesive side up. After constructing the garment, fold the hem up, fuse it in place, and topstitch from the right side.

For a nearly invisible hem, press the hem up and catchstitch it by hand.

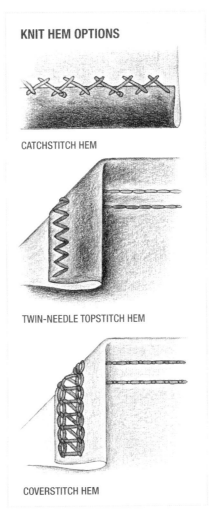

KNIT HEM OPTIONS

CATCHSTITCH HEM

TWIN-NEEDLE TOPSTITCH HEM

COVERSTITCH HEM

See "Catchstitch," on page 284.

For a quick hem by machine, install a 4-mm-wide twin needle and topstitch with a stitch length of about 3 mm. A serged cover-hem stitch is suitable and also creates a double or triple row of topstitching for a sporty, ready-to-wear effect.

See "Coverstitch," on page 172.

On lightweight knits, you can create a decorative lettuce edge by stretching the fabric as you serge a rolled hem.

Buttonholes

Stabilizing buttonholes in knit fabrics is important, or they may permanently distort. The easiest way to do this is to interface the area and use a machine-sewn corded buttonhole (page 241). For added stability, sew through clear elastic and trim it away after stitching. Some sewing machines feature a stretch buttonhole, which is appropriate for some knits. Test any buttonhole method on fabric scraps first.

TIP

If an existing buttonhole has stretched, you can run heavy thread under the satin stitches on the wrong side of the garment, pull the thread, and knot the ends to tighten up the buttonhole.

FINISHING EDGES WITH ELASTIC

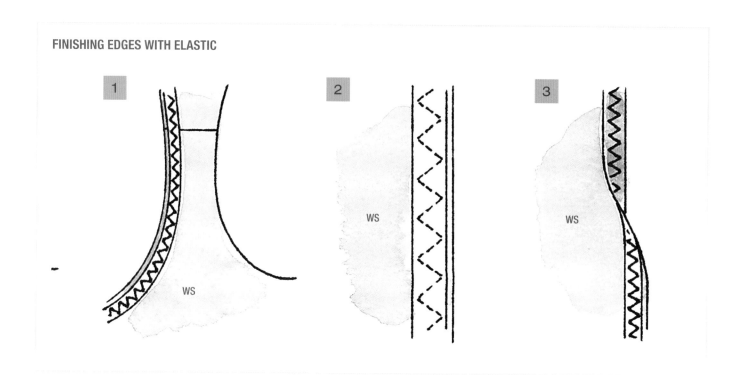

Elastic Application

It's easy to finish edges with elastic, especially for sportswear and bathing suits. Select a narrow elastic (¼-in.- to ⅜-in.-wide) that can be sewn through. If making swimwear, be sure the elastic is chlorine resistant.

1. Cut a strip of elastic the length indicated on the pattern or to fit the body snugly, plus ½ in. If you're elasticizing a circular opening, such as a neckline or leg opening, sew the elastic into a circle. Divide and mark the elastic into equal quarters; repeat for the garment edge. On the garment wrong side, align one edge of the elastic, matching and pinning at the quarter marks. Zigzag the elastic to

the garment, keeping the edges aligned and stretching the elastic to fit as you sew. Don't stretch the garment edge.

2. In highly stretched areas, such as the back of a leg, switch to a multiple-stitch zigzag. (Alternatively, apply the elastic with a three-thread serged overlock stitch.)

3. Turn the elastic to the inside of the garment and topstitch, using either a twin needle or a zigzag stitch, enclosing the raw fabric edge on the underside. (Alternatively, use a serger cover stitch to topstitch the elastic.)

Sheers

Transparent fabrics aren't just for bridal and eveningwear. Lightweight and cool, sheer fabrics offer endless design opportunities, from extravagant gowns to a crisp organdy collar on a cotton blouse. On the dress at right, the "stripes" in the sheer fabric are engineered with tucks. The key to making the most of these fabrics is to sew seams, edges, and hems that are lightweight, sturdy, and nearly invisible. Thoughtful handling during layout, cutting, and stitching can tame even the most flyaway fabrics, so there's no need to fear these lovely textiles.

TYPES OF SHEERS

A sheer fabric is one that's transparent or translucent. This includes chiffon, gauze, organza, organdy, netting, tulle, voile, gazar, georgette, cotton lawn, and dévoré (burnout) or cut velvet. While we often think of silk when considering sheers, many of these fabrics come in a variety of fibers. Polyester chiffon; rayon georgette; silk, wool, and rayon voile; and wool or linen gauze are just a few examples.

Sheers come in a rainbow of solids, ideal for layering, as well as stripes, checks, and prints.

If you're not planning to layer a sheer garment over another piece of clothing, you must line or underline it, either with an opaque lining, or with several additional layers of sheer fabric. Experiment with lining colors, as the lining can change the overall hue significantly. To maintain the transparent fabric's color most effectively, match the lining to it, or choose a shade lighter or darker. White lining brightens pale to medium shades; black dulls and darkens all colors. A lining that matches the wearer's skin tone gives the impression of no lining at all. Adding a lining in an entirely different color can create unusual, almost iridescent effects.

You can also find sheer knits. Sew these combining the general principles for sheers (narrow, lightweight, supple seams and finishes), with the guidelines for sewing knits (see pages 299–304).

LAYOUT AND CUTTING

If you're working with a sheer fabric that has some tooth (that is, its surface texture enables the layers to cling

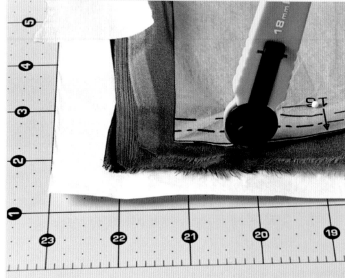

together), you can cut it as you would any woven. Cutting slippery sheers accurately is a greater challenge, and it calls for an extra step or two. In the skirt shown above, layers of sheer fabric are caught in an elastic waistband.

Because many sheers easily slide out of position—on the table, under the pattern, and between the blades of your scissors—it's helpful to pin or tape the fabric down before you cut. The methods shown can be used to cut a single layer or multiple layers of sheer easily and accurately. Sometimes it helps to cover the fabric with another piece of paper and then pattern pieces.

When working with a rotary cutter, lay out the fabric layers as follows: Cover the cutting mat with lightweight paper, such as tissue paper or medical exam-room paper.

Find the crosswise grain of the fabric, align it with a line on the mat, and tape the fabric to the paper with removable tape. Next, align and tape the selvage or lengthwise edge to the paper along a perpendicular line on the cutting mat. To smooth the airy fabric, lean close to the edge of the cutting table and blow on the fabric.

If you want, you can layer multiple pieces of sheer fabric. Layer the next fabric on top of the first, taping and smoothing as you did before. For added control, you can place another layer of paper between the layers to prevent slippage. Place the pattern on the top layer, and pin through all of the fabric and paper layers. With a fresh, sharp blade, cut the garment through all of the layers simultaneously.

If you prefer to cut with shears, use a cardboard cutting mat or a large sheet of foam-core board. Lay out the fabric as described above. When you pin the pattern, stick the pins upright into the fabric, paper, and cardboard mat. This prevents the layers from slipping. Then cut through all the layers with your shears.

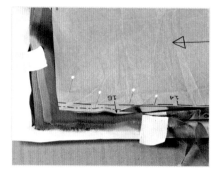

TIPS FOR WORKING WITH SHEERS

- Cut with a rotary cutter, ruler, and mat.

- Use fine, extra-sharp pins with glass heads.

- Sew with a walking foot.

- Mark with tailor's tacks or thread tracing. Waxed chalk can stain.

- Trim with serrated shears.

- Stitch with silk thread.

- Press with a dry iron on the silk setting. Steam can water-spot.

- Construct with French or enclosed seams (pages 157–159).

- Hold the thread ends taut as you begin sewing so the fabric doesn't sink into the throat plate. If your machine has one, use a straight stitch pressure foot and throat plate with a single round hole.

CONSTRUCTION TECHNIQUES

Keep seams and hems as narrow and lightweight as possible, so they don't overwhelm the fabric itself or look obtrusive. Work with finer-than-normal thread, such as 50- to 100-weight silk or cotton, a size 60/8 to 70/10 sharp needle, and a medium-short stitch length. Use taut sewing to stitch long seams or hems.

See "Taut Sewing and Eased Seams," on page 142.

Every 6 in. or so, stop sewing, with the needle down, and lift the presser foot to release the tension in the fabric. Then lower the presser foot and resume sewing. This pause helps prevents rippled seams.

Sheers have a reputation for slipping as you sew. To prevent slippage, apply temporary spray adhesive along the edges, or use a water-soluble or tear-away stabilizer (see page 336) to sandwich the layers when stitching. Alternatively, you can apply spray starch to the edges before stitching. Whichever method you choose, be sure to test it on scraps before you begin sewing to make sure you like the results.

Seams

These two seam options yield very narrow seam allowances. Use the French seam for straight or slightly curved seams, and the double-stitched seam for curved or angled seams.

REDUCED FRENCH SEAM

A French seam is just two parallel seams. These directions are intended for patterns that include a ⅝-in.-wide seam allowance. The result is a narrow seam allowance that encloses all raw edges.

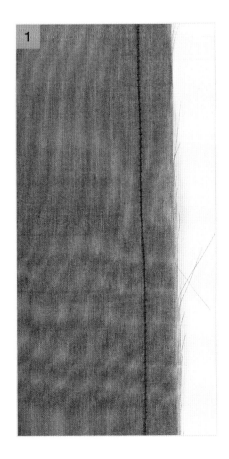

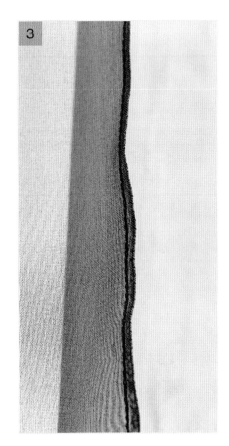

1. Position the two layers of fabric with wrong sides together. Sew the seam with a ½-in.-wide seam allowance.

2. Trim the seam allowances to about ¹⁄₁₆ in., then press them to one side.

3. Fold the two layers along the seamline with right sides together. Press the fold. Stitch ⅛ in. away from, and parallel to, the first seam to create a nearly invisible enclosed seam.

DOUBLE-STITCHED SEAM

Sewing angled or sharply curved seams can be difficult with a French seam, because it's difficult to fold the fabric and enclose the seam allowances. This double-stitched seam works better when navigating sharp curves or angles on necklines or armholes and also as a straight seam.

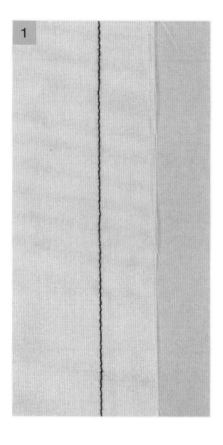

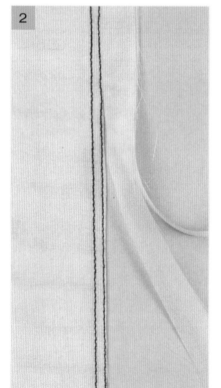

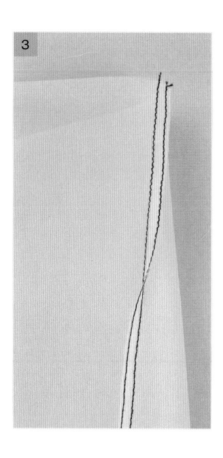

1. With right sides together, stitch the seam, using the designated seam allowance width.

2. Then stitch a second time, ⅛ in. or ¼ in. to the right of the first row of stitching, within the seam allowance. Trim close to the second stitching.

3. Press the seam allowances flat, then to one side. (Although this technique results in a raw edge, the second row of stitching helps keeps the seam allowance from raveling. A narrow zigzag stitch may be substituted for the second row of straight stitching.)

Hems

Before marking the hem on any sheer garment, let it hang at least 24 hours. Try one of these subtle, machine-sewn hem finishes to keep your edges neat, clean, and elegant.

NARROW ZIGZAG HEM

The narrow zigzag hem works especially well on the bias, because it has a tiny bit of stretch. (Hang your bias-cut sheer garment for 48 hours before hemming.)

1. Mark the hemline, then trim the hem allowance to ½ in. Press the hem allowance to the wrong side of the garment on the hemline.

2. Set the machine for a short, narrow zigzag stitch. (Test on a scrap to get the best stitch results.)

Sewing from the right side of the fabric, begin stitching, allowing the needle to just catch the folded edge of the fabric when it swings to the right. Stitch all the way around the hem in this manner.

3. Trim away the excess hem allowance using appliqué scissors (page 25).

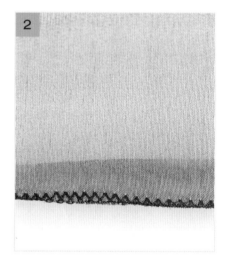

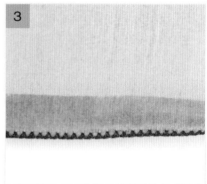

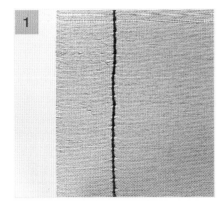

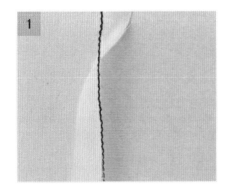

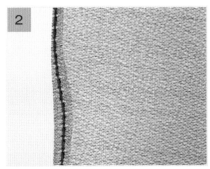

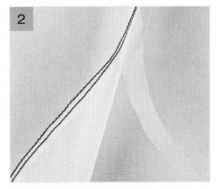

NARROW CHIFFON HEM

Even though there is a raw edge in the chiffon hem, the second stitching holds it close and prevents raveling. Use this technique to hem large, square scarves as well as garments.

1. Mark the hemline. Trim the hem allowance to ½ in. Stitch on the hemline all the way around the garment. Press the hem allowance to the wrong side along the stitched hemline.

2. Edgestitch again through all layers, close to the original hemline. Trim the excess hem allowance with appliqué scissors, close to the second row of stitching.

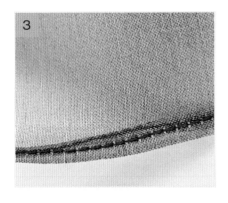

NARROW ROLLED HEM

This rolled hem is a double-fold hem, but the hem allowance is only ⅛ in., so it looks almost like a roll.

1. Mark the hemline, then trim the hem allowance to ⅝ in. Stitch ½ in. from the raw edge.

2. Press the hem allowance to the garment wrong side, along the stitched line. Trim the hem allowance to ⅛ in.

3. Fold the edge over once more. Edgestitch close to the inner fold from the right side of the garment.

3

Special Occasion Fabrics

Sewing your own special occasion garments guarantees you a look that's unique and truly you. It's inspiring to work with silk, lace, beaded, and sequined textiles. You may not sew these fabrics often, though, so it's worthwhile to review the techniques best suited to them before beginning. The extra care you take in sewing these fabrics will be richly repaid in a garment that flatters the wearer—so her event is special, indeed.

SILK AND SILKY FABRICS

Lustrous fabrics—whether they're fluid and slinky, like charmeuse or crepe de Chine, or crisp like organza, dupioni, and taffeta—have a wonderful sheen and feel luxurious against the skin. They're lovely for evening and bridal wear, as well as for lingerie.

Types of Silky Fabrics

Silky fabrics come in many fibers, weaves, colors, and patterns, and at a wide range of price points. While all lustrous fabrics have a smooth surface, some are drapey and malleable, and others have a crisp, almost paperlike hand. The effect these fabrics give are quite different, so explore your options before buying and consider the garment's requirements.

Fiber content influences how a fabric behaves in the presence of heat and humidity, which in turn determines how easy it is to press and mold, and how it feels when worn. Pure silk insulates and absorbs, is wearable in warm or cool climates, resists wrinkles, presses well, and can be eased and shaped without difficulty. It comes in a gamut of colors, weights, and weaves, and is always a classic.

Synthetic silklike fabrics (which can be made of cellulose fibers, like rayon, or petroleum-based fibers, like polyester) are often less expensive than pure silk, and in some cases are easier to care for. Polyester fabrics tend to wrinkle very little, but some people find them uncomfortable in hot or cold temperatures. Rayon fabrics, while comfortable to wear, can shrink, pill, or sag. Hand-wash, press, and gently rub a swatch of the fabric to see how it will react to wear.

A fabric's weave structure, as well as surface finishes, contribute to its texture and body. Satin weaves, with long yarns lying on the surface, are quite shiny. Heavier satins, while liquid-looking, can be quite firm. Crepes, made from fibers that are slightly crimped, have a fine, pebbled surface and drapey hand. Charmeuse, which has one satin-finished side and one crepelike side, combines the look of both, but with a light, fluid hand.

Fabrics like taffeta, faille, dupioni, and shantung glisten softly and are very crisp in drape unless laundered first. They're somewhat easier to sew than the slippery, very shiny fabrics described above, due to their stable structure.

Layout and Cutting

As for all fabrics, pretreat the yardage and find the straight grain.

See "Pretreating Fabric," on page 70 & "Finding the Straight Grain," on page 104.

If the fabric is slippery or tends to shift as you lay it out, pin or tape it to a layer of paper, as described for sheer fabrics (see page 306). For accuracy, use a single-layer layout. Place fine, glass-head silk pins within the seam allowance, and secure the center with weights. Cut with serrated scissors or a rotary cutter. After cutting, and before moving the pieces, transfer the pattern markings with a double strand of silk or cotton thread.

Firm silky fabrics, like taffeta, dupioni, and faille, can usually be laid out in a double layer as for any stable woven. Use fine pins, and mark with thread tracing and tailor's tacks.

Construction Techniques

Always start with a new, sharp needle and fine cotton or silk thread. Use a short stitch length (1.5 mm), and

test it on scraps of fabric. If the fabric puckers, try shortening the stitch length to 1 mm. Handle the fabric without pulling it, allowing the machine to feed it through.

Interface silk or silky fabric with self-fabric or silk organza, which gives stability without adding stiffness to the garment. To create stability when stitching buttonholes, place a piece of silk organza between the feed dogs and the fashion fabric, then when opening the buttonhole, trim the excess organza from the back of the buttonhole.

SEAMS AND SEAM FINISHES

Select the seam and seam finish that create the strongest seam needed for that part of the garment, while minimizing bulk and preventing raveling. Fluid and crisp textiles typically call for different seam types. Make seam samples of fabric swatches, working on the straight and cross-grains, and along the bias if it occurs in the garment you're planning.

A French seam is suitable for lightweight silky fabrics, such as three- or four-ply crepe, crepe de Chine, and charmeuse. For these fabrics, follow the instructions for a reduced French seam provided on page 307, but sew the first seam at ⅜ in., trim the allowance to

Underline a draped bodice for shapely folds that stay put.

Soft fullness is the hallmark of gathered dupioni, especially when it's underlined with silk organza.

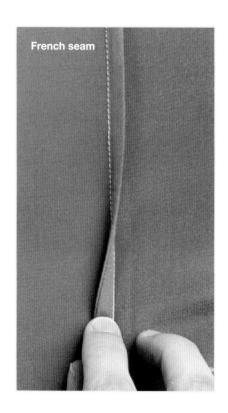

French seam

Double zigzag seam

Turned and stitched finish

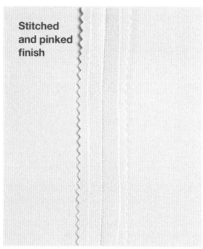

Stitched and pinked finish

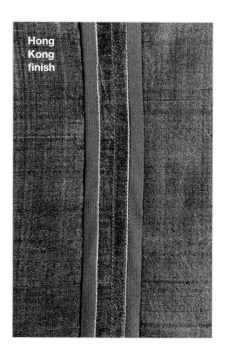

Hong Kong finish

⅛ in., press, and sew the second seam at ¼ in.

Also for lightweight fabrics, and for seams on the bias, a double zigzag seam works well. Although there is a raw edge, the seam is extremely flexible and stretches slightly. Start with a ¾-in.-wide seam allowance. Set the machine for a zigzag stitch that's 1.5 mm long and 1.5 mm wide. Sew at ¾ in. Adjust the zigzag to a slightly wider and longer stitch (2.5 mm long and 2.5 mm wide), and sew another row next to the first row, within the seam allowance. Trim close to the stitching.

A turned and stitched finish is a good choice for opaque fabrics, and in places where the seam allowances are pressed open. Press the raw edges of the seam allowances under ¼ in., and edgestitch along the fold, sewing only through the seam allowance (not the garment).

If removing bulk is your main goal in a seam finish, use a stitched and pinked finish. This can be ideal for gowns that

won't receive a lot of wear. The look is less finished than with a finish that completely encloses the raw edges, but there's no worry of ridges showing. Sew the seam, press the seam allowances open, and sew a row of straight stitches ¼ in. from the cut edge. Then pink the raw edges.

For firm medium- to heavyweight fabrics, a Hong Kong or serged finish is appropriate. Make a test swatch and press it to determine if the seams create a ridge on the garment right side.

BROCADE

Brocade—which can be made of silk, silk and rayon, or polyester—has floating threads that create a satinlike texture, and is patterned with complex, woven designs. It's dense, firm, stable, and easy to sew. Because it has plenty of body, brocade is best suited to fitted garments, from jackets and coats to dresses, vests, straight skirts, and narrow pants. Choose patterns with dart or seam shaping to avoid a stiff, boxy look.

Note that silk-faced brocade (that is, fabric that's mostly silk on the right side, with a rayon backing) becomes spongy, crepey, and supple when washed and dried. Experiment with washing brocade if you're interested in a softer, slightly antique look.

LACE

Lace is often considered suitable only for wedding gowns, lingerie, and children's clothing. But it comes in a vast range of colors and types, and can take on a variety of characteristics. From frothy white trims to heavy, luxurious black fabric, you can find lace that's appropriate for any special occasion garment.

Alençon

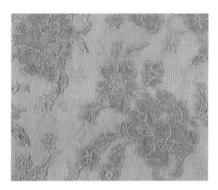

Chantilly

Guipure

Most brocade yardage is relatively narrow, from just 30 in. to 45 in. in width. Plan carefully when purchasing to be sure you have enough for your garment.

Construction Techniques

When sewing brocade, follow the guidelines for sewing silk fabrics, but note that brocade frays excessively at the cut edges. If the garment won't be lined, finish the edges either by serging, by binding, or with a Hong Kong finish.

Brocade is easy to press, but if you accidentally press a crease in the fabric, it's very hard to get out. The glossy surface shows needle marks, so plan ahead and avoid having to remove stitching. The satin weave can look puckered when topstitched, so consider replacing topstitching with some other edge or seam detail, such as piping.

TIP

To avoid pressing imprints that show on the right side of the garment, slip a piece of craft paper between the edge of a dart or the cut edge of the seam allowance and the wrong side of the garment fabric.

Types of Lace

Although there are many varieties of lace, three types are used most often in dressmaking: Alençon, Chantilly, and Guipure (pronounced ghi-PYUR). Each has its own qualities and handling requirements. They're generally woven in widths of 36 in. or less and have lovely borders. Guipure and some Alençons can be cut apart and pieced together to take full advantage of their intricate designs. All types are delicate and should be handled gently during construction and wear.

Once you've fallen in love with a piece of lace, study it to familiarize yourself with the density and repeat of its pattern and symmetry of motifs. Many lace fabrics are made with wide, ornate borders; these borders can be cut off and used separately as a perfectly coordinating trim for the garment.

ALENÇON

Alençon lace features a fine net backing, intricate patterns, and corded embroidery around its motifs. As long as the motifs are densely placed, you can cut around them and piece the lace into the desired shape, without an underlay. This type of lace has a light, delicate appearance similar to Chantilly, but is stronger due to its cording. It can be cut apart and reassembled to fashion darts or shaping seams.

CHANTILLY

Chantilly lace is weightless and softly feminine; with lightweight motifs on a delicate net backing. Use it as an embellishment added to a foundation fabric. It's too fragile to stand on its own, but is lovely as an overlay, especially when its decorative borders are used as part of the garment design. It can be gathered, but is not suitable for a lot of seaming or shaping.

GUIPURE

This heavy, densely patterned lace, which doesn't have a net backing, works best when tacked to a structured underlayer and lining, which are shaped to fit the body and which provide support for the lace's weight. It's ideal for simple styles like the straight skirt shown on the facing page, where side seams can be eliminated or converted to darts. To create shaping in guipure lace, cut between the motifs and overlap or join the cut edges.

Layout and Cutting

To make a lace garment, or portion of a garment, begin with a well-fitting muslin pattern. Be sure to make a full, labeled pattern, with both right and left sides, minus hem and seam allowances. Take this pattern to the shop and use it to make a provisional layout, so you know exactly how much lace to purchase.

Lay a length of lace yardage, right side up, on a table, and arrange the pattern pieces under it, also right sides up. Use the lace's borders for hems and

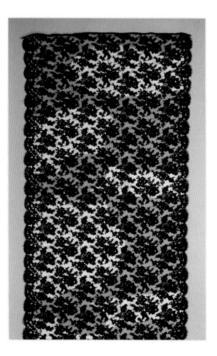

edges, and try to maintain symmetry between right and left halves of the garment. When possible, arrange adjoining seamlines so that border motifs will appear continuous when the garment is sewn. This trial layout shows exactly how much lace you need.

For the actual layout, reposition the pattern pieces as desired, and pin them to the lace through the motifs (not through the netting). Thread-trace around the perimeter of each pattern piece to transfer its outlines, and mark darts in the same way. Then cut the pattern pieces, leaving wide seam allowances and preserving any full motifs that straddle a seamline.

Construction Techniques

Each piece of lace is unique, so you need to decide ahead of time which of the techniques described here are best suited to your fabric. You can sew lace by hand or machine; match the thread color to the lace so the stitches disappear into the fabric's weave. When machine stitching lace, use polyester thread and a standard presser foot.

STANDARD SEAMS AND EDGES

Sew seams that receive stress, such as sleeve and armscye seams, by machine, with right sides together. Keep seam allowances out of sight by binding them with organza that matches the wearer's skin tone.

For edge finishing, facings are often out of the question. Instead, use a narrow strip of bias-cut organza or charmeuse to bind the edge. First staystitch along the seamline, and remove any ornamentation (beads, sequins, and so on) from the lace in the seam allowance. Machine-stitch the binding to the edge, fold it over, and slipstitch or fell-stitch the folded edge in place.

When using Chantilly lace, with or without an underlay, you can try sewing a French seam for any straight seams. If the seam is too bulky, use a standard seam, with bound or overcast edges as shown in the top left photo below.

Darts can be sewn the same way. In the vicinity of the marked dart (it's not necessary to be exactly on the markings), define a route that follows the corded edge of one or more motifs—the "leading edge." Cut open the dart on this line and overlap

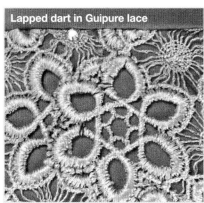

Lapped dart in Guipure lace

the leading edge, aligning the dart markings. Pin the dart closed, and sew it by hand, stitching through all layers along the corded leading edge. On the interior of the garment, trim away the lace underlap of the dart, fairly close to the stitching.

UNDERLINING AND UNDERLAYS

Most lace works best when sewn with an underlayer of some sort for support, opacity (if desired), and structure. For Chantilly and Alençon lace, make an underlay of lightweight fabric, such as silk charmeuse (for an opaque underlayer), sheer illusion (available where you purchase bridal fabrics), netting or organza (for a transparent underlayer). Apply these as you would a standard underlining (see page 267). To stabilize Alençon lace, hand-tack the lace to the underlayer here and there, through the

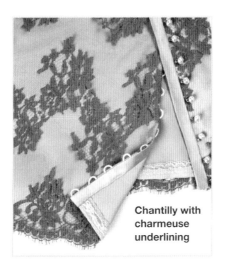

Chantilly with charmeuse underlining

Alençon with sheer illusion underlay

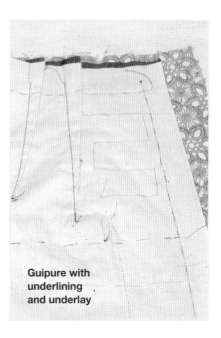

Guipure with underlining and underlay

lace motifs. If desired, you can cut the underlay with extra-wide seam allowances, and use the excess to enclose the raw edges.

Guipure lace's weight calls for greater support than is needed for Alençon or Chantilly. For best results, attach it to a structured underlayer. Start by sewing the garment in sections, with a stable underlining (such as muslin) beneath the fashion fabric underlay. Baste the layers together and use thread tracing to indicate the centers and the straight and cross-grain lines on the underlining.

Lay out the lace facedown, and spread a garment section facedown over it. Trim the lace around the section, then tack the layers together, working from the right side of the lace. Tack the hem edge, then the center-front and center-back lines, and finally tack in parallel, vertical rows. Use tiny backstitches. Once the layers have been joined, proceed to create lapped or standard seams, and lapped darts (see above).

SEQUINED AND BEADED FABRIC

Embellished fabrics are wonderful options for special occasion garments, but must be handled with care so the sequins or beads aren't damaged during sewing and pressing.

Line garments made from embellished fabrics to protect the wearer from any beads or sequins left in the seam allowances, to support the seams, and to prevent snagging. Cut and fit the lining before cutting the embellished fabric. Make the outer layer slightly bigger than the lining so the lining takes the strain of wear.

When purchasing embellished fabrics, save all the scraps, and consider buying a little extra. The remnants provide spare sequins and beads to replace any that you remove during construction.

Sequined Fabric

There are two categories of sequined fabric: Those with densely overlapped sequins, for a raised, scaly texture, and those with sequins sewn flat, either closely spaced or widely scattered.

Cut sequined fabric using a single-layer, with-nap layout. For overlapped sequins, the smooth direction of the fabric should run from top to bottom of the garment. Cut with a sharp rotary cutter, with the fabric facedown.

Sequins tend to be sensitive to heat, so test before pressing. If the sequins can withstand the heat of the iron, press the fabric facedown, with a layer of paper over it and a low-temperature, dry iron. Opt for sew-in interfacings, to avoid fusing at high temperatures.

When sewing fabric with overlapped sequins, sew by hand. Fold under the seam allowances and place the fabric

LADDER STITCH FOR JOINING SEQUINED SEAMS

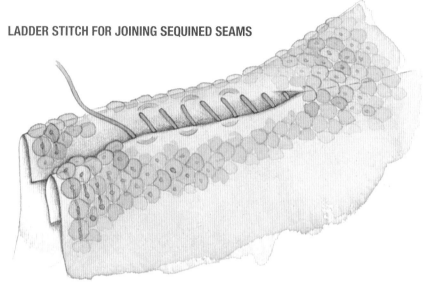

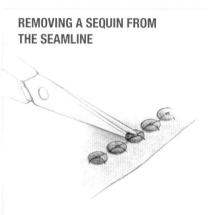

REMOVING A SEQUIN FROM THE SEAMLINE

REMOVING A BEAD FROM THE SEAMLINE

wrong sides together. Join them with a loose ladder stitch, pulling stitches tight every 1½ in. This merges the sequins, flattens the fabrics, and conceals the stitches. Stitch in place to lock the seam, and repeat.

If the sequins are attached flat to the fabric, remove them from the seam allowances before sewing. You can then sew the seams by machine. To remove individual sequins without cutting the thread that's holding them to the fabric, push the sequin away from the thread and cut through the center of the sequin. If you happen to leave a sequin along a seamline, don't worry. You can machine-sew through sequins with little trouble. Sew the seam by machine, and

fill in any bare spots by hand-sewing sequins harvested from fabric remnants.

Beaded Fabric

Because you can't sew through beads, you must remove them from the seamline before sewing. Avoid cutting the threads that attach the beads, because if you cut one, the neighboring beads are likely to fall off as well. Instead, push a pin through the bead's hole to protect the thread, then use needle-nose pliers to break the beads off the thread. Remove as few as possible, and install a zipper foot so you can sew along the narrow track you've formed.

WHITE FABRIC

White fabrics are no more difficult to sew than any other, but it's important to plan ahead when working with them so the finished garment is as clean as the fabric was when you started. Start by cleaning your sewing area thoroughly, including your machine, your iron, and your ironing board cover.

Avoiding Show-Through

White fabrics are notoriously transparent, so test for opacity before sewing. Use a lining and, if necessary, an underlining. In most cases, white is best, but occasionally you may find that one matching the wearer's skin tone works better. Layer the fashion fabric over its underlayers and check that the white or the fabric isn't altered. Even a slightly off-white lining can dull bright white fabric.

White Notions

When choosing thread, match the color as closely as possible to the particular white of the fabric (it may be snow white, ecru, cream, and so on). To sew very lightweight fabrics, use fine silk thread in natural blends with any shade of white. Skip beeswax or thread conditioner when you're hand sewing, as they may discolor the fabric.

Because white fabric is often more transparent than a colored version of the same textile, fusible interfacings can show through unexpectedly. Test any fusible first, and if you're able to see the adhesive dots, opt for a sew-in, such as silk organza or cotton batiste.

Look for white or clear plastic snaps and white hooks and eyes. These hide nicely on white garments. To keep zippers as unobtrusive as possible, move them to the side seam.

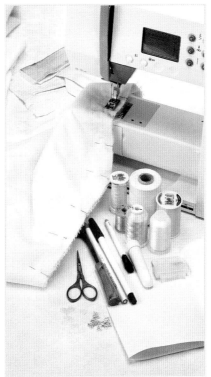

Handling White Fabrics

Avoid marking white fabric with anything but white. Use white tracing paper, white chalk, or white thread for thread tracing and tailor's tacks. Any other color marking may leave permanent traces on the fabric. If the garment is underlined, transfer marks to the underlining (see page 287) rather than to the outer fabric.

Before sewing, wash your hands, and don't use hand lotion, which might stain the fabric. Check that your clothing doesn't shed dark lint or transfer dye.

When pressing, use a white press cloth; it can be organza, batiste, or even wool. If the garment is large and drapes to the floor, place a clean sheet on the floor under the ironing board to keep it clean.

Pile & Napped Fabrics

4

The sewing term *nap* refers to the raised fibers on the surface of a textile. Napped fabrics can be woven or knit and made from many different fibers. Wool and cotton flannel, melton cloth, camel's hair, mohair, brushed denim, and even Ultrasuede®, a nonwoven synthetic fabric, all have nap.

Pile fabrics like chenille, corduroy, terry cloth, velour, and velvet are knitted or woven with an extra set of yarns to make a looped pile on one or both sides; these loops may or may not be cut. Both napped and pile fabrics reflect light differently from different directions, and must be cut with this in mind.

TYPES OF NAPPED AND PILE FABRICS

Any fabric that has a fuzzy or brushed surface should be treated as a napped or pile fabric. Even if the surface seems uniform in all directions, it's possible that, when worn, subtle differences in shading may show up.

Some of the most common pile or napped fabrics include corduroy, velvet and velour, and real or faux fur.

Corduroy

Corduroy is usually made of cotton or cotton blended with polyester, and sometimes spandex is added for stretch. It's characterized by pile that's cut in a striped pattern called wales, which run parallel to the fabric's straight grain. The wales vary from 22 per in., on lightweight corduroy, to 3 per in. You can find corduroy in a large range of colors, as well as prints. Prewash corduroy yardage to soften and shrink it.

Velvet

Velvets range in weight from chiffon to heavy upholstery fabrics. Originally made of silk, velvet is now available in cotton, rayon, acetate, polyester, and

Corderoy

Glossary of Common Velvets

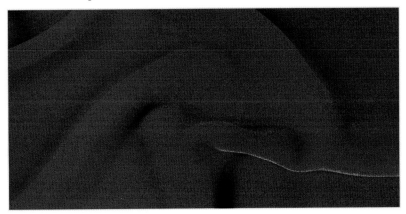

Velvet is available in a variety of types, distinguished primarily by how the pile is treated.

BURNOUT VELVET (DÉVORÉ)
Burnout velvet starts with plain velvet in which the pile is made of protein fiber, such as silk, and the backing of a cellulose fiber, typically rayon. The fabric is printed with a protein-eating chemical that removes the pile from the printed areas, creating a textured pattern made up of sheer areas and areas with pile.

CRUSHED VELVET
The velvet's pile is textured by pressing in different directions to create a pattern.

CUT VELVET
A brocaded pattern is woven on a jacquard loom to create a distinct pattern in the pile on a plain fabric background. The background can range from sheer fabrics such as chiffon, georgette, or voile, to heavy satins.

EMBOSSED VELVET
A textured, nonpermanent surface is created by pressing the velvet with engraved rollers and heat.

PANNÉ VELVET
A lightweight, highly lustrous velvet with flattened pile, which is laid in one direction, finished with very heavy roller pressure. This is usually a knit.

SCULPTURED VELVET
The velvet's pile is trimmed to various heights to create a sculptured pattern.

VELOUR
This term is loosely applied to all types of fabric, woven or knit, with nap or cut pile on one side.

VELVET AND VELVETEEN
True velvet is made with a warp pile (that is, on the straight grain), and velveteen is made with a weft, or cross-grain, pile. When folded with wrong sides together, velveteen "breaks" on the lengthwise grain, and velvet breaks on the crossgrain. Velveteen pile unravels on the cross-grain between filling rows and velvet pile unravels on the lengthwise grain between warp piles.

various blends. It's usually woven as double cloth. Two layers of fabric are woven simultaneously, one on top of the other. The pile, which joins the two layers, is then cut to create that signature, luxurious nap.

Faux Fur

Although you can purchase natural pelts, it's much easier and usually more cost-effective to work with faux fur. Faux fur is made of synthetic fibers—usually nylon, acrylic, or polyester—on a synthetic knit backing or a woven cotton backing. Knit-backed faux furs are typically less expensive than woven, cotton-backed types.

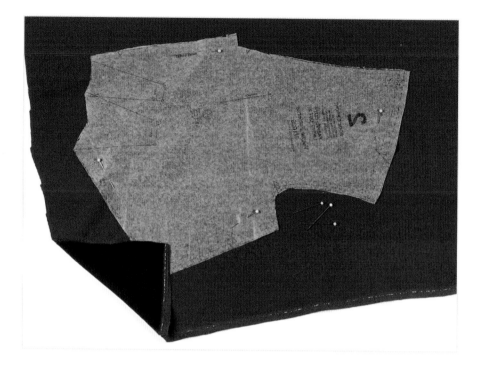

With synthetic fur, you'll find myriad colors and textures, some mimicking natural fur textures and colors, others in completely artificial colors and styles.

LAYOUT AND CUTTING

All napped and pile fabrics should be cut using a consistent "with-nap" layout (see page 106). This prevents differences in shading from appearing on the finished garment.

Decide the direction in which the nap or pile will run on the finished garment either by feel or by look. Rub your hand over the fabric following the straight of grain, or selvage edge. If the surface feels smooth, you're brushing with the nap or pile. If it feels rough, you're brushing against it. Many sewers cut napped fabrics with the nap running from the top of the garment down so the nap stays flat and the fabric wears better.

Alternatively, hang the fabric yardage around your neck, so the nap or pile runs up on one side, and down on the other. Choose the side that looks best to you, and cut the garment in that direction. Some pile fabrics look darker when the pile runs up from the hem. Mark the desired nap direction on the wrong side of the fabric.

To cut faux fur, make a full set of pattern pieces, with both right and left sides. Lay faux fur wrong side up in a single layer on a cutting table, and place the pattern pieces facedown on the fabric backing. Pin them to the backing. Trace around the pattern with a felt-tip pen, then remove the pattern paper to cut through the faux fur backing.

Cut pile fabrics with scissors, cutting carefully through the backing, without cutting the pile. Alternatively, cut fur with a craft knife, cutting only through the backing.

For easily visible but completely removable marks that don't damage or crush the surface of napped and pile fabrics, use tailor's tacks and thread tracing. Mark notches by clipping into the seam allowance.

CONSTRUCTION TECHNIQUES

The pile on velvet or fur fabrics can interfere with standard sewing and pressing techniques, because it inhibits the fabric from layering smoothly. The methods described here help you manage these textiles easily.

Seams

For velvet, velveteen, and velour, follow these guidelines:

- Hand-baste, with a double row of basting, a large backstitch, or diagonal basting.
- Loosen the machine tension.
- Install a universal or sharp machine needle, size 70/10 or 80/12.

- Thread the machine with cotton or silk thread.
- Hold the fabric taut as you sew.
- Use a walking foot, Teflon® foot, or roller foot.
- Stitch with tissue paper or a stabilizer between the layers and/or between the fabric and the feed dogs.
- Stitch in the direction of the pile.
- Trim and grade seam allowances to reduce bulk.

If basting doesn't hold the layers well enough, use temporary spray adhesive.

See "Spray Adhesives," on page 48.

Mask the garment section with a sheet of paper, if desired, leaving only the seam allowance exposed. Spray a light line of adhesive along the seam allowance, on the fabric's right side. Then place the right side of the corresponding piece along the seamline, aligning the cut edges, and gently press to adhere the layers before sewing. The adhesive dissipates cleanly, but test first to be sure it doesn't damage your fabric. Seam allowances can be treated with a pinked, serged, or Hong Kong finish.

Sew faux fur by machine, using a large sharp or ballpoint needle (size 90/14 or 100/16), and either a long straight stitch or a long, wide zigzag stitch. As you stitch, use a pin or awl to push the pile fibers between the fabric layers and away from the cut edge. After sewing, comb the fibers out of the seamline on the right side so they cover the seamline. On the garment wrong side, clip or shave the pile from the seam allowances.

Pressing

Pressing velvet is always delicate work. It is easy to mar the pile with an iron, so use only steam. Never allow the iron to touch the fabric. There are several pressing board surfaces you can use to safely position the velvet pile-side down while steaming from the wrong side.

Always "hover" the iron; never press directly on the fabric.

See "Pressing Techniques," on page 147.

Never press faux fur; the fibers are heat sensitive and can be damaged by the iron. A low-temperature garment steamer may be used to gently fluff crushed fur, but test first in an unobtrusive spot on the garment to see if this method is safe for your fabric.

Stripes, Plaids & Large Prints

Stripes, plaids, and large prints inject bold design into even the simplest garment style. Whether you like your plaid, stripe, or print perfectly matched or purposefully not, proper planning is essential to a successful garment. To work successfully with these fabrics, analyze both the fabric, focusing on the horizontal and vertical repeat of the pattern, and the style lines of the garment. The size of the repeat may be in conflict with the garment design. For example, many seams and small garment sections may not work well with large plaids. But if you find a fabric you love, you can find a pattern that will result in a stand-out garment you love to wear.

STRIPES

For the most attractive striped garments, select designs that have few section seams. For example, favor darted bodices over those shaped by princess seams, and consider pant styles that have no side seam. Avoid patterns in which a longer fabric section must be eased to a shorter one.

On most garments, some basic matching of stripes is desirable, although you don't need to match the stripes at every seam or edge. Decide which seams are most obvious, and try to match the stripes there. A general rule to observe is to match vertical stripes at horizontal seams (such as waistline and shoulder seams), and to match horizontal stripes at vertical seams (such as side seams, and center front or back). It's nearly impossible to match stripes perfectly at armscye seams, so (with horizontal stripes) match a few stripes at the front armscye curve, and let the rest fall as they may.

Before you lay out and cut the pattern, assess the fabric's stripe pattern to determine whether the stripe is balanced (even) or unbalanced (uneven). Balanced stripes are composed of symmetrical repeats, so the stripes are the same in either direction. Unbalanced stripes have asymmetrical repeats, so you need more yardage to match stripes on these fabrics.

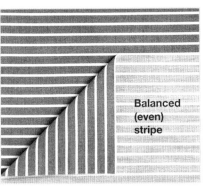

Balanced (even) stripe

Unbalanced (uneven) stripe

WHERE TO MATCH STRIPES

MATCH AT SIDE SEAMS, FRONT OF SLEEVES.

MATCH AT SHOULDER SEAMS.

PARALLEL AT CENTER FRONT.

MATCH AT CENTER FRONT, THEN SIDE SEAMS.

CHEVRON AT SIDES, PARALLEL AT CENTER SEAM.

Layout and Matching

To ensure that the stripes match properly, use a single-layer layout. Make a full pattern with both right and left sides of each piece.

For horizontal stripes, aim to place a dominant stripe at the hemline, and to avoid placing dominant stripes in unflattering positions, such as across the fullest part of the torso. Lay out the garment front first, then match the remaining pieces to this one by aligning corresponding notches at the same part of the stripe repeat.

With vertical stripes, try to center the bodice and sleeves in the middle of a stripe repeat, or on a dominant stripe. If the stripe repeat is unbalanced, you must decide whether you want the stripes mirrored symmetrically on the garment or moving in a single direction around the garment.

PLANNING A STRIPE LAYOUT

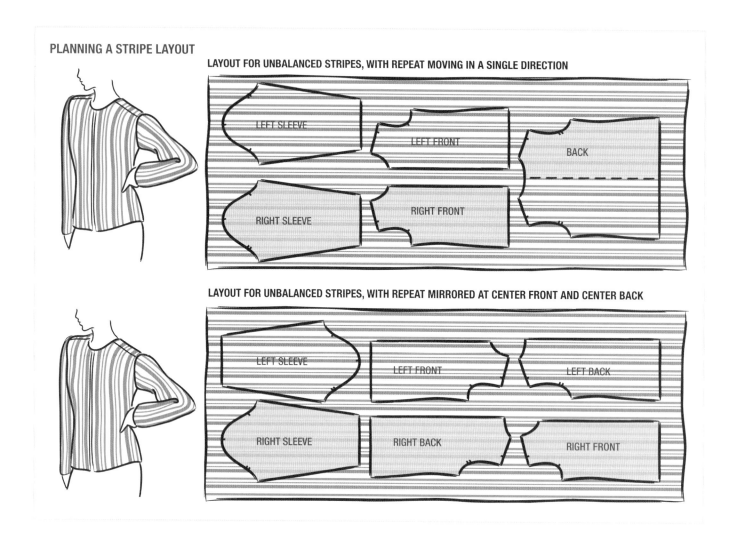

LAYOUT FOR UNBALANCED STRIPES, WITH REPEAT MOVING IN A SINGLE DIRECTION

LEFT SLEEVE

LEFT FRONT

BACK

RIGHT SLEEVE

RIGHT FRONT

LAYOUT FOR UNBALANCED STRIPES, WITH REPEAT MIRRORED AT CENTER FRONT AND CENTER BACK

LEFT SLEEVE

LEFT FRONT

LEFT BACK

RIGHT SLEEVE

RIGHT BACK

RIGHT FRONT

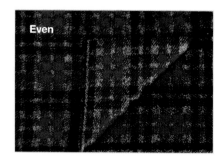

Even

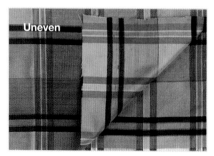

Uneven

PLAIDS

Like stripes, plaid patterns can be either even or uneven; your layout must take into account the plaid structure and repeat in order to match the lines in both directions.

In an even plaid, the line configuration is the same in the lengthwise and crosswise directions. In an uneven plaid, the spacing is different in one or both directions. Uneven plaids and stripes require a special layout to get a matched look.

To determine whether a plaid is even or uneven, fold a corner of the fabric (on the straight grain) at a 45-degree angle through the center of any repeat.

If it is even, the lines and colors match in both directions, and form a mirror image when folded horizontally through a repeat.

Layout and Matching

Successful matching is determined at the cutting table. For a perfectly matched layout, it's often helpful to make a full pattern, and lay the fabric out in a single layer. If you prefer to use a double-layer (folded) layout, fold the fabric along the center of a vertical repeat, and pin the layers to keep the plaid lines aligned as you work.

If your fabric is an even plaid, you can, in theory, lay the pattern out in any direction. With an uneven plaid, all the pattern pieces must be laid out with their bottom edges facing the same direction, as in a with-nap layout. It's your choice whether the vertical stripes are arranged in a mirror image on the body or go around the body in one direction.

In all cases, place bodice and sleeve centers on a dominant vertical stripe, and position the horizontal stripes as desired for the most flattering effect. The priority for matching the vertical stripes is high at the center back bodice and collar, at the shoulder seams, and on pockets or pocket welts. Elsewhere, give higher priority to matching the horizontal stripes. Always begin by positioning a major garment section—the bodice front or back, for example—and work outward from there.

1. Carefully fold the fabric in half on the centering line you choose, pinning the layers together to keep the lines together. Lay patterns marked "place on fold" (for example, the bodice back, or the collar) along the fold, aligning the horizontal stripes as desired.

2. For each adjoining pattern piece, align the notches on the same horizontal line (or a corresponding one on a different part of the fabric), so the horizontal lines match when the pieces are joined. To

Creative Striping

Stripes lend themselves to great design opportunities, and by shifting the grain on stripes, you can solve matching problems while creating interesting visual effects. When making mitered or chevron patterns at a seamline, remember that the stripes must intersect the joining seam at equal angles from each side, to ensure that they match properly.

Sewing Plaids and Stripes

Once you've laid out and cut the garment so the stripes or plaid is perfectly matched, baste the seams so the layers don't shift out of place during stitching.

Fold one seam allowance under along the seamline. Lay this piece on top of the adjoining section, aligning the seamlines and matching any notches. Pin through all layers to secure. Then, slipstitch the top layer to the bottom layer along its folded edge, making sure that all horizontal and vertical stripes match or chevron as planned.

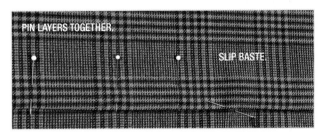

Remove the pins, and fold the top layer back so the pieces are right sides together with raw edges aligned. Sew the seam, and remove the basting stitches.

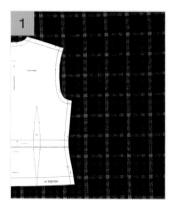

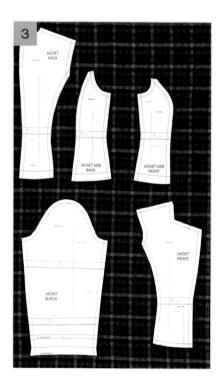

make this easier, trace some of the plaid lines onto the pattern tissue to use as a matching guide. Once these pieces are properly placed on a horizontal stripe, shift them right or left to position them as desired on the vertical stripes.

3. To match set-in sleeves, first center the sleeve pattern piece on a dominant vertical stripe. Then move it up or down, using the armscye and sleeve-cap notches as guides. Place the sleeve-cap notches as close as possible to the corresponding front and back notches on the armscye. The sleeves will match from the notch down. They may not match perfectly above the notch, where the ease in the sleeve cap makes the sleeve seamline slightly longer than the armscye seamline.

4. With right sides together, line up the seamlines carefully and pin the layers together. Place the pins perpendicular to the seam to prevent slippage while you

sew. For longer seams, or when the fabric is slippery, slipstitch first (see page 325). Then fold the right sides back together and machine-stitch the seamline.

LARGE PRINTS

Like plaids and stripes, large prints have a repeat, or interval at which a decorative motif or pattern is duplicated along the width (horizontal repeat) and length (vertical repeat) of the fabric. For a fabric pattern to be included in the extra-large category, the horizontal and vertical repeats must be at least 6 in. The motifs themselves, however, may not be that large.

It's always useful to identify the size, type, and direction of a fabric's repeat so you can strategically position pattern pieces and estimate yardage. To determine the repeat, select a prominent motif at the fabric edge, and mark it with a pin. Scan the fabric until you find the next instance of that motif, and pin. After you have pin-marked several motifs, step back to get the big picture. The repeat should become crystal clear.

For many prints, you need to use a with-nap layout so the motifs all face the same way on the finished garment (see the chart "Understanding Large Print Repeats" on page 327). To control the position of the motifs on the body, make a full set of pattern pieces, and lay them out on a single layer of fabric.

Style and Positioning

- Use a print in a garment that flatters your figure. Remember, a print draws the eye. If you have a trim torso, try a jacket. If you're slim-hipped, make a skirt or pants.

- Opt for tailored silhouettes rather than boxy shapes.

- Plan around fitting details, like darts or pleats. These small tucks of fabric can interfere with large motifs.

- Try to achieve key matches: the center front closure of a top, front armhole and sleeve cap, center-front and center-back skirt seams, and crotch seams of pants.

- Don't center a prominent motif on a breast, your abdomen, or derrière.

- Don't reject a print because you can't match it at all seams. Just match where you can.

Understanding Large Print Repeats

The print repeat determines your pattern layout. It also helps you to determine the yardage required. First ascertain the type of repeat: straight (motifs are aligned in horizontal and vertical rows) or half-drop (the motifs are staggered for a diagonal or zigzag effect). Then decide if the pattern is nondirectional (it looks the same upside down) or directional (it has a definite top/bottom and does not look the same upside down).

STRAIGHT, NONDIRECTIONAL REPEAT

(Requires the least yardage and is the easiest to work with)

You can turn and flip pattern pieces without fear of including an upside-down motif, and therefore fit the pieces closer together.

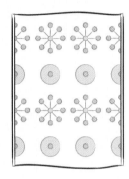

STRAIGHT, DIRECTIONAL REPEAT

(Requires the most yardage)

You need to make sure the tops of all pattern pieces point in the same direction (follow the "with nap" layout on your pattern instruction sheet). And to capture a dominant motif and/or achieve a critical match, you'll need to drop your pattern piece down to the next vertical repeat.

HALF-DROP, NONDIRECTIONAL REPEAT

(Looks intimidating, but is easy to work with, and doesn't require much yardage)

You can turn and flip pattern pieces, and because the motifs are offset, you don't need to drop down as far to capture a dominant motif and/or achieve a critical match. This print is also a good choice for a bias-cut garment.

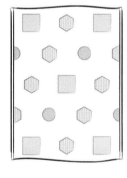

HALF-DROP, DIRECTIONAL REPEAT

(Is downright challenging)

It doesn't usually require as much yardage as a straight, directional repeat. You need to make sure the tops of all pattern pieces point in the same direction (use the "with nap" layout) and then strategically position the zigzagging motifs within each pattern piece.

XV
SURFACE EMBELLISHMENT

Decorative Machine Stitching

You can do more with your sewing machine than just construct garments. With specialized needles and decorative threads, you can create unique embellishments, too. From basic topstitching (see page 151) to delicate openwork, such as hemstitching and fagoting, most contemporary sewing machines are able to produce an assortment of effects that will suit any style. By mastering these decorative techniques, you'll get to know your machine better and improve your overall sewing skills.

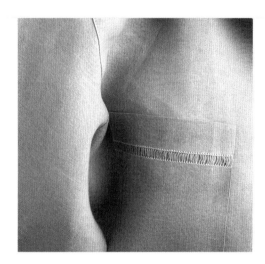

MACHINE HEMSTITCHING

This decorative technique, often associated with heirloom sewing, adds a delicate embellishment while finishing and securing an edge. Historically, hemstitching was an involved process of pulling out threads parallel to the hemline and then hand sewing the hem in a manner that grouped the remaining vertical threads to create spaced openings in the fabric. Today, hemstitching is easy to do by machine, using a wing needle, which has two finlike projections along its shaft, and an appropriate multistep stitch.

The hemstitch isn't only an embellishment. It's also intended to anchor the free edge of a hem allowance, while applying a decorative finish at the same time. You can use it on standard, fold-under hems or on edges that are finished with facings.

Tools and Materials

For the best results when hemstitching, use 100 percent linen fabric, although other natural-fiber fabrics can be used as well. Synthetic fibers don't retain the openwork definition as well as linen and cotton. If the fabric is lightweight or lacks body, starch it before hemstitching, or use tear-away stabilizer.

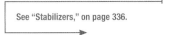

See "Stabilizers," on page 336.

Install a wing needle, which is essential for creating an open, lacy effect.

See "Specialty Needles," on page 13.

During the formation of the hemstitch, the wing needle separates the yarns, and the thread holds the holes open. Machine-embroidery thread is ideal for this purpose, as it's lightweight and has a subtle sheen. Experiment with different thread weights to find the one that produces the effect you want.

Stitch Selection

As the wing needle goes through the fabric, the wings spread the yarns and make a hole without cutting or tearing the fabric. For the best results, select a stitch that penetrates the fabric in the same place more than once (to create a defined hole), and that is wide enough to prevent the hem or facing's raw edge from raveling.

Be sure to test the stitch and needle on the machine by hand cranking through the stitch pattern several times. If the needle touches the presser foot or stitch plate at any point, change stitches or adjust the stitch width. Examples of standard stitches that are well suited to

Decorative Threads

Any time your stitching shows, you want it to look perfect. For added emphasis, choose a decorative thread. The texture and weight of these threads enhances stitching and stands out from the fabric. Test the thread on a swatch of fabric, and note that you might need a special needle to accommodate a thicker or more delicate-than-usual thread (see page 13).

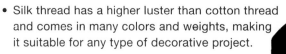

- Metallic thread, which is available in fine, medium, and heavy weights, usually requires a stronger thread in the bobbin for stability (cotton or polyester).

- Silk thread has a higher luster than cotton thread and comes in many colors and weights, making it suitable for any type of decorative project.

- Buttonhole twist, also known as topstitching thread, is thicker than regular sewing thread and is available in cotton, polyester, and silk.

- Machine embroidery thread is smoother and glossier than standard sewing thread and comes in various weights and fibers, including silk, acrylic, rayon, polyester, and cotton.

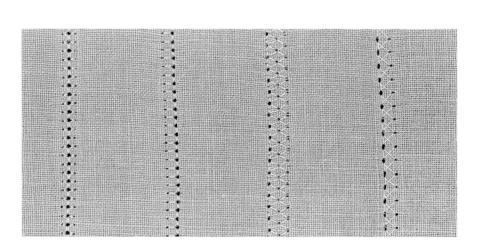

hemstitching are the ladder, overedge, smocking, honeycomb, blanket, and decorative daisy chain stitches. Refer to your owner's manual for the stitches available on your machine, and experiment with them.

Hemstitching Technique

Hemstitching is as easy as topstitching. Prepare the garment by folding under the desired hem allowance and pressing. There's no need to clean-finish the edge. If you're hemstitching along a faced edge, don't interface or clean-finish the facing. Sew it to the garment with right sides together, trim and clip the seam allowances as needed, and turn it to the garment wrong side. Press the opening edge, rolling the seamline slightly to the wrong side.

Install a wing needle, thread the machine with embroidery thread, and set it for the desired stitch. Position the garment faceup under the needle. If necessary, slide lightweight tear-away stabilizer under the work to support the stitches. Sew, keeping the stitches an even distance from the edge. When the stitching is complete, gently tear away the stabilizer, if present. Then, use appliqué scissors to trim the excess hem allowance or facing close to the stitching.

TWIN NEEDLE EFFECTS

Place a twin needle in your machine, and a wonderful array of embellishments can be easily, and sometimes magically, created. Attached to a single shaft, twin, or double, needles are inserted into the machine just like a single needle. The machine throat plate and presser foot need to have a hole wide enough to accommodate both needles, and some machines limit the usable stitch width for twin needle use.

Tools and Materials

Fine needles, closely spaced, are for lightweight fabrics. As the needles go up in size, the space between them increases. These larger needles are intended for heavier fabrics. The options for needle types include sharp, metallic, stretch, denim, and machine

Short rows of twin needle tucks texturize a plain fabric.

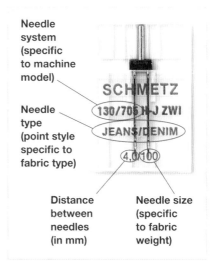

Needle system (specific to machine model)

Needle type (point style specific to fabric type)

SCHMETZ
130/705 H-J ZWI
JEANS/DENIM
4,0 100

Distance between needles (in mm)

Needle size (specific to fabric weight)

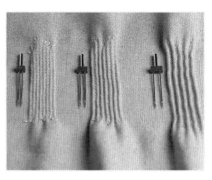

embroidery. A twin hemstitch needle set is also available, with a straight needle and a wing needle combination.

A flat presser foot ensures that the fabric stays flat between the two lines of stitches. Loosen the upper thread tension and use stabilizer to ensure flat stitching. A ridged or grooved foot encourages the fabric to form raised tucks between them, forming a pin-tuck effect. Feet with smaller grooves should be paired with close-set needles; the wider the space between the needles, the larger the grooves on the presser foot need to be. Tighten the upper tension to encourage the fabric to form pin tucks.

See "Presser Feet," on page 10.

Twin-Needle Threading

Each of the two needles is threaded from its own spool on top of the machine. A single bobbin serves both needles. When the machine is set to a straight stitch, the needle threads form two parallel rows of straight stitches on the fabric right side, and the bobbin thread forms a zigzag pattern on the wrong side. Triple needles (one shaft, three needles) work similarly.

FAGOTING

Fagoting is the process of filling a narrow space between garment sections with an open, decorative stitch. When done by hand, this technique requires extensive marking, measuring, and basting, in addition to the stitching itself. If you have a machine that makes decorative stitches at least 4 mm wide, you can duplicate this effect quickly and easily.

Tools and Materials

Choose fabric with enough body or stiffness to provide sharp, creased edges to define the space that will be filled with stitches, and resist puckering or pulling during stitching. Woven linens and cottons are usually perfect, but almost any light- to medium-weight natural-fiber or blended woven will fill the bill, or can be spray-starched to do so.

Straight-grain or cross-grain lines of fagoting are the easiest to control when stitching, but even curves and bias edges can be fagoted if the fabric is starched stiffly enough.

Work with cotton or rayon threads and use whatever needle suits your fabric and thread choices. Start with a basic zigzag presser foot, but also consider using a pin-tucking foot or

any other foot that has grooves and/or markings that will simplify guiding the two fagoted edges accurately under the needle. Equally important is that the foot holds both pieces being joined securely over the feed dogs.

Always make a practice sample. Adjust the space between the practice pieces until the stitches are properly centered between the finished fabric edges.

Stitch Selection

Almost any stitch that's at least 4 mm wide can be used for fagoting. Adjust the stitch length to create an effect you like. The stitches shown here are only some of the possibilities. Experiment with stitch width and length, as well as thread weight.

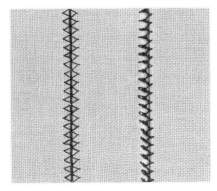

Venetian hemstitch

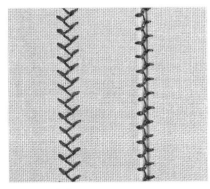

**Featherstitch
(with two strands of embroidery thread)**

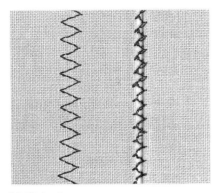

Multiple zigzag

Fagoting Technique

To stabilize the fagoting stitches and ensure that the edges along the open-work seam are clean and ravel-free, fold the raw edges under. The raw edges should then be serged, zigzagged, or clean-finished in some other way that suits the fabric. On each side of the seam that is to be fagoted, fold the raw edge under about 1 in. and spray-starch the folds several times. To reduce sticking, let the starch soak into the fabric for at least 10 seconds before ironing.

To begin stitching, hold the folded edges parallel, about ⅛ in. apart, and feed them under the foot. The stitch should swing from one edge to the other, catching each fold and making stitches across the space between. The stitches should look the same on each side of the space, and with most stitch patterns, there will be only a single edgestitch on each side.

To maintain a parallel and centered space, tape a flat plastic coffee stirrer directly in front of the presser foot, trimming it off if necessary where the sewing surface of your machine starts to tilt away from horizontal. This gives you an easy-to-follow guide for positioning and maintaining two parallel edges. Or you can cut a narrow strip of cardboard to the exact guide width you want and use it in the same manner.

Here are a few additional tips for successful guiding:

- Use a sewing table or bed extension on your machine, rather than just the free arm, when fagoting.

- Sit directly in front of the needle. It's much harder to guide if you're looking at the fabric from an angle.

- Use a slow, even rhythm when stitching.

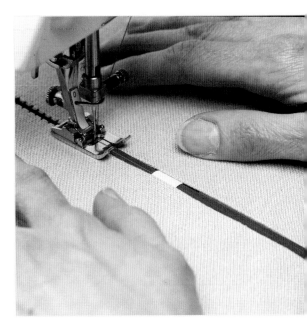

- Don't watch the needle going into the fabric (except at first as you center the stitch). Instead, watch the fabric as it moves past the guides on the foot.

- Work with wider pieces, because they're easier to guide. Trim them later, or baste extra fabric, stabilizer, or interfacing to the outer edges if you're trying to handle narrow strips.

- Apply more starch before stitching if your fabric is rippling.

- Loosen the upper thread tension a little, if the two pieces of fabric are being pulled together by the stitches.

Brother   AlphaSew

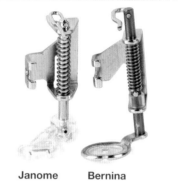

Janome   Bernina

Bernina   Pfaff

FREE-MOTION EMBROIDERY

Also referred to as "thread painting," free-motion embroidery can be done on any sewing machine. Lower (or cover) the feed dogs of your machine, and take control of the movement of the fabric as you're stitching, giving you total freedom to stitch in any direction, in any pattern, and at any stitch length.

Tools and Materials

The easiest way to manage fabric when free-motion stitching is with a free-motion or darning presser foot. This holds the fabric against the throat plate, and usually includes a ring around the area where the needle moves. You can find a free-motion foot for almost any brand of sewing machine; consult your dealer for more details. Alternatively, many embroiderers work without a presser foot, and simply avoid moving their fingers anywhere near the needle.

Free-motion embroidery can be done with or without an embroidery hoop. If you choose to hoop the fabric, hoop it so the fabric is at the bottom of the hoop rather than the top (as it would be for hand-embroidery). If you prefer not to use a hoop, you'll likely need a firm stabilizer to ensure that the fabric stays flat.

The real glamour comes from using beautiful rayon, polyester, or metallic embroidery threads. If you are using metallic thread, use a sewing machine needle designed for that purpose.

See "Specialty Needles," on page 13.

You definitely need a stabilizer that supports your fabric through a free-motion stitching marathon.

See "Stabilizers," on page 336.

Use fusible interfacing when you want something that has body but isn't stiff. Organza allows the fabric to drape, stay soft, and look good from the wrong side if it's exposed. Water-soluble or wash-away stabilizer leaves no sign that it was ever used once it's rinsed out. Experiment with various stabilizers or interfacings under your fabric during test stitching to see which you prefer.

Free-Motion Technique

If you're working with hooped fabric, slide the hoop under the needle, tilting it if necessary to move it past the presser foot. If you're not using a hoop, position the stabilized fabric under the needle, and use your hands as a "hoop" to keep the fabric flat around the needle. To avoid skipped stitches, make sure the fabric doesn't lift off the bed of the machine with each upstroke of the needle. Remember to lower the presser-foot lever so the tension disks are engaged, even if you're not using a presser foot. Otherwise, you'll end up with long loops of thread underneath.

The basic stitch for free-motion embroidery is a straight stitch, set to a length of zero. However, you can select any pattern when free-motion stitching. Experiment to see how to move the fabric for the best effects.

Begin stitching at a slow speed, and move the fabric in smooth, regular motions. Work at creating a consistent stitch length. As you get more confident, increase your speed. After a bit of practice, you'll discover that you can get the best results by stitching quickly, but moving the fabric at a steady, medium to slow pace under the needle. Don't pivot the fabric. Instead, move it as required by your design with your hands straight out in front of you on either side of the needle. Typically, you'll move the fabric forward and

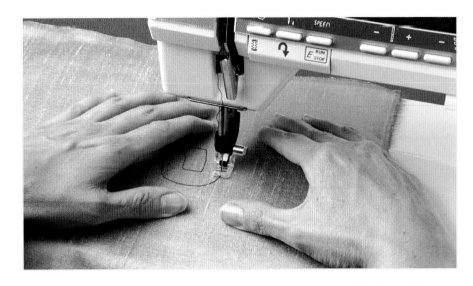

back, side to side, and in looping shapes.

One way to begin learning free-motion technique is by sewing geometric or repeated designs. Plan a stitching route along the design so you can stitch it without stopping or breaking the thread.

Another easy exercise is to outline a motif on printed fabric with free-motion stitching. If you include batting on the wrong side, this adds dimension to the printed design.

DIGITIZED MACHINE EMBROIDERY

If you've invested in a computerized embroidery machine, you can embellish

any fabric or project that fits inside the machine's hoop. Unlike free-motion or other decorative stitching you can create with your regular sewing machine, digitized embroidery is executed entirely by the machine, which is guided by software. It's not an exaggeration to say that

Stabilizers

For most decorative stitching techniques, you need to support and reinforce your fabric with a stabilizer. These products (sometimes called backing, although some are used on the top of the fabric) help to hold fabric as flat as possible for embroidery and decorative stitching.

Stabilizers are available in various weights and application methods, such as fusible, nonfusible, and adhesive. Some stabilizers remain permanently affixed to the fabric, while most are temporary and are removed once the embroidery is finished. Match the stabilizer to the fabric type, weight, and color, as well as to the type of decorative stitching you're planning to do. If you use decorative techniques often, keep a clearly labeled supply of several types of stabilizers in your sewing studio. Store heat-away and wash-away products in a zip-sealed plastic bag to prevent drying out or degrading due to humidity.

CUT-AWAY STABILIZERS

Used for: Permanent support
Best used on: Knits, unstable and loose wovens
Comes in: Light to heavy weights
Removal: Cut away excess around stitching area
Cut-away stabilizers are permanent and keep the fabric stable during and after embroidery. They prevent the fabric and stitched designs from stretching or distorting with frequent wearing and washing. Remove the excess stabilizer by rough cutting around the design. Then, using sharp embroidery scissors, trim close to the stitching.

TEAR-AWAY STABILIZERS

Used for: Temporary support
Best used on: Firmly woven natural-fiber fabrics
Comes in: Light to heavy weights: fusible and nonfusible
Removal: Torn away, but not always completely removable from under the stitching
Tear-aways are generally easy to remove, but take care not to pull or stretch the fabric in the process. Pull the excess stabilizer away from the stitched design, keeping it as flat against the surface of the fabric as you can while you pull laterally. To use tear-away on a project that requires strong support, combine several layers of a light- to medium-weight stabilizer, rather than one heavy product, and gently remove the layers individually. Some tear-aways, called toppings, are intended for use on top of, rather than beneath, the fabric to prevent stitches from getting lost in a dense nap or pile fabric surface.

HEAT-AWAY STABILIZERS

Used for: Temporary support
Best used on: Nonwashable, delicate fabrics and for off-the-edge stitching techniques
Comes in: Woven sheets, plastic film
Removal: Completely removable with heated iron
Heat-away stabilizers offer temporary support and are perfect for use on nonwashable fabrics that can stand the heat needed for removal. The woven heat-away stabilizer turns brown and flakes when heated, and the flakes can be gently brushed away. A second type of heat-away stabilizer, a plasticlike film, is used mainly as a topping to prevent stitches from getting lost in a dense nap or pile. It remains under the stitching, continuing to support it during washings. The excess stabilizer around the stitches disappears when heat is applied.

WASH-AWAY STABILIZERS

Used for: Temporary support
Best used on: Delicate, meshlike, and difficult-to-mark fabrics; also for cutwork and embroidered appliqués
Comes in: Plastic film, paper sheets, brush-on or sprayable liquid
Removal: Completely removable with water
Wash-away stabilizers are designed to dissolve when wet, so use them only on fabrics that can be washed. There are adhesive-backed wash-away stabilizers, too. Test any wash-away stabilizer on your garment fabric to ensure that you can remove it successfully without affecting the fabric. Some wash-away products can be used on top of the fabric to keep the embroidery stitches from sinking into a nap or pile. For free-motion stitching, or anywhere you need a guideline but can't mark the fabric directly, draw the marking lines on wash-away stabilizer, adhere it to the fabric's right side, and stitch, following the lines.

The challenges for a machine embroiderer lie in matching the digitized motif to the fabric, selecting the correct stabilizer and hooping method (see "Hooping Methods" below), successfully marking and hooping the fabric so that the motif stitches out in the right place, and, of course, choosing and positioning the motifs for the most flattering, attractive effect on the finished garment.

Digitized Designs

Each embroidery motif is formatted digitally (with different brands using different formats). Most machines come preloaded with an assortment of digitized designs, but you can purchase additional designs, which are loaded via a special memory card, memory stick, CD, diskette, flash drive, or by downloading directly from the Internet.

Digitized designs range from tiny, individual motifs to complex designs that can embellish entire garment sections. The density of the design—that is, the number of stitches per square inch—determines its suitability for a specific fabric. Outline-only, or very open designs, are appropriate for lightweight or unstable fabrics. Very dense designs, in which fill stitches completely cover the fabric, should be reserved for medium- to heavyweight fabrics, and call for a sturdy stabilizer.

Before embroidering your garment, test the motif on a scrap of fabric to decide what type of stabilizer best supports the stitching.

Hooping Methods

How you hoop the fabric and stabilizer depends on the fabric's surface texture, weight, size, and shape. Standard hooping, in which the fabric is gripped between the inner and outer frames of

the hoop, provides the greatest control, but there are alternatives for fabrics that require gentler treatments, such as sheers, thick fabrics, and fabrics with nap.

For nearly any fabric, one or more of the hooping methods described below can be used. Refer to the chart on page 338 to determine your fabric characteristics, then use the numbered hooping method indicated there and explained here to secure the fabric in the hoop.

1. Standard hooping: Lay the fabric on top of the stabilizer, and hoop the layers together. Use for stable, firm fabrics.

2. Hooped stabilizer plus adhesive spray: Hoop the stabilizer (cut-away, tear-away, or wash-away) alone, spray it with temporary adhesive, and press the fabric onto the stabilizer without distorting the fabric grain. The fabric is not gripped within the hoop, but instead adheres to the stabilizer. Use for unstable fabrics, knits, or fabrics that will be damaged if hooped directly.

3. Adhesive stabilizer: Hoop adhesive stabilizer alone, remove the protective paper within the hooped area, and finger-press the fabric onto the sticky surface, without distorting the fabric grain. To remove the paper easily, peel it up before hooping, tear into it, restick it to the

today's embroidery machines are essentially computers that stitch. And they're updated constantly, so the technology changes every year. These machines are user-friendly, but most new owners benefit from classes and lessons in learning about all the features.

Although all the information for embroidering is contained in the machine's computerized insides, the actual stitching takes place very much the same way that free-motion embroidery does: The needle stitches up and down, and the fabric moves under it in different directions to create outlines and fills that form the digitized motif. In digitized embroidery, the fabric is inserted into a hoop, which in turn is attached to the machine's embroidery module. This module moves the hoop, starting and stopping so you can change thread colors.

See "Specialty Machines," on page 8.

Solve Embroidery Problems before They Happen

The structure and stability of each fabric determine the manner in which it must be handled for successful embroidery. Each row on the chart explains how to work with fabrics that share specific characteristics.

FABRIC TYPE	COMMON PROBLEMS	CAUSE OF PROBLEM	STABILIZER	HOOPING METHOD
WOVENS	Generally problem-free		Tear-away	1, 2, 3, 4
	Puckering around embroidery on very tightly woven fabrics	Fabric fibers so tightly woven that there isn't room for embroidery threads; overcrowding causes puckers	Tear-away	1, 2, 3, 4
	On some dark colors, permanent hoop marks may occur	Damage to surface fibers is caused by stress from hoop	Tear-away or sticky tear-away	2, 3
DELICATE OR SLIPPERY: OPAQUE	Fabric distortion during hooping	Grain of fabric is distorted as fabric is pressed into hoop	Sticky stabilizer or temporary spray adhesive used on tear-away stabilizer; select a stabilizer that tears off easily	2, 3
	Hand of fabric altered by embroidery	Overly dense design stiffens or weakens fabric		
DELICATE OR SLIPPERY: SHEER	As for opaque delicates, plus stabilizer show-through	Transparency of fabric	Heat-away or wash-away	1 (heat-away); 2 (wash-away)
NAP OR PILE: FUR, VELVET, VELVETEEN, CORDUROY, TERRY CLOTH	Fabric too thick to fit between hoops	Pile fabrics are often too thick to hoop easily	Tear-away or cut-away stabilizer with temporary spray adhesive, or sticky stabilizer	2, 3
	Fabric surface damaged by hoop	Hoop pressure can permanently crush nap or pile		
	Pile pokes through embroidered design	Stitches get lost among surface fibers	Water-soluble or permanent topping to prevent stitches from sinking into nap; water-soluble topping eventually washes away, allowing pile to emerge between stitches; permanent toppings may prevent project from drying thoroughly; choose topping on the basis of the project's cleaning requirements	5 (in conjunction with other stabilizer)
STRETCH FABRICS: KNITS AND WOVENS	Puckering around stitched design	Fabric was stretched and distorted during hooping	Cut-away stabilizer only; avoid tear-aways	1, but use temporary adhesive to stick fabric to stabilizer before hooping; 2, 3, but to embroider, slip a sheet of cut-away stabilizer under hoop; first stitches will attach stabilizer to embroidery
	Machine jams during stitching	If you used a tear-away stabilizer, it may be perforated during embroidery, and won't provide stability during stitching, causing needle to push down into needle hole and jam machine		
LEATHER/ SIMULATED LEATHER	As for stretch fabrics, plus damage to fabric surface from needle perforations	Intrinsic nature of material	Cut-away stabilizer only; avoid tear-aways	2, 3, with a sheet of cut-away stabilizer under hoop

stabilizer, and hoop. The pretorn edges enable you to peel the topping off without the risk of cutting the stabilizer itself. Another type of adhesive stabilizer is moisture activated. Hoop this stabilizer alone, dampen slightly, and adhere the fabric to it. Use for unstable fabrics that require tear-away stabilizer but would be damaged by direct hooping, and for knits.

4. Iron-on stabilizer: Iron this tear-away stabilizer to the back of the fabric and hoop both layers together. Use for fabrics that slip off grain during standard hooping, but can withstand the pressure of the hoop.

Additional Software for Machine Embroidery

If you want to manipulate existing digitized designs, or digitize your own, you can do so with the help of extra software. These programs are loaded onto your home computer, and enable you to convert designs from one machine format to another, adjust the size of motifs, combine several motifs into one larger design, edit designs (removing elements, changing fill stitch style, etc.), and more. Once you've changed the design, you save it as a new file, then export it on disk, flash drive, or other medium to your embroidery machine.

Digitizing software enables you to create original embroidery designs from artwork. You can scan artwork, then use the file as the basis for a digitized motif, or create the design directly in the digitizing program. This type of software is routinely updated and improved, making it easy for a computer-savvy home sewer to work with.

DESIGN CHOICE	THREAD	NEEDLE
Any	30- or 40-wt. embroidery thread	Size 75/11 embroidery needle; size 90/14 embroidery or titanium needle on very heavy fabrics or with very dense designs
Avoid extremely dense designs	40- or 50-wt. thread (finer thread will distort fabric less)	
Any	30- or 40-wt. embroidery thread	
Light density or outline only	Generally 40-wt. thread; finer thread may be substituted to decrease stiffness of dense designs	Size 75/11 embroidery needle
Light density or outline only	Generally 40-wt. thread; finer thread may be substituted to decrease stiffness of dense designs	Size 75/11 embroidery needle
Avoid outline designs or sparsely digitized designs; dense designs will show up more clearly; prefer designs with underlay stitches to control nap	30- or 40-wt. embroidery thread	Size 90/14 embroidery needle or titanium needle
Dense designs change hand of fabric; test first to see if you find change objectionable	40- or 50-wt. embroidery thread	Size 75/11 embroidery needle
Avoid dense designs	40- or 50-wt. embroidery thread	Size 90/14 embroidery needle; do not use a leather needle, as it will sever thread

5. Topping: *Cut a piece of topping larger than the embroidery area, and lay it on the right side of the hooped fabric. Hold it in place with your fingers and embroider. The first few stitch passes will secure the* *topping. Toppings can be attached with adhesive spray but may then be difficult to remove. Use for fabrics with a deeply textured surface to keep the stitches from sinking into the pile or nap.*

Appliqué

Appliqué—an old and cherished technique used in quilting—is simply the application of one layer of fabric on the surface of another. It's easy to do, but can make a big impact in a garment design. There are many ways of appliquéing by hand and by machine. You can choose the one that's best suited to your fabric and garment design, as well as your sewing skills. Don't underestimate the potential of this tried-and-true decorative technique.

APPLIQUÉ BY HAND

Hand-sewn appliqué is time-consuming, but it enables you to apply a fabric embellishment with no visible stitches.

Needle-Turn Appliqué

Needle-turn appliqué is a traditional technique in which you use the point of the needle to turn under the appliqué's

raw edge as you stitch. Work from right to left if you're right-handed; reverse if you're left-handed. Use a long, thin needle, such as a size 10 sharp, and a single strand of fine thread.

Cut each appliqué shape with a ⅛-in.-wide allowance around all edges. Position the pieces as desired on the background fabric, and baste them in place, ½ in. from the cut edges. Fold under and finger-press the ⅛-in.-wide allowance at the point where you want to start stitching. Thread the needle with a single strand of thread, knot the end, and bring the needle up just inside the fold of the appliqué. Insert the tip into the background fabric, exactly opposite the point where the thread

emerges. Swivel the needle slightly so it reemerges from the edge at the fold, ¹⁄₁₆ in. farther along the appliqué edge. Continue around the edge of the appliqué, using the point of the needle to push the seam allowance under as you go. When the appliqué is complete, knot the thread on the wrong side.

Lined Appliqué

Instead of turning each edge under by hand, let your sewing machine help. Use an ultra-lightweight fabric such as tulle or organza, and machine-sew it as a lining for each appliqué piece. Then turn the appliqué right side out through a slit cut in the lining and hand-sew it, using the same stitch as for the needle-turn technique.

1. Cut the appliqué with a ¹⁄₈-in.-wide seam allowance around all edges. Place the appliqué right side down on a larger piece of organza or tulle. Using short, straight stitches, sew around the appliqué, ¹⁄₈ in. from the raw edge, overlapping the stitches at the beginning and end. Trim off excess organza.

2. Cut an opening in the organza layer.

3. Turn the piece to the right side through the cut hole. Finger-press the edges flat, then sew the appliqué to the garment.

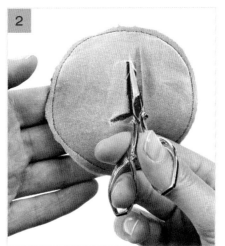

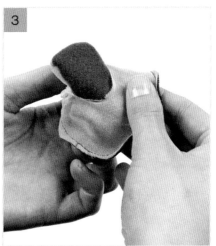

APPLIQUÉ BY MACHINE

To attach appliqués more quickly, use a machine-sewn satin stitch. Cut the appliqué to the desired finished size, and pin, baste, fuse, or glue it in position. Satin-stitch around it, using a thread color to match the appliqué, a color to match the background, or a contrasting color if desired. Follow these guidelines for the best results.

- Start with a test swatch of the appliqué and background fabric used in your project.

- Install an embroidery foot or satin-stitch foot (a foot that's got a shallow groove on the underside to accommodate the extra height of the satin-stitch column).

- Thread the machine with high-quality embroidery thread. Select a fiber content that's compatible with the eventual care requirements of the project.

- Set your machine for a very short zigzag stitch (begin with a length just above 0 and test), and find a stitch width that will swing from appliqué to background and completely enclose the appliqué edge. Only the upper thread should show on the right side of the fabric; if the bobbin thread is visible, try loosening the tension of the upper thread.

- For clearly delineated designs, exaggerate details as you satin-stitch: swoop deeply into and out of curved areas; pivot and turn carefully to avoid gaps; and create sharp points and angles by cornering very slightly beyond the tip and stitching over the outbound stitch pass on the way back in.

- To negotiate curves, stop with the needle down on the outside edge of the curve, lift the presser foot, and pivot the fabric slightly.

Trims & Embellishments

To make any garment—ready-to-wear or custom-sewn—truly special, add embellishments. Decorative trims, beads, and sequins can enhance a fabric, define style lines, and express your personal aesthetic. Many embellishments can be sewn by machine, but some require hand stitching. Take your time and enjoy the process; you'll love the one-of-a-kind results.

APPLYING TRIM BY MACHINE

There are many wonderful trims, perfect for easy embellishment. Just make sure the weight and handling characteristics of the trim and fabric are compatible.

Begin by sketching your embellishment design on the pattern tissue, then transfer the guidelines for the design to the right side of the garment piece. Transfer key dots and lines; you don't need to transfer the entire design. If you plan to add

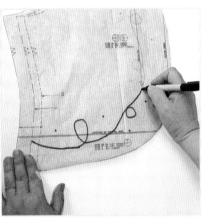

embellishments along a seam, you don't need to mark guidelines because the seam will act as the guide. Then, either topstitch or couch the trim to the fabric.

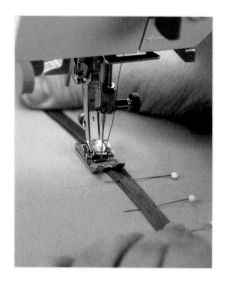

Topstitching Ribbon and Flat Trim by Machine

Thread the machine needle with thread that matches the trim or with monofilament thread. Match the bobbin thread to the fabric. Pin the trim along the marked design lines. Pull it taut to prevent puckers, and sew very close to one edge, using a straight stitch. Sew the remaining edge, stitching in the same direction as for the first edge. Alternatively, choose a decorative thread and stitch, and use the stitching to enhance the trim as it secures it.

Couching Trim by Machine

Trims that aren't flat, such as cord, gimp, and strings of beads or sequins, can't be topstitched easily, and instead should be attached with couching stitches. To couch trim or cord to a fabric surface, stitch over the trim instead of through it, using a wide stitch such as a zigzag or decorative stitch.

A grooved presser foot keeps the couching material in place without crushing it. Choose one with slots large enough to accommodate the

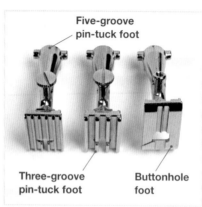

Five-groove pin-tuck foot

Three-groove pin-tuck foot

Buttonhole foot

trim. For low-profile trim or strings of very small beads, a satin stitch or buttonhole foot may work. Pin-tuck feet have various groove sizes and offer an advantage for stitching parallel rows of beading. You just keep moving over one or two grooves for each subsequent row. Presser feet labeled for cording, beading, or sequins all have a groove or tunnel on the sole, so the trim passes through easily as the machine stitches over it.

Apply tear-away stabilizer to the fabric's wrong side to keep the fabric taut and support it. Thread the machine with monofilament thread if you don't want the thread to show, or with contrasting thread. Set the machine for a wide stitch, and stitch slowly. The trim will feed through the presser foot as the machine stitches over

it. When the stitching is complete, knot the thread ends on the wrong side and remove the stabilizer.

If you are couching loose beads, string them on a strong beading thread, such as Nymo®, using a beading needle. String the beads in lengths as long as your desired row. Leave a long, unknotted tail on both ends. Loop both ends of the string together in a loose knot to prevent the beads from sliding off.

Shaping and Applying Soutache Braid

Soutache braid, a narrow braid consisting of two cords woven together, comes in many colors and fibers. It's typically used to create intricate, looping motifs. Once you've created the motifs, you can sew them on by hand or machine. It's a good idea to prewash or steam the braid with a damp cloth before attaching it, taking care not to crush the fibers.

1. Unravel one end of the soutache to expose the cording.

2. Holding one cord firmly with one hand, gently push the soutache away from you with the other hand, pulling the cord toward you. A loop will begin to form.

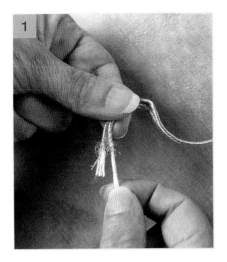

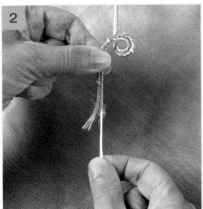

3. Push the loop up the soutache by gently nudging it up the trim. Secure it with a pin. To loop in the opposite direction, pull the opposite cord and repeat. Secure the loops with fabric glue, then sew them in place.

For machine sewing, use a grooved foot to hold the braid in place. But for most designs with small, intertwining curves, it's easier to get good results when stitching the braid by hand. Baste the braid in place with long (½-in. to 1-in.) stitches, or pin it before sewing. Then, working from the wrong side, use small stitches to catch the braid securely along its center.

BEADING BY HAND

Hand beading is an easy way to add sparkle to a garment. It requires few supplies and more patience than skill. A couple of basic stitches can be combined as desired to create an endless number of designs. When choosing beads, consider their care requirements. Some can't be washed, and others lose their color in dry cleaning.

For hand beading, use Nymo beading thread (all-purpose/size D), a thin, sharp sewing needle, and an embroidery hoop if you're working on lightweight fabric. For very lightweight fabrics, underline (with the fashion fabric, if possible) to add body and conceal the beading threads. Transfer your design to the fabric using one of the methods described on page 347.

Basic Beading Stitches

To get started, thread the needle with one strand of thread, and knot the end.

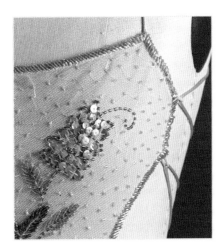

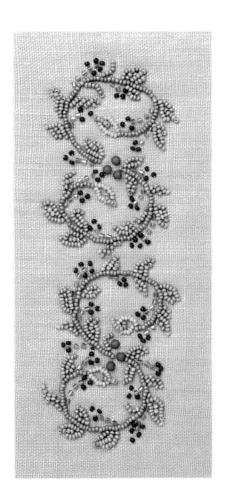

Then bring the needle up from the wrong side of the fabric on one of the marked design lines. Pick up one bead with the needle and let the bead fall down the thread until it hits the fabric surface. Lay the bead on its side (with its hole parallel to the surface), and insert the needle into the fabric a bead-length away. Either knot the thread on the wrong side (see tip on page 346), or repeat, bringing the needle back up and attaching the next bead. If the individual beads are spaced more than an inch apart, take a tiny stitch between them to secure the floating thread on the wrong side.

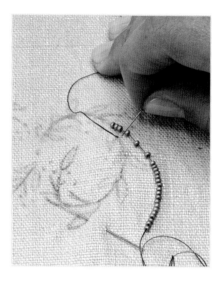

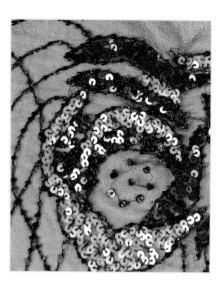

To sew multiple beads, pick up several beads. Let the beads fall down the thread. Lay them on their sides flush against each other (with bead holes parallel to the surface), and insert the needle into the fabric right next to the last bead. Knot or bring the needle back up and repeat.

TIP

KNOT TO SECURE THE BEADS

During the beading process, knot the thread frequently to minimize bead loss if a thread breaks within the beadwork. Simply loop and pull: Catch one or two yarns of the fabric with the needle, then pull the needle until a loop forms. Pass the needle through the loop, and pull to form a knot. To finish a thread, knot first; then cut the end close to the knot.

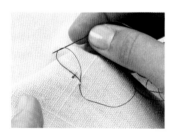

Couching Beads by Hand

To couch strung beads by hand, use two needles, threaded with Nymo beading thread. Knot the thread. Bring up one threaded needle from the wrong side of the fabric, and string the desired number of beads. Let them fall down the thread. Lay the thread along the fabric, leaving spaces between the beads. Temporarily secure the needle in the fabric.

Next, bring the second needle up near the beginning of the bead string. Stitch over the beaded thread between every three or four beads, or as desired. Continue down the line of beads, pushing the beads together as you stitch. Add more beads to the first needle as needed. To finish, insert both needles into the fabric, and knot on the fabric wrong side.

SEQUINS AND PAILLETTES

Sequins and their larger cousins, paillettes, add lightweight shine and are easy to sew. Scatter a few here and there, or place them close together for a shimmery, textured effect.

Sequins

For sequins, mark the sequin location with chalk or a removable marking pen (if you plan to distribute them randomly, you can skip this step). Thread a hand-sewing needle with machine-embroidery thread. Work with a double strand, 18 in. long or shorter. Knot the thread and hide the knot on the wrong side. Bring the needle to the right side through the hole in the sequin. Carry the thread over the sequin and back through the fabric, right at the edge of the sequin. If you want the sequin to lie flat, repeat on the other side of the sequin, so there are two straight stitches holding the sequin in place. For greater security or decorative effect, you can add more stitches. If the next sequin is less than 1 in. away, carry the thread on the wrong side. Otherwise, knot the thread on the wrong side, and stitch each sequin individually.

Paillettes

Paillettes are larger than sequins, are usually entirely flat (rather than faceted, as many sequins are), and have an off-center hole. They're usually spaced fairly widely, and often attached loosely

Transferring a Design

For most embellishment techniques, you need to plan the design, then transfer it to the fabric before stitching. For freehand designs, you can simply draw on the fabric, using a marker that is either removable, or leaves marks that can be covered by the stitching or trim.

For more complex designs, it's best to work out the design on paper, then transfer it to the fabric using one of the following methods. Test each one on your fabric to see if it leaves a sufficiently clear—and removable—trace.

CARBON-COPY METHOD

Draw the motif on bond paper. Place the fabric on a hard surface, and cover it with the bond paper, motif side up. Slip a sheet of dressmaker's tracing paper, coated side down, between the layers; pin along the edges of the bond paper,

avoiding the tracing paper. Trace the motif with a pencil, tracing wheel, stylus, or knitting needle.

IRON-TRANSFER METHOD

Trace the motif onto tracing paper with a regular pencil. Then, turn the paper over and trace over the lines with a heat-sensitive transfer pencil. This reverses the motif. Place the paper on the fabric, with the transfer-pencil side against the fabric's right side, and pin in place. Following the pencil manufacturer's instructions, press the paper with a dry iron. Unpin the paper and lift it straight up, then allow the fabric to cool.

SEE-THROUGH METHOD

This method is good for thin, light-colored fabrics only. Draw the motif with a marker on tracing or bond paper, then tape it to a window or light box. Smooth the fabric over the paper, tape it in place, then trace the motif with a fabric marker that's suited to your fabric.

BLEED-THROUGH METHOD

Draw the motif on bond paper, then tape a layer of tulle over it. Trace the motif onto the tulle with permanent marker. Pin the tulle on the fabric's right side, marked side up, and lightly retrace with a marker or chalk. The ink or chalk will bleed through the tulle to the fabric.

so they can swing enough to create a shimmery effect. To sew them, use two strands of thread and knot one end. Come up through the garment through the hole of the paillette. Take two somewhat loose stitches over the edge,

then knot on the fabric wrong side to secure. To avoid puckers and pulling between paillettes, sew and knot each individually, and don't float the thread between them on the wrong side.

XVI
GARMENT MENDING & REPAIR

Common Quick Fixes

1

Mending a damaged garment is usually a simple and surprisingly satisfying job. Many repairs can be accomplished quickly and by hand, while some are better done by machine. If you want to extend the lifespan of your favorite garments, take the time to mend holes, broken zippers, and torn buttonholes.

MENDING A TEAR

If a tear occurs at a seamline, simply resew the seam, using a stitch length and seam allowance width to match the existing seam. If the tear is in the body of the fabric, you can repair it by hand, by machine, or by turning the tear into a tuck. (The following techniques are shown using contrasting thread, but you should match the thread to the fabric as closely as possible.)

Mending by Hand

Depending on the position and size of the tear, and the type of fabric, mending by hand is easier and results in a less-visible repair.

349

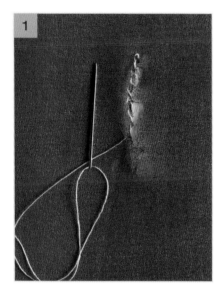

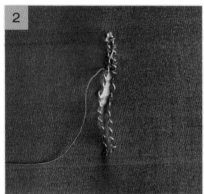

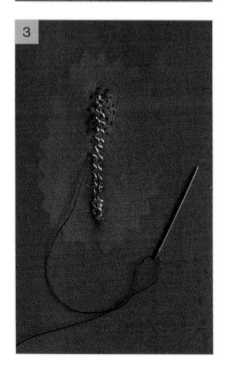

1. Thread a thin needle with a single strand of fine thread; don't knot the thread. Work a few tiny running stitches to secure the thread, then overcast the raw edges with loose stitches. Finish with running stitches to secure the thread.

2. Butt the overcast edges together. Work hand zigzag stitches down the length of the tear to close it.

3. Stabilize the repair by backing the mended tear with self-fabric, China silk, or organza. Work tiny backstitches around the mend to secure the stabilizer.

Mending by Machine

To machine-sew a tear, you can either darn or pinch out the rip.

DARNING A TEAR

A. On the wrong side of the fabric, fuse the tear closed with a patch of lightweight interfacing.

B. Zigzag over the cut with a short, medium-width stitch (contrasting thread shown for clarity).

CAMOUFLAGING A TEAR WITH TUCKS

C. Close the tear by fusing a patch of lightweight interfacing on the wrong side.

D. Create a pin tuck by stitching the right sides of the slit edges together. Then, sew a series of additional decorative tucks in the same area, either randomly or regularly spaced, to create a larger design.

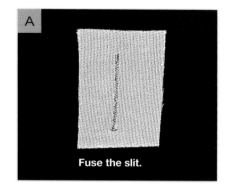

Fuse the slit.

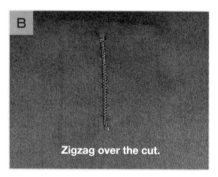

Zigzag over the cut.

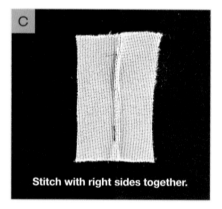

Stitch with right sides together.

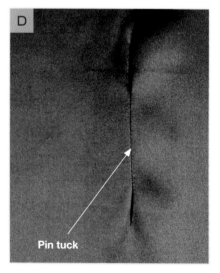

Pin tuck

PATCHING A HOLE

For most holes that can't be simply sewn closed, you want a patch that's nearly invisible. Alternatively, for casual wear, you can make the mend into a design feature.

Patching a Hole with Stitches

On jeans and other deliberately worn-looking items, a visible mend or patch can contribute to the distressed character of the garment. To patch a hole in jeans, first neaten the hole by trimming away loose threads. Stabilize the area on the wrong side with fusible interfacing. From the right side, darn the hole by sewing multiple rows of a wide zigzag stitch or a three-step zigzag stitch (sometimes referred to as a mending stitch). If desired, use slightly contrasting thread and scatter similar fake mends all over.

Before

After

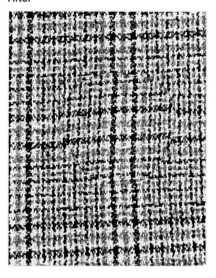

Patching a Hole with Self-Fabric

To invisibly eliminate a stain or to patch a hole, such as a moth hole, use fabric that matches the garment. If you don't have fabric that matches, try cutting a scrap from the hem allowance, or, if necessary, shorten the sleeves to obtain the fabric.

The technique is shown here with a stain, but it can be used for patching a hole as well.

1. Cut a piece of paper-backed fusible web about ½ in. to 1 in. larger all around than the stain or hole. Fuse it to the wrong side of the garment, directly over the damaged area, following the manufacturer's instructions. If you're fusing it over a hole, place the garment on a Teflon press cloth or sheet of waxed paper to prevent the fusible web from adhering to the ironing board.

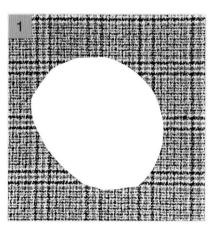

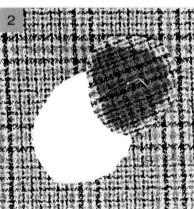

2. From the right side, cut around the stain or hole, just outside its edge. Remove the protective paper covering from the fusible patch on the wrong side of the garment.

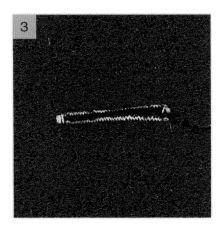

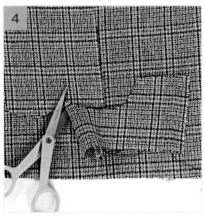

3. Turn the garment right side up. Place a patch of fabric under the hole, matching the pattern of the patch to the pattern on the edges of the hole. Finger-press to secure, then fuse the layers together.

4. Trim the excess fabric from the patch on the wrong side, cutting as close as possible to the edge of the fusible web. Press again from the right side, and the patch is complete. If desired, sew by hand or machine around the edges of the hole for further reinforcement. These stitches can blend in closely with busy patterns.

You can always topstitch a patch of fabric over a hole to prevent it from getting larger, as long as it doesn't detract from the look and feel of the garment.

REWEAVING

Reweaving is a special method of mending a damaged area by closing or covering the area with a self-fabric patch or yarns that are woven into the fabric, rather than sewn to it. This technique is easiest to work on fabrics that have some texture and pattern, and medium-to-coarse yarns. You'll need to harvest a patch or yarns from scrap fabric or from the garment itself. Look at hem allowances, pocket backs, or seam allowances as sources for the fabric or yarns you need.

Patching a Hole by Reweaving

To cover a clean-cut hole, such as a burn hole or a large insect hole, weave in a patch of matching fabric. In the steps on the facing page, the hole has been outlined with red thread for visibility.

For the best results, begin by making a weighted worksurface. Cover a brick with leather. Cut three layers of felt to the size of the brick's largest side, lay them on the leather-covered brick, then cover the entire brick with an additional layer of felt. Finally, wrap the brick tightly with a layer of muslin, and hand-sew the muslin to permanently upholster the brick.

1. Cut a matching patch that's at least ½ in. larger than the hole all around. Trim the patch along the grainlines so it's square, and precisely align it with the garment grainlines. If the fabric has a pattern, such as plaid, make sure the patch matches. Secure the patch with glass-head pins.

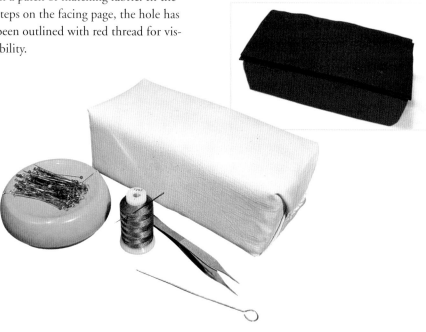

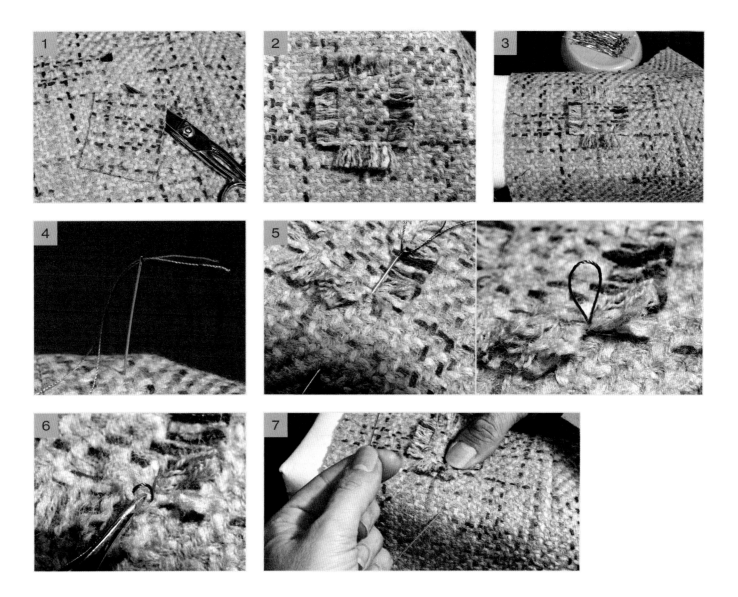

2. Baste the patch to the right side of the garment, using contrasting thread. Then, unravel at least ⅜ in. from the patch edges.

3. Pin the work to the brick. Make sure the fabric's grainlines are at 90 degrees throughout the work, and that the fabric is as smooth as possible. Push the pins in so their heads rest against the fabric.

4. Choose a needle that will accommodate a doubled nylon filament thread. When you thread both ends into the eye of the needle, the opposite end forms a loop. This

loop is used to draw the patch threads through the fabric. (Note: For visual clarity, the thread shown is not a nylon filament; a colored spun thread is easier to see in the photos.)

5. Insert the needle under a patch corner. Move the needle away from the patch along the grain, just skimming the fabric's weave, for ½ in., and drop under and out of the fabric for 1 in. on the wrong side. Then bring the needle back up to the surface, leaving a small loop of thread on the fabric surface, close to the patch corner.

6. Use tweezers to guide one free yarn tail from the patch through the thread loop. There should be about ⅛ in. between the end of the yarn and the thread loop.

7. Place your thumb firmly on the patch, and with a gentle tug, pull the thread in the direction of the grain. This catches and buries the yarn tail in the fabric. Keep your thumb on the patch to ensure that you don't pull the yarn completely out of the patch and through the fabric.

8. Repeat pulling patch tails on each edge until all tails have been woven into the garment fabric. Here, one side of the patch is completed, and the second is half finished. The thread basting remains so you can see where the edge of the patch is.

9. Steam-press the patch from the wrong side to set the yarns.

Closing a Tear or Small Hole by Reweaving

To close a tear or a small moth hole, pull yarns from the fabric that match the pattern (if there is a pattern) in the fabric in the area to be repaired. Thread a yarn through a needlepoint needle, which has a rounded point that enables you to weave the yarns easily. Weave the yarn across the center of the hole, or the middle section of a tear, following the fabric's grain exactly. Leave a ⅜-in. tail of yarn at each end of the woven section. Repeat, working from the middle of the repair toward its outer edges or ends, and alternating horizontal and vertical threads, until the hole or tear is completely closed.

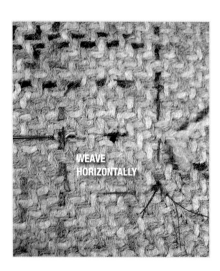

FIXING PULLS AND SNAGS

Pulls on woven fabrics occur when one thread gets caught on something and forms what looks like a line across the fabric. You can often stroke them out with a fingernail. Snags on knits need to be pulled inside of the garment to avoid unraveling. Do not clip the thread, or you may end up with holes.

A knit picker is a tiny latch hook available from sewing supply stores and notions catalogs. To use one, insert the hook from the wrong side of the garment, hook the snag, close the latch, and gently pull the snag to the wrong side of the garment. Rub the right side of the area with your fingernail to smooth.

Or, use a needle and thread. Insert the threaded needle eye end from the wrong side of the garment through the base of the snag. Manipulate the snag into the loop formed by the eye end of the needle and the thread, then grasp both the needle and thread underneath, and pull the snag to the wrong side.

MENDING A TORN BUTTONHOLE

When a buttonhole is too close to the garment edge, or is subjected to lots of wear, it can tear. There's no invisible way to mend such a tear, but you can cover it up attractively with a matching or contrasting patch. Make the repaired buttonhole part of an overall design by

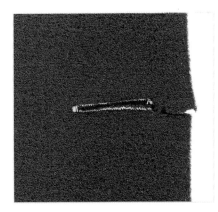

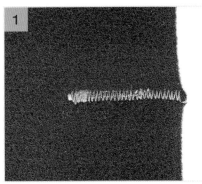

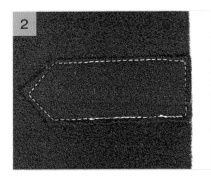

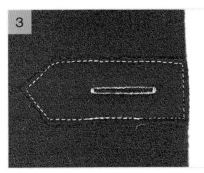

adding patches over some or all of the remaining buttonholes.

1. Zigzag over the torn buttonhole to close and reinforce it. Add a scrap of interfacing underneath if desired.

2. Cut a patch of contrasting fabric large enough to cover the mended area. On the right side of the garment, topstitch the patch over the mended buttonhole.

3. Stitch a new buttonhole on the patch. Sew a new buttonhole on the patch. Avoid sewing directly over the stitching you used to mend the original buttonhole.

REPAIRING AND REPLACING ZIPPERS

Zippers break in several ways. The teeth or coil can break, or the slider can fall off or jam. Sometimes the zipper is reparable, and sometimes you must replace it or discard the garment.

Broken Teeth

If the zipper teeth break close enough to the bottom of the zipper, and you can still wear the garment without unzipping it fully, you can simply create a new stop above the break. Working by hand and with heavy thread, take several straight stitches just above the break.

Broken or Loose Slider

If the slider separates from one column of teeth, or the zipper separates below the slider, this may indicate that the slider is loose or broken. To replace the slider, look for zipper repair kits at sewing supply stores.

For zippers with metal teeth, move the slider up to the top, and force it off between two teeth. Force a new slider on in the same way. For coil-type zippers, open the seam that holds the zipper's top in place, remove the slider, slide a new one on, and resew the seam. If there's a metal zipper stop at the top, remove it with wire snippers, replace the slider, and install a new stop or take several stitches over the zipper to form a thread stop.

Broken Fly Zippers

When replacing a fly zipper, it can be difficult to replace the topstitching so that it matches the original. The method shown here avoids that by leaving the original topstitching in place.

If you need to shorten the new zipper to fit into the fly opening, do so from the bottom. After removing the original zipper in step 1, measure the length of the teeth portion of the original zipper, and measure down from the top stop of the new zipper. Stitch a new bottom stop by zigzagging across the zipper teeth, then cut off the bottom of the zipper. If necessary, use wire cutters or diagonal cutters to remove the excess teeth.

See "Preparing the Zipper and the Garment," on page 243.

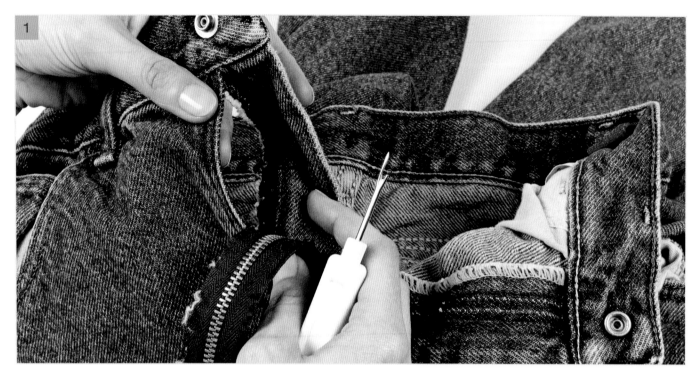

you created between the fly shield and the pants front. Fold the top of the tape under. Pin or baste the zipper tape in position. Install a zipper foot on the sewing machine, and stitch the zipper close to the edge of the pants front, sewing from the top of the zipper as far down the tape as you can.

3. Close the zipper. Working from the inside of the pants, pin the free tape in place on the wrong side of the fly overlap. Align the tape along the original stitching line, and fold the top of the tape under. Open the zipper. Using a sturdy needle and a double strand of thread, hand-sew the tape firmly to the pants, using a backstitch (see page 284). Stitch through only the fly facing fabric so no stitches show on the outside of the pants.

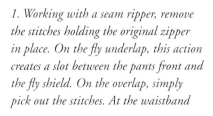

1. Working with a seam ripper, remove the stitches holding the original zipper in place. On the fly underlap, this action creates a slot between the pants front and the fly shield. On the overlap, simply pick out the stitches. At the waistband

and bottom of the fly, cut the zipper tape to release the zipper. Don't unstitch the waistband.

2. With the new zipper right side up, slide one side of the tape into the opening

Removing Stains

2

The key to successful stain removal is prompt treatment geared to the type of stain and fabric. The longer the stain is left in place, the darker and more stubborn it becomes. A staining agent reacts chemically with the fibers of a fabric, so if you know the characteristics of the stain, you can counteract its chemistry. No two stains are alike, but a few basic techniques can help you restore the garment to its original condition.

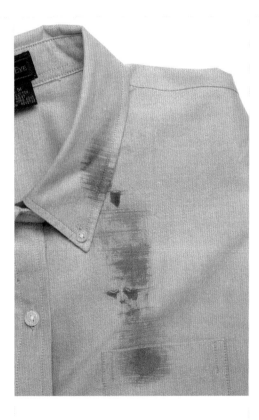

BASICS OF STAIN REMOVAL

When attempting to remove a stain, keep in mind a few basic rules. These will improve your chances of success, and limit the chance that you'll further set the stain.

- Act quickly. The sooner you notice a stain and can begin treating it, the more likely you are to remove it completely.

- Never rub a stain. Rubbing breaks the fabric's surface fibers and removes dyes, causing blotching and fading. Instead of rubbing, use a gentle blotting or feathering motion.

- Don't wash, dry, or iron a garment before treating the stain. The chemicals and heat from these processes can set some stains permanently.

- Avoid sunshine. Exposure to ultraviolet light can increase the damage caused by acid stains on cellulose fibers.

TYPES OF STAINS

The more you know about a stain, the easier it is to remove it. If you know exactly what caused the stain, you can proceed with the approaches given on the following page. If you're not sure, use the information here to make your best guess.

Treating Water-Based Stains

Most garment stains are water based. They can be caused by everything from vinegar to coffee to carbonated soft drinks. Don't scrub the stain with a wet cloth, as the water can cause a ring to form around the stain (a virtual certainty with dyed silks).

Instead, gently blot the stained area—on both sides if possible—with a clean, dry cloth, to absorb the offending liquid. If the garment is washable and colorfast, carefully blot it a second time with water to pull off excess residue. Make a note of the location of the stain and treat it promptly.

If you stain a garment with a colorless liquid (other than water), it's still important to blot it, then treat it promptly, as if it were more noticeable. If left untreated, it's likely to oxidize and turn brown, either on its own or through dry cleaning, washing, ironing, or machine drying.

Oil-Based Stains

Grease and oil stains can be caused by many culprits, including cooking oils, mayonnaise, salad dressings, cosmetics, and car grease. You can identify oil stains because they tend to follow the weave of the fabric, form a cross shape, and turn yellow if left untreated. Don't treat oil stains with water; it makes the stain harder to remove. A dry cleaning solvent is much more effective.

Acid-Based Stains

These stains are commonly caused by sodas, fruit juices, and alcoholic beverages. Acid stains can cause fibers to deteriorate if left to set in the fabric and then exposed to the agitation of washing. Acidity can also cause color changes and splotching. Cellulose fibers like cotton, rayon, and ramie are most vulnerable to the effects of acidity. With these stains, the key to success is to act quickly and take care to prevent exposure to sunlight, which can cause the stain to darken.

Perspiration Stains

Body perspiration can stain and cause dyes to bleed if it sits in a garment too long. Antiperspirants themselves can yellow and weaken fibers if they're left on fabric (liquid antiperspirants with aluminum salts tend to be far more damaging to fabrics than sticks or creams). To avoid perspiration and antiperspirant stains, clean garments that come in contact with the body every time they're worn, and try to launder them soon after wearing. Dress shields can help prevent perspiration damage, and they're easy to make from scraps of leftover fabric.

TREATING WASHABLE GARMENTS

Washable garments can be spot-treated or soaked before regular laundering, then machine-washed. When you use stain-removal products, read the instructions first, paying special attention to fabric restrictions. Test all products on an inconspicuous part of the garment, such as a seam allowance. It's also important to test the garment for colorfastness in water.

TIP

When you're constructing a new garment, try soaking a scrap of the fabric in water and note how it responds. You'll eliminate frustrating guesswork later.

Here are some common treatment methods for washable fabrics:

Soaking

Simple soaking in water is occasionally enough to "lift" certain water- and acid-based stains, but make sure that the fabrics are colorfast. It's also important to soak garments individually in order to prevent colors from running together. Use cool to tepid water, and don't agitate the garment.

Enzyme Presoak Products

These are your best bet for removing hardy protein stains such as egg, blood, grass, chocolate, and baby formula.

Prewash Soil and Stain Removers

These products work well for many stains, including oil, but not for those with a protein base. When using a spray product, place a cloth under the fabric you're spraying, to help absorb the dissolving stain.

Prewash gel sticks are helpful when you want to limit the application to a specific area. They can be applied immediately to the stain and left in until washing. The longer you leave prewash gel on stains, the longer it has to work.

Bleaching

When using bleach, treat the entire garment to avoid uneven color change. Fabric testing is especially important with these powerful products.

There are three basic types of bleach: chlorine, oxygen (or hydrogen peroxide), and color remover. Chlorine is the most common bleach. It's an

Removing Specific Stains

STAIN	REMEDY
ADHESIVE RESIDUE, CHEWING GUM, RUBBER CEMENT	1. Apply ice to harden the surface; scrape with a dull knife. 2. Saturate with a prewash stain remover or Carbona® cleaning fluid. 3. Rinse, then launder.
BLOOD	Fresh stains: Soak in cold water; launder immediately. Dried stains: Pretreat or soak in warm water with an enzyme product; launder. If the stain remains, wash the item again using appropriate bleach.
BROWN OR YELLOW DISCOLORATION FROM IRON, RUST, MANGANESE	Use rust remover recommended for the fabric; launder. Note: Don't use chlorine bleach to remove rust stains as it may intensify the stain. For a rusty water problem, use Calgon® water softener (liquid or powder) in wash and rinse water. For severe problems, install an iron filter.
CANDLE WAX	1. Scrape off surface wax with a dull knife. 2. Place the stain between clean paper towels and press with a warm iron. Replace the paper towels frequently. 3. Place the stain facedown on clean paper towels. Sponge the remaining stain with a prewash stain remover or Carbona cleaning fluid; blot with paper towels. Let dry. 4. Launder. If color remains, wash again using an appropriate bleach.
CHOCOLATE	Pretreat or prewash in warm water with an enzyme product, or treat with a prewash stain remover; launder. If the stain remains, wash again using an appropriate bleach.
COFFEE	Blot with cold water. If the stain remains, apply liquid dish detergent; rinse. If the stain persists, apply white vinegar, then rinse.
COSMETICS	Treat with a prewash stain remover, laundry detergent, and water; launder.
DAIRY PRODUCTS, EGG	1. Pretreat or soak stains using an enzyme product. 2. Soak for at least 30 minutes (several hours for set-in stains); launder.
INK	Some inks may be impossible to remove. Try one of the following: Treat with a prewash stain remover; launder. Sponge the area around the stain with denatured alcohol or cleaning fluid. Place the stain facedown on clean paper towels. Apply alcohol or dry-cleaning fluid to the back of the stain. Replace the paper towels frequently. Rinse thoroughly; launder. (Alternate method: Place the stain over the mouth of a jar or glass; hold the fabric taut. Drip alcohol or cleaning fluid through the stain, so the ink drops into the container. Rinse thoroughly, then launder.)
MUD	Let dry, then gently brush off as much mud as possible. Light stains: Pretreat with a paste of granular detergent and water, or liquid laundry detergent; launder. Heavy stains: Pretreat or presoak with laundry detergent or an enzyme product; launder.
PERFUME	Treat with a prewash stain remover or liquid laundry detergent; launder.
PERSPIRATION	1. Apply a prewash stain remover. If perspiration changed the fabric's color, apply ammonia (for fresh stains) or white vinegar (for old stains); rinse. 2. Launder using the hottest water that's safe for the fabric. For stubborn stains, try an enzyme product or oxygen bleach.
WINE AND ALCOHOLIC BEVERAGES	1. While the stains are fresh, blot with cold water, even for white wine and colorless drinks. 2. Pretreat with a prewash stain remover, laundry detergent, and water; rinse. 3. If the stain persists, spot-treat it with white vinegar; rinse. Finally, try an appropriate bleach.

effective weapon against mildew and helps deodorize and brighten garments. However, chlorine will destroy or yellow the fibers of some fabrics, such as silk, wool, and linen. In these cases, you should use oxygen bleach. To remove rust, dyes, or dye stains from fabrics, use color remover.

TREATING STAINS WITH SOLVENTS

Some stains, especially those containing oil, require solvents. When you use solvents, place cheesecloth under the garment to absorb the dissolving stain and prevent it from dispersing.

Rest the garment on a stable surface, such as a pressing ham (which you've protected with a layer of muslin). Spray the stain lightly with solvent, blot with a clean cloth, flush with a little more solvent, and feather out the spot, moving from the center outward with gentle blotting and pressing strokes. Continue this procedure until the stain disappears. For lipstick, candle wax, or tar, treat the stain from the wrong side to prevent it from being driven into the fabric.

CLEANING A STAINED GARMENT

Once you've treated the stain, make sure that the garment is thoroughly cleaned to remove all traces of the stain and the treatment product. Garments that can be laundered can simply go into the wash as usual. For nonwashable garments, you have two options: wet or dry cleaning.

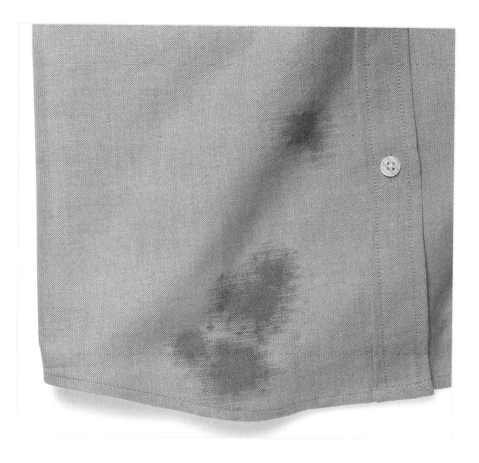

Wet Cleaning

If your fabric can be soaked (not laundered) in water, wet cleaning is a safe, gentle alternative to dry cleaning or machine washing, as it involves no heat or agitation. To wet-clean, soak the garment with water and the appropriate cleaning additives long enough for the cleaning agent to dissolve any remaining traces of the stain. Rinse gently and air-dry. Bear in mind that garments with decorative trim or multiple colors may require dry cleaning to avoid shrinking or color loss.

Dry Cleaning

If you decide that you need professional assistance, take the garment to a dry cleaner within a few days of the staining. Point out the spot to the dry cleaner and explain its cause. Let them know if you've used any stain-removal products; they may need to adjust their own treatment process. If you don't tell your dry cleaner about the stain, they'll proceed with a regular cleaning, and the heat can make the stain harder to remove.

Stains penetrate to the core of porous wool fibers. Unless they're scrupulously removed, stains, both from food and body oils, make wool even more tempting to insects. Clean woolen items thoroughly before storing them.

Pressing Marks and Crushed Pile

Whether through wear or pressing with the iron, fabrics can develop crushed lines or patches. It's often possible to revive the surface with steam or brushing.

to a solution of equal parts white vinegar and water, but you should test the solution on a fabric scrap before using to see that it doesn't stain.

CRUSHED PILE

Sometimes the nap on pile fabrics becomes crushed due to incorrect pressing or ordinary wear. For washable fabrics, simply wash and machine-dry the garment to fluff up the pile. For dry-clean-only garments, use steam from the iron or a steamer. Steam will make the pile "bloom" before your very eyes. Encourage the pile by brushing gently with a stiff-bristled clothes brush.

PRESS MARKS

Overly enthusiastic pressing can leave ridge lines, smashed-looking threads and fibers, and other unwanted creases and shine marks on garments. To remove them, apply steam and brush the area with your fingers or a clothes brush. The steam fluffs up the fibers and usually eliminates the marks.

Alternatively, dampen the area by spraying with a mister, gently massage it with your fingers, and lightly repress. Always test for water spotting on dry-clean-only fabrics. Some creases respond well

Photo Credits

pp. ii, vi (roping), 1 (dress): Photos by Scott Phillips © The Taunton Press, Inc.

Illustrations:

p. v: Carol Ruzicka © The Taunton Press, Inc.

p. vi: Sue Mattero © The Taunton Press, Inc.

p.1: Michael Gellatly © The Taunton Press, Inc.

CHAPTER 1

pp. 2, 4, 10, 18, 20 (right), 21, 22 (right), 23 (left), 25 (photo of seam ripper), 26 (right), 27, 28 (photos of the tweezers, dress form, and glove): Photos by Scott Phillips © The Taunton Press, Inc.

pp. 6–7, 11, 12, 13, 16, 19, 20 (top & bottom left), 22 (left photos), 23 (right), 24, 25 (all photos except the seam ripper), 26 (left photos), 28 (photos of awl, point turners, bodkins, hem gauge, and tube turners), 29: Photos © Sloan Howard

p. 17: Photos by David Page Coffin © The Taunton Press, Inc.

Illustrations:

p.10: Michael Gellatly © The Taunton Press, Inc.

p. 14: Karen Meyer © The Taunton Press, Inc.

p. 22: Carol Ruzicka © The Taunton Press, Inc.

CHAPTER 2

pp. 30–36, 38, 39, 40, 43 (top right), 44–49: Photos by Scott Phillips © The Taunton Press, Inc.

p. 37 Photos: by Jennifer Sauer © The Taunton Press, Inc.

pp. 41, 42, and p. 43 (top left): Photos © Sloan Howard.

CHAPTER 3

pp. 50, 52, 53, 56, 57 (right photos), 61 (right top & right bottom), 66 (left),

70, 71: Photos by Scott Phillips © The Taunton Press, Inc.

pp. 54, 57 (left photos), 58, 59, 60, 63 (top), 66 (right), 68, 69, 72, 73: Photos © Sloan Howard.

p. 61(bottom left), 62: Photo by Judith Neukam © The Taunton Press, Inc.

p. 63: © The Taunton Press, Inc.

Illustrations:

p. 57: Carol Ruzicka © The Taunton Press, Inc.

p. 59: Glee Barre © The Taunton Press, Inc.

p. 64: Karen Meyer © The Taunton Press, Inc.

CHAPTER 4

pp. 74, 79, 81 (bottom), 89, 90, 91, 95, 96: Photos by Scott Phillips © The Taunton Press, Inc.

p. 76: Photo courtesy of Simplicity Patterns

pp. 77, 81(top), 84, 85, 92, 93, 100, 101: Photos © Sloan Howard

p. 78: Photo by Susan Kahn © The Taunton Press, Inc.

p. 99: Photo by David Page Coffin © The Taunton Press, Inc.

Illustrations:

p. 80: by Roseann Berry © The Taunton Press, Inc.

p. 82: Karen Meyer© The Taunton Press, Inc.

pp. 83, 97 (left), 99: Carol Ruzicka © The Taunton Press, Inc.

pp. 86–87: Linda Boston © The Taunton Press, Inc.

pp. 94, 95 (left), 96, 97 (left): Christine Erikson © The Taunton Press, Inc.

p. 95 (right): Maryellen McGoldrick © The Taunton Press, Inc.

p. 97(center & right), 98: Gloria Melfi © The Taunton Press, Inc.

CHAPTER 5

pp. 102, 104 (left), 106 (bottom), 107–113: Photos by Scott Phillips © The Taunton Press, Inc.

p. 103: Photo by Linda Boston © The Taunton Press, Inc.

pp. 104 (right), 106 (top): Photos by Jennifer Sauer © The Taunton Press, Inc.

p. 114: Photo © Sloan Howard

Illustrations:

p. 105: Christine Erikson © The Taunton Press, Inc.

p. 107: Bob LaPointe © The Taunton Press, Inc.

pp. 115–117: Carol Ruzicka © The Taunton Press, Inc.

CHAPTER 6

pp. 118, 120, 121, 123, 127, 128, 129: Photos by Scott Phillips © The Taunton Press, Inc.

pp. 119, 130, 134: Photos by Jack Deustch © The Taunton Press, Inc.

pp. 122, 124, 126, 135: Photos © Sloan Howard

p. 125: Photo by Cathy Cassidy © The Taunton Press, Inc.

p. 132: Photo by David Page Coffin © The Taunton Press, Inc.

Illustrations:

p. 119: Scott Phillips © The Taunton Press, Inc.

p. 122: Karen Meyer © The Taunton Press, Inc.

pp. 125, 127, 129 (bottom): Christine Erikson © The Taunton Press, Inc.

p. 129 (top): Heather Lambert © The Taunton Press, Inc.

pp. 131, 132, 133: Kathy Bray © The Taunton Press, Inc.

CHAPTER 7

pp. 136–138, 139 (top left & bottom right), 140 (top left), 146–148, 150,

151(bottom right), 152 (top right), 159 (bottom right), 160, 163: Photos by Scott Phillips © The Taunton Press, Inc.

pp. 139 (top right), 140 (right photos), 141, 142, 149, 151 (top left), 152 (bottom right), 153–156, 158, 161: Photos © Sloan Howard

pp. 159 (top right), 162 (top left): Photos by Jack Deutsch © The Taunton Press, Inc.

p. 162 (top right): Photo by David Page Coffin © The Taunton Press, Inc.

Illustrations:

pp. 142–144, 163: Kathy Bray © The Taunton Press, Inc.

pp. 145, 157 (top): Michael Gellatly © The Taunton Press, Inc.

p. 152 (left): Frank Habbas © The Taunton Press, Inc.

pp. 152 (right), 159 (bottom left): Leigh Ann Smith © The Taunton Press, Inc.

p. 153: Carol Ruzicka © The Taunton Press, Inc.

pp. 155, 157 (bottom), 159 (top), 162: Karen Meyer © The Taunton Press, Inc.

p. 158: Bob LaPointe © The Taunton Press, Inc.

CHAPTER 8

pp. 164, 171–175: Photos by Scott Phillips © The Taunton Press, Inc.

p. 165: Photo by David Page Coffin © The Taunton Press, Inc.

p. 170: Photos © Sloan Howard

Illustrations:

pp. 166,168,169, 170: Christine Erikson © The Taunton Press, Inc.

CHAPTER 9

pp. 176, 177, 178 (left), 180 (left), 184 (top right), 185 (yoke construction photos), 186, 187 (left top & bottom), 191 (bottom), 194, 195, 199, 200,

202, 205: Photos by Scott Phillips © The Taunton Press, Inc.

pp. 178 (right top & bottom), 179, 182, 183, 192, 193, 202, 203 (left top & left bottom; right top, middle and bottom), 204: Photos © Sloan Howard

pp. 180 (bottom right), 181, 185 (top), 187 (middle), 191 (top) 203 (top center): Photos by Jack Deutsch © The Taunton Press, Inc.

pp. 184 (left top & left bottom), 206 (top left): Photos by Susan Kahn © The Taunton Press, Inc.

p. 206 (top right, bottom left & right): Photos by Boyd Hagan © The Taunton Press, Inc.

Illustrations:

p. 178: Amy Russo © The Taunton Press, Inc.

pp. 180, 181, 187, 188 (left top & bottom), 189, 190 (left top & bottom), 192, 193, 200 (top & bottom left), 201 (all drawings except bottom left), 202 (top left, middle left, & top right), 207 (top drawings): Christine Erikson © The Taunton Press, Inc.

pp. 184, 194, 195, 200 (top right), 201 (bottom left), 202 (bottom left): Kathy Bray © The Taunton Press, Inc.

p. 188: (drawings 1–6) Bob LaPointe © The Taunton Press, Inc.

p. 189 (right): Patricia Keay © The Taunton Press, Inc.

p. 205: Robbin Mazzola © The Taunton Press, Inc.

p. 207 (bottom drawing): Sue Mattero © The Taunton Press, Inc.

CHAPTER 10

pp. 208, 209 (left), 211 (bottom photos), 223 (right photos), 225 (bottom), 226, 228 (middle & bottom), 229, 230 (top left, bottom left & bottom right), 231(bottom), 233: Photos by Scott Phillips © The Taunton Press, Inc.

pp. 209 (right), 211(top), 217 (left top, left middle & left bottom) : Photos by Susan Kahn © The Taunton Press, Inc.

pp. 215, 216 (left top, left bottom & middle), 217 (right top, right bottom), 218, 219, 221 (right), 222 (right photos), 223 (top center), 224, 225 (top & middle photos), 227, 231 (top): Photos © Sloan Howard

pp. 216 (right), 221 (left), 228 (left): Photos by Jack Deutsch © The Taunton Press, Inc.

p. 223 (bottom left photos): Photos by Jennifer Sauer © The Taunton Press, Inc.

p. 230 (top right): David Page Coffin © The Taunton Press, Inc.

Illustrations:

pp. 210, 212 (left top, left bottom & right bottom), 213 (top & middle), 214, 215, 220: Christine Erikson © The Taunton Press, Inc.

pp. 212 (right top), 213 (bottom left & right): Kathy Bray © The Taunton Press, Inc.

p. 222: Donna Kern © The Taunton Press, Inc.

p. 228: Steve Buchanan © The Taunton Press, Inc.

p. 232: Carol Ruzicka © The Taunton Press, Inc.

p. 233: Leigh Ann Smith © The Taunton Press, Inc.

CHAPTER 11

pp. 234, 235, 236, 237, 244, 247, 252, 254 (right), 256, 257: Photos by Scott Phillips © The Taunton Press, Inc.

pp. 238, 241: Photos by Jennifer Sauer © The Taunton Press, Inc.

pp. 240, 245, 246, 248, 249, 250, 251: Photos © Sloan Howard

pp. 242, 254 (left photos): Photos by Kenneth D. King © The Taunton Press, Inc.

p. 243: Photo by Jack Deutsch © The Taunton Press, Inc.

p. 255: Photo by Judi Rutz © The Taunton Press, Inc.

Illustrations:

pp. 236, 237, 239, 240, 241: Carol Ruzicka © The Taunton Press, Inc.

p. 242: Carolyn Fanelh © The Taunton Press, Inc.

p. 244, 246, 253 (right top, right middle & right bottom): Christine Erikson © The Taunton Press, Inc.

p. 253: (left top, left bottom & top center) Sue Mattero © The Taunton Press, Inc.

CHAPTER 12

pp. 258, 263 (top center, top right & bottom right), 264, 270, 278 (left), 279 (right): Photos by Scott Phillips © The Taunton Press, Inc.

pp. 259–263 (left), 267–268, 274, 275–278 (right), 279 (left): Photos © Sloan Howard

p. 265: Photo by Kenneth D. King © The Taunton Press, Inc.

pp. 266, 269, 273: Photos by Jack Deutsch © The Taunton Press, Inc.

pp. 280–281: Photos by Jennifer Sauer © The Taunton Press, Inc.

Illustrations:

p. 264: Carol Ruzicka © The Taunton Press, Inc.

pp. 265, 266: Heather Lambert © The Taunton Press, Inc.

p. 267: David Rohm © The Taunton Press, Inc.

pp. 270, 271, 272 (bottom): Christine Erikson © The Taunton Press, Inc.

p. 272: (top left & right): Karen Meyer © The Taunton Press, Inc.

CHAPTER 13

pp. 282, 283, 284, 287 (right), 290 (right), 291, 294: Photos by Scott Phillips © The Taunton Press, Inc.

pp. 285, 286: Photos by Kenneth D. King © The Taunton Press, Inc.

pp. 287 (left top & bottom), 288, 290 (left), 292, 293 (left), 295: Photos © Sloan Howard

p. 289: Photo by Pamela Metcalf © The Taunton Press, Inc.

p. 293 (right): Photo by Peter Saskas © The Taunton Press, Inc.

Illustrations:

pp. 284, 285, 296, 297: Christine Erikson © The Taunton Press, Inc.

p. 286 (top) Martha Garstang Hill © The Taunton Press, Inc.

p. 286 (middle & bottom) Christine Erikson © The Taunton Press, Inc.

CHAPTER 14

pp. 318, 320 (left), 322, 323 (top), 326 (right): Photo by Jack Deutsch © The Taunton Press, Inc.

pp. 319 (left), 321 (center top & bottom), 323 (middle & bottom): Photos by Scott Phillips © The Taunton Press, Inc.

pp. 319 (right), 320 (right), 321 (left & right top), 324, 325, 326 (left top & bottom, middle): Photos © Sloan Howard

Illustrations:

pp. 323, 324, 325, 327: Christine Erikson © The Taunton Press, Inc.

CHAPTER 15

pp. 328, 329 (bottom), 330, 331, 333, 334, 335 (bottom), 337 (right), 342, 345 (top right & bottom), 347: Photos by Scott Phillips © The Taunton Press, Inc.

p. 329 (top): Photo by Marcus Tullis © The Taunton Press, Inc.

pp. 332, 337 (left): Photos by Jack Deutsch © The Taunton Press, Inc.

p. 335 (top), 336, 339, 340 (right), 341 (middle, bottom left & bottom right), 343 (top left & top right), 344 (top right & bottom right), 345 (left photos), 346: Photos © Sloan Howard © The Taunton Press, Inc.

p. 340 (left): Photo by Joseph Kugielsky © The Taunton Press, Inc.

p. 341 (top): Photo by Susan Kahn © The Taunton Press, Inc.

p. 343 (bottom), 344 (top left): Photos by Jennifer Sauer © The Taunton Press, Inc.

Illustrations:

p. 335: Karen Meyer © The Taunton Press, Inc.

p. 344: Linda Boston © The Taunton Press, Inc.

CHAPTER 16

pp. 348, 350 (left photos), 354 (seam ripper), 355 (bottom right), 361: Photos by Scott Phillips © The Taunton Press, Inc.

pp. 349, 350 (right photos), 351, 352 (top photos), 355 (left photos), 356, 357, 360: Photos © Sloan Howard

pp. 352 (bottom photos), 353, 354 (left & center photos): Photos Kenneth D. King © The Taunton Press, Inc.

Index